Fodor's

1st EDITION

Egypt

The complete guide, thoroughly up-to-date

Packed with details that will make your trip

The must-see sights, off and on the beaten path

What to see, what to skip

Mix-and-match vacation itineraries

City strolls, countryside adventures

Smart lodging and dining options

Essential local dos and taboos

Transportation tips, distances, and directions

Key contacts, savvy travel tips

When to go, what to pack

Clear, accurate, easy-to-use maps

Books to read, videos to watch, background essays

Fodor's Travel Publications, Inc.
New York • Toronto • London • Sydney • Auckland
www.fodors.com

P9-DML-383

Fodor's Egypt

EDITOR: Stephen Wolf

Editorial Contributors: Magda Abdou, David Brown, Maria Golia, Salima Ikram, Jill Kamil, Nora el-Samahy, Rami el-Samahy, Sean Rocha, Helayne Schiff, M.T. Schwartzman, Cassandra Vivian, Nathalie Walschaerts

Editorial Production: Linda K. Schmidt

Maps: David Lindroth, *cartographer*; Robert Blake, Steven Amsterdam, *map editors*

Design: Fabrizio La Rocca, *creative director*; Guido Caroti, *associate art director*; Jolie Novak, *photo editor*

Production/Manufacturing: Mike Costa

Cover Photograph: Glen Allison/Tony Stone Images

Copyright

First Edition

ISBN 0–679–00014–3

Special Sales

Fodor's Travel Publications are available at special discounts for bulk purchases for sales promotions or premiums. Special editions, including personalized covers, excerpts of existing guides, and corporate imprints, can be created in large quantities for special needs. For more information, contact your local bookseller or write to Special Markets, Fodor's Travel Publications, 201 East 50th Street, New York, NY 10022. Inquiries from Canada should be directed to your local Canadian bookseller or sent to Random House of Canada, Ltd., Marketing Department, 2775 Matheson Boulevard East, Mississauga, Ontario L4W 4P7. Inquiries from the United Kingdom should be sent to Fodor's Travel Publications, 20 Vauxhall Bridge Road, London SW1V 2SA, England.

PRINTED IN THE UNITED STATES OF AMERICA

10 9 8 7 6 5 4 3 2 1

CONTENTS

ON THE ROAD WITH FODOR'S

WHEN I PLAN A VACATION, the first thing I do is cast around among my friends and colleagues to find someone who's just been where I'm going. That's because there's no substitute for a recommendation from a good friend who knows your tastes, your budget, and your circumstances. Unfortunately, such friends are few and far between. So it's nice to know that there's *Fodor's Egypt*.

In the first place, this book won't stay home when you hit the road. It will accompany you every step of the way, steering you away from wrong turns and wrong choices. That's because it's written and assiduously updated by the kind of people you *would* hit up for travel tips if you knew them. In these pages, they don't send you chasing down every town and sight in Egypt, but have instead selected the best ones, the ones that are worthy of your time and money. To make it easy for you to put it all together in the time you have, they've created short, medium, and long itineraries and, in cities, neighborhood walks that you can mix and match in a snap. Will this be the vacation of your dreams? We hope so.

About Our Writers

Magda Abdou became a Red Sea addict the first time she visited Sinai and the coast around Hurghada about 10 years ago. Since then she has worked summers at hotels and diving companies, explored the desert, camped out under the stars, and made hundreds of dives among some of the most amazing marine life on the planet. She also writes on film and women's issues for the Cairo fashion magazine *Pose*.

Cairo Times columnist **Maria Golia** believes that travel creates time lines, in significant destinations, through which an individual's life gains dimensions of immortality. A woman who regards cities as lovers, she has resided in Rome, Paris, Buenos Aires, Kathmandu, Moscow, and St. Jean Cap Ferrat on France's Cote d'Azur. Of course, no capital has captured her attentions as completely as Cairo, whose name appropriately means "the city victorious." Ms. Golia divides her time between working on her first novel and travel writing about expeditions in Oman's Wahiba Sands, the Empty Quarter, and Egypt's southwestern desert. She wrote the bulk of our Nile Valley chapter.

Dr. Salima Ikram is Assistant Professor of Egyptology at the American University in Cairo. She is the author of *Choice Cuts: Meat Production in Ancient Egypt, The Mummy in Ancient Egypt* (with A. Dodson), *Royal Mummies* (with A. Dodson), five children's books on ancient Egypt, and numerous articles. Her areas of expertise on matters ancient are daily life, mummification, ethnoarchaeology, fauna, and zooarchaeology, and she has excavated in Egypt, the Sudan, Turkey, and Greece.

Sean Rocha moved to Egypt in 1994 to write his first novel, leaving behind an investment banking career in Hong Kong. Frequently asked "Why Cairo?" at the time, he still has no compelling explanation, apart from a partisan's love for the place that borders on obsession. That obsession is with the contemporary, clandestinely hip Cairo—not the camels-and-Pyramids Egypt of the mind's eye—and that is where he set his novel. This often overlooked side of the country is what he has captured in writing our Destination: Egypt and Alexandria chapters, and in covering modern Cairo. With his novel completed—and likewise his stint as a regular columnist for the Cairo Times—Sean has recently returned to New York.

Bi-national—and in perpetual motion— **Nora el-Samahy** will always consider Cairo home. (The fact that her family and friends remain there gives her a viable excuse to return frequently.) Nora has carefully nurtured her affection for the Sinai over the past decade, most recently with heavy doses of scuba diving. She is now pursuing an acting career in San Francisco.

Rami el-Samahy's contributions to *Fodor's Egypt* range from lyrical evocations of Cairo's Islamic architecture to an incisive account of the past 5,000 years of Egyptian history to attempts to teach the editor how to pronounce the complicated Arabic letter *ayn*—and convincing arguments why we should spell the Arabic word for street *shar'a* instead of *shari'a*. After a nine-month stint project-managing ongoing construction at the Red Sea resort of al-Gouna, he is currently completing his architecture degree at Harvard University's Graduate School of Design.

Nathalie Walschaerts wrote on the monuments of Luxor—the great temples of Karnak and Luxor and the wonders of the Theban Necropolis—and on the jewellike Temple of Isis on Philae. She is a research assistant on the team of Dr. Kent Weeks' Theban Mapping Project at the American University in Cairo. A native of Ixelles, Belgium, she obtained her degree in Oriental Philology and History, section of Egyptology, at the Free University in Brussels, where she specialized in ancient languages.

Our roster of thank yous begins to sound like a biblical list of begats: Gay Robins (Associate Professor of Art History and Faculty Curator of Ancient Egyptian Art in the Michael C. Carlos Museum at Emory University) led us to Terry Walz at the American Research Center in Egypt (in New York), who led us to a long line of Egyptologists and expatriates in Cairo. He also put us on the trail of Drs. Salima Ikram (*above*) and Susan Allen (Research Associate in the Department of Egyptology at the Metropolitan Museum of Art in New York), whose recommendations proved invaluable in building a solid Egyptological foundation for this guide.

We'd also like to thank Cassandra Vivian, author and expert on the geography of Egypt's deserts and the cultures of their oases, whose suggestions breathed life into our Western Desert Oases chapter, and Egypt Air for their generous assistance with air travel to Egypt.

Connections

We're pleased that the American Society of Travel Agents continues to endorse Fodor's as its guidebook of choice. ASTA is the world's largest and most influential travel trade association, operating in more than 170 countries, with 27,000 members pledged to adhere to a strict code of ethics reflecting the society's motto, "Integrity in Travel." ASTA shares Fodor's devotion to providing smart, honest travel information and advice to travelers, and we've long recommended that our readers—even those who have guidebooks and trav-

eling friends—consult ASTA member agents for the experience and professionalism they bring to your vacation planning.

On Fodor's Web site (www.fodors.com), check out the new Resource Center, an online companion to the Gold Guide section of this book, complete with useful hot links to related sites. In our forums, you can also get lively advice from other travelers and more great tips from Fodor's experts worldwide.

How to Use This Book

Organization

Up front is the **Gold Guide,** an easy-to-use section arranged alphabetically by topic. Under each listing you'll find tips and information that will help you accomplish what you need to in Egypt. You'll also find addresses and telephone numbers of organizations and companies that offer destination-related services and detailed information and publications.

The first chapter in the guide, Destination: Egypt, helps get you in the mood for your trip. New and Noteworthy cues you in on trends and happenings; What's Where gets you oriented; Pleasures and Pastimes describes the activities and sights that make Egypt unique; Fodor's Choice showcases our top picks; and Festivals, Seasonal Events, and National Holidays alerts you to special events you'll want to seek out.

Chapters in Egypt start with Cairo—the place to begin either to get the pulse of Africa's most interesting city or to take in the nearby pyramids at Giza and Saqqara. The next chapter covers Alexandria, Egypt's cosmopolitan Mediterranean city. Then two chapters focus on the wonders of the Nile: The Nile Valley and Lake Nasser is where you'll read about the tombs and temples, the Aswan High Dam, and dining and lodging options; Nile and Lake Nasser Cruises is our guide-within-a-guide to the top 15 boats—also called floating hotels—that will give you the classic experience of the river and its ancient waterside pharaonic monuments.

Chapter 6 turns to the coast and waters of the Red Sea, home of some of the world's most spectacular undersea life—which means fantastic diving—and to the desert interior of the Sinai Peninsula, where Mount Sinai is a great hiking site and the Monastery of St. Catherine. The next chapter covers the mystical terrain of the Western Desert and its four oases, Bahariyya, Farafra, Dakhla, and Kharga. With the Western Desert Oases we include Siwa Oasis, just east of Egypt's border with Libya.

To help you decide what to visit in the time you have, all chapters begin with our recommended itineraries. The A to Z section that ends all chapters covers getting there and getting around. It also provides helpful contacts and resources.

At the end of the book you'll find Portraits, which include a brief romp through 5,000 years of Egyptian history, short pieces about life and death in ancient Egypt, and suggestions for pretrip reading and Egyptian films to see.

Icons and Symbols

★   Our special recommendations
✕   Restaurant
🏨   Lodging establishment
✕🏨   Lodging establishment whose restaurant warrants a special trip
⚠   Campgrounds
☞   Sends you to another section of the guide for more information
✉   Address
☎   Telephone number
☉   Opening and closing times
💲   Admission prices (those we give apply to adults; substantially reduced fees are almost always available for children, students, and senior citizens)

Numbers in white and black circles ③ ❸ that appear on the maps, in the margins, and within the tours correspond to one another.

Dining and Lodging

The restaurants and lodgings we list are the cream of the crop in each price range. Price charts appear in the Pleasures and Pastimes section that follows each chapter introduction.

Hotel Facilities

We always list the facilities that are available—but we don't specify whether you'll be charged extra to use them: When pricing accommodations, always ask what's included. Assume that all rooms have private baths unless noted otherwise.

Restaurant Reservations and Dress Codes

Making reservations is always a good idea; we mention them only when they're essential or not accepted. Unless otherwise noted, restaurants listed are open daily for lunch and dinner. We mention dress only when men are required to wear a jacket or a jacket and tie. Look for an overview of local dining-out habits in the Pleasures and Pastimes section that follows each chapter introduction.

Credit Cards

The following abbreviations are used: **AE,** American Express; **DC,** Diners Club; **MC,** MasterCard; and **V,** Visa.

Don't Forget to Write

You can use this book with the confidence that all prices and opening times are based on information supplied to us at press time; Fodor's cannot accept responsibility for any errors. Time inevitably brings changes, so always confirm information when it matters—especially if you're making a detour to visit a specific place.

Were the restaurants we recommended as described? Did our hotel picks exceed your expectations? Did you find a museum we recommended a waste of time? Keeping a travel guide fresh and up-to-date is a big job, and we welcome your feedback, positive *and* negative. If you have complaints, we'll look into them and revise our entries when the facts warrant it. If you've discovered a special place that we haven't included, we'll pass the information along to our correspondents and have them check it out. So send us your thoughts via e-mail at editors@fodors.com (specifying the name of the book on the subject line) or on paper in care of the Egypt editor at Fodor's, 201 East 50th Street, New York, NY 10022. In the meantime, have a wonderful trip!

Karen Cure
Editorial Director

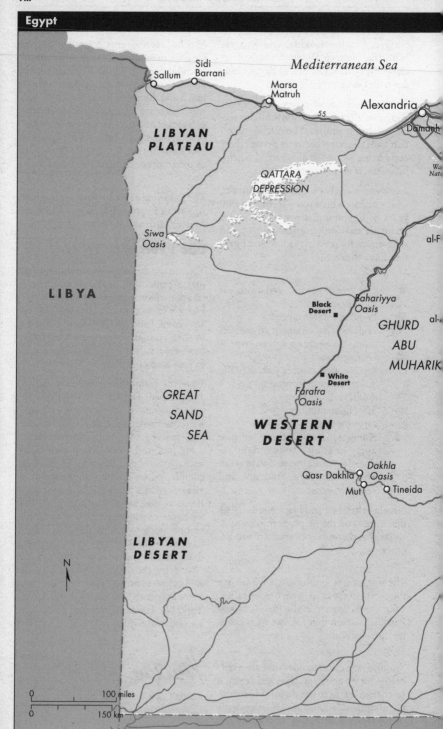

Egypt

Mediterranean Sea

Sallum
Sidi Barrani
Marsa Matruh
55
Alexandria
Damanh

LIBYAN PLATEAU

QATTARA DEPRESSION

Siwa Oasis

al-F

LIBYA

Black Desert ■
Bahariyya Oasis

GHURD

al-

ABU

MUHARIK

GREAT SAND SEA

White Desert ■
Farafra Oasis

WESTERN DESERT

Qasr Dakhla
Mut
Dakhla Oasis
Tineida

LIBYAN DESERT

N

Wa Nat

0   100 miles
0   150 km

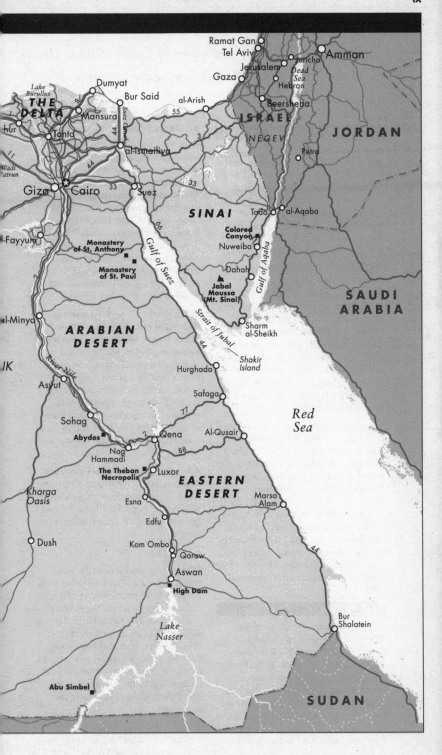

SMART TRAVEL TIPS A TO Z

Basic Information on Traveling in Egypt, Savvy Tips to Make Your Trip a Breeze, and Companies and Organizations to Contact

ADDRESSES

As a rule, street addresses in Egypt are generally useless when it comes to locating a museum or a hotel or a restaurant. In fact, there are whole towns, like Sharm al-Sheikh, that do not really have street names, but nonetheless have plenty of travelers passing through. This might sound unsettling, but you will manage just fine.

More often than not, landmarks are used to give directions, not street names or numbers. This might be because street names often change every three blocks, and streets are often referred to by their pre-revolutionary names, which don't appear on any maps. Local people go by place names and landmarks, which often means that you'll have to ask pedestrians where to go at various points on your way to wherever you're going.

When giving directions to a taxi driver, name a major landmark near your destination, rather than a street address. This might be a square in the area that you're going—in Cairo, for example, Maydan Tahrir (Liberation Square), or al-Azhar University. As you get closer to the destination, give more specifics; this will avoid confusion between you and your driver. For mailing addresses, postal codes have been recently instituted. However, like street names, they are not commonly used.

AIR TRAVEL

Most flights from North America stop over in Europe en route to Cairo. EgyptAir and TWA fly nonstop to Cairo from New York. From other parts of the United States, connect either through New York or a European city: Lufthansa, for example, flies from San Francisco to Frankfurt and on to Cairo. Most major European cities have nonstop flights to Cairo.

BOOKING YOUR FLIGHT

Price is just one factor to consider when booking a flight: frequency of service and even a carrier's safety record are often just as important. Major airlines offer the greatest number of departures. On the other hand, so-called low-cost airlines usually are cheaper, and their fares impose fewer restrictions, such as advance-purchase requirements. Safety-wise, low-cost carriers as a group have a good history—about equal to that of major carriers.

When you book, **look for nonstop flights** and **remember that "direct" flights stop at least once.** Try to **avoid connecting flights,** which require a change of plane. Two airlines may jointly operate a connecting flight, so ask if your airline operates every segment—you may find that your preferred carrier flies you only part of the way. International flights on a country's flag carrier are almost always nonstop; U.S. airlines often fly direct.

Ask your airline if it offers electronic ticketing, which eliminates all paperwork. There's no ticket to pick up or misplace. You go directly to the gate and give the agent your confirmation number.

CARRIERS

When flying internationally, you usually have the choice of flying with a carrier from your home country, a national flag carrier of the country you are visiting—EgyptAir in this case—and a foreign carrier from a third country. National flag carriers have the greatest number of nonstops. Domestic carriers may have the best connections to the city nearest you. Third-party carriers may have the best prices.

➤ FROM THE U.S.: **British Air** (☎ 800/247–9297); **El Al** (☎ 800/223–6700); **EgyptAir** (☎ 212/315–0900 in New York; 310/670–8496 in Los

Angeles); **KLM/Northwest** (☎ 800/361–5073); **Lufthansa** (☎ 800/645–3880); **TWA** (☎ 800/892–4141).

➤ FROM THE U.K.: **EgyptAir** (☎ 0171/734–2343 in London); **British Air** (☎ 0345/222–1111 in London); **Lufthansa** (☎ 0345/73–7747); **Northwest** (☎ 0990/561000).

➤ FROM AUSTRALIA: **Ansett** (☎ 13–1300); **EgyptAir** (☎ 02/9232–6677); **British Air** (☎ 02/9258–3399); **Lufthansa** (☎ 029/3673–7747 in Melbourne); **Qantas** (☎ 13–1313).

➤ FROM SOUTH AFRICA: **British Air/Comair** (☎ 011/921–0222); **EgyptAir** (☎ 880–4126); **Lufthansa**(☎ 011/484–4722); **South African Airways** (☎ 011/356–1111).

CONSOLIDATORS

Consolidators buy tickets for scheduled international flights at reduced rates from the airlines, then sell them at prices that beat the best fare available directly from the airlines, usually without restrictions. Sometimes you can even get your money back if you need to return the ticket. Carefully read the fine print detailing penalties for changes and cancellations, and **confirm your consolidator reservation with the airline.**

➤ CONSOLIDATORS: **Cheap Tickets** (☎ 800/377–1000). **Up & Away Travel** (☎ 212/889–2345). **Discount Travel Network** (☎ 800/576–1600). **Unitravel** (☎ 800/325–2222). **World Travel Network** (☎ 800/409–6753).

CUTTING COSTS

The least-expensive airfares to Egypt are priced for round-trip travel and usually must be purchased in advance. It's smart to **call a number of airlines, and when you are quoted a good price, book it on the spot**—the same fare may not be available the next day. To get the lowest airfare, **check different routings.** Compare prices of flights to and from different airports if your destination or home city has more than one gateway. Also price off-peak flights, which may be significantly less expensive.

Travel agents, especially those who specialize in finding the lowest fares (☞ Discounts & Deals, *below*), can be especially helpful when booking a plane ticket. When you're quoted a price, **ask your agent if the price is likely to get any lower.** Good agents know the seasonal fluctuations of airfares and can usually anticipate a sale or fare war. However, waiting can be risky: The fare could go *up* as seats become scarce, and you may wait so long that your preferred flight sells out.

CHECK IN & BOARDING

On internal Egyptian flights, **be absolutely sure to confirm your flight 72 hours before your departure** or else you risk being bumped off the flight. By the same token, get to the gate and check in 45 minutes or more in advance of your departure.

Although the trend on international flights is to drop reconfirmation requirements, many airlines still ask you to reconfirm each leg of your international itinerary. Failure to do so may result in your reservation being canceled.

ENJOYING THE FLIGHT

For more legroom, **request an emergency-aisle seat.** Don't sit in the row in front of the emergency aisle or in front of a bulkhead, where seats may not recline.

If you don't like airline food, **ask for special meals when booking.** These can be vegetarian, low-cholesterol, or kosher, for example.

When flying internationally, try to maintain a normal routine, to help fight jet-lag. At night, **get some sleep.** By day, **eat light meals, drink water (not alcohol), and move around the cabin** to stretch your legs.

Many carriers have prohibited smoking on all of their international flights; others allow smoking only on certain routes or certain departures, so **contact your carrier regarding its smoking policy.**

FLYING TIMES

The flight time from New York to Cairo is 10 hours. The total time in the air on the San Francisco–Frankfurt–Cairo flight is about 17 hours. Direct flights from London take about 7 hours. Travel time to Cairo from Sydney, with connections in

Frankfurt, is about 20 hours; from Johannesburg, 19 hours.

HOW TO COMPLAIN

If your baggage goes astray or your flight goes awry, complain right away. Most carriers require that you **file a claim immediately.**

AIRPORTS

Egypt's main port of entry is Cairo International Airport. There are additional international airports in Alexandria, Luxor, Hurghada, and Sharm al-Sheikh that receive nonstop flights from Europe.

➤ AIRPORT INFORMATION: **Cairo International Airport** (☎ 02/291–4277 or 02/291–4255); **Luxor** (☎ 095/384–655); **Hurghada** (☎ 065/546–788); **Sharm al-Sheikh** (☎ 062/601–140).

BUS TRAVEL

For extensive information on bus travel throughout Egypt, *see* Arriving and Departing By Bus *in* Cairo A to Z.

BUSINESS HOURS

The Egyptian weekend starts Friday. For some people it includes Saturday; others work Saturdays.

Businesses are usually open by 8 AM and close by 4 or 5 PM Sunday through Thursday. Most shops are open by 9 AM in summer and 10 AM in winter; they stay open until about 10 PM. Many shops close Sundays and are open the latter half the day on Saturday. Many shops close during Friday prayers, which begin at noon (1 PM in summer) and last for 15 minutes.

Cairo's celebrated Khan al-Khalili bazaar is open Monday–Saturday 10–9.

CAMERAS

EQUIPMENT PRECAUTIONS

Always **keep your film, tape, or computer disks out of the sun.** Carry an extra supply of batteries, and **be prepared to turn on your camera, camcorder, or laptop** to prove to security personnel that the device is real. Always **ask for hand inspection of film,** which becomes clouded after successive exposure to airport X-ray machines, and **keep videotapes and computer disks away from metal detectors.**

TRAVEL PHOTOGRAPHY

➤ PHOTO HELP: **Kodak Information Center** (☎ 800/242–2424). *Kodak Guide to Shooting Great Travel Pictures,* available in bookstores or from Fodor's Travel Publications (☎ 800/533–6478; $16.50 plus $4 shipping).

CAR RENTAL

The following agencies have offices in several cities, including Cairo, Hurghada, Sharm al-Sheikh, and Alexandria. The average daily rate for a basic, standard transmission car with air-conditioning is approximately $55, $330 per week.

➤ MAJOR AGENCIES: **Alamo** (☎ 800/522–9696, 0800/272–2000 in the U.K.). **Avis** (☎ 800/331–1084, 800/879–2847 in Canada, 008/225–533 in Australia). **Budget** (☎ 800/527–0700, 0800/181181 in the U.K.). **Dollar** (☎ 800/800–4000; 0990/565656 in the U.K., where it is known as Eurodollar). **Hertz** (☎ 800/654–3001, 800/263–0600 in Canada, 0345/555888 in the U.K., 03/9222–2523 in Australia, 03/358–6777 in New Zealand). **National InterRent** (☎ 800/227–3876; 0345/222525 in the U.K., where it is known as Europcar InterRent).

CUTTING COSTS

To get the best deal, **book through a travel agent who is willing to shop around.**

Also **ask your travel agent about a company's customer-service record.** How has the company responded to late plane arrivals and vehicle mishaps? Are there often lines at the rental counter? If you're traveling during a holiday period, does a confirmed reservation guarantee you a car?

Be sure to **look into wholesalers,** companies that do not own fleets but rent in bulk from those that do and often offer better rates than traditional car-rental operations. Prices are best during off-peak periods. Rentals booked through wholesalers must be paid for before you leave home.

➤ RENTAL WHOLESALERS: **Auto Europe** (☎ 207/842–2000 or 800/223–5555, FAX 800–235–6321; in London: ☎ 0800/89–9893).

INSURANCE

When driving a rented car you are generally responsible for any damage to or loss of the vehicle. You also are liable for any property damage or personal injury that you may cause while driving. Before you rent, **see what coverage you already have** under the terms of your personal auto-insurance policy and credit cards.

REQUIREMENTS

In Egypt an International Driver's Permit and your driver's license are required. Permits are available from the American or Canadian automobile association, and, in the United Kingdom, from the Automobile Association or Royal Automobile Club. These international permits are universally recognized, and having one in your wallet may save you a problem with the local authorities.

SURCHARGES

Before you pick up a car in one city and leave it in another, **ask about drop-off charges or one-way service fees,** which can be substantial. To avoid a hefty refueling fee, **fill the tank just before you turn in the car,** but be aware that gas stations near the rental outlet may overcharge.

CAR TRAVEL

If you are into the adrenaline rush of driving in Egypt and have the flexibility of adapting to an entirely different set of rules, then renting a car has many benefits. You are guaranteed the flexibility to leave when you please and explore the many virgin territories remaining on the route to the Red Sea or the Western Desert. You are spared the discomfort of blasting pop Arabic music on buses and similarly unpleasant sights and sounds. However, buses, trains, or planes are a much more sensible option if you want to play it safe (statistics prove that car accidents are the greatest danger facing foreigners in Egypt). Drive at your own peril!

If you decide to risk it, make sure that you leave in the daylight: at night most roads are dimly lit at best, drivers sometimes try to save power by driving without lights, and to add to the adventure truckers often neglect to pull over to the side of the road when taking their tea breaks.

If, again, you decide to risk it, purchase Mary Megalli's book *On the Road in Egypt: A Motorist's Guide,* which is full of road maps and practical information that you'll need when driving.

The best route between **Cairo and Alexandria** is the Desert Road (200 km, 125 mi, to central Alexandria). To get to it, head to Maydan Lebnan (Lebanon Square) in Mohandiseen and get onto the new ring road, which brings you to the Desert Road, just before the toll booth. The Desert Road is known to be dangerous, so drive slowly (speed limit is 100 km/hr).

Al-Qattamia Road is the main route to **Hurghada** (500 km, 312 mi), **Safaga,** (570 km, 355 mi), and **al-Quseir** (700 km, 435 mi). It also takes you past the monasteries of St. Paul and St. Anthony. It is strongly recommended that you do not drive in the dark because of the extremely steep curbs on the road.

The Ismailiya Road goes to the Suez Canal town of **Ismailiya** (120 km, 75 mi). The **Suez Road** takes you to **Sharm al-Sheik** (510 km, 320 mi), **Nuweiba** (680 km, 425 mi), and **Taba** (740 km, 460 mi).

To get to the **Western Desert Oases,** take the **Fayyum Road,** which branches off the Shar'a al-Haram (Pyramids Rd.).

AUTO CLUBS

Auto clubs generally have limited reciprocity with clubs in Cairo. The Cairo club will provide touring and planning assistance but not roadside help with breakdowns. Your best bet for getting coverage for these types of crises is through a car rental insurance policy—companies may include towing as part of an insurance option. The best option often is to hire a car with a driver. The cost is little more than renting your own car.

SMART TRAVEL TIPS / THE GOLD GUIDE

➤ IN CAIRO: **Automobile et Touring Club D'Egypte** (✉ 10, Shar'a Qasr al-Nil, Cairo, ☎ 02/574–3355, FAX 02/574–3115).

➤ IN AUSTRALIA: **Australian Automobile Association** (☎ 06/247–7311).

➤ IN CANADA: **Canadian Automobile Association** (CAA, ☎ 613/247–0117).

➤ IN NEW ZEALAND: **New Zealand Automobile Association** (☎ 09/377–4660).

➤ IN THE U.K.: **Automobile Association** (AA, ☎ 0990/500–600), **Royal Automobile Club** (RAC, ☎ 0990/722–722 for membership, 0345/121–345 for insurance).

➤ IN THE U.S.: **American Automobile Association** (☎ 800/564–6222).

CHILDREN & TRAVEL

CHILDREN IN EGYPT

Be sure to plan ahead and **involve your youngsters** as you outline your trip. When packing, include things to keep them busy en route. On sightseeing days try to schedule activities of special interest to your children. If you are renting a car don't forget to **arrange for a car seat** when you reserve. Most hotels in Egypt **allow children under 10 to stay in their parents' room at no extra charge,** but do charge those children for breakfast. Be sure to **ask about the cutoff age for children's discounts.**

FLYING

If your children are two or older, **ask about children's airfares.** As a general rule, infants under two not occupying a seat fly at greatly reduced fares or even for free.

In general the adult baggage allowance applies to children paying half or more of the adult fare. When booking, **ask about carry-on allowances for those traveling with infants.** In general, for babies charged 10% of the adult fare you are allowed one carry-on bag and a collapsible stroller, which may have to be checked; you may be limited to less if the flight is full.

When making your reservation, **request children's meals or a free-standing bassinet** if you need them; the latter are available only to those seated at the bulkhead, where there's enough legroom. Remember, however, that bulkhead seats may not have their own overhead bins, and there's no storage space in front of you—a major inconvenience.

CONSUMER PROTECTION

Whenever possible, **pay with a major credit card** so you can cancel payment or get reimbursed if there's a problem, provided that you can provide documentation. This is the best way to pay, whether you're buying travel arrangements before your trip or shopping at your destination.

If you're doing business with a particular company for the first time, **contact your local Better Business Bureau and the attorney general's offices** in your state and the company's home state, as well. Have any complaints been filed?

Finally, if you're buying a package or tour, always **consider travel insurance** that includes default coverage (☞ Insurance, *below*).

➤ LOCAL BBBs: **Council of Better Business Bureaus** (✉ 4200 Wilson Blvd., Suite 800, Arlington, VA 22203, ☎ 703/276–0100, FAX 703/525–8277).

CUSTOMS & DUTIES

When shopping, **keep receipts** for all of your purchases. Upon reentering the country, **be ready to show customs officials what you've bought.** If you feel a duty is incorrect, appeal the assessment. If you object to the way your clearance was handled, get the inspector's badge number. In either case, first ask to see a supervisor, then write to the appropriate authorities, beginning with the port director at your point of entry.

IN AUSTRALIA

Australia residents who are 18 or older may bring back $A400 worth of souvenirs and gifts (including jewelry), 250 cigarettes or 250 grams of tobacco, and 1,125 ml of alcohol (including wine, beer, and spirits). Residents under 18 may bring back $A200 worth of goods.

➤ INFORMATION: **Australian Customs Service** (Regional Director, ✉ Box 8, Sydney, NSW 2001, ☎ 02/9213–2000, FAX 02/9213–4000).

IN CANADA

Canadian residents who have been out of Canada for at least 7 days may bring in C$500 worth of goods duty-free. If you've been away less than 7 days but more than 48 hours, the duty-free allowance drops to C$200; if your trip lasts 24–48 hours, the allowance is C$50. You may not pool allowances with family members. Goods claimed under the C$500 exemption may follow you by mail; those claimed under the lesser exemptions must accompany you. Alcohol and tobacco products may be included in the 7-day and 48-hour exemptions but not in the 24-hour exemption. If you meet the age requirements of the province or territory through which you reenter Canada, you may bring in, duty-free, 1.14 liters (40 imperial ounces) of wine or liquor *or* 24 12-ounce cans or bottles of beer or ale. If you are 16 or older you may bring in, duty-free, 200 cigarettes and 50 cigars.

You may send an unlimited number of gifts worth up to C$60 each duty-free to Canada. Label the package UNSOLICITED GIFT—VALUE UNDER $60. Alcohol and tobacco are excluded.

➤ INFORMATION: **Revenue Canada** (✉ 2265 St. Laurent Blvd. S, Ottawa, Ontario K1G 4K3, ☎ 613/993–0534, 800/461–9999 in Canada).

IN NEW ZEALAND

Although greeted with a "Haere Mai" ("Welcome to New Zealand"), homeward-bound residents with goods to declare must present themselves for inspection. If you're 17 or older, you may bring back $700 worth of souvenirs and gifts. Your duty-free allowance also includes 4.5 liters of wine or beer; one 1,125-ml bottle of spirits; and either 200 cigarettes, 250 grams of tobacco, 50 cigars, or a combo of all three up to 250 grams.

➤ INFORMATION: **New Zealand Customs** (✉ Custom House, 50 Anzac Ave., Box 29, Auckland, New Zealand, ☎ 09/359–6655, ☎ 09/309–2978).

IN THE U.K.

From countries outside the EU, including Egypt, you may import, duty-free, 200 cigarettes or 50 cigars; 1 liter of spirits or 2 liters of fortified or sparkling wine or liqueurs; 2 liters of still table wine; 60 milliliters of perfume; 250 milliliters of toilet water; plus £136 worth of other goods, including gifts and souvenirs.

➤ INFORMATION: **HM Customs and Excise** (✉ Dorset House, Stamford St., London SE1 9NG, ☎ 0171/202–4227).

IN THE U.S.

U.S. residents may bring home $400 worth of foreign goods duty-free if they've been out of the country for at least 48 hours (and if they haven't used the $400 allowance or any part of it in the past 30 days).

U.S. residents 21 and older may bring back 1 liter of alcohol duty-free. In addition, regardless of your age, you are allowed 200 cigarettes and 100 non-Cuban cigars. Antiques, which the U.S. Customs Service defines as objects more than 100 years old, enter duty-free, as do original works of art done entirely by hand, including paintings, drawings, and sculptures.

You may also send packages home duty-free: up to $200 worth of goods for personal use, with a limit of one parcel per addressee per day (and no alcohol or tobacco products or perfume worth more than $5); label the package PERSONAL USE, and attach a list of its contents and their retail value. Do not label the package UNSOLICITED GIFT, or your duty-free exemption will drop to $100. Mailed items do not affect your duty-free allowance on your return.

➤ INFORMATION: **U.S. Customs Service** (Inquiries, ✉ Box 7407, Washington, DC 20044, ☎ 202/927–6724; complaints, Office of Regulations and Rulings, ✉ 1301 Constitution Ave. NW, Washington, DC 20229; registration of equipment, Resource Management, ✉ 1301 Constitution Ave.

NW, Washington DC 20229, ☎ 202/927–0540).

DINING

See Dining *in* the Pleasures and Pastimes setion of Destination: Egypt for information on food and eating in Egypt.

DISABILITIES & ACCESSIBILITY

MAKING RESERVATIONS

When discussing accessibility with an operator or reservations agent, **ask hard questions.** Are there any stairs, inside *or* out? Are there grab bars next to the toilet *and* in the shower/tub? How wide is the doorway to the room? To the bathroom? For the most extensive facilities meeting the latest legal specifications, **opt for newer accommodations,** which are more likely to have been designed with access in mind. Older buildings or ships may have more limited facilities. Be sure to **discuss your needs before booking.**

TRANSPORTATION

➤ COMPLAINTS: **Disability Rights Section** (✉ U.S. Department of Justice, Civil Rights Division, Box 66738, Washington, DC 20035–6738, ☎ 202/514–0301 or 800/514–0301, TTY 202/514–0383 or 800/514–0383, FAX 202/307–1198) for general complaints. **Aviation Consumer Protection Division** (☞ Air Travel, *above*) for airline-related problems. **Civil Rights Office** (✉ U.S. Department of Transportation, Departmental Office of Civil Rights, S-30, 400 7th St. SW, Room 10215, Washington, DC, 20590, ☎ 202/366–4648, FAX 202/366–9371) for problems with surface transportation.

TRAVEL AGENCIES & TOUR OPERATORS

As a whole, the travel industry has become more aware of the needs of travelers with disabilities. In the U.S., the Americans with Disabilities Act requires that travel firms serve the needs of all travelers. Note, though, that some agencies and operators specialize in making travel arrangements for individuals and groups with disabilities.

➤ TRAVELERS WITH MOBILITY PROBLEMS: **Access Adventures** (✉ 206 Chestnut Ridge Rd., Rochester, NY 14624, ☎ 716/889–9096), run by a former physical-rehabilitation counselor. **Flying Wheels Travel** (✉ 143 W. Bridge St., Box 382, Owatonna, MN 55060, ☎ 507/451–5005 or 800/535–6790, FAX 507/451–1685), a travel agency specializing in customized tours and itineraries worldwide. **Hinsdale Travel Service** (✉ 201 E. Ogden Ave., Suite 100, Hinsdale, IL 60521, ☎ 630/325–1335), a travel agency that benefits from the advice of wheelchair traveler Janice Perkins.

DISCOUNTS & DEALS

Be a smart shopper and **compare all your options** before making any choice. A plane ticket bought with a promotional coupon may not be cheaper than the least expensive fare from a discount ticket agency. For high-price travel purchases, such as packages or tours, keep in mind that what you get is just as important as what you save. Just because something is cheap doesn't mean it's a bargain.

CLUBS & COUPONS

Many companies sell discounts in the form of travel clubs and coupon books, but these cost money. You must use participating advertisers to get a deal, and only after you recoup the initial membership cost or book price do you begin to save. If you plan to use the club or coupons frequently, you may save considerably. Before signing up, find out what discounts you get for free.

➤ DISCOUNT CLUBS: **Entertainment Travel Editions** (✉ 2125 Butterfield Rd., Troy, MI 48084, ☎ 800/445–4137; $20–$51, depending on destination). **Great American Traveler** (✉ Box 27965, Salt Lake City, UT 84127, ☎ 801/974–3033 or 800/548–2812; $49.95 per year). **Moment's Notice Discount Travel Club** (✉ 7301 New Utrecht Ave., Brooklyn, NY 11204, ☎ 718/234–6295; $25 per year, single or family). **Privilege Card International** (✉ 237 E. Front St., Youngstown, OH 44503, ☎ 330/746–5211 or 800/236–9732; $74.95 per year). **Sears's Mature Outlook** (✉ Box 9390, Des Moines, IA 50306, ☎ 800/336–6330; $19.95

per year). **Travelers Advantage** (⊠ CUC Travel Service, 3033 S. Parker Rd., Suite 1000, Aurora, CO 80014, ☎ 800/548–1116 or 800/648–4037; $59.95 per year, single or family). **Worldwide Discount Travel Club** (⊠ 1674 Meridian Ave., Miami Beach, FL 33139, ☎ 305/534–2082; $50 per year family, $40 single).

CREDIT-CARD BENEFITS

When you use your credit card to make travel purchases you may get free travel-accident insurance, collision-damage insurance, and medical or legal assistance, depending on the card and the bank that issued it. American Express, MasterCard, and Visa provide one or more of these services, so **get a copy of your credit card's travel-benefits policy.** If you are a member of an auto club, always **ask hotel and car-rental reservations agents about auto-club discounts.** Some clubs offer additional discounts on tours, cruises, and admission to attractions.

DISCOUNT RESERVATIONS

To save money, **look into discount-reservations services** with toll-free numbers, which use their buying power to get a better price on hotels, airline tickets, even car rentals. When booking a room, always **call the hotel's local toll-free number** (if one is available) rather than the central reservations number—you'll often get a better price. Always ask about special packages or corporate rates.

When shopping for the best deal on hotels and car rentals, **look for guaranteed exchange rates,** which protect you against a falling dollar. With your rate locked in, you won't pay more, even if the price goes up in the local currency.

➤ AIRLINE TICKETS: ☎ 800/FLY–4–LESS.

PACKAGE DEALS

Packages and guided tours can save you money, but don't confuse the two. When you buy a package, your travel remains independent, just as though you had planned and booked the trip yourself. Fly/drive packages, which combine airfare and car rental, are often a good deal.

DIVING

Most dives in Sharm al-Sheikh are wall dives, rich in fan, fire, and plate coral; napoleon fish; puffer fish; barracudas; and an occasional shark (usually in slumber). Shore diving is virtually nonexistent in Sharm al-Sheikh and Hurghada, but it is available most everywhere else—Dahab, Nuweiba, Taba. The most popular dive sites in Sharm al-Sheikh are at Ras Muhammad National Park, the Straits of Tiran, and Ras Nusrani.

Although the Red Sea is tropical, it can get very cold. Scorching on-land summer temperatures of 104°F are deceiving, because temperatures at depth can be as low as 68°F. When diving, avoid the temptation to dispense with a wet suit altogether. Between April and November, 3-mm or Lycra suits are sufficient thermal protection; 7-mm suits with hoods are ideal for the rest of the year.

For some of Egypt's least spoiled, most precious sites—which include top shark diving areas—opt for a three- to seven-day dive safari on a live-aboard boat. Various dive centers can arrange these trips to reefs like the Elphin Stone Reef, Sha'ab Abu Dahab, Marsa Nakari, and Dolphin Reef, which are all south of Hurghada on the Red Sea coast. Boats range in size and number of berths.

All dive centers rent full gear, including torches for night dives. If you are certified, don't forget your C-card and logbook. If you plan to take any dive courses, you will need to bring a copy of a recent medical examination from a doctor back home.

ELECTRICITY

To use your U.S.-purchased electric-powered equipment, **bring a converter and adapter.** The electrical current in Egypt is 220 volts, 50 cycles alternating current (AC). Most wall outlets take rounded plugs, so North American travelers will need both a converter and an adapter.

If your appliances are dual-voltage, you'll need only an adapter. Don't use 110-volt outlets, marked FOR SHAVERS ONLY, for high-wattage appliances such as blow-dryers. Most laptops operate equally well on 110 and 220 volts and so require only an adapter.

GAY & LESBIAN TRAVEL

In a country like Egypt, where sexuality is not widely discussed, homosexuality remains a taboo. Therefore an open gay population is hard to come by and a general acceptance from the people is also not prevalent. However, as in every country in the world, there is a gay and lesbian population that remains underground.

➤ GAY- AND LESBIAN-FRIENDLY TRAVEL AGENCIES: **Corniche Travel** (✉ 8721 Sunset Blvd., Suite 200, West Hollywood, CA 90069, ☎ 310/854–6000 or 800/429–8747, FAX 310/659–7441). **Islanders Kennedy Travel** (✉ 183 W. 10th St., New York, NY 10014, ☎ 212/242–3222 or 800/988–1181, FAX 212/929–8530). **Now Voyager** (✉ 4406 18th St., San Francisco, CA 94114, ☎ 415/626–1169 or 800/255–6951, FAX 415/626–8626). **Yellowbrick Road** (✉ 1500 W. Balmoral Ave., Chicago, IL 60640, ☎ 773/561–1800 or 800/642–2488, FAX 773/561–4497). **Skylink Travel and Tour** (✉ 3577 Moorland Ave., Santa Rosa, CA 95407, ☎ 707/585–8355 or 800/225–5759, FAX 707/584–5637), serving lesbian travelers.

HEALTH

Your first concern in Egypt should be with the sun. In this lattitude sunburn happens very quickly, and the heat itself—shade temperatures are very often in the upper 90s (Fahrenheit)—is intense. In the dry desert areas, you might not feel that you are sweating, when in fact your body is losing considerable amounts of water.

Take extreme care to **protect yourself from the sun** by covering your skin and using high-level sunblocks. **Always carry bottled water and keep up your water intake.** Dehydration can be a serious problem, so replenish your fluid levels regularly.

FOOD & DRINK

In Egypt the major health risk is "gippy tummy"—traveler's diarrhea varying in intensity from mild to disablingly severe. It is almost certainly attributable to contaminated water, and, consequently, you are strongly advised to drink only bottled water (or water that has been boiled for at least 20 minutes), avoid uncooked vegetables with a high water content (lettuce, green salads, watermelon), and be very wary of taking ice in drinks. However, precautions are often of no avail. A cruise of some 90 British medical doctors and their spouses found 70 members out of action for three days. People who consumed identical meals at the same table were hit randomly. Staying at the very best international hotels won't necessarily protect you from this.

Mild cases may respond to Imodium (known generically as loperamide) or Pepto-Bismol (not as strong), both of which can be purchased over the counter; paregoric, another antidiarrheal agent, requires a doctor's prescription in Egypt.

Drink plenty of purified water or tea—chamomile is a good folk remedy. In severe cases, rehydrate yourself with a salt-sugar solution (½ teaspoon salt and 4 tablespoons sugar per quart of water).

HOSPITALS AND PHARMACIES

Many hotels will have a doctor on call or will be able to recommend a good doctor to contact if you need one. Otherwise the best places to seek medical attention are in Cairo and Alexandria. Hospitals work on a cash basis and do not accept foreign medical insurance. Some hospitals accept credit cards, however most do not. In cases of serious illness, your best option might be to return home for treatment.

The following is a list of Cairo hospitals: **Anglo-American Hospital Zohoreya** (✉ next to the Cairo Tower, Zamalek, ☎ 02/341–8630); **As-Salam International Hospital** (✉ Corniche al-Nil, Maadi, ☎ 02/363–8050 or 02/363–4196); **Nile Badrawi Hospital** (✉ Corniche al-Nil, Maadi, ☎ 02/363-8688 or 02/363–8167).

Pharmacies are generally open from 10 AM to 10 PM daily and are run by qualified pharmacists. Medicine is inexpensive because it is government subsidized. The crescent with a snake around it is the national sign for a pharmacy.

Twenty-four hour pharmacies in Cairo include the following: **Attaba Pharmacy** (⊠ 17 Maydan Attaba, ☎ 02/910–831); **Isaaf Pharmacy** (⊠ 3 Shar'a 26 July, ☎ 02/743–369); **Zamalek Pharmacy** (⊠ 3 Shagaret al-Dorr, Zamalek, ☎ 02/340–2406).

MEDICAL PLANS

No one plans to get sick while traveling, but it happens, so **consider signing up with a medical-assistance company.** Members get doctor referrals, emergency evacuation or repatriation, 24-hour telephone hot lines for medical consultation, cash for emergencies, and other personal and legal assistance. Coverage varies by plan, so **review the benefits of each carefully.**

➤ MEDICAL-ASSISTANCE COMPANIES: **International SOS Assistance** (⊠ 8 Neshaminy Interplex, Suite 207, Trevose, PA 19053, ☎ 215/245–4707 or 800/523–6586, ℻ 215/244–9617; ⊠ 12 Chemin Riantbosson, 1217 Meyrin 1, Geneva, Switzerland, ☎ 4122/785–6464, ℻ 4122/785–6424; ⊠ 10 Anson Rd., 14-07/08 International Plaza, Singapore, 079903, ☎ 65/226–3936, ℻ 65/226–3937).

SHOTS & MEDICATIONS

According to the U.S. government's National Centers for Disease Control (CDC) there is a limited risk of malaria and dengue fever, diseases carried by insects, and some risk of schistosomiasis, a parasitic infection acquired by swimming in fresh water. Malaria poses almost no risk to travelers visiting major tourist areas in North Africa. One exception is al-Fayyum oasis.

Swimming in the Nile, or fresh water anywhere in Egypt, is highly discouraged and should be reserved for well-chlorinated pools or salt water. Prepare yourself for the most common illness which befalls travellers by bringing anti-diarrhea tablets with you from home. Also as a preventative, adults and children should complete Hepatitis A and B and tetanus shots at least a month before traveling.

➤ HEALTH WARNINGS: **National Centers for Disease Control** (⊠ CDC, National Center for Infectious Diseases, Division of Quarantine, Traveler's Health Section, 1600 Clifton Rd. NE, M/S E-03, Atlanta, GA 30333, ☎ 404/332–4559, ℻ 404/332–4565).

HOLIDAYS

Egypt's national holidays are **Sinai Liberation Day** (Apr. 25), **Labor Day** (May 1), **Evacuation Day** (June 18), and **Revolution Day** (July 23).

The **Muslim lunar calendar** is normally 10 to 11 days earlier than the Gregorian year. The month of Ramadan lasts for anywhere from 28 to 30 days. It is followed by Ead al-Fetr, known as the "small feast" in English. The "big feast" is Eid al-Adha, which occurs at the end of the Pilgrimage Period. The other two main Muslim holidays are the Muslim New Year (early Apr.), and the Prophet Muhammad's birthday (mid- to late June). **Coptic holidays** are observed by Coptic citizens only. They are Christmas (Jan. 7), Baptism (Jan. 20), Palm Sunday (the Sunday before Easter), and Easter. See also Festivals and Seasonal Events in Destination: Egypt for holiday dates.

INSURANCE

Travel insurance is the best way to **protect yourself against financial loss.** The most useful plan is a comprehensive policy that includes coverage for trip cancellation and interruption, default, trip delay, and medical expenses (with a waiver for preexisting conditions).

Without insurance, you will lose all or most of your money if you cancel your trip, regardless of the reason. Default insurance covers you if your tour operator, airline, or cruise line goes out of business. Trip-delay covers unforeseen expenses that you may incur due to bad weather or mechanical delays. It's important to compare the fine print regarding trip-delay coverage when comparing policies.

For overseas travel, one of the most important components of travel insurance is its medical coverage. Supplemental health insurance will pick up the cost of your medical bills should you get sick or injured while traveling. U.S. residents should note that Medicare generally does not cover health-care costs outside the United States, nor do many privately issued policies. Residents of the United Kingdom can buy an annual travel-insurance policy valid for most vacations taken during the year in which the coverage is purchased. If you are pregnant or have a pre-existing condition, make sure you're covered. British citizens should buy extra medical coverage when traveling overseas, according to the Association of British Insurers. Australian travelers should buy travel insurance, including extra medical coverage, whenever they go abroad, according to the Insurance Council of Australia.

Always **buy travel insurance directly from the insurance company**; if you buy it from a cruise line, airline, or tour operator that goes out of business you probably will not be covered for the agency or operator's default, a major risk. Before you make any purchase, **review your existing health and home-owner's policies** to find out whether they cover expenses incurred while traveling.

➤ TRAVEL INSURERS: In the U.S., **Access America** (✉ 6600 W. Broad St., Richmond, VA 23230, ☎ 804/285–3300 or 800/284–8300). **Travel Guard International** (✉ 1145 Clark St., Stevens Point, WI 54481, ☎ 715/345–0505 or 800/826–1300). In Canada, **Mutual of Omaha** (✉ Travel Division, 500 University Ave., Toronto, Ontario M5G 1V8, ☎ 416/598–4083, 800/268–8825 in Canada).

➤ INSURANCE INFORMATION: In the U.K., **Association of British Insurers** (✉ 51 Gresham St., London EC2V 7HQ, ☎ 0171/600–3333). In Australia, the **Insurance Council of Australia** (☎ 613/9614–1077, FAX 613/9614–7924).

LANGUAGE

Arabic is Egypt's language. Semitic in origin, in its classical form it is known as the language of Islam. Colloquial Arabic is significantly different than classical, written Arabic and is spoken most commonly in Egypt. Egypt's colloquial dialect differs from other Arab countries' dialects. Egyptian Arabic is nonetheless understood across the Arab world because of Egypt's popular film and television reputation.

Egyptians are gesture-oriented people. Plenty of large arm and hand movements will explain a lot that words aren't needed for. This non-verbal communication can be especially effective if you do not necessarily understand what someone is trying to tell you. Most Egyptians understand and speak at least a little (if not a lot) English or French. Both languages are requirements in the school system and Egyptians are accustomed to having English speakers around.

Arabic is not an easy language to speak. In addition to there being two kinds of *h*, *s*, *d*, and *t* sounds, there are a few letters that we don't even have in English. The first of these is the *kha*, as in *Khan al-Khalili* (the famous Cairo bazaar), which sounds much like the German *ch* in Bach.

Another letter not found in English is the *ayn*. Difficult to prononounce (and even more difficult to explain in text), it is a lengthened *a* sound interrupted by a guttural extension that sounds a bit like the *ah* in Bach with a hint of the *ch* to terminate the word. It appears in such words as shar'a (Arabic for street). No one will expect you to get this right; just give it your best shot and you're sure to be understood.

We spell the Arabic word for street *shar'a*. You may see it rendered elsewhere as *shari'a*. It has been noted however that this encourages people to pronounce the word *shar-ee-ah*, which in Arabic means Islamic law, rather than street. Consequently, we have omitted the *i*.

There seem to be innumerable ways to transliterate Arabic into the Roman alphabet. We have aimed for the closest approximation of correct pronunciations. One example is the name al-Husayn, which is often spelled el-Hussein. Considering that it is pronounced hu-*sayn*, not hus-*ayn*, we do not double the *s*. In that spirit

we do not generally double conso-
nants unless correct pronounciation
demands it. In the same spirit, *ayn* is
thought to be more akin to the Arabic
sound of the word than is *ein*.

This system of transliteration is one
that many scholars, among them
Albert Hourani, author of *A History
of the Arab Peoples,* now use.

LODGING

The Egyptian Hotel Association rates
all hotels in the country on a five-star
scale. While it might seem like these
stars are more generously given here
than in Europe or the United States,
top-end hotels do have all the facilities and modern conveniences you
need to recuperate after a long day.
The great chasm in Egyptian hotel
standards is much of the rest of the
options: a healthy mid-range of hotels
by and large doesn't exist, and the
quality of low-cost hotels leaves a lot
to be desired.

Two rays of hope shine out from this,
however. One is the good buying
power of U.S. and European currency.
The other is that there are affordable
hotels in the country, and we include
them in this guide.

Most hotel rooms in Egypt come with
a private bathroom and shower. A
standard continental breakfast buffet
is usually included in room rates.
Finer hotels are well equipped with
large swimming pools, an excercise
room, several restaurants, bars, tennis
courts, and room service. Smaller
pensions around Cairo and in southern Egypt are less lavish and much
cheaper.

The practice remains, left over from
the early and mid-1980s when the
Egyptian pound fell in value from
month to month, of hotels charging
room rates in U.S. dollars. At the
time, this kept prices more stable.
Now, its annoyance is lessened by the
likelihood that you will pay for your
room with a credit card. You can, of
course, pay in Egyptian currency if
you prefer.

CAMPING

Guided trips are the best way to ful-
fill that urge to sleep in the desert:
going off on your own is not wise.

See the A to Z sections of Chapters
6 and 7 for guides who can arrange
desert trips.

HOSTELS

No matter what your age, you can
**save on lodging costs by staying at
hostels.** In some 5,000 locations in
more than 70 countries, Hostelling
International (HI), the umbrella
group for a number of national youth
hostel associations, has single-sex,
dorm-style beds and, at many hostels,
"couples" rooms and family accommodations. Membership in any HI
national hostel association, open to
travelers of all ages, allows you to
stay in HI-affiliated hostels at member rates (one-year membership is
about $25 for adults; hostels run
about $10–$25 per night). Members
also have priority if the hostel is full.

➤ HOSTEL ORGANIZATIONS: **Hostelling
International—American Youth
Hostels** (✉ 733 15th St. NW, Suite
840, Washington, DC 20005, ☎ 202/
783–6161, FAX 202/783–6171).
Hostelling International—Canada
(✉ 400-205 Catherine St., Ottawa,
Ontario K2P 1C3, ☎ 613/237–7884,
FAX 613/237–7868). **Youth Hostel
Association of England and Wales**
(✉ Trevelyan House, 8 St. Stephen's
Hill, St. Albans, Hertfordshire AL1
2DY, ☎ 01727/855215 or 01727/
845047, FAX 01727/844126); member-
ship in the U.S. $25, in Canada
C$26.75, in the U.K. £9.30).

MAIL

The quality of the mail service in
Egypt has improved dramatically in
the late 1990s. Egypt's 1,470 postal
offices nationwide are open from 8:30
AM–3 PM. The larger post offices in
Cairo, Muhammad Farid (Downtown), Ataba Square (next to the
Postal Museum), and the Maadi offices are open until 6pm daily. All
post offices are closed on public
holidays and the first days of the
Greater and Lesser Birams.

Postcards to countries outside of the
Middle East cost £e1.25 and take a
minimum of seven days to reach their
destination. If you are mailing a letter
within Egypt it will cost you a mere
20 piasters and take two days to
reach its destination. A more costly

THE GOLD GUIDE / SMART TRAVEL TIPS

THE GOLD GUIDE / SMART TRAVEL TIPS

express mail service is also available: same-day service within the country costs £e5, within the Arab world next-day service costs £e30, anywhere else in the world costs £e45 and arrives within 48 hours. Note that these dates are what the postal service advises; they do not reflect how long mail will actually take to arrive. If in doubt, double these times.

RECEIVING MAIL

If you decide to use Poste Restante you will be notified of your package within 24 hours and will be expected to pick it up within 30 days.

MONEY

Traveler's checks are a good option to use at hotels and four- and five-star restaurants. Actually cashing them, however, is a bit more difficult, as working hours of exchange offices and banks are short. ATMs are in abundance in Cairo and are located in major shopping areas of most smaller cities and tourist areas. Carrying cash is not much of a worry here (as long as you are not riding on public buses).

Credit cards are accepted almost everywhere, except in most town bazaars. If you are planning on doing any bargaining, cash is your best option. If you are bargaining and the stall or shop owner accepts credit cards, know that you won't be getting the best deal.

At press time, the exchange rate was £e3.43 to the U.S. dollar; £e2.20 to $1 Canadian; £e5.71 to £1 Sterling; £e2.11 to $1 Australian.

COSTS

At press time, the cost of a cup of coffee at a hotel was £e5; a falafel sandwich £e1; a bottle of Coke 75p; a 2km taxi ride in Cairo £e5.

CREDIT & DEBIT CARDS

Should you use a credit card or a debit card when traveling? Both have benefits. A credit card allows you to delay payment and gives you certain rights as a consumer (☞ Consumer Protection, *above*). A debit card, also known as a check card, deducts funds directly from your checking account and helps you stay within your budget. When you want to rent a car, though, you may still need an old-fashioned credit card. Although you can always *pay* for your car with a debit card, some agencies will not allow you to *reserve* a car with a debit card.

Otherwise, the two types of plastic are virtually the same. Both will get you cash advances at ATMs worldwide if your card is properly programmed with your personal identification number (PIN). Both offer excellent, wholesale exchange rates. And both protect you against unauthorized use if the card is lost or stolen. Your liability is limited to $50, as long as you report the card missing.

➤ ATM LOCATIONS: **Cirrus** (☎ 800/424–7787). **Plus** (☎ 800/843–7587) for locations of ATMs worldwide.

CURRENCY

The Egyptian pound (£e) is divided into 100 piasters (p). Bank notes currently in circulation are the following: 10p, 25p, and 50p notes; £e1, £e5, £e10, £e20, £e50, and £e100 notes. There are also 5p, 10p, 20p, and 25p coins.

EXCHANGING MONEY

As a rule of thumb, the best place to exchange your money is at banks, which charge a small fee. Bank hours are 8:30 AM to 2 PM, Saturday–Thursday. There are also some exchange offices that charge no fee.

Although fees charged for ATM transactions may be higher abroad than at home, Cirrus and Plus exchange rates are excellent, because they are based on wholesale rates offered only by major banks. You won't do as well at exchange booths in airports or rail and bus stations, in hotels, in restaurants, or in stores, although you may find their hours more convenient. To avoid lines at airport exchange booths, **get a bit of local currency before you leave home.**

➤ EXCHANGE SERVICES: **Chase *Currency To Go*** (☎ 800/935–9935; 935–9935 in NY, NJ, and CT). **International Currency Express** (☎ 888/842–0880 on the East Coast, 888/278–6628 on the West Coast). **Thomas Cook Currency Services**

(☎ 800/287–7362 for telephone orders and retail locations).

TRAVELER'S CHECKS

Lost or stolen traveler's checks can usually be replaced within 24 hours. To ensure a speedy refund, buy your own traveler's checks—don't let someone else pay for them: irregularities like this can cause delays. The person who bought the checks should make the call to request a refund.

PACKING

Above all, bring light clothing made of breathable fabric, preferably cotton. In summer or early fall, pants, skirts, and dresses are most appropriate for women. Remember that although Egypt is the one of the more liberal of the Arab countries, it remains essentially conservative. It is not mandatory, but many Muslim Egyptian women chose to cover their hair and dress very modestly in loose clothing, long sleeves, and long skirts. For this reason it is advisable that women visiting Egypt dress discreetly. Egyptians are accustomed to travelers dressing differently than they do themselves, but it still best not to attract undue attention. Short-sleeve clothing is acceptable, but stay away from tank tops and shorts, short skirts, and short dresses—baring shoulders, upper arms, and knees is considered immodest. In beach resorts in the Sinai or along the Red Sea Coast, shorts are acceptable. Men should stick to pants in the city, as Egyptians tend to see shorts as boys' clothing, or something akin to underwear. Do bring a light sweater or jacket, as Egypt has a desert climate, and temperatures tend to drop at night.

Do not forget to **bring a hat and sunglasses for long days in the sun.** Likewise, sunscreen is a must. Daytime heat can be more overwhelming than you would expect. Also bring bug repellent, tissues, and some premoistened face cloths. All of these items will come in handy along the way.

In winter, it is essential to bring sweaters and other warm clothing. Buildings generally aren't centrally heated, which can make them even colder than it is outside.

Bring an extra pair of eyeglasses or contact lenses in your carry-on luggage, and if you have a health problem, pack enough medication to last the entire trip or have your doctor write you a prescription using the drug's generic name, because brand names vary from country to country. It's important that you don't put prescription drugs or valuables in luggage to be checked: it might go astray. To avoid problems with customs officials, carry medications in the original packaging. Also, don't forget the addresses of offices that handle refunds of lost traveler's checks.

LUGGAGE

How many carry-on bags you can bring with you is up to the airline. Most allow two, but the limit is often reduced to one on certain flights. Gate agents will take excess baggage—including bags they deem oversize—from you as you board and add it to checked luggage. To avoid this situation, make sure that everything you carry aboard will fit under your seat. Also, get to the gate early, and request a seat at the back of the plane; you'll probably board first, while the overhead bins are still empty. Since big, bulky baggage attracts the attention of gate agents and flight attendants on a busy flight, make sure your carry-on is really a carry-on. Finally, a carry-on that's long and narrow is more likely to remain unnoticed than one that's wide and squarish.

If you are flying internationally, note that baggage allowances may be determined not by piece but by weight—generally 88 pounds (40 kilograms) in first class, 66 pounds (30 kilograms) in business class, and 44 pounds (20 kilograms) in economy.

Airline liability for baggage is limited to $1,250 per person on flights within the United States. On international flights it amounts to $9.07 per pound or $20 per kilogram for checked baggage (roughly $640 per 70-pound bag) and $400 per passenger for

THE GOLD GUIDE / SMART TRAVEL TIPS

unchecked baggage. You can buy additional coverage at check-in for about $10 per $1,000 of coverage, but it excludes a rather extensive list of items, shown on your airline ticket.

Before departure, **itemize your bags' contents** and their worth, and label the bags with your name, address, and phone number. (If you use your home address, cover it so that potential thieves can't see it readily.) Inside each bag, **pack a copy of your itinerary.** At check-in, **make sure that each bag is correctly tagged** with the destination airport's three-letter code. If your bags arrive damaged or fail to arrive at all, file a written report with the airline before leaving the airport.

PASSPORTS & VISAS

When traveling internationally, make **two photocopies of the data page of your passport** (one for someone at home and another for you, carried separately from your passport). If you lose your passport, promptly call the nearest embassy or consulate and the local police.

ENTERING EGYPT

Egypt requires that all visitors have a valid passport and a visa. You cannot enter Egypt with a passport that's due to expire within six months. Visas may be obtained in advance through an Egyptian consulate office or, for one-month stays or less, upon arrival at Cairo, Luxor, or Hurghada airports. Expect to pay $15–$20 for the visa.

PASSPORT OFFICES

The best time to apply for a passport or to renew is during the fall and winter. Before any trip, be sure to check your passport's expiration date and, if necessary, renew it as soon as possible. (Some countries won't allow you to enter on a passport that's due to expire in six months or less.)

➤ AUSTRALIAN CITIZENS: **Australian Passport Office** (☎ 131–232).

➤ CANADIAN CITIZENS: **Passport Office** (☎ 819/994–3500 or 800/567–6868).

➤ NEW ZEALAND CITIZENS: **New Zealand Passport Office** (☎ 04/494–0700 for information on how to apply, 0800/727–776 for information on applications already submitted).

➤ U.K. CITIZENS: **London Passport Office** (☎ 0990/21010), for fees and documentation requirements and to request an emergency passport.

➤ U.S. CITIZENS: **National Passport Information Center** (☎ 900/225–5674; calls are charged at 35¢ per minute for automated service, $1.05 per minute for operator service).

SAFETY

Egypt is far safer than you think. Indeed, it is a sad irony that the handful of terrorist attacks involving foreigners has given Egypt a reputation as a dangerous place, because it is blissfully free of the sort of ordinary social violence—murder, mugging, vandalism, and so on—that is all too common in the West. Even in Cairo there are no "bad" neighborhoods, only poor ones, and you can freely walk anywhere at any hour, which is why the city was recently ranked the second safest in the world, after Tokyo.

Pickpocketing is a minor concern in heavily touristed areas like bazaars, and women can reduce **unwanted advances** by dressing in a way that reveals little skin. Generally, you will find that you are more likely to be assaulted by hospitality than by violence.

What Egypt does have, unfortunately, are rare but shocking attacks that seek to destabilize the government by scaring tourists away: Tourism revenues are the lifeblood of the country. The government has stepped up security following the Luxor massacre in November 1997—which was likely the last gasp of the Islamist groups rather than a sign of their resurgence—but it is impossible to stop every radical, so the threat of future attacks remains. Once you land in Egypt, however, you will realize how remote this threat feels.

SENIOR-CITIZEN TRAVEL

To qualify for age-related discounts, **mention your senior-citizen status up front** when booking hotel reservations (not when checking out) and before you're seated in restaurants (not when paying the bill). Note that discounts may be limited to certain menus, days, or hours. When renting a car, **ask about promotional car-rental discounts,** which can be cheaper than senior-citizen rates.

➤ ADVENTURES: **Overseas Adventure Travel** (✉ Grand Circle Corporation, 625 Mt. Auburn St., Cambridge, MA 02138, ☎ 617/876–0533 or 800/221–0814, ℻ 617/876–0455).

➤ EDUCATIONAL PROGRAMS: **Elderhostel** (✉ 75 Federal St., 3rd floor, Boston, MA 02110, ☎ 617/426–8056).

SHOPPING

By far the most interesting shopping in Egypt is found at the *souks* (bazaars). Cairo's age-old Khan al-Khalili is the most outstanding souk in the country. Alexandria's Attarine Market, Luxor's old and new souks, and Aswan's souk are also well worth a look.

Negotiating is the name of the game at bazaars—a fact that will be unsettling to some Westerners. Three brief pointers: never make the first offer; start negotiating from about half of what is asked if the price seems farfetched; and try to look disinterested (a gleam in your eye will make it harder to bargain down the seller).

STUDENT TRAVEL

Note that student prices for ancient monuments—from the pyramids outside Cairo to the Nile Valley sights—are half that of prices quoted throughout this guide.

➤ STUDENT I.D.s & SERVICES: **Council on International Educational Exchange** (✉ CIEE, 205 E. 42nd St., 14th floor, New York, NY 10017, ☎ 212/822–2600 or 888/268–6245, ℻ 212/822–2699), for mail orders only, in the United States. **Travel Cuts** (✉ 187 College St., Toronto, Ontario M5T 1P7, ☎ 416/979–2406 or 800/667–2887) in Canada.

TAXES

Egypt has no V.A.T. (Value-Added Tax) for tourists.

The taxes you will have to reckon with are in restaurants and hotels. Meal taxes vary around the county; in Cairo they are as high as 26%. Hotel taxes in Cairo, Sharm al-Sheikh, and Hurghada are 19%; 21% in Luxor and Aswan. Restaurant tabs and hotel rates listed in this guide include these taxes.

TAXIS

Riding in a taxi anywhere in Egypt is an adventure you shouldn't miss. All taxis have meters. The catch is that they don't really work.

Taxis in Cairo are black and white and can be seen on every street. Be sure that you discuss the fare with the taxi driver (here and throughout the country) before you embark on your trip. Most jaunts within downtown Cairo itself should cost no more than £e5.

Most drivers will speak a bit of English. The best way to get where you want to go is to have someone at your hotel write down the name of the street you are going to in Arabic. If you know where you are going and wish to direct the driver yourself, remember the following words: *ala toul* and *doughri* (straight ahead), *yameen* (right), *shamal* (left), and *hina kwais* (here is fine).

TELEPHONES

Egypt's telecommunications system is improving. You can now rent mobile phones upon arrival from most 5-star hotels, although roaming is not yet on par with the United States. Landlines are government run and therefore very affordable.

COUNTRY CODES

The country code for Egypt is 20. Various city codes within Egypt are Cairo 02, Alexandria 03, Luxor 095, Aswan 097, Sharm al-Sheikh 062, Hurghada 065. When dialing an Egyptian number from abroad, drop the initial 0 from the local area code.

DIRECTORY & OPERATOR INFORMATION

There is no toll-free directory information service. If you dial 140, you can reach a very effective directory assistant if you speak fluent Arabic. With a little bit of creativity and some luck you might still be able to get the number you need in English.

INTERNATIONAL CALLS

International calls are most cost effective when made from the Telephone Central. After 8 PM calls are cheapest. Give the number and name of your party to the operator along with the number of minutes you would like to speak.

Another option for making international calls is the business centers around Egypt, but their fees can be 20–30% higher. Calls from your hotel room can cost anywhere from double to triple the fee of Telephone Central.

International calling cards make the task very accessible and reliable. Access numbers of major calling card companies are listed below.

AT&T, MCI, and Sprint international access codes make calling the United States relatively convenient, but you may find the local access number blocked in many hotel rooms. First ask the hotel operator to connect you. If the hotel operator balks, ask for an international operator, or dial the international operator yourself. One way to improve your odds of getting connected to your long-distance carrier is to travel with more than one company's calling card (a hotel may block Sprint, for example, but not MCI). If all else fails, call from a pay phone in the hotel lobby.

➤ ACCESS CODES: **AT&T Direct** (in Cairo: ☎ 520–0200; elsewhere in Egypt: ☎ 02/520–0200). **MCI WorldPhone** (in Cairo: ☎ 355–5770; elsewhere in Egypt: ☎ 02/355–5770). **Sprint International Access** (in Cairo: ☎ 395–5513; elsewhere in Egypt: ☎ 02/356–4777).

LOCAL CALLS

You can make local calls from just about anywhere: kiosks, grocery stores, craft stores, coffee shops, et cetera. Most of these places charge 25p–50p per call.

PUBLIC PHONES

Throughout towns in Egypt there are Telephone Centrals from where you can make domestic long distance calls as well as international calls. Ask at your hotel reception desk if you want to try this option.

Archaic yellow public phones are few and far between, and when you do find one, you'll need the right-sized coin. They take silver 10p coins, but the coins have changed so many times over the past decade that you never know if the ones you have will fit the slot. You'll be better off using a kiosk phone than the old yellow jobs.

Newer card phones are scattered throughout the major cities and all around major tourist attractions, but finding the pre-paid calling cards will take some luck. Try big supermarkets.

TIPPING

Baksheesh is a word that every traveler to Egypt gets well acquainted with. It means tip, and many people expect one. For this reason it is important to carry around a good number of 50p notes and £e1 bills in your pocket. Porters, taxi drivers, doorkeepers, and many others will expect this of you. There is no need to give a lot of money, small tips are fine. It is customary to leave a 10% tip (before taxes) at a restaurant. The bill already has a 12% service charge, a 5% government tax, and a 2% city tax included in the total.

TOUR OPERATORS

Buying a prepackaged tour or independent vacation can make your trip to Egypt less expensive and more hassle-free. Because everything is prearranged, you'll spend less time planning.

Operators that handle several hundred thousand travelers per year can use their purchasing power to give you a good price. Their high volume may also indicate financial stability. But some small companies provide more personalized service; because they tend to specialize, they may also be more knowledgeable about a given area.

BOOKING WITH AN AGENT

Travel agents are excellent resources. In fact, large operators accept bookings made only through travel agents. But it's a good idea to **collect brochures from several agencies,** because some agents' suggestions may be influenced by relationships with tour and package firms that reward them for volume sales. If you have a special interest, **find an agent with expertise in that area**; ASTA (☞ Travel Agencies, *below*) has a database of specialists worldwide.

Make sure your travel agent knows the accommodations and other services. Ask about the hotel's location, room size, beds, and whether it has a pool, room service, or programs for children, if you care about these. Has your agent been there in person or sent others you can contact?

BUYER BEWARE

Each year consumers are stranded or lose their money when tour operators—even very large ones with excellent reputations—go out of business. So **check out the operator.** Find out how long the company has been in business, and ask several travel agents about its reputation. If the package or tour you are considering is priced lower than in your wildest dreams, **be skeptical.** Try to **book with a company that has a consumer-protection program.** If the operator has such a program, you'll find information about it in the company's brochure. If the operator you are considering does not offer some kind of consumer protection, then ask for references from satisfied customers.

In the U.S., members of the National Tour Association and United States Tour Operators Association are required to set aside funds to cover your payments and travel arrangements in case the company defaults. It's also a good idea to choose a company that participates in the American Society of Travel Agent's Tour Operator Program (TOP). This gives you a forum if there are any disputes between you and your tour operator; ASTA will act as mediator.

➤ TOUR-OPERATOR RECOMMENDATIONS: **American Society of Travel Agents** (☞ Travel Agencies, *below*). **National Tour Association** (✉ NTA, 546 E. Main St., Lexington, KY 40508, ☎ 606/226–4444 or 800/755–8687). **United States Tour Operators Association** (✉ USTOA, 342 Madison Ave., Suite 1522, New York, NY 10173, ☎ 212/599–6599

or 800/468–7862, FAX 212/599–6744).

COSTS

The more your package or tour includes, the better you can predict the ultimate cost of your vacation. Make sure you know exactly what is covered, and **beware of hidden costs.** Are taxes, tips, and service charges included? Transfers and baggage handling? Entertainment and excursions? These can add up.

Prices for packages and tours are usually quoted per person, based on two sharing a room. If traveling solo, you may be required to pay the full double-occupancy rate. Some operators eliminate this surcharge if you agree to be matched with a roommate of the same sex, even if one is not found by departure time.

GROUP TOURS

Among companies that sell tours to Egypt, the following have a proven reputation and offer plenty of options. The classifications used below represent different price categories, and you'll probably encounter these terms when talking to a travel agent or tour operator. The key difference is usually in accommodations, which run from budget to better, and better-yet to best.

➤ SUPER-DELUXE: **Abercrombie & Kent** (✉ 1520 Kensington Rd., Oak Brook, IL 60521-2141, ☎ 630/954–2944 or 800/323–7308, FAX 630/954–3324). **Travcoa** (✉ Box 2630, 2350 S.E. Bristol St., Newport Beach, CA 92660, ☎ 714/476–2800 or 800/992–2003, FAX 714/476–2538).

➤ DELUXE: **Globus** (✉ 5301 S. Federal Circle, Littleton, CO 80123-2980, ☎ 303/797–2800 or 800/221–0090, FAX 303/347–2080). **Maupintour** (✉ 1515 St. Andrews Dr., Lawrence, KS 66047, ☎ 785/843–1211 or 800/255–4266, FAX 785/843–8351).

➤ FIRST-CLASS: **Brendan Tours** (✉ 15137 Califa St., Van Nuys, CA 91411, ☎ 818/785–9696 or 800/421–8446, FAX 818/902–9876). **Collette Tours** (✉ 162 Middle St., Pawtucket, RI 02860, ☎ 401/728–3805 or 800/340–5158, FAX 401/

THE GOLD GUIDE / SMART TRAVEL TIPS

728–4745). **Insight International Tours** (⊠ 745 Atlantic Ave., #720, Boston, MA 02111, ☎ 617/482–2000 or 800/582–8380, FAX 617/482–2884 or 800/622–5015). **Trafalgar Tours** (⊠ 11 E. 26th St., New York, NY 10010, ☎ 212/689–8977 or 800/854–0103, FAX 800/457–6644).

➤ BUDGET: **Trafalgar** (☞ *above*).

THEME TRIPS

➤ ADVENTURE: **Himalayan Travel** (⊠ 110 Prospect St., Stamford, CT 06901, ☎ 203/359–3711 or 800/225–2380, FAX 203/359–3669). **Wilderness Travel** (1102 Ninth St., Berkeley, CA 94710, ☎ 510/558–2488 or 800/368–2794).

➤ ARCHAEOLOGY: **Archaeological Tours** (⊠ 271 Madison Ave., New York, NY 10016, ☎ 212/986–3054, FAX 212/370–1561). **Crow Canyon Archaeological Center** (2339 Road K, Cortez CO 81321, ☎ 970/565–8975 or 800/422–8975, FAX 970/565–4859). **Journeys of the Mind** (⊠ 221 N. Kenilworth Ave. No. 413, Oak Park, IL 60302, ☎ 708/383–9739, FAX 708/254–5154. **Smithsonian Study Tours and Seminars** (⊠ 1100 Jefferson Dr. SW, Room 3045, MRC 702, Washington, DC 20560, ☎ 202/357–4700, FAX 202/633–9250).

➤ ART HISTORY: **Travel With the Met** (⊠ Metropolitan Museum of Art, 1000 Fifth Ave., New York, NY 10028, ☎ 212/570–3956, FAX 212/396–5040).

➤ HORSEBACK RIDING: **Equitour Worldwide Riding Holidays** (⊠ Box 807, Dubois, WY 82513, ☎ 307/455–3363 or 800/545–0019, FAX 307/455–2354).

➤ LEARNING: **IST Cultural Tours** (225 W. 34th St., New York, NY 10122-0913, ☎ 212/563–1202 or 800/833–2111, FAX 212/594–6953). **Smithsonian Study Tours and Seminars** (☞ Archaeology, *above*).

➤ SCUBA DIVING: **Rothschild Dive Safaris** (900 West End Ave., #1B, New York, NY 10025-3525, ☎ 800/359–0747, FAX 212/749–6172).

➤ WALKING/HIKING: **Wilderness Travel** (☞ Adventure, *above*).

TRAIN TRAVEL

There is a direct correlation between how much you are willing to spend on a train ticket and the quality of the train you'll ride. In all first-class cars the no smoking policy is strictly adhered to, and you will enjoy a comfortable air-conditioned ride to your destination. The food is nothing to write home about and ranks right alongside airplane food. Train trips are very scenic, taking you through agricultural villages and vast deserts.

Although the sleeper train to Luxor and Aswan has a charm all its own, the ride is long and cramped. Flying to Luxor and Aswan is really the best option. The train is the best option to Alexandria—it is easier, less expensive, and, believe it or not, faster.

RESERVATIONS

It is strongly advised to purchase your ticket at least a day before your planned departure. That actually allows you to plan your trip with a degree of certainty, because train schedules often seem to be random.

Cairo–Alexandria first-class one-way tickets cost £e40; second-class tickets costs £e20. On this run trains operate from 6 AM until 10 PM on the hour. Cairo–al-Minya (the principle city of the Middle Nile Valley) first class tickets cost £e30; second class £e20. On that line the trains run from 5 AM until 1 AM every 45 minutes. Luxor–Aswan–Cairo trains run from 6:20 AM until 9 PM every 90 minutes. When you purchase your ticket, ask if your train is an express or local.

For exact schedules and ticket prices, inquire and purchase tickets a few days before departing at the Egyptian Tourist Authority in Cairo (⊠ Maydan Ramses, ☎ 02/764–214), or at your hotel reception desk.

TRAVEL AGENCIES

For listings of travel agencies within Egypt, *see* the A to Z sections in chapters throughout this book.

A good travel agent puts your needs first. Look for an agency that has been in business at least five years, emphasizes customer service, and has someone on staff who specializes in your destination. In addition, **make sure the agency belongs to a professional trade organization,** such as ASTA in the United States. If your travel agency is also acting as your tour operator, *see* Buyer Beware in Tour Operators, *above.*

➤ LOCAL AGENT REFERRALS: **American Society of Travel Agents** (ASTA, ☎ 800/965–2782 24-hr hot line, ℻ 703/684–8319). **Association of Canadian Travel Agents** (⊠ Suite 201, 1729 Bank St., Ottawa, Ontario K1V 7Z5, ☎ 613/521–0474, ℻ 613/521–0805). **Association of British Travel Agents** (⊠ 55–57 Newman St., London W1P 4AH, ☎ 0171/637–2444, ℻ 0171/637–0713). **Australian Federation of Travel Agents** (☎ 02/9264–3299). **Travel Agents' Association of New Zealand** (☎ 04/499–0104).

TRAVEL GEAR

Travel catalogs specialize in useful items, such as compact alarm clocks and travel irons, that can **save space when packing.** They also offer dual-voltage appliances, currency converters, and foreign-language phrase books.

➤ CATALOGS: **Magellan's** (☎ 800/962–4943, ℻ 805/568–5406). **Orvis Travel** (☎ 800/541–3541, ℻ 540/343–7053). **TravelSmith** (☎ 800/950–1600, ℻ 800/950–1656).

U.S. GOVERNMENT

Government agencies can be an excellent source of inexpensive travel information. When planning your trip, **find out what government materials are available.**

➤ ADVISORIES: **U.S. Department of State** (⊠ Overseas Citizens Services Office, Room 4811 N.S., Washington, DC 20520; ☎ 202/647–5225 or ℻ 202/647–3000 for interactive hot line; ☎ 301/946–4400 for computer bulletin board); enclose a self-addressed, stamped, business-size envelope.

➤ PAMPHLETS: **Consumer Information Center** (⊠ Consumer Information Catalogue, Pueblo, CO 81009, ☎ 719/948–3334 or 888/878–3256) for a free catalog that includes travel titles.

VISITOR INFORMATION

For information about traveling to and within Egypt before you go, contact the nearest office of the **Egyptian Tourist Authority** (ETA).

➤ EGYPTIAN TOURIST AUTHORITY: **U.S.:** ⊠ 630 5th Ave., Suite 1706, New York, NY 10111, ☎ 212/336–3570, ℻ 212/956–6439; ⊠ 645 N. Michigan Ave., Suite 829, Chicago, IL 60611, ☎ 312/280–4666, ℻ 312/280–4788; ⊠ 8383 Wilshire Blvd., Suite 215, Beverly Hills, CA 90211, ☎ 213/653–8815, ℻ 213/653–8961. **Canada:** ⊠ 1253 McGill College Ave., Suite 250, Montréal, PQ H3B2Y5, ☎ 514/861–4420, ℻ 514/861–8071. **South Africa:** ⊠ Box 6298, Parklands, Johannesburg 2121, ☎ 011/880–9602, ℻ 011/880–9604. **U.K.:** ⊠ Egyptian State Tourist Office, Egyptian House, 170 Picadilly, London W1V9DD, ☎ 0171/493–5282, ℻ 0171/408–0295.

WHEN TO GO

It's best to visit Egypt in the cooler season, which begins in November and ends in March. Summers can be oppressive, especially in Cairo, Luxor, and Aswan. And forget about going to the desert oases in summer.

Generally speaking, it doesn't rain in Egypt. In cooler months, Alexandria and the Mediterranean coast can get cloudy, and a few wet days aren't uncommon. Considering how arid and relentlessly sunny the rest of the country is, these brief wet conditions can be a welcome relief.

Weather along the Mediterranean or Red Sea coast remains temperate throughout the year. The water does get a bit cold between December and March, but never frigid.

CLIMATE

Egypt's climate is characterized by hot and dry summers in most of the country. The areas that are most humid are the Delta and along the Mediterranean coast. Summer lasts from the end of April until the beginning of October. Spring is very short, if not nonexistent. Winter is mild, but nights do get cool.

The most important time of year to keep in mind is the 50 days of the *Khamseen*. Between the end of March and mid-May, dust storms whip up occasionally and blot out the sky.

Southern Egypt becomes brutally hot in summer. So if your trip includes a few days in Luxor, we highly recommend that you go between November and March—for your own comfort.

➤ FORECASTS: **Weather Channel Connection** (☎ 900/932–8437), 95¢ per minute from a Touch-Tone phone.

Climate in Egypt

CAIRO

Jan.	66F	19C	May	90F	32C	Sept.	90F	32C
	46	9		63	17		68	20
Feb.	69F	21C	June	94F	34C	Oct.	86F	30C
	49	9		64	18		64	18
Mar.	75F	24C	July	94F	34C	Nov.	77F	25C
	52	11		71	22		57	14
Apr.	83F	28C	Aug.	95F	35C	Dec.	69F	21C
	57	14		71	22		50	10

ALEXANDRIA

Jan.	65F	18C	May	80F	27C	Sept.	85F	29C
	49	9		62	17		70	21
Feb.	67F	19C	June	83F	28C	Oct.	86F	30C
	50	10		68	20		64	18
Mar.	70F	21C	July	85F	30C	Nov.	76F	24C
	52	11		73	23		59	15
Apr.	75F	23C	Aug.	87F	30C	Dec.	69F	20C
	56	14		73	23		52	11

LUXOR

Jan.	73F	23C	May	103F	39C	Sept.	101F	39C
	42	5		69	21		71	22
Feb.	78F	25C	June	105F	41C	Oct.	95F	35C
	44	7		73	23		64	18
Mar.	84F	29C	July	105F	41C	Nov.	85F	30C
	51	11		75	24		54	12
Apr.	95F	35C	Aug.	106F	41C	Dec.	77F	25C
	60	16		75	24		46	8

SHARM AL-SHEIKH

Jan.	75F	24C	May	91F	33C	Sept.	93F	34C
	56	13		75	24		79	26
Feb.	77F	25C	June	99F	37C	Oct.	90F	32C
	57	14		79	26		73	23
Mar.	78F	26C	July	101F	38C	Nov.	82F	28C
	57	14		80	27		66	19
Apr.	84F	29C	Aug.	100F	38C	Dec.	73F	23C
	64	18		80	27		61	16

1 Destination: Egypt

LIVING IN AN ANTIQUE LAND

PEOPLE COME TO EGYPT for its antiquities, and Egypt is ancient on a scale most of us can barely begin to comprehend. The civilizations that we in the West see as occupying the outermost reaches of antiquity—the Greece of Homer, say—are only middle-aged by Egyptian standards. When Alexander the Great extended the Hellenic world to include the Nile Delta 2,300 years ago, Egypt was already in its 30th Dynasty. And by the time the Romans erected the Colosseum, the great king Ramesses II had been entombed for 1,300 years. By the calendar that most of the world uses, time starts with the birth of Jesus Christ. Today, we are closer to that beginning than Christ himself was to the pharaoh Djoser, who built the Step Pyramid in Saqqara.

To say the least, the land is rich with temples: soaring lotus-bud columns; enormous stone portals laced with delicate carvings of gods, wars won, people honored; elaborate underground tombs as brilliantly colored as the day they were painted; windswept desert monasteries where Christian monks first retreated from the world; and richly decorated mosques with minarets that pierce the sky. It was here that science, architecture, and astronomy first achieved genuine sophistication. And it was here that an unimportant young king's treasure—that of Tutankhamun, a modest display by the standards of his day—would come to light some 3,300 years after his death and stun the world with its opulence. Indeed, there is hardly a stretch of the Nile Valley from Aswan in the south to the Delta in the north that does not exhibit the physical remains of the 5,000 years of civilization that have clung to life at the river's edge.

As extraordinary as these sights are, they will probably not be the things that linger in your memory after you return home. It is the rhythm of life in Egypt—from the Mediterranean feel of Alexandria to the electric pace of Cairo to the timelessness of desert villages—that is unforgettable. In a world that seems to get smaller and more homogeneous by the day, Egypt lives defiantly by its own rules. Because in spite being the recipient of a century's worth of organized tourism, Egypt, outside a few pockets, is still a place that exists for its residents, not its visitors. It is the real thing. As a visitor you will have to learn how to accommodate Egypt and not hope that Egypt, with 5,000 years of momentum behind it, will accommodate you.

Egyptians are keenly aware of the degree to which the world misunderstands them. Cairo is the second safest city in the world behind Tokyo, and Egypt is one of the least violent societies, yet most foreigners come expecting the terrorism and bloodshed that the news media almost exclusively report. Egyptians practice two religions—Islam and Christianity—that preach peace, yet they have been branded as fanatics. And they live in a present that is in so many ways a pale shadow of the grandeur of their past, even though, for the past 2,000 years, Egypt has been either the capital or the crown jewel of every empire in the region. It has long been the cultural and intellectual center of the Arab world. It has been the home of al-Azhar, Islam's most prestigious university, for 1,000 years. But today it is a country struggling under the combined challenges of a population explosion, slow job growth, administrative neglect, and a diminished standing in the Middle East.

One of the ironies of the Middle East is that the least populous countries have the most oil. So while fabulous wealth is concentrated in the hands of relatively few Saudis and Kuwaitis, most of the 60 million Egyptians face a more dire situation. In the last two decades, many young men have been forced to leave behind their wives and small children, sometimes for years at a time, to take the jobs in the Persian Gulf that Gulf Arabs, bloated with petrol dollars, no longer care to do themselves. During oil's boom years, their hard, thankless work allowed them to send back to Egypt money that transformed their villages with new concrete homes, refrigerators, and televisions. Now those boom years are over. The price of oil has fallen sharply, and many Egyptian workers have been sent home.

Opportunity doesn't exactly await them back home. Agriculture is still the main industry in the countryside, and the state is the largest employer in the cities—and neither of these count as growth industries. Recently the government has expressed a new commitment to private enterprise and economic reform. And ads for cellular phones and luxury cars have increased as a result. But so far this has created few jobs for the general population. The latest twist of this economic inertia is that in Cairo, where housing is in short supply, parents will rarely let their daughter marry a man without an apartment. Few men can afford an apartment without a good job, and because a good job is so hard to find, there are legions of single men in their late twenties and early thirties unable to marry.

ENTER THE PERENNIAL EGYPTIAN capacity for adapting and surviving—an evolutionary adjustment, perhaps, to the variability of centuries of annual Nile floods. Far from being a nation of angry, desperate souls, the people not only survive, but they do so with a lingering humanity that is astounding. This might not be obvious from the locals you'll see hanging around tourist sights like the pyramids and the Khan al-Khalili; they've been hardened by the trade. But elsewhere in Cairo, generosity and compassion are more readily apparent. Few people on Earth enjoy a joke as much as Egyptians do, and you'll see them in cafés at all hours of the day and night laughing with their friends over shared hardships. And for all of Egypt's other problems, there are few of the social ills that plague richer societies: crime is low, drug use uncommon, divorce rare, and only a tiny fraction of babies are born out of wedlock. That America of the 1950s, so bathed in the glow of nostalgia—the small-town life of tight communal bonds where the butcher has known your family for generations and everyone looks out for each other—is alive and well in Egypt at the turn of the millennium.

It is these communal bonds that give Egypt its strength as a nation and enable its people to cope with the absence of opportunities. Family members look out for one another, giving when they can and taking when they need to. Egyptians take great pride in the force of those ties. For many, admiration for the West's opportunities is tempered by a sense of despair at what they see as our social decay. Looking at us through the distorted lens of American movies and pop culture, Egyptians often say that we have lost God. And if there is one thing that is immediately palpable in Egypt, it is the degree to which religion, whether it is Islam or Christianity, is woven into the fabric of everyday life. It is a touchstone of identity, a source of comfort and hope, a constant presence.

This religious revival from a more politically secular period earlier in the century has mostly taken the form of private choices—prayer, devotion to God, and commitment to family and friends. For most people these are not political choices, and they don't imply support for fundamentalists who want to overthrow the government. This does make Egypt a fairly conservative place in other ways. It is a good idea, for example, to try to respect some of the basic social rules, the kinds of things that you would learn by watching how Egyptians themselves behave: men don't wear shorts (which are seen as underwear), women dress modestly, and no one kisses or drinks alcohol in public.

There is another side to life in Egypt, of course, behind the closed doors of bars and hotels and private parties, where many of these same rules are broken without concern. Learning which rules you can break and where you can break them is one of the intriguing aspects of Egyptian life. It is something Egyptians themselves are still trying to figure out.

—Sean Rocha

NEW AND NOTEWORTHY

Security has been tightened at most monuments following the massacre at Deir al-Bahri (Hatshepsut's Mortuary Temple) in Luxor in November 1997. The new measures consist of an increased presence of armed guards at major sites and greater patrolling of the surrounding areas, even though the underlying grievances of most Islamist groups—poverty, lack of jobs, corruption—have hardly been addressed.

The massacre notwithstanding, Egypt has always felt astonishingly safe, which often comes as a shock, considering the fears that news reports abroad understandably raise. The fact remains that there is no public support whatsoever in Egypt for terrorist violence or bloodletting. You are far more likely to remember Egyptians for their hospitality toward visitors and patience in the face of adversity than for any sense of hostility toward Westerners.

Air quality in Cairo has improved considerably—although first-time visitors are not likely to believe it could ever have been worse—following the introduction of unleaded gasoline. Airborne dust particles remain a problem—inevitably, in a city so close to the desert. But lead levels, once among the world's most toxic, have fallen substantially. Ingeniously, the government introduced unleaded gasoline by stealth, witholding news of the change from Cairo drivers in an effort to preempt any perceived reduction in motor power.

The **second line of the Cairo metro,** which will run from the northern district of Shubra to the Giza suburbs near the pyramids, is currently under construction and will be completed in stages by the year 2000. It will connect with the first line (already in operation) at Maydan Ramesses and Maydan Tahrir (Ramesses and Tahrir squares). Not only will this provide visitors with a convenient, if sometimes crowded, means of getting around the city, but it should also noticeably reduce road traffic, making life easier even if you never use the metro.

Word has leaked out of a plan to **restore Islamic Cairo,** but in the absence of public dialogue the details are sketchy. The district, home to the world's richest concentration of Fatimid and Mamluk monuments, was badly damaged by an October 1992 earthquake, so the restoration plans are long overdue. Early reports are that the government intends to tear down one of al-Azhar University's administrative buildings (not medieval, but attractive nonetheless) to create a large, sterile square linking the mosques of al-Azhar and al-Hussein. Even more disturbing, the many workshops and vendors that give the area such vitality—and admittedly increase wear and tear on the monuments—have been put on notice that they could be evicted to make way for "tourist-oriented" businesses, which will supposedly be cultural in nature but are more likely to be yet more T-shirt and knickknack shops.

In mid-1998 rumors surfaced of a **corniche road** to be built **on Luxor's West Bank**—where there are abundant ancient temples but blessedly little modern development—along with rows of landing docks for tourist cruise ships. If the road proceeds, it will inevitably bring with it tacky souvenir shops and heinous concrete buildings, forever altering the rural feel of the West Bank and cutting it off from the Nile. The president may intervene to halt the project. If not, please do not hesitate to voice the view, to tourism authorities in Luxor, that this road would destroy much of what it is that brings people to Luxor in the first place.

The government's latest pet megaproject is the **Toshka Canal,** an ambitious waterway that would run from Lake Nasser to the Western Desert oases. Its purpose is to open up vast tracts of arable land in what is now largely desert. Although much work has been done already, almost everything about the massive scale and cost of the project suggests that it will not go forward as planned. Nevertheless, if you are interested in seeing what remains of the ancient lifestyles in the Western Desert oases, go soon, because progress on the canal will erode the oases' idyllic sense of isolation.

WHAT'S WHERE

Geography

There is only one reason why 5,000 years of civilization could survive in Egypt: the Nile. Without the river that flows north from Ethiopia and from Lake Victoria in Tanzania, Egypt would be a largely barren waste, traversed by nomads and settled along the coast by fishermen and seafarers. But the river flows on, cutting a jagged green line through the dust-brown sands, then fanning into the verdant sprawl of the Delta. More than 60 million people squeeze themselves into this sliver of life next to the Nile, which constitutes just 4% of the country's total area of 1,000,000 square km (386,000 square mi).

Egypt stands at the crossroads of Africa, Asia, and Mediterranean Europe, a position that has been both a blessing and a curse: Egypt has been the envy of empire-builders everywhere. In ancient times it marked a terminus of the spice trade, whose caravan routes reached all corners of the (known) world. In more modern times, once the Suez Canal started functioning in the 1860s, Egypt became the key to Britain's control over India. All of this has made Egypt a culturally rich, incredibly diverse society, because several millennia of exposure to foreign peoples and ideas have been woven into the very fabric of the country.

It comes as a surprise to many foreigners imagining a land of rolling sand dunes that Egypt is, in parts, quite mountainous—the result of the African and Eurasian plates' grinding together for eons. The Sinai Peninsula and the Red Sea coast near Hurghada are lined with rugged, atmospheric mountains, and Egypt's highest point, Gebel Katherina in the Sinai, stands at 8,652 ft. Most of the country is near sea level. The area known as Lower Egypt begins at Cairo, runs north to the Mediterranean, and is remarkable mainly for the wide delta of lush agricultural land watered by the branches of the Nile. The north coast has long been a summer retreat for Egyptians escaping the heat of the rest of the country, and development now extends west from Alexandria along the shore to Marsa Matruh.

Middle and Upper Egypt run south from Cairo to the border of Nubia, a region within Egypt, near Aswan. After the completion of the Aswan High Dam in the 1960s, most of ancient Nubia was flooded to create Lake Nasser, the largest man-made body of water in the world.

The eastern end of the Sahara Desert surrounds the Nile. The Western Desert, bordered by the Libyan Desert, has four central oases, Bahariyya, Farafra, Dakhla, and Kharga. In this desert's northwest corner, tucked in between the edges of the Libyan Plateau and the formidable Great Sand Sea, resides Siwa Oasis, where its famous oracle is said to have told Alexander the Great that he was descended from the gods. Between the Nile and the Red Sea, the Eastern Desert is the final, forbidding band of the Sahara, the edge of the continent.

Cairo

For well over 1,000 years one of the world's great cosmopolitan cities, Cairo is infinite and inexhaustible. Different religions, different cultures—sometimes, it seems, even different eras—coexist amid the jostling crowds and aging monuments gathered here at the head of the Nile Delta. Don't expect to find a city frozen in layers of ancient history: Cairo's current vitality is as seductive as its rich past.

Alexandria

Home to polyglot communities in ancient and modern times alike, Alexandria embodies the Mediterranean side of Egypt's character: breezy, relaxed, oriented toward the sea. It is a city of cafés and late-night dinners, of horse-drawn carriages and long strolls along the Corniche. And it is a city of history—numerous overlapping histories.

The Nile Valley

From the implacable nobility of its pharaonic monuments to the raw strength of the Aswan High Dam, the Nile Valley is arguably the world's most enduring nexus of human striving for greatness. Natural beauty has fused with historic destiny as nowhere else on the planet. Stark desert borders verdant fields and silvery palm groves; and the diamond gleam of the late afternoon sun plays on the mighty river. Prepare yourself for a dose of pure iconography.

Nile and Lake Nasser Cruises

Roman emperors and their ladies, medieval travelers and historians, 19th-century romantics and antiquarians—all have fallen for the legendary Nile, the majestic ghostly presence of its pharaohs, its healthy climate. Until the completion of the High Dam at Aswan in 1971, the land of Nubia was the age-old link between Egypt and the Sudan. Now it lies under Lake Nasser, on the shores of which stand fabled monuments like Ramesses II's great temple at Abu Simbel.

The Sinai Desert, the Red Sea Coast, and the Suez Canal

Leaving Cairo, at first you see nothing but miles of flat, sandy landscape that seems to extend well beyond the horizon. A barren desert, seemingly lifeless—and the beauty is just beginning. Cross the Suez Canal and the Sinai Desert will take your breath away. As you snake through the rust-colored mountains toward the coast of the Gulf of Aqaba, the crystal sea peeks out between peaks that join it to the sky. Mysteries both on land and under the sea fairly beg to be explored. From the mountains of the eastern Sahara, hills and sands tumble right down into the Red Sea. The Suez Canal Zone isn't much to look at, but remnants of colonial building put up for French canal employees are highlights in neighborhoods in Ismailiya and Port Said.

Western Desert Oases

Turn west from the Nile, and the desertscapes seem to echo with the haunting melodies of the Bedouin flute. Start the day with bread baked in the hot sand, and finish it with a plunge into a hot spring with the moon as your lantern, shining out from the stellar sea of the Milky Way. You'll sip strong, sweet oasis tea or thick Arabic coffee roasted over a desert fire. Embrace all of this and feel like you've crossed into another world.

PLEASURES AND PASTIMES

Egyptians love to socialize, sharing a joke or a tale of woe, and as a result almost everything is organized around large groups. Solitary activities are just not on the agenda. Among city dwellers there is also a former farming culture's bias against physical labor, which shows up in the enormous bellies worn as badges of honor, and in scant demand for outdoor activities or sports—with the exception of soccer, which more people watch than play. All of this might owe something to the fact that there is hardly a shred of nature left in Cairo and Alexandria. When urban life becomes too much even for Egyptians, those who can afford to go to the resorts on the coasts of the Mediterranean, the Red Sea, and the Sinai Peninsula—in big groups, of course, with their friends or families.

Beaches

The beaches of the Mediterranean, the Sinai Peninsula, and the Red Sea are Egypt's outdoor playgrounds—not surprisingly in a country as arid as this. As attractive as the beaches of the Sinai are, and less so those

on the Red Sea coast, it's as much what's beyond them that make them so appealing: in many places the spectacular reefs of the Red Sea and Gulf of Aqaba are a short snorkel or dive right off of the sand.

Cafés

The primary forum of social life, cafés are a second home for most Egyptian men. Each man has his favorite—based on his passion for, say, chess, or the music of Umm Kalthoum—which he will diverge from only with the greatest reluctance. As a result, even in a city as large and overwhelming as Cairo, each café is a microcommunity in which everyone seems to know everyone else. It is worth stopping at as many as you can, although the basic elements are always the same: People debate life, play *towla* (backgammon) or *domino* (dominoes), and while away the hours with as little stress as possible. Cafés are largely a male preserve, but even the most traditional café will usually indulge a foreign-looking woman without issue, and there are numerous more modern cafés with a regular female clientele.

Coffee is called *'ahwa* (stress the *h*), and it can be ordered *saada* (no sugar), *mazboot* (medium), or *ziya'ada* (sweet). *Shai* (tea) is dark and bitter, offset with plenty of sugar, and sometimes available *bi-laban* (with milk) or *bi-n'an'a* (mint). You can also try *karkedeh* (hibiscus tea), *helba* (fenugreek), or *'erfa* (cinnamon). Alcohol is rarely available, but many places will serve the usual soft drinks, which Egyptians often order generically as *hagga sa'a* (which literally means "something cold"). Only fancier places will serve mineral water (*izazat mayya*), although you will always be given a glass of perfectly drinkable tap water with your coffee. Don't be surprised if pedestrians stop and drink your water—sometimes asking first but often not—because it is customary to share. Water pipes (*shisha*) come with honey (*'asal*) or apple (*tuffaha*) tobacco, but definitely *not* hashish.

Cinemas

Being the center of the Arab film world, Egypt has always been a great place for moviegoers. Unfortunately, the decline in the local film industry over the past couple of decades has meant that few Egyptian films appeal to a Western audience (it doesn't help that they're usually not subtitled). There are a number of cinemas that show American or European films, some of them in the sort of enormous movie palaces that no longer exist in the West.

There are a few local peculiarities to keep in mind when you go to watch a movie. First, films usually start at least 30 minutes after the scheduled time. Then there are the intermissions, during which key footage is occasionally lost, so that the movie picks up in a different place than it left off. Seats are assigned at the ticket counter, but you can usually sit any place that's open. You might need that flexibility, because you should expect the ringing of cellular phones and nonstop conversation from the audience. English-language films are generally shown with Arabic subtitles, and films from the United States are censored for nudity and arrive two to six months late. Keep an eye out for listings of films at embassies, which have cultural centers that show uncensored, original-language films.

Dining

In Cairo you can sample everything from French to Thai, but outside the capital it's a different world. Alexandria offers superb seafood due to its proximity to the Mediterranean, but the rest of the country is mostly limited to Egyptian food. This is no bad thing, as Egyptian cuisine is a delicious if somewhat heavy mix of Turkish, Arabic, and indigenous influences, with a French touch thrown in. But for a country so long at the crossroads of the world's spice trade, Egypt makes surprisingly little use of elaborate seasonings and favors freshness over complexity.

Meals start with a soup, like *shorbat 'ads* (lentil), for which Egypt is famous throughout the Middle East, or *molukhiyya*, a thick green-leaf soup sometimes called "Jew's mallow." A wide range of *mezze* (appetizers) follows, and this can make a meal in itself. You'll taste dips like tahina (sesame-seed paste) or *baba ghanouj* (eggplant), *wara einab* (stuffed grape leaves), a crispy local *ta'amiya* (falafel), and *ful* (stewed fava beans). The main course is invariably grilled chicken, often roasted whole in a rotisserie oven, or lamb shish kebab (skewered in chunks) or *kofta* (minced lamb on skewers). Beef is expensive and rarely served in Egyptian restaurants, but *hamam mashwi* (stuffed pigeon) is immensely popular. Fresh vegetables are hard to come by, except in the rather generic cucumber salad, but stewed vegetables such as *bamia* (okra) are common. Every meal comes with round loaves of pita-style bread, either *'aish baladi* (coarse-grain wheat) or *'aish shami* (white).

Diving

Blessed with some of the world's greatest diving sites in the Red Sea, off the Eastern Desert and Sinai coasts, Egypt has become a requisite stop for divers, although Egyptians themselves have mostly been priced out of the sport. The variety of marine life is stunning. Beach dives, wrecks, wall dives, hole dives, anemone gardens, crevice pools, shark caves, and strong currents in places mean that there is a wide variety of diving for divers of all experience levels. If you don't dive, it's a great place to learn. If you do, consider spending a few days on a live-aboard vessel that will take you to a series of wonderful reef and wreck sites.

Ramadan

The month-long Ramadan holiday is a remarkable experience, exciting and, yes, potentially frustrating. Fasting during Ramadan from sunrise to sunset is one of the five requirements of Islam, and it involves abstaining from food, water, cigarettes (the real trial for most Egyptians), sex, and impure thoughts. It is the month when everyone is on their best behavior, and even those who only loosely abide by the strictures of Islam for the rest of the year will give up things like alcohol and gambling.

It is also a time of great community and charity, when wealthy benefactors set up makeshift restaurants, called "tables of mercy," where the poor can break the fast for free. As a visitor you will not be expected to fast, but you may find it is easier, and more satisfying, to fall into the natural rhythm of abstaining all day and then breaking the fast at *iftar* with everyone else. Egyptians will greatly appreciate your solidarity. If you decide not to join in, it is polite to be discreet about it.

If all of this suggests a rather somber month, that mood only applies during the day. Ramadan nights are the liveliest of the year, with entire families making the trek down to al-Hussayn in Islamic Cairo to eat or visit cafés until all hours of the morning. Traditional Arabic music concerts are given throughout the city, and there are plenty of other performances, including the recitation of the oral epic of Abu Zeid—a spectacle worth seeing even if you don't understand the words. There are, as well, all-night feasts held in large elaborately decorated tents that end with the *sohour,* the predawn meal that enables those fasting to get through the next day.

On a practical level, it has to be said that nothing meaningful gets done during Ramadan. Museum, restaurant, and business hours go haywire, and everyone claims to be delirious with hunger and thus unable to function. When the month falls during the short days of winter, people leave work around 3 to beat the traffic home—an impossibility, but still they try—for iftar around 5:30. One great and unexpected pleasure reigns supreme: after the frenzied half hour before iftar, a beautiful, almost eerie calm settles in, and the city appears to empty of its residents. You can walk through even the busiest square and not see a soul.

Soccer

On the night of a big game the streets empty, even in Cairo, as Egypt's soccer fanatics crowd cafés, their eyes glued to the television sets. The big teams are Ahli and Zamalek, both from Cairo, and there are numerous other teams throughout the country. Allegiance is nurtured at birth and taken to the grave.

The quality of play is mixed, and generally sloppy gamesmanship is mixed with occasional flashes of brilliance. Local fans had rounded on the Egyptian national team for not qualifying for the 1998 World Cup in France—a failure chalked up to a chronic unwillingness to get in shape—until the team turned around and won the prestigious African Nations' Cup in Burkina Faso and returned to a hero's welcome. Inevitably, fans now claim they had faith all along. The local season runs from September to May.

FODOR'S CHOICE

Urban Culture

★ Of all of Cairo's cafés, **al-Fishawi** is the living legend, where Turkish coffee and hibiscus-leaf tea have been the fuel for gen-

erations of local talk, that indispensible lubricant of society. Khan al-Khalili, Islamic Cairo.

★ Cairo's **Khan al-Khalili** is the quintessential Egyptian market experience. Parts are touristy, parts are decidedly old world. A trip to Cairo isn't complete without seeing the Khan. Islamic Cairo.

★ From the Bab al-Futuh (the Futuh Gate) in the north, past a millennium of Islamic architecture, coppersmiths' lanes, and into al-Khayammiyya (the tentmakers' bazaar) to the south, **Shar'a al-Mu'iz** is the very lifeline of old Qahira (Cairo). Islamic Cairo.

★ The small **Cavafy Museum** has been reopened in the apartment of Alexandria's great poet Constantine Cavafy, who died largely unknown outside his native city but is now regarded as the finest Greek poet of the 20th century. Downtown Alexandria.

★ The **Grand Trianon** is a tea salon that evokes the old-world grandeur of pre-revolutionary Alexandria, where old women go to keep up their French and young Egyptian couples go for courtship. Downtown Alexandria.

Monuments, Mosques, and Churches

★ The **Chaar-Hachamaim Synagogue** is a spectacular (and often overlooked) Art Nouveau remnant of Egypt's once-powerful Jewish community. Downtown Cairo.

★ The **Mosque of Sultan Hassan,** built, some believe, with stone from the Giza pyramids, is one of the largest Islamic buildings in the world. Islamic Cairo.

★ Delicately carved stucco archways, a minaret wrapped with a staircase, tremendous scale yet purity of design—the **Mosque of Ibn Tulun** is a one-of-a-kind Islamic masterpiece in a city chock-full of exotic architecture. Islamic Cairo (Citadel section).

★ The **Egyptian Antiquities Museum** is a monument to the arts of this ancient land. The museum is a repository of phenomenal works of art, and in it you'll find Tutankhamun's gold, the mummies of mighty pharaohs, and the elegant Amarna-style images of Akhenaten and Nefertiti. Downtown Cairo.

★ The 9th-century **Hanging Church,** so-named because it was built on the gatehouse of a Roman fortress, is Coptic Cairo's most spectacular house of worship, remarkable for its marble pulpit, inlaid screens, and paintings.

★ There's just no denying **Khufu's Pyramid,** the Great Pyramid, in spite of the urban sprawl that's crept into the desert around it. As the only one remaining of the seven wonders of the ancient world, it is arguably *the* essential sight to see in Egypt. Giza.

★ The pharaoh Djoser's **Step Pyramid** at Saqqara, Egypt's first great architectural triumph, gained its architect, Imhotep, patron sainthood in his craft and near-equal fame to the pharaoh who hired him. Outside Cairo.

★ Seti I's **Temple of Horus** at Abydos is one of the high points of refinement in 3,000 years of Egyptian artistic expression. Upper Nile Valley.

★ Built on an almost superhuman scale, the **Temple of Karnak** demonstrates the beauty, intelligence, ambition, and power of ancient Egyptian culture. Luxor, Upper Nile Valley.

★ Carved and extended out of the bottom of a cliff face in Luxor, **Deir al-Bahri,** Queen Hatshepsut's mortuary temple, with its rows upon rows of colonnades, is the Nile's architectural masterpiece. The fact that it was commissioned by the only queen to reign as pharaoh makes it that much more intriguing. Theban Necropolis, Upper Nile Valley.

★ The **Double Temple of Haroeris and Sobek** at Kom Ombo is unique for its concurrent honoring of two deities, and equally worth seeing for its picturesque bend-in-the-Nile setting. Kom Ombo, Upper Nile Valley.

★ Surrounded by the waters of the Nile on Agilquiyya Island, lovely **Philae** (the Temple of Isis) is where the gods of ancient Egypt took their last rites, their priests driven upriver by the advance of Christianity in the early centuries of the first millennium AD. Outside Aswan, Upper Nile Valley.

★ There's no denying Ramesses II, and his temple at **Abu Simbel** towers over the south end of Lake Nasser as he towered over his kingdom some 3,200 years ago. Lake Nasser Monuments.

★ Of all of the rock-cut tombs in the Valleys of the Kings and Queens, the **Tomb of Nefertari** stands out for its exquisite paintings of ancient Egyptian gods.

★ Kings and queens aside, the **Tombs of the Nobles** give us scenes—such beautifully painted scenes—from the daily lives of the people of pharaonic Egypt.

★ In the country that introduced wilderness hermitages to the Christian church, the **Monastery of St. Catherine,** which harbored crusaders during their invasion of the holy land, is a picture-perfect walled bastion of stalwart faith. Sinai Peninsula.

Natural Wonders

★ Outside of Farafra Oasis in the midst of the Western Desert, the chalk mountains and cliffs and otherworldly outcrops of the **White Desert** are endlessly fascinating.

★ **Mt. Sinai,** rising out of the desert above the Monastery of St. Catherine, is part of a rugged chain of mountains that provide Egypt's finest opportunities for hiking.

★ **Ras Muhammad National Park** on the very tip of the Sinai Peninsula is one of the world's great dive sites, where miles of beaches and 10 reefs provide shore dives, boat dives, and endlessly colorful marine life.

Dining

★ **Justine.** The best French restaurant in the country for more than a decade remains in top form thanks to the consistent inventiveness of executive chef Vincent Guillou. Cairo. $$$$

★ **The Moghul Room.** Prepare for a dining experience like no other: rich, sophisticated Indian cuisine served in the Moorish-fantasy setting of the Mena House at the base of the pyramids. Cairo. $$$$

★ **El Saraya** is a notch above the standard fish-on-ice seafood place, with a gorgeous view of the sea to match. Alexandria. $$$$

★ **Abu Ahsraf** consists of no more than a few tables in an alley, but it serves the most succulent fresh seafood to be found on this side of the Mediterranean. Alexandria. $$

★ **La Mamma.** This is just the Nile-side patio to come to for that fix of Italian that you've been craving: a little proscuitto; calamari with lemon, olive oil, and garlic; and tasty gnocchi. Luxor. $$$

Tut Ankh Amun. Fantastic vegetable dishes, meat tagines, grilled chicken with rosemary—this hearty Egyptian cooking is the local answer to fast food, and it will keep you coming back for more. Luxor. $

The 1902. In the Old Cataract Hotel, gentility is perhaps a better reason to come than culinary finesse, but dining on the Nile doesn't get any grander than it is here. Aswan. $$$$

Rangoli. It's surprising, perhaps, but true: some of Sharm al-Sheikh's best fare is Indian—from tangy *lassi* (the yogurt drink) to soothing *biryani* (an aromatic stew) to a fragrant cup of spiced *chai* (tea) with milk. Na'ama Bay. $$$

TamTam. Sharm al-Sheikh might not feel terribly Egyptian, but the Egyptian food at TamTam is so authentic that you're likely to think that you're back in Cairo, if it weren't for all that white sand just across the boardwalk. Na'ama Bay. $

Lodging

The **Cairo Hilton World Trade Center Residence** has palatial 2,000-square-ft apartments, fully furnished, at the capital's most exclusive address, for less than the price of a standard suite at most hotels—and you can still get room service. Cairo. $$$$

The **Cairo Marriott** is the largest hotel in the Middle East, built around a stunning old palace that originally hosted French Empress Eugénie's visit for the opening of the Suez Canal. The hotel is also a perfect forum for late-night drinks out in its gardens. Cairo. $$$$

The **Mena House Oberoi** is exquisitely sited at the foot of the pyramids and in-corporates an old khedival lodge, built with a wild mix of arches, arabesque, and romance. Cairo. $$$$

al-Zalamlek Palace, set amid the grounds of the royal gardens, is the height of decadence, with a few luxurious suites in a palace Khedive Abbas II built for his Austrian mistress. Alexandria. $$$$

Paradise Inn–Metropole is the best deal in Alexandria, with tasteful rooms in a turn-of-the-century building smack in the center of town. Alexandria. $$$

Mövenpick Jolie Ville. While Luxor still bustles with sightseers at day's end, you can be taking in fantastic Nile views from Crocodile Island, its gardens filled with flowering trees and colorful birdlife. Luxor. $$$$

St. Joseph's. Serious cleanliness, rooms with spacious balconies, and a friendly staff make this the best affordable option in Luxor. $

Old Cataract. A Moorish interior and late-Victorian grace still enchant at this *non plus ultra* of colonial hotels. The views of the Nile and Elephantine Island aren't so bad, either. Aswan. $$$$

Sofitel Sharm al-Sheikh. Moorish inside and out—from Moroccan tilework and *mashrabiya* (fretted-screen) windows to the brilliant white exterior—this Sofitel has the right approach for an Egyptian seaside resort. Sunsets from your own balcony are fabulous. Na'ama Bay, Sharm al-Sheikh. $$$$

Mövenpick Quseir. Decidedly tranquil, this waterside haven is *the* resort to choose on the Red Sea. Seafood at its Seagull restaurant is superb. Quseir. $$$

FESTIVALS, SEASONAL EVENTS, AND NATIONAL HOLIDAYS

With Muslim and Coptic Christian holy days, days commemorating military events and the revolution, and internationally celebrated holidays like Labor Day, Egypt's calendar is full to overflowing. Only "official" holidays are non-working days, however, and except for a few Muslim holidays most others are largely unnoticable, because they receive little popular expression outside particular areas in Cairo.

While military events are fixed against the Western calendar, religious holidays use different calendars. This can make scheduling somewhat tricky. As a rule, the lunar-based Islamic calendar rotates *backward* against the Western calendar by about 11 days per year. Thus the Muslim New Year began on May 8 in 1997 and April 27 in 1998. Copts, in turn, go by the solar-based Orthodox calendar, which sees them celebrating Christmas, for example, in early January. Fasting is a major part of both religions.

SPRING

➤ EARLY–MID-APR.: **Muslim New Year** (official) marks the start of Muharram, which is the first month by the Islamic calendar. Celebrations are relatively low-key.

➤ MID-APR.: **Coptic Easter** is preceded by 55 days of fasting and ends at a prayer on Holy Saturday that runs until midnight.

➤ LATE APR.: **Ashura** is a day of mourning (10 days after the new year) marking the martyrdon of Hussein at Kerbala, which is an event of great symbolic importance to Shi'a Muslims. According to legend, Hussein's head was brought to Egypt and is in the mosque that bears his name in Islamic Cairo (☞ Islamic Cairo North *in* Chapter 2).

➤ LATE APR.: **Sham al-Nessim** ("sniffing the breeze," official) is a pharaonic-era holiday commemorating the start of spring. All Egyptians celebrate, marking the day with picnics, but the holiday is particularly loved by Copts, who see themselves as direct descendants of the pharaonic peoples.

➤ APR. 25: **Sinai Liberation Day** (official) marks the 1978 return of the Sinai Peninsula, which Egypt lost to Israel in the 1967 War.

➤ MAY 1: **Labor Day** (official).

➤ JUNE 18: **Evacuation Day** (official).

➤ MID–LATE JUNE: **The Prophet's Birthday** (official) is one of the most colorful holidays, especially in the area around al-Azhar mosque in Islamic Cairo. An all-night *mulid* is held with Quranic readings, Sufis, and a flood of farmers in from the countryside.

SUMMER

➤ JULY 23: **Revolution Day** (official) marks the date in 1952 when the Free Officers, a group of young military men, launched a coup that sent King Faruq into exile and brought Egypt its first independence in 2,000 years.

➤ AUG. 22: **Feast of the Virgin Mary** commemorates her assumption into heaven. Copts fast for two weeks in preparation and break the fast with a church service on the morning of the feast.

➤ EARLY SEPT.: The **Cairo Experimental Theater Festival** is, inevitably, less experimental than it sounds, because most of the participating foreign theater troupes are selected by their local embassies. Nonetheless, it does draw some excellent performers, including many of Egypt's best drama and dance groups.

➤ SEPT. 11: **Coptic New Year.**

AUTUMN

➤ OCT. 6: **Armed Forces Day** (official) commemorates the storming of the Bar-Lev Line near Suez in the 1973 War, when Egyptian forces had Israeli troops briefly on the run. It is remembered as Egypt's greatest military triumph.

➤ OCT. 24: **Suez City Day** (official).

➤ EARLY DEC.: For two weeks, the **Cairo International Film Festival** offers a rare chance to see uncensored foreign movies. There are a few screenings of interesting art films, particularly those from the Arab world, but the festival in its current, chaotically organized incarnation is mostly an opportunity for Egyptian men to cram into theaters to watch whatever fleeting on-screen nudity they can find.

➤ DEC. 23: **Victory Day** (official).

➤ MID-DEC.– TO MID-JAN.: **Ramadan** is the Muslim month of fasting—*the* major holiday event in Egypt. Muslims are supposed to forsake food, drink, smoking, and sex during daylight hours, and the fast is almost universally observed, particularly in public. Although businesses stay open during the month, the work day is severely curtailed because people leave early to be home with their families for *iftar,* the sunset meal that breaks the fast. At night, the area around the Khan al-Khalili surges with life as people gather in cafés to socialize until the *sohour* meal, which comes just before dawn and will get them through another day's fast. There are music performances and traditional storytelling throughout the city.

➤ JAN. 7: **Coptic Christmas.** Copts fast for 43 days in advance of Christmas, during which time most monasteries are closed to visitors.

➤ MID-JAN.: Cairo shuts down completely during **Eid al-Fitr** (official), a family-oriented, three-day holiday celebrating the end of Ramadan. The city is never quieter than during the Eid: traffic disappears, sidewalks empty, the air miraculously seems clean, and distances you once thought endless suddenly seem walkable. It is traditional practice to buy new clothes for the holiday, especially for children.

➤ JAN. 19: The **Epiphany** commemorates the baptism of Jesus Christ by John the Baptist.

➤ MID–LATE MAR.: **Eid al-Adha** (official) is a four-day holiday commemorating Abraham's willingness to sacrifice his son, Isaac, to God. God allowed Abraham to replace the child with a ram at the last moment, and it is traditional during Eid for the wealthy to slaughter a sheep and distribute the meat among the poor.

2 Cairo

*With Side Trips to
the Pyramids, the Fayyum,
and Wadi Natrun Monastery*

*For well over 1,000 years one of the
world's great cosmopolitan cities,
Cairo is infinite and inexhaustible.
Different religions, different cultures—
sometimes, it seems, even different
eras—coexist amid the jostling crowds
and aging monuments gathered here
at the head of the Nile Delta. Don't
expect to find a city frozen in layers of
ancient history: Cairo's current vitality
is as seductive as its rich past.*

By Sean
Rocha, Rami
al-Samahy,
and Salima
Ikram

ON FIRST IMPRESSION, there is hardly a superlative too vast to capture the epic scale of this city of twelve million—or fourteen, or sixteen; no one really knows for sure—that sprawls in all directions. The traffic, the people, the chaotic rhythm of Cairo all reinforce this impression, all threatening to overwhelm. So take your time, relax over a mint tea in a café or wander the quiet back alleys, and you'll step into a different world. In many ways Cairo is the proverbial overgrown village, full of little districts and communities much smaller and more intimate than the city of which they're part.

Cairo's juxtaposition of the monstrous and the humane breeds an almost heart-wrenching partisanship among Cairenes, for whom a two-hour lament about the city's failings and frustrations always merges, without a hint of contradiction, into a testimony of undying love. Likewise, if your first and most powerful impression is that this is an umanageable beast of a city, the second and more lingering impression should be that Cairo bountifully rewards the patience and faith required to take it in.

Like so much else in Egypt, Cairo's charm is a product of its history, and its network of districts and communities is the physical remains of 1,000 years of being conquered and reconquered by different groups. The city didn't really begin, as you might expect, with the pharaohs; they quartered themselves in nearby Memphis and Heliopolis, areas only recently overtaken by Cairo's outward urban spread. Even the pyramids at Giza, on the west bank of the Nile, mislead the eye in search of the seeds of Cairo. For this has always been an east-bank city—albeit one creeping west with the Nile as it silted its east bank and pushed itself west. It's only in the past 40 years that the city has moved faster than the river, leaping the banks and drawing in the endless new suburbs on the west bank.

No, Cairo's history begins with a Roman trading outpost now called Babylon—referred to as Old or Coptic Cairo—at the mouth of an ancient canal that once connected the Nile to the Red Sea. Seventh-century AD Arab invaders founded the city with their encampment at Fustat, just north of Old Cairo. Under their great leader, Amr Ibn al-As, the Arabs took over a land that Greeks, Persians, and Romans had conquered before them. In the millennium that followed Amr Ibn's conquest, the city was ruled by the Fatimids (969–1171), the Mamluks (1250–1517), and the Ottomans (1517–1798), then periodically influenced by French and British muscle during the khedival period (1805–1919) and the monarchy (1919–53).

What makes Cairo unique is that each new ruler, rather than destroying what he had conquered, chose to build a new city, upwind from the old one. Thus from a bird's-eye view above the Nile, you can follow the progression of the historic center of Cairo, cutting a question mark–shaped path from Old Cairo in the south, curving north through Fustat and east to Islamic Cairo, and then west to the colonial Downtown district until you reach Maydan Tahrir (Liberation Square), where it has settled for the moment. But as the city continues to expand, the heart threatens to relocate again, perhaps to Maydan Sphinx, or Boulaq, or somewhere in Giza.

Cairo's districts have changed, of course, since the time when they were founded, and with 10 million new residents pouring in since the revolution in 1952 that brought an end to colonial rule, even more new districts have grown around them. Each district retains a distinct identity, not only in its buildings, but also among its residents and their ways of life. Pre-Islamic Babylon is, to this day, a disproportionately Christian area, with more crosses visible than crescents. And the medieval precinct of Islamic Cairo is still where families traditionally flock during Ramadan to spend the night eating and smoking after a day of abstinence. Indeed, one of the joys of Cairo is that its historic areas are still vibrant, living spaces and not open-air museums. The past here is more a state of mind than a historical fact. Ultimately, that is the way in which the city is truly overwhelming.

Cairo Glossary

Ablaq masonry (the striped walls of Islamic buildings); *amir* (prince); *baraka* (blessings or good luck); *hammam* (bathhouse); *haramlik* (a family's private chambers); *khanqah* (Sufi school); *kuttab* (the traditional equivalent of a primary school, where children would learn Qur'an and other sciences); *liwan* (a sitting room with a raised floor that opened onto a courtyard; also the vaulted areas off of a central court of a mosque or madrasa); *madrasa* (religous school); *mashrabiyya* (a type of woodwork in which small pieces are fitted together, forming a grill that filters in air and light; like a veil, mashrabiyya screens are useful in that they allow those inside to see out without being seen); *maydan* (square); *mihrab* (the prayer niche in a *qibla* wall); *minbar* (wooden pulpit); *mulid* (the celebration of a saint or holy person's birthday, when people gather around the saint's shrine and play devotional music and dance, sometimes reaching an ecstatic trance state, while the children play on swings and other amusements brought in for the occasion; these are very local, very popular, somewhat chaotic events); *qa'a* (great hall); *qasr* (palace); *qibla* (the direction of mecca, which in Cairo is southwest; all mosques and madrasas are oriented in this way); *sabil* (a place where water, drawn from a man-made well, was dispensed to the public); *shar'a* (street, pronounced *shar*-eh); *ziyada* (a walled-off space); *wikala* (caravansery, an inn for medieval merchants).

Pleasures and Pastimes

Ancient Monuments

With the pyramids of Giza, Abu Sir, Saqqara, and Dahshur anchoring the western flank of Cairo, it would seem like architectural time began here. And to the extent that Saqqara has the world's oldest stone building, it might as well have. In addition to seeing the Great Pyramid of Khufu and the Sphinx on the Giza Plateau, don't miss the Egyptian Antiquities Museum in downtown Cairo. Full of wonders like Tutankhamun's gold funerary mask, the vast collections of the museum are an essential supplement to all of the country's ancient monuments.

Dining

Providing food for guests is a central element in Egyptian hospitality. As a result, the best dining experiences typically occur in Egyptian homes. Also as a result, even Cairo did not have what might be called a restaurant scene until recently: five-star hotels catered to the wealthy, modest sidewalk kitchens in popular districts served the poor, and there was relatively little in between. That has changed—and continues to change so rapidly that entrepreneurs seem to be opening new restaurants every month or two. Eating out is now a regular form of entertainment affordable to a growing upper and middle class.

Naturally, Egyptian food remains the local favorite, and Cairo is the place to find the best of the country's specialties. Restaurants compete mainly on quality of ingredients rather than refinement of preparations. But lately the range of options has expanded dramatically to include other cuisines: Lebanese and Turkish, Indian, Thai, French, Italian, Jap-

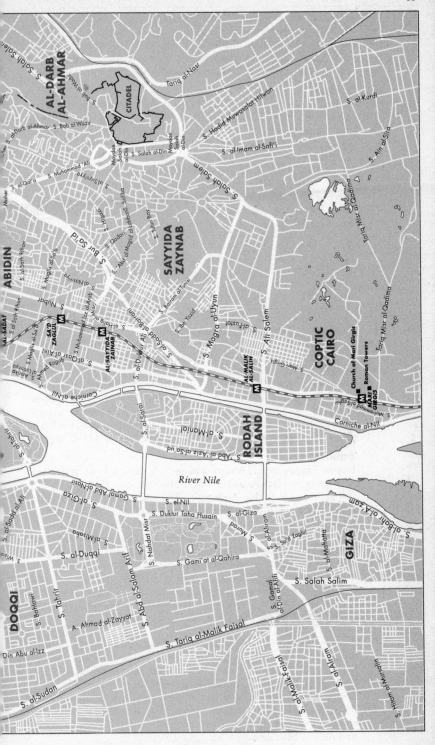

AL-DARB
AL-AHMAR

CITADEL

ABIDIN

SAYYIDA
ZAYNAB

COPTIC
CAIRO

RODAH
ISLAND

DOQQI

GIZA

River Nile

Tariq al-Nasr

S. al-Kurdi

S. Hadia Muwasalat Hilwan

S. al-Imam al-Safi'i

S. Ain al-Sira

Tariq Misr al-Qadima

Tariq Misr al-Qadima

Church of Mari Girgis

Roman Towers

MARI
GIRGIS

S. Muhammad al-Sagha

Corniche al-Nil

S. Ali Salem

S. Salah al-Din

S. Salah Salem

Maydan
Salah
al-Din

Maydan
Salah
al-Din

S. Salah al-Din

S. Muhammad 'Ali

S. al-Suyufiya

S. al-Qal'a

Maher

S. al-Darb al-Ahmar

S. Bab al-Wazir

S. Bab al-Wazir

S. Solah Salim

AL-MALIK
AL-SALIH

SAID
ZAGLUL

AL-SAYYIDA
ZAINAB

AL-SADAT

S. Nubar

Corniche al-Nil

S. Mari Girgis

S. al-Fustat

S. Magra al-Uyun

S. Barram al-Tunsi

S. Ibn Yazid

S. al-Sadd al-Barrani

S. al-Qasr al-Aini

S. Dukur Ali

S. al-Sarai

S. al-Manial

S. Abd al-'Aziz al-Sa'ud

S. Gamal Abd al-Nasir

S. el-Nil

S. Duktur Taha Husain

S. al-Giza

S. Nahdat Misr

S. Murad

S. al-Ahram

S. Sa'd Zaglul

S. Gami'at al-Qahira

GIZA

S. al-Mahatta

S. al-Giza

S. al-Sudan

S. Tariq al-Malik Faisal

A. Ahmad al-Zayyat

S. Abd al-Salam Arif

S. Tahrir

S. Bahlawi

Din Abu al-Izz

S. Wizar

S. al-Sadd al-Ali

S. al-Tahrir

S. al-Duqqi

S. al-Misaha

S. al-Duqqi

S. al-Malik Faisal

S. Gamal al-Din al-Afifi

S. al-Ahram

S. Hisham al-Muralim

S. al-Bahr al A'zam

anese, almost everything except Mexican, which hasn't quite caught on with Egyptians. Culinary creativity is still constrained by limited access to unusual ingredients—don't expect to find wild mushrooms or sun-dried tomatoes—but gradually that too is improving. Service, except at the very finest restaurants, tends to be friendly but lethargic.

Lodging

Cairo has a number of five-star hotels scattered across the city, all of which are quite affordable by international standards. If you are dreaming of a place with Old World charm or a distinctive Egyptian atmosphere, most Cairo hotels will disappoint, as they are in the characterless-modern vein. A few exceptions still have a turn-of-the-century air, and they are that much more precious for being so rare. The modern hotels do have their compensating virtues, above all that top end hotels are near either the Nile or the pyramids—so request a room with a view. Nile views are good, but Cairo's skyline, dotted with minarets and domes, can be even more spectacular.

The Egyptian Hotel Association rates all hotels in the country on a five-star scale. While few if any Cairo hotels merit their full set of stars, you'll find that those at the top end have all the facilities and modern conveniences you need to recuperate after a long day. It is when you get out of the five-star range that Cairo's options quickly grow more limited, although there are a few hotels that fill the gap adequately.

Mosques, Churches, Synagogues

Cairo is known as the city of a thousand minarets. When you're looking out from the Citadel, it is that and much more. On the east bank lie the remains of the Roman town that house the city's oldest Coptic churches, as well as a medieval synagougue. And directly below the Citadel sits the Islamic city. Within its dense fabric are the vast open spaces of mosques and public squares, including the huge courtyard Mosque of Ibn Tulun, the sublime Sultan Hasan Mosque and the Maydan al-Husayn, where you'll find the famous Khan al-Khalili bazaar.

Sailing

One of Egypt's eternal images is of the tall white sails of traditional feluccas as they tack up and down the Nile. You can take a felucca trip in Luxor or Aswan, but don't wait—you might need the therapeutic value of one in Cairo to escape from the stresses of urban life. Within minutes you can be floating in total peace, massaged by a light summer breeze (you'll probably find winter too cold for a sail). Most feluccas can seat up to 10 people comfortably, if not luxuriously. So the craft are still intimate even when you're with strangers. Boat captains congregate on the banks. Haggling is part of the process, but a one-hour boat ride is never expensive.

EXPLORING CAIRO

Cairo is big: just how big you'll see on the drive in from the airport, which sometimes takes so long you'll think you're driving to Aswan. What you'll see on the way into town, amazingly, is only half of it—Cairo's west bank sister city, Giza, stretches to the pyramids, miles from downtown. If by instinct you happen to have a built-in compass, you'll find exploring Cairo a breeze, because the Nile works like a giant north–south needle running through the center of the city. If not, you might find the city bewildering at first.

Taxi drivers generally know only major streets and landmarks, and pedestrians rarely know the name of the street they stand on—when they do, it's as often the old names as the new ones—but they'll gladly steer you in the wrong direction in an effort to be helpful. Just go with the flow and try to think of every wrong turn as a chance for discovery.

Thankfully, too, you don't have to conquer all of Cairo to get the most out of it. Much of the city was built in the last 40 years or so, and the new areas hold relatively little of historical or cultural interest. The older districts, with the exception of Giza's pyramids, are all on the east bank and easily accessible by taxi or metro. And the city's evolution has left it conveniently divided into districts, which, while they may blur together at the edges, become relatively straightforward targets for a day's exploration on foot.

Old Cairo, on the east bank a couple miles south of most of current-day Cairo, was the city's first district. Just north of it is Fustat, the site of the 7th-century Arab settlement. East of that is the Citadel. Running north of the Citadel is the medieval walled district of al-Qahira that gave the city its name. It is better known as Islamic Cairo. West of that is the colonial district. Known as Downtown, it is one of several—including Ma'adi, Garden City, Heliopolis, and Zamalek—laid out by Europeans in the past two centuries. (The west-bank districts of Mohandiseen and Doqqi, by comparison, have only sprouted up since the revolution in 1952.) The most interesting sights are in the older districts; the newer ones have the highest concentrations of hotels, restaurants, and shops.

You're likely to spend as much of your time around Cairo as in it—at the ancient west bank monuments in Giza, Saqqara, and Abu Sir, or north of the city at the Coptic Wadi Natrun monastery, or south at the Fayyum, the nearest of the oasis towns. Seeing the pyramids is essential. Wadi Natrun and the Fayyum are equally informative, and they open up perspectives on ancient lifestyles that are still very much alive.

Numbers in the text correspond with numbers in the margin and on the Cairo, Islamic Cairo, and Coptic Cairo maps.

Great Itineraries

There are so many distinct chapters in Cairo's millennium-long existence that three days will only give a sense of its most distant past—the pyramids and Islamic Cairo—with little opportunity to explore what makes it tick today. Five days allows you to mix in some of the modern history, including the colonial-era Downtown. A week is ideal, because it will give you time to discover not only the city's tremendous history but also how it functions today as the living, breathing home of fourteen million residents—*and* find a few favorite haunts of your own.

IF YOU HAVE 3 DAYS
Although the pyramids are usually at the top of everyone's itinerary, it is more interesting to work your way back through the city's history and end with its pharaonic origins. So start with **Khan al-Khalili,** the great medieval marketplace, and wander the narrow alleys of nearby **Islamic Cairo** to get a feel for the texture of life in the city. Stop in at the spectacular **Museum of Islamic Arts** for a glimpse of the range of Persian, Turkish, and Arab cultures that shaped that period of Cairo's history. The next day, dive farther back in time by visiting the city's pre-Islamic roots in **Old Cairo,** including the 7th-century **Hanging Church** and **Coptic Museum.** Spend the afternoon at the **Citadel** on the Muqattam hills, exploring the mosques and palaces within the fortress walls and savoring the view of the sun as it sets over the city spread out below you. On your final day, get an early start and quickly visit the **Egyptian Antiquities Museum.** This will give you a smidge of background for an afternoon jaunt to **Giza** and the pyramids, the eternal

monuments of the ancient world. While there, take a camel ride in the desert.

IF YOU HAVE 5 DAYS

With a little more time, you can plan to spend the first day in **Islamic Cairo** as above but then take the full second day to explore the area around the **Citadel.** In addition to everything that is within the Citadel walls, at its base there are two of Cairo's most beautiful monuments, the **Sultan Hassan** and **Rifa'i mosques,** standing dramatically only a few feet apart. Also in the area is the tranquil **Ibn Touloun Mosque,** one of Cairo's earliest, and the adjacent **Gayer-Anderson House.** On the third day, make your way to **Old Cairo,** but then wander over to the ruins of **Fustat,** the site of the first Islamic settlement and for many centuries, until their forced eviction in 1998, a traditional potter's community. End the day with a sail in a **felucca** on the Nile. On the fourth day get an early start at the **Egyptian Antiquities Museum,** then head outside and explore the fascinating colonial quarter called **Downtown:** take in the Art Nouveau **Chaar-Hachamaim Synagogue,** the **old red-light district,** and the small bookstores and antiques shops in the area. On day five, plan to go back in time to see **Giza**'s pyramids and move on through palm groves to the very early Step Pyramid and the decorated mastabas at **Saqqara.**

IF YOU HAVE 7 DAYS

With a week in Cairo, keep expanding on your itinerary and consider your four great advantages. First, you can go at a more leisurely pace that will keep this sometimes exhausting city from getting the better of you. Divide up the Egyptian Antiquities Museum for one day and spend a full day in Giza, Saqqara, and Abu Sir. Second, you can explore some of the contemporary aspects of Cairo life: **art galleries,** the **Opera House,** and a couple of the more beautiful residential districts like **Garden City, Heliopolis,** or **Zamalek.** Third, you can take longer day trips out of the city: to less-visited pharaonic sights at **Abu Sir** and **Dahshur** or to the **Fayyum,** the most accessible of Egypt's oases, or to the monastery—monastic life was an Egyptian contribution to Christianity—at **Wadi Natrun.** Most rewarding of all, you can take the extra time to fall into Cairo's natural rhythm, which for all the frenzy of traffic and noise means stopping for unhurried coffees, good conversation, and a game of backgammon in a café.

WHEN TO TOUR CAIRO

Cairo is blessed with great weather and is only uncomfortable for a couple of months a year. Spring and autumn are both gorgeous, with warm days and cool nights. The only unpredictable factor in spring is the *khamiseen,* the dust storms that turn the air yellow for a couple of days and then disappear. Summer *is* very hot, but relatively dry, so if you avoid the peak sun hours it is not unbearable. Winter is brief, eight weeks at most, and chillier than you might expect, even if it's never truly cold. It rains perhaps 10 days a year, mostly in winter, and the rain is rarely more than a light shower. The big seasonal wildcard is Ramadan, the holy month of fasting, which rotates with the lunar calendar. In 1999 and 2000 it will straddle December and January—on New Year's Eve only five-star hotels will serve alcohol. Ramadan has its rewards and its inconveniences: Egypt is most Egyptian, and you'll find more music and folkloric performances than at other times, but many restaurants close by day, drinking alcohol becomes even more illicit, and little productive work gets done.

Islamic Cairo North: al-Husayn Mosque to Bab al-Futuh

By Rami
el-Samahy

The magic of Islamic Cairo isn't on its busy main thoroughfares—those modern impositions on the old city—but in its smaller side streets, some of which were, in their time, main roads themselves. Take Shar'a al-Mu'iz bi Din Allah—call it Shar'a Mu'iz for short. The city's main artery from the Fatimid to the Ottoman period, about 969–1848, Mu'iz occupies a cherished place in world cultural history. Lined with beautiful monuments from the Fatimid, Ayyubid, Mamluk, and Ottoman eras, Shar'a al-Mu'iz is an open-air museum displaying a millennium of Cairo's Islamic architecture. More significant than the individual buildings is the scale of the structures and the width of the street in relation to the body, which allows for an experience not only of old Egypt, but of the face of premodern urban life.

The locale around al-Husayn Mosque is also known as the Khan al-Khalili—for the huge bazaar that fronts the Maydan al-Husayn. With al-Azhar University, the tent makers' market (al-Khayammia), and al-Ghuri Palace across Shar'a al-Azhar, this is the heart of medieval Islamic Cairo. Currently, plans are being made to convert the whole area into a pedestrian walkway by depressing the part of Shar'a al-Azhar that cuts it in two. The following section covers the area north of al-Azhar.

A Good Walk

If you are coming from Downtown, take a cab. Tell the driver that you want to go to al-Husayn, or al-Azhar, or the Khan al-Khalili; he's bound to understand one of these. Or take the metro to Attaba Square Station and walk 15 minutes up Shar'a al-Azhar (the street with the overpass above it) to al-Azhar University, which is on the wrong side of the street. In front of al-Azhar is an underpass that will bring you up just to the left of **Sayyidna al-Husayn Mosque** ① and its square. If you are coming from Heliopolis, Ma'adi, or any of the suburbs to the south or west of the Khan, chances are you'll arrive via Shar'a Salah Salem, on the right side of the street. If so, you will get out of the taxi by the bus/cab stop across from al-Azhar in front of the mosque.

From here, there are several ways to take on this walk. If shopping at the bazaar is your sole goal, go directly to the **Khan al-Khalili** ②, which is right in front of you. If you are here for the sights only, skip the Khan, turn left down Shar'a al-Muski, and walk until you hit Shar'a al-Mu'iz. If you're here for sights and shopping, see the sights first then double back to the stores, because haggling with shopkeepers may tire you out early; likewise lugging your purchases around the streets.

When you get to al-Mu'iz, turn right. On either side of the road are gold- and coppersmiths, who give this segment of the street the name *al-Nahhasseen* (the coppersmiths). Slightly off the main street on the right is the **Madrasa and Mausoleum of Sultan al-Salih al-Ayyubi** ③, the last of Salah al-Din's relatives to rule Egypt in the 13th century. The complex is not altogether obvious from the street; it appears to be part of the adjoining buildings, and its ground floor is largely obscured by shops.

Diagonally across the street is the **Complex of Qalaun** ④, which includes a mosque, mausoleum, madrasa, and hospital. This was the site of the original Fatimid (10th- to 12th-century Shi'ite rulers) western palace. Opposite Qalaun's mausoleum, abutting the tomb of al-Salih al-Ayyubi, lie the remains of the **Madrasa of Sultan al-Zahir Baybars I** ⑤. Al-Zahir built his structure where the eastern Fatimid palace once stood. The area between them is known as *Bayn al-Qasrayn* (between the two

22

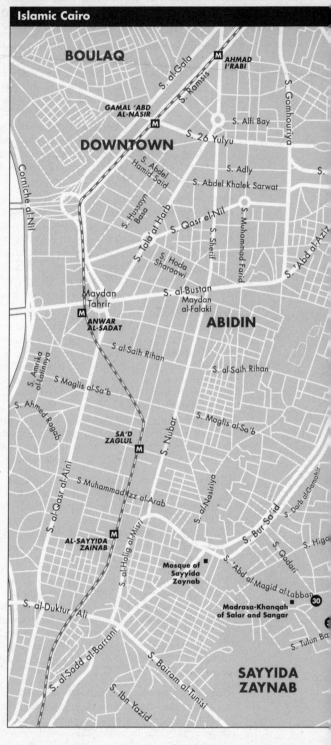

Islamic Cairo

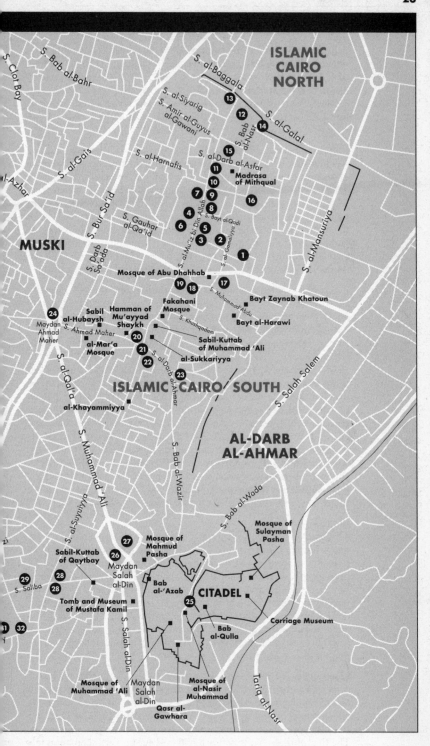

ISLAMIC CAIRO NORTH

S. al-Baggala

S. al-Siyarig

S. Amir al-Guyus al-Gawani

S. al-Galal

Bab al-Nasr

13

12

14

15

S. al-Harnafis

S. al-Darb al-Asfar

11

10

Madrasa of Mithqual

7

9

8

16

S. al-Mu'iz bi Din Allah

S. Bayt al-Qadi

4

5

6

3

2

S. al-Gamaliyya

1

S. Gauhar al-Qa'id

S. Darb Sa'ada

MUSKI

S. Bur Sa'id

S. Gais

l-Azhar

S. Clot Bay

S. Bab al-Bahr

S. al-Mansuriya

Mosque of Abu Dhahhab

19

18

17

S. Muhammad Abdu

Bayt Zaynab Khatoun

Fakahani Mosque

S. Khuhgadam

Bayt al-Harawi

Sabil al-Hubaysh

Hamman of Mu'ayyad Shaykh

24

Maydan Ahmad Maher

S. Ahmad Maher

al-Mar'a Mosque

20

Sabil-Kuttab of Muhammad 'Ali

21

22

al-Sukkariyya

S. al-Darb al-Ahmar

23

S. Salah Salem

ISLAMIC CAIRO SOUTH

al-Khayammiyya

S. al-Qal'a

AL-DARB AL-AHMAR

S. Bab al-Wazir

S. Muhammad 'Ali

S. al-Khuyush

S. Bab al-Wada

Mosque of Sulayman Pasha

27

Mosque of Mahmud Pasha

Sabil-Kuttab of Qaytbay

26

Maydan Salah al-Din

Bab al-'Azab

CITADEL

29

28

28

S. Saliba

Tomb and Museum of Mustafa Kamil

25

Carriage Museum

32

Bab al-Qulla

S. Salah al-Din

Mosque of Muhammad 'Ali

Maydan Salah al-Din

Mosque of al-Nasir Muhammad

Qasr al-Gawhara

Tariq al-Nasr

palaces). You are now standing in the very center of the original city of al-Qahira, which was founded in 969 AD.

Adjacent to Qalaun is the **madrasa** of Sultan al-Zahir Baybars I's son **al-Nasir Muhammad** ⑥, one of the longest reigning Mamluks—a total of 41 years in three separate periods. Next to al-Nasir Muhammad up al-Mu'iz is the **Madrasa of Barquq** ⑦. Across the street from al-Nasir is Shar'a Bayt al-Qadi, a smaller street on which you'll find one of the best kept secrets of Islamic Cairo, the **Qa'a of Muhib al-Din** ⑧ (alternatively known as the House of Uthman Katkhuda).

Return to Shar'a al-Mu'iz, walk past al-Nasir and Barquq, and you will find another side street to the right where the entrance to the **Palace of Bishtak** ⑨ is on the right side. Get back on the main thoroughfare and go to the **Sabil-Kuttab of Abdul Rahman Katkhuda** ⑩, which occupies the triangular island that divides al-Mu'iz. Before you take the left-hand fork, stop by the bakery on the right-hand fork for a fresh sweet bread. Retrace your steps to the left fork and take it up Mu'iz for several blocks to the **Mosque of al-Aqmar** ⑪, a small but well-preserved example of Fatimid architecture. There is also a junk-and-antiques shop on the left side of al-Mu'iz between al-Aqmar and the city walls.

A few blocks after al-Aqmar is the **Mosque of al-Hakim** ⑫. From inside the mosque, to the left of the entrance, climb the stairs to the roof, which gives access to the two extant northern gates of the Fatimid city, **Bab al-Futuh** ⑬ and **Bab al-Nasr** ⑭. When you come down from the roof, go through Bab al-Futuh, turn right, then reenter the city through Bab al-Nasr on Shar'a al-Gamaliyya. There are a couple of facades to check out on the way back. Immediately on the right after Bab al-Nasr is the **Wikala of Qayt Bay**, once a famous inn for medieval Mamluk merchants. At the end of the next block, also on the right, is the **Wikala of Oda Bashi**, an Ottoman inn. A few minutes walk leads you to **Darb al-Asfar**, an alley perpendicular to al-Gamaliyya. Turn left into this street, and halfway up on the right is **Bayt al-Suhaymi** ⑮, one of the best examples of domestic Islamic architecture in Cairo. Return to Gamaliyya and continue south until you reach an alley called **Darb al-Tablawi** on your left, where you find another exquisite piece of domestic architecture, **al-Musafirkhana Palace** ⑯. Return to al-Gamaliyya and proceed south to get back to the Mosque of al-Husayn and the Khan al-Khalili.

TIMING

This walk could easily take you a day and more, depending on how much shopping you can withstand. The walk alone could take up to four hours. Spend about fifteen minutes at any given site, but plan a little more time at the complex of Qalaun and Musafirkhana Palace. For the Khan, the amount of time you spend will depend on your interest and saturation point in bazaars. If you are into haggling, don't do this walk on a Sunday, when most of the shops are closed. If the merchant's hustle and bustle isn't your thing, use Sunday as an opportunity to explore the area in relative peace and quiet. Friday before noon is also a downtime for the neighborhood.

Islamic sights are open from 8 or 9 AM to 4 or 5 PM, depending on whether or not the custodians get bored and want to go home. Prayers usually last 15 minutes or so except for Friday noon prayers (1 PM in summer), which render mosques off limits to tours for about an hour. There are five daily prayers, the times of which vary depending on the season. The first of these is just before dawn (al-Fagr prayer), then noon (al-Duhr), midafternoon, around 3 or 4 (al-'Asr), sunset (al-Maghrib), and evening (al-'Esha) at about 8 or 9 PM.

Sights to See

⑯ al-Musafirkhana Palace. Built in the 1700s, the palace was purchased by Ibrahim, Egypt's second khedive (ruled 1863–79); his famous son Isma'il—who instigated the construction of downtown Cairo, the Suez Canal, and plunged the country into devastating debt—was born here. Renovations have been in the works since the late 1980s, but a 1992 earthquake wrought havoc with the structure. Nevertheless, its interior spaces and decorative elements are worth seeing.

The first qa'a immediately to your left after you enter is a lofty hall where you can almost imagine lavish entertainments taking place. Through the courtyard and up the stairs, the haramlik has huge mashrabiyya windows and carved mahogany ceilings. Note the colored glass in the bathrooms. Although they seem like additions from the '70s they are actually original. ⊠ *Darb al-Tablawi,* ☎ *no phone.* ☞ *£e6.*

⑬ Bab al-Futuh (the Futuh Gate). To the left inside the entrance to the Mosque of al-Hakim (☞ *below*) is a small passageway that leads to a stairway to the roof of the mosque. From here, you can get to the Bab al-Futuh, one of the main gates of the Islamic city. Built in 1087 by Badr al-Gamali al-Gayushi, it was designed to protect al-Qahira from the Seljuk Turks who held Syria and were threatening Egypt. But the gate was never put to the test.

From up above, there is a fantastic view south down al-Mu'iz all the way to the southern gate of Bab Zuwayla—as well as the minarets of the Mosque of al-Hakim. Turning the other way gives you a view of the city outside the walls and the Northern Cemetery. When you climb back down, try to find the custodian of the gate, who will let you into the interior of the two rounded towers. Check out the thin slit windows for firing arrows and the holes in the floor for pouring hot oil on potential attackers. ⊠ *Shar'a al-Mu'iz.* ☞ *£e6 (to get inside).*

⑭ Bab al-Nasr (the Nasr Gate). This gate is similar to Bab al-Futuh, except that it is flanked by two square towers. On one of the towers is the inscription: TOUR CORBIN, a memento of French arrogance from the Napoleonic expedition (Bab al-Futuh also has TOUR JUNOT and TOUR PERRAULT carved into its towers). The wall between the two gates is fun to explore, so try to get inside. Tunnels with slit windows to provide light once connected the entire wall and its 60 (yes, 60) gates with rooms and storehouses within the girth of the wall, making it possible for an army to defend the city without ever having to leave the wall. The keeper of the keys is usually around the corner in the al-Hakim mosque from 9 to 4; tip him if he lets you in. ⊠ *Shar'a Bab al-Nasr.*

⑮ Bayt al-Suhaymi. Considered the best example of domestic Islamic architecture in Cairo, this 16th-century merchant's house is cool and comfortable. Typically the entrance passageway leads to a lush courtyard that is totally unexpected from the outside. On the ground floor are the *salamlik* (public reception rooms), upstairs the haramlik. The house is currently undergoing active restoration efforts, which might make getting in difficult, but do try your luck. ⊠ *19 Shar'a al-Darb al-Asfar,* ☎ *no phone.*

★ ❹ Complex of Qalaun. One of the early Mamluk rulers of Egypt, Mansur Qalaun was originally a Tartar (Mongol) brought to Egypt as a slave. *Mamluk*s (literally, those owned) were first imported from the Volga to Egypt by al-Salih Ayyubi, the man buried in the tomb across the street, who used them as his personal bodyguards. Aybak, the first Mamluk ruler, was one of al-Salih's slaves. The man who took over from him, Baybars al-Bunduqdari, was too. Qalaun was acquired by Baybars. In short, one's lot in life could be worse than being a slave to the Sultan in medieval Cairo.

Qalaun died at the ripe old age of 70, on his way to attack the Crusader fortress of Acre in 1290. The complex that he had built is noteworthy for its workmanship and the diverse styles that it displays.

A *bimaristan* (hospital and psychiatric ward) has existed on the site since Qalaun first saw the need for one. Only fragments of the original hospital remain, having been replaced by a modern (not necessarily better) one. In its heyday, Qalaun's bimaristan was famous for its care of the physically and mentally ill, and it staff was said to include musicians and storytellers as well as surgeons capable of performing delicate eye surgery.

The madrasa and mausoleum present the complex's impressive street facade, a series of pointed arch recesses, almost Gothic in their proportions, each one pierced with groups of three windows, a much-seen feature of Islamic architecture. Look up at the the 194-foot minaret with its horseshoe-shape arched recesses and its corniced overhang, a device used since pharaonic times. The entrance is set slightly forward up a set of steps; its semicircular arch was the first of its kind in Egypt. Beyond the entrance is a long, tall corridor with the madrasa to the left and the tomb to the right. Note the beamed and coffered ceiling. A door at the end of the corridor used to lead to the bimaristan, but has been sealed off.

The madrasa is undergoing restoration at the moment, making it an odd mix of prefab caravans and faded medieval splendor. Because it stands on the site of the Fatimid western palace there has been much archaeological interest in the renovation efforts. The stuccowork above the mihrab is original, and quite impressive.

The gem of the complex, however, is the mausoleum, the burial place of Qalaun and his son al-Nasir Muhammad. The chamber is dark, cool, and mammoth. In its center is a wooden grille that encloses the tombs. There is much here to suggest that Qalaun was deeply influenced by what he saw on his exploits in Palestine. The plan of the mausoleum is similar to that of the Dome of the Rock in Jerusalem, in that it contains an octagon fit within a square. The stained glass and tall proportions have a Gothic quality that are reminiscent of Crusader churches that he saw in the Levant. ✉ *Shar'a al-Mu'iz*, ☎ *no phone*. ✆ *£e6*.

❷ Khan al-Khalili. The Khan has been a marketplace since the end of the 14th century; commercial activity is its life blood. A maze of small streets and narrow alleys charts its way around the bazaar, and these passages are filled with scores of vendors hawking their wares and attempting to draw customers into their small shops. It is a chaotic mixture of Egyptians and tourists, smells of perfume and incense, fragments of age-old buildings next to modern amenities—and always noise and confusion. With a little determination, you can find just about anything you want to take home to prove you've come to Cairo. Carpets, gold, silver, clothing, belly dancing outfits, spices, perfumes, water pipes, woodwork, books, pottery, blown glass, leather, papyrus, pharaonic replicas— you name it. There are hundreds of little stores that will attract or repel.

To describe the bazaar in further detail would require an entire book on its own—in fact, Ola Seif has written just such a book: *Khan al-Khalili: A Comprehensive Mapped Guide* (£e30).

A few words of advice: never take something at the first price; bargaining is the modus operandi in the Khan, and if you do not show interest, the price will likely drop. In the case of a silver- or goldsmith, for example, while a fixed price for the weight of the piece exists, one may bargain on the quality of the workmanship. If a shopkeeper offers you tea or coffee and you take it, you are in no way obligated to buy something from his shop; it's just Middle Eastern hospitality. If someone offers to take you to their workshop on the second floor, accept if you have time; most of these crafts are fascinating to see in progress. If you pay by credit card, there may be a service charge, 3 to 6 percent; ask before handing over the plastic. Finally, if someone offers to sell you marijuana or hashish, don't accept; you're likely to get oregano or compressed henna or a stay in a dreadful local jail.

The Khan has plenty of places to eat, including the grilled meat restaurants on the corner of Maydan al-Husayn and Shar'a Muski and places that serve *fiteer,* Egyptian pancakes that are filled with everything from feta cheese to raisins. They form a row just outside of the Khan, between Shar'a Muski and Shar'a al-Azhar.

Stores in the Khan are generally open from 10 AM to 9 PM. Most shops close on Sundays and during Friday prayer (the hour around noon; 1 PM between April and October during daylight saving time).

NEED A
BREAK?

Al-Fishawi Café is just one of many coffeehouses that line the corner closest to the mosque of al-Husayn, but it is the oldest and best-known—and usually the most crowded. Here you can sip a Turkish coffee, a tea, or myriad other local beverages including *karkadeh,* hibiscus leaves, served hot or cold, and *sahleb,* a warm milk-based drink sprinkled with coconut and nuts. Enter the Khan from al-Husayn Square along Sikkit al-Badestan, the main thoroughfare, and take the first left. ⊠ *5 Sikkit Khan al-Khalili,* ☏ *02/590–4792.*

Naguib Mahfouz Café isn't a coffeehouse in the traditional sense. This well-managed, upscale café has reasonably tasty samples of local dishes, and clean bathrooms. ⊠ *5 al-Badestan La.,* ☏ *02/590–3788.*

❸ **Madrasa and Mausoleum of al-Salih al-Ayyubi.** Although not significant in appearance from the street, this building occupies an important place in Cairo's history as a point of architectural and political transition. The last descendant of Salah al-Din to rule Egypt, al-Salih Nejm al-Din al-Ayyubi died in 1249 defending the country against the Crusader attack lead by Louis IX of France. Following his death, his wife, the famous Shagarat al-Dor, ruled for a brief time as queen and then as wife to Aybak, the first Mamluk ruler of Egypt.

This madrasa was the first in Cairo to have a liwan for more than one legal school. It was also the first to have a tomb attached. These two unique traits became standard features of a Mamluk madrasa. During Mamluk times, the madrasa of al-Salih was used by judges when hearing cases and issuing judgments. The street in front, the Bayn al-Qasrayn section of Shar'a al-Mu'iz, was used for meting out punishments to those deemed guilty. This was the city center for centuries.

Above the madrasa's minaret sits a top in the shape of a incense burner, in Arabic known as a *mabkhara.* It is the only one of its kind remaining from the Ayyubid period (1171–1250). Beneath the minaret, very little remains of this structure—part of an arched liwan in the courtyard, and the fragments of another arch opposite that suggest something of its former scale and importance. Some details, like the keel arch recess on the minaret with shell-like ornamentation, and the shallow relieving arch over the doorway, deserve notice.

The building is in effect a soccer field and throughway for the neighborhood's denizens. The tomb is usually locked, but if you are determined and ready to tip, the custodian with the key can more than likely be found (ask at nearby storefronts). The room is an early example of a dome with *muqarnasat,* the squinches and stalactites that Cairenes often used to fit a round dome onto a square room. The cenotaph and a pair of Quranic friezes display the fine skill of the era's woodworkers. ⊠ *Shar'a al-Mu'iz.* ☏ *Free.*

❻ Madrasa of al-Nasir Muhammad. Considered the greatest Mamluk sultan, al-Nasir ruled on three different occasions, for a total of 42 years (1293–1340). It was during al-Nasir's reign that Egypt took advantage of its geographical location and gained control of the lucrative maritime trade routes that connected England with China. Al-Nasir built more than 30 mosques, the aqueduct from the Nile to the Citadel, and a canal from Cairo to Alexandria. Eight of his sons ruled Egypt in the 21 years following his death.

If Qalaun's complex had Gothic influences, all the more so his son's madrasa. In fact the entrance was literally lifted from a Crusader church in Acre. The minaret, with its delicate stucco work, is one of the finest in the city. Little of interest can be found inside, but it is nevertheless significant because this was the first madrasa in Cairo to have a liwan for each of the four Sunni schools of jurisprudence, giving it a cruciform plan. ⊠ *Shar'a al-Mu'iz,* ☏ *no phone.* ☏ *£e6.*

❼ Madrasa of Barquq. The first of the Circassian Mamluk Sultans, Barquq assumed power after a series of political intrigues that led to the downfall (and often deaths) of the Bahri (Tartar) Mamluks. His madrasa, completed in 1386, is strikingly different in appearance from those of Qalaun and al-Nasir. Compare, for example, the difference between his slender octagonal minaret and that of the **Complex of Qalaun** (☞ *above*). Also, the high narrow entrance of stripes of black and white marble and the bronze door with silver inlay suggest a monumentality unseen in its neighbors. This type of portal was to become a standard in Mamluk architecture, reaching its high point in the magnificent entrance of the mosque of Sultan Hassan (☞ The Citadel section, *below*). The columns supporting the ceiling of the qibla liwan were most likely taken from a pharaonic monument. ⊠ *Shar'a al-Mu'iz,* ☏ *no phone.* ☏ *£e3.*

❺ Madrasa of Sultan al-Zahir Baybars I. Al-Zahir Baybars' reign (1260–77) marked the real beginning of the Mamluk state, due in large part to his skills as a commander, administrator, and builder. It was he who halted the Mongols' western expansion by defeating them at Ayn Jalout in Palestine (1260), and he staged a series of successful campaigns against the Crusaders. All that survives of this once great madrasa is the restored corner across the street from Qalaun's mausoleum. Check out the panthers above the window; this was Baybars' insignia (Baybars means panther). ⊠ *Shar'a al-Mu'iz,* ☏ *no phone.* ☏ *£e6.*

⓫ Mosque of al-Aqmar. The name of the mosque means "the moonlit" and refers to the way the stone catches the moon's reflection at night. Built in 1125, it is one of a few Fatimid buildings that have escaped major alterations. The shell-like recesses in the stone facade, later to become a common decorative element, were used here for the first time. This little mosque was also the first in Cairo to have an ornamented stone facade, and the first to alter its plan according to the existing urban structure, as the street existed before the mosque. ⊠ *Shar'a al-Mu'iz,* ☏ *no phone.* ☏ *£e6.*

⓬ Mosque of al-Hakim. Originally built in 1010 by the Fatimid Khalifa (caliph) al-Hakim bi Amr Allah, this gigantic mosque has recently been restored under the aegis of the Aga Khan, spiritual leader of the Isma'ili Shi'a sect.

Al-Hakim was, to put it nicely, an eccentric character. Some of the strangest edicts were declared during his caliphate, including a ban on *mulokhia,* a favorite Egyptian dish (he didn't care for it), and a ban on women's shoes, to prevent them from going out in public. Rumors began to circulate that he was claiming to be divine, creating extreme unrest among the populace. In order to quell the riots, he sent his main theologian, al-Darazi, to Syria (where he established the Druze religion), and then ordered his troops to attack Fustat, which at the time was the local town outside the royal city of al-Qahira. However, half his troops sided with the people, and the ensuing violence resulted in the burning of Fustat. He was given to riding around town on his donkey to ensure that his orders were being obeyed. One night after riding off into the Muqattam hills, he disappeared, never to be seen again, although the Druze claim that he has vanished only temporarily and will return to lead them to victory.

Built outside the original walls of Cairo (those standing now were constructed in 1087), the mosque has seen varied usage during its lifetime. During the Crusades, it held European prisoners of war who built a chapel inside it. Salah al-Din (1137–1193) tore the chapel down when he used it as a stable. For Napoléon's troops it was a storehouse and fortress. Under Muhammad 'Ali in the 1800s, part of it was closed off and used as a *zawya* (small Sufi school). By the end of the century, until the establishment of the **Museum of Islamic Arts** (☞ Islamic Cairo South, *below*) in 1896, it was a repository for Islamic treasures.

Architecturally, the mosque does not compete among the finest in the city; the most significant element is its minarets, which were restored and reinforced by Baybars II in 1303, giving them that impressive trapezoidal base. Nevertheless, its scale and history are important, and its courtyard is large and breezy, making it a comfortable place to rest or meditate. ✉ *Shar'a al-Mu'iz,* ☎ *no phone.* 🎫 *£e6.*

❾ Palace of Bishtak. Bishtak was a wealthy amir who married one of Sultan al-Nasir Muhammad's daughters. Completed in 1339, the original palace was purported to be five stories high, with running water on each floor. Only the women's quarters have survived the centuries, and even they are so impressive in scale as to give an idea of what the whole complex must have been like. The main qa'a is not unlike that of the Qa'a Muhib al-Din, but it is wider and more truly Mamluk in style. It also possesses a mezzanine level with mashrabiyya galleries for people to watch events in the main hall below without being seen. The coffered wooden ceilings in these galleries are worth the climb, as are the views both of the qa'a itself and the city outside. The palace entrance—the building itself fronts Shar'a al-Mu'iz—is on the side street across from the Madrasa of Sultan Barquq. Public bathrooms here are reasonably clean. ✉ *Shar'a al-Mu-iz,* ☎ *no phone.* 🎫 *£e6.*

OFF THE
BEATEN PATH
Madrasa of Mithqal. When you leave the Palace of Bishtak, turn right instead of returning immediately to al-Mu'iz. The little road winds past the small mausoleum of Shaykh Sinan and deposits you in front of a beautifully restored Mamluk madrasa. Mithqal, chief eunuch to two Mamluk sultans, built this cruciform madrasa in 1361. The most interesting part of the complex is the tunnel that passes underneath it. Dare yourself to go through it and try to get back to al-Mu'iz this way. It can be done. (The tunnel takes you out to a small street that leads to the open Maydan Bayt al-Qadi. The last right off the square leads you down Shar'a Bayt al-Qadi—where you'll find ☞ **Muhhib al-Din**—which in turn feeds onto al-Mu'iz.) ✉ *Darb al-Qirmiz,* ☎ *no phone.* 🎫 *£e6.*

★ ❽ Qa'a of Muhhib al-Din. Halfway up a street called Shar'a Bayt al-Qadi, on the west side of al-Mu'iz, this qa'a has little to distinguish it save a small plaque (if the door isn't open, knock and the custodian will appear; otherwise just walk in and find him). Inside is one of the greatest spaces in Islamic Cairo: a hall that towers 50 feet, with exquisite wood and stone carving. Also known as the house of Uthman Kathkhuda, after the 18th-century Ottoman lieutenant who converted the original 14th-century Mamluk qa'a, the hall has superb features from both periods. The marble mosaic around the fountain is remarkable, and if you can get up to the roof, take a look at the *malqaf* (wind catcher) once used to ventilate Cairo houses. ⊠ *Shar'a al-Mu'iz,* ☏ *no phone.* 🎟 *Baksheesh suggested.*

🔟 **Sabil-Kuttab of Abdul Rahman Katkhuda.** Before running water was available to the majority of the city's inhabitants, it was customary for wealthy patrons to build a sabil to provide people with potable water. Often attached to a sabil was a kuttab for teaching children Qur'an and other subjects. This 17th-century Ottoman monument is one of the most impressive in the city, in part because of its location at the head of an island along the main road of medieval Cairo. Restorations are currently underway in an attempt to revitalize it, which means that you will probably be allowed in only if you persist. Do so, because there are some gorgeous Turkish tiles on the ground floor, and the roof is also quite outstanding, both for its woodwork and its view down Shar'a al-Mu'iz. ⊠ *Shar'a al-Mu'iz,* ☏ *no phone.* 🎟 £e6.

1️⃣ **Sayyidna al-Husayn Mosque.** One of the holiest sites in Egypt, the mosque was originally built by the Fatimids in the 12th century as a shrine said to contain the head of Husayn, the Prophet's grandson. Al-Husayn is the spiritual heart of the Islamic city. It is here that the president and his ministers come to pray on important religious occasions. Many of the Sufi orders in the neighborhood perform Friday prayers at al-Husayn. During the mulid of al-Husayn, held during the Muslim month of Rabi'a al-Akhiri (the fourth month in the Muslim calendar), the square in front of the mosque becomes a carnival. In Ramadan, the area is the packed with people from sunset to dawn.

Not only was Husayn the grandson of the Prophet, but he was also the son of 'Ali, the fourth caliph and cousin of the Prophet. A group of followers who believed that 'Ali and his descendants should lead the faithful broke ranks with the majority (known as the Sunnis) when the Ummayads took control of the *umma* (the Islamic nation). This group became known as "the group of 'Ali" or Shi'a 'Ali, later Shi'a for short. Husayn is greatly revered by the Shi'a for his role as a martyr to the cause when, in 680, he and a band of his followers were massacred at the battle of Kerbala in Iraq.

If it seems strange that the head of a Shi'a martyr be given such importance in a country that is overwhelmingly Sunni, it should be noted that the Fatimids, the original builders of al-Qahira, were Shi'a. The 200 years in which they ruled the city left an impact on the traditions of the people. Not only did the Shi'a found the most prestigious Islamic university, al-Azhar, but they were also responsible for inculcating in the populace a veneration for saints, holy men, or relatives of the Prophet—a practice not at all in keeping with a strict interpretation of Sunni Islam. Thus, although the head of Husayn was brought to Cairo for safekeeping by a ruling minority, the Sunni majority quickly accepted the shrine as part of its heritage.

The mosque itself is a 19th-century stone building heavily influenced by the Gothic Revival; only elements of older structures remain. On the south end of the southeast facade stands a partial wall with a gate, known as Bab al-Akhdar (the Green Gate), which probably dates from the Fatimid dynasty. Inside the mosque, past the main prayer hall, is the tomb of Husayn, a domed chamber built by 'Abd al-Rahman Katkhuda in the 1760s. The grave itself is enclosed with a silver mashrabiyya screen.

The mosque is technically closed to non-Muslims. However, while large tour groups are not allowed to enter, there is more leeway for the individual traveler, provided that one avoids prayer times (the hour around noon; 1 PM between April and October during daylight saving time) and Fridays. ⊠ *Maydan al-Husayn.* ☜ *Free.*

NEED A BREAK?	On the roof of **al-Husayn Hotel,** you'll find a restaurant and café with a great view of the area—not to mention a rest room. The hotel is on the southeast corner of Maydan al-Husayn. ⊠ *2 Sikkit Khan al-Khalili,* ☎ *02/590-6935.*

Islamic Cairo South: al-Azhar to Bab Zuwayla

Shar'a al-Mu'iz bi Din Allah continues south on the other side of Shar'a al-Azhar. No tourist magnet like that of the Khan al-Khalili bazaar exists on this southern stretch of the road. Like the Khan, it was and remains a commercial area, albeit with far more contemporary local color than its more famous counterpart. You'll find on sale here everything from plastic sandals to brightly colored lingerie. Interspersed among the kitsch are a number of places for good buys—as well as some significant architectural sites and the remarkable Museum of Islamic Arts. There are also a few detours—including one to the longest running university in history, al-Azhar, which lends its name to the modern street that bisects the Islamic city.

A Good Walk

As in the Islamic Cairo North section, begin in front of **al-Azhar Mosque and University** ⑰. Immediately to the right of al-Azhar, the **Mosque of Abu Dhahhab** is an excellent example of Ottoman mosque design and construction. Because it is being restored, it might be inaccessible. The entrance to al-Azhar is through the pair of arched doors known as **Bab al-Muzayyinin,** or the barber's gate, so named because this is the where Azhar students got their hair cut.

After poking around the university, take some time to explore **Shar'a Muhammad 'Abdu,** the road behind al-Azhar. Turn east and look for the **Sabil-Kuttab and Wikala of Qayt Bay,** a culmination of Mamluk proportion and decoration, worth seeing even though it is in poor condition; the **Qayt Bay Hawd** (watering trough), currently under restoration; and, farther up the road, three fine examples of Islamic domestic architecture, the **Bayt Zaynab Khatoun, Bayt Um al-Wasil,** and **Bayt Abd al Rahman al-Harawi.** The first of these is Mamluk in origin, but was extended in the 18th century, about the same time the other two were constructed. The last of the three has been restored, and cultural events are sometimes held in its main hall.

Retrace your steps on Shar'a Muhammad 'Abdu to where you entered it and continue until you approach, on the left, the **Wikala of al-Ghuri** ⑱, a 16th-century merchant's inn, now a center for producing and exhibiting traditional crafts. Back on Shar'a Muhammad 'Abdu, resume in the same direction until the street feeds into Shar'a al-Azhar. Keep going straight until you see two medieval buildings on your left. Flanking the continuation of Shar'a al-Mu'iz, the central spine of old Cairo, these buildings are the **Madrasa and Mausoleum of al-Ghuri,** collectively known as **al-Ghuriyya** ⑲. Turn left onto al-Mu'iz and you are in the heart of commercial Islamic Cairo. Its products have changed, but the style here is mostly as it was 500 years ago: small shops where prices are negotiated between buyer and seller in narrow streets crowded with shoppers, suppliers, and passersby.

Your mission from here is to successfully reach Bab Zuwayla, al-Mu'iz's southern gate. The 10-minute walk is littered with monuments in various states of disrepair. The first of these, on the second left-hand corner, is the **Fakahani Mosque**—only its beautifully carved, 12th-century Fatimid doors remain. At the next corner is the **Sabil-Kuttab of Muhammad 'Ali,** dedicated to his favorite son, Tususn. The complex of **Nafisah al-Bayda',** a powerful woman of the late 1700s, is also on this block; it includes a hammam, a wikala, and a sabil-kuttab. Collectively they are known as **al-Sukkariyya.** Check out the mashrabiyya windows, still used to look out into the street without being seen. Across the street is the **Mosque of Mu'ayyad Shaykh** ⑳. Mu'ayyad Shaykh was a 15th-century Mamluk sultan whose pleasant mosque abuts **Bab Zuwayla** ㉑, the most impressive gate of al-Qahira still standing.

Through the gate is a open area that was used from the time of the Fatimids to the Ottomans as the site for public executions. To the right is the small **Zawiyah and Sabil of Sultan Farag.** This structure, built in 1408, was designed as a center for Islam's Sufi mystics. On the left is the Fatimid **Wazir al-Salih Tala'i Mosque** ㉒, and immediately ahead the last covered market from medieval Cairo, **al-Khayammiyya,** the tent makers' bazaar. Other parts of al-Mu'iz still have the names of the crafts once sold there—farther down al-Mu'iz there is a Sievers' Bazaar and a Saddle-makers' Bazaar, although the sievers and saddle-makers are no longer. But al-Khayammiyya is to this day the place to get those beautifully stitched appliqué panels that are used to make tents, pillowcases, and wall hangings. Incorporated into the Tent-makers' Bazaar are several small monuments—including the facades of apartments built for the influential Mamluk of Ottoman times, Radwan Bek, which flank the entrance to the bazaar. Farther into the covered bazaar on the left are the **Madrasa and Mausoleum of Mahmud al-Kurdi** and the **Madrasa and Mausoleum of Inal al-Yusufi,** both Mamluk functionaries of the late 1300s.

If you're pressed for time, or just plain bushed, skip ahead to the Museum of Islamic Arts by taking Shar'a Ahmad Maher, the road to your left as you face Bab Zuwayala.

The first left turn after al-Khayammiyya leads down a small side street to the remnants of a small palace, the **Pavilion of Sultan Qaytbay.** It remains unclear why this most prolific Mamluk builder put this place up, but the quiet and elegance even in its ruined state suggests that it may have been used as a retreat from the official life of the Citadel. Immediately following the pavilion is a fork in the road; go right until you reach the **Mosque of Altunbugha al-Maridani,** a 14th-century Mamluk prince who rose to prominence, fell, then rose again all before an early death at age 24. Walk around the mosque until you are on a main street known as **Shar'a al-Tabbana** and turn left.

On the left-hand side at the end of the first block stands the Mosque and Tomb of Mihmandar, a complex whose facades reveal both its Mamluk origins and Ottoman additions. At the next intersection, on the right, is the fantastic **Mosque and Tomb of Qijmas al-Ishaqi** ㉓. By the end of the 15th century, this was a fairly dense urban area, and building new large-scale civic structures on irregular plots of land was a fairly common problem, one that the designer of this mosque solved beautifully. As you continue along Shar'a al-Tabbana, the street's name changes to **Darb al-Ahmar,** which is also the name for the entire neighborhood, before you return to Bab Zuwalya. Walking farther past the gate, the street again changes its name, this time becoming **Shar'a Ahmad Maher;** follow Ahmad Maher until your next destination: the **Museum of Islamic Arts** ㉔.

Several Islamic monuments on the way to the museum along Ahmad Maher deserve attention. To the right are the remains of the **Hammam of Mu'ayyad Shaykh,** across from which are the **Takiyyah and Tomb of Ibrahim al-Gulshani.** Al-Gulshani was a Sufi teacher who came to Mamluk Egypt seeking refuge from persecution for his religious beliefs. About 150 yards farther down the road on the right are the adjoining water fountains, the **Sabil al-Habaysh** and the **Sabil of Hasan Agha Arzingan,** both Ottoman structures intended to provide fresh water to the growing urban population. A few steps later, across the street, is the **Mosque of al-Mar'a** (Mosque of Women). Originally built during the Mamluk era, it has undergone several Ottoman and modern renovations. The Museum of Islamic Arts is five minutes on foot from here, at the busy **Maydan Ahmad Maher** intersection. From the museum, a 20-minute walk west down Shar'a al Barudi will take you to Maydan Tahrir (Liberation Square). Or hop in a cab and just enjoy the somewhat chaotic ride back to your hotel.

TIMING

The territory covered along this walk is substantial. Although there are only nine major sights to see, just getting around will take some time—four to five hours for the entire tour. If time is short, go only to al-Azhar (30 minutes), the Wikala of al-Ghuri (10 to 15), al-Ghuriyya (10 minutes), Bab Zuwayla (a two-minute look), al-Khayammiyya (30 minutes for shoppers, five minutes otherwise), and the Museum of Islamic Arts (at least an hour). This abbreviation avoids the detour up Shar'a Muhammad 'Abdu and the trek through Darb al-Ahmar. The walking alone will still take up three-quarters of an hour, so this is still a three-hour excursion.

Either way, begin early in the morning to minimize exposure to the midday heat (especially in summer) or come back in late afternoon or evening to shop and just look around. Again, Sundays are calmer because many stores close, which of course won't interest shoppers. **For Islamic sights' hours and prayer times,** *see* Timing *in* Islamic Cairo North, *above.*

Sights to See

⑰ **Al-Azhar Mosque and University.** Originally built in 970 by the conquering Fatimid caliph al-Mu'iz, al-Azhar is the oldest university in the world. Although the Fatimids were Shi'ite, the Sunni Mamluks who ousted them recognized the importance of the institution and replaced the Shi'ite doctrine with the Sunni orthodoxy. Today the university has faculties of medicine and engineering in addition to religion, and it has auxiliary campuses across the city.

Al-Azhar's primary significance remains as a school of religious learning. All Egyptian clerics must go through the program here before they are certified—a process that can take up to 15 years. Young men from all over the Islamic world come to study here, learning in the traditional Socratic method where students sit with a tutor until both agree that the student is ready to go on. The Shaykh of al-Azhar is not just the director of the university, but also the nation's supreme religious authority.

Built in pieces throughout the ages, al-Azhar is a mixture of architectural styles. The stucco ornamentation and the open courtyard represent early Islamic tastes; the solid stone madrasas and the ornate minarets are Mamluk; additions in the main sanctuary and its walls are Ottoman. The enclosure now measures just under 3 acres.

After you enter through the **Gates of the Barbers,** an Ottoman addition constructed under the auspices of Abd al-Rahman Katkhuda in 1752, remove your shoes and pay for your ticket. Then turn left to the **Madrasa and Tomb of Amir Atbugha.** Until recent renovations, this Mamluk hall used to house the university's collection of rare manuscripts. Check out the recess in the qibla wall; an organic shaped mosaic pattern rare to Islamic ornamentation can be found near the top.

Return to the ticket and shoe-removing men and look up at the **Gates of Sultan Qayt Bay,** the second set on the way into the university. Built in 1483, they have a quality of ornamentation that verifies this Mamluk leader's patronage of architecture. The composition as a whole is masterful: from the recessed lintel to the multitier stalactite arch above the doorway, the grilles and medallions above the arch, and finally the finely carved minaret placed off center.

To the right of this lobby is the **Madrasa of Taybars.** Once ranked among the most spectacular madrasas in Mamluk Cairo, only the qibla wall remains. It is said that the ceiling was gold-plated and that Taybars, the patron, so wanted to glorify Allah that he specifically asked not to see any bills until it was completed, in 1309.

Sultan Qayt Bay's gateway opens to a spacious courtyard, quite typical of early Islamic design. Originally this court must have appeared similar to that of the **Mosque of al-Hakim** (☞ Islamic Cairo North, *above*), but changes over the centuries have diminished that effect. The keel arches of the arcades and the stucco decoration, however, remain true to that era. The raising of the arch that indicates entrance to the main sanctuary, while a common feature of Persian and Indian Islamic architecture, remains an oddity in Arab buildings.

The main sanctuary, which was traditionally a place to pray, learn, and sleep, is part Fatimid, part Ottoman. The Ottoman extension is distinguished by a set of steps that divides it from the original. Take some time to soak in the atmosphere, and look for the two qibla walls, the painted wooden roof, the old metal gates that used to open for prayer or the poor, and the ornate stucco work of the Fatimid section. To the right of the Ottoman qibla wall is the **Tomb of 'Abd al-Rahman Katkhuda,** the greatest builder of the Ottoman era and the man most responsible for the post-Mamluk extension of al-Azhar. To the extreme left along the Fatimid qibla wall is the small **Madrasa and Mausoleum of the Eunuch Gawhar al-Qunqubay,** treasurer to Sultan Barsbay. Although it is diminutive in size, the quality of the intricately inlaid wooden doors, the stained-glass windows, and the interlacing floral pattern on the dome make it a deserved detour.

Return to the courtyard. To the right of the **minaret of Qayt Bay** is the **minaret of al-Ghuri,** the tallest in the complex. Built in 1510, it is similar to, but not a copy of Qayt Bay's: it is divided into three sections (the first two are octagonal) like its predecessor, but it is tiled rather than carved. The final section, consisting of two pierced rectangular blocks, is unusual, and not at all like Qayt Bay's plain cylinder. With an extra tip, a custodian would be glad to escort you to the top of the minaret, a great spot for looking at the city and taking photographs.

A recently completed restoration project has left the complex shiny and clean, and has made the custodians especially sensitive about its upkeep. But a strange rule is currently in effect: foreigners are allowed in all day (except during Friday prayers), but Egyptians are permitted entrance only during prayer time. An effort to discourage the poor from coming and sleeping in the cool sanctuary, this rule is contrary to all traditions of this place. The beauty of al-Azhar, unlike many of the other monuments, stems in part from the fact that it is alive and much in use. ⊠ *Gama' al-Azhar, Shar'a al-Azhar,* ☏ *no phone.* ☞ *£e12.*

⑲ Al-Ghuriyya. This medieval landmark stands on either side of Shar'a al-Mu'iz where it crosses Shar'a al-Azhar. The area between the two buildings was the site of the Silk Bazaar, a covered space far grander than the remaining Tent-maker's Bazaar.

Built by Sultan al-Ghuri, who constructed the **Wikala al-Ghuri** three years later, al-Ghuriyya is the last great Mamluk architectural work before the Ottomans occupied Egypt. On the east side of the street is the madrasa; opposite it stands the mausoleum. The former is a large-scale project, with almost Brutalist (large, modern, exposed concrete buildings') proportions. The interior cruciform plan is divided by great arches. The central court is relaxing and cool, a pleasant break from the hustle and bustle outside its doors. The minaret, with its square base topped by five chimney pots, has an unusual design.

The wooden roof of the mausoleum is a later addition—originally a blue-tiled dome, similar to those in Iran, covered the tomb. It was rebuilt three times during al-Ghuri's reign and finally collapsed in 1860. After spending a reported 100,000 dinars on the complex, al-Ghuri was never buried here; the bodies of a son, a daughter, a concubine, Tumanbay II (his successor), and Tumanbay's daughter are interred in the vault.

Al-Ghuriyya's official name today is the al-Ghuri Cultural Palace: a restoration converted the site for displays of art and other cultural events. Sufi dancers perform in the madrasa Wednesday and Saturday nights (9 PM in summer; 9:30 PM in winter). This is one of the best things you can see in Cairo, and it's free, so arrive early. ⊠ *Qasr al-Ghuri, Shar'a al-Mu'iz,* ☏ *02/510–0823.* ☞ *Free.* ☉ *Daily 9–5.*

OFF THE BEATEN PATH **House of Gamal al-Din al-Dhahabbi.** The second right after al-Ghuriyya along al-Mu'iz leads to a small alley named Shar'a Khushqadam. Fifty yards up on the right, look for the well-preserved, 16th-century, wealthy merchant's house. Enter through the massive wooden doors that feed into the courtyard. Of particular interest are the mashrabiyya and stained-glass windows, the stone Mamluk-style facia panels, the marble floors, and the reception room's wooden ceilings. ⊠ *6 Shar'a Khushqadam,* ☏ *no phone.* ☞ *£e3.*

㉑ Bab Zuwayla. Built in 1092, this is one of three remaining old gates from the city of Cairo and, with its rounded towers and arched supports, it is by far the most refined. There were once 60 such entrances to al-Qahira. This one is named Zuwayla because warriors from the Berber tribe Zuwayli settled here after the Fatimid conquest of Egypt.

The gate has another name as well: Bab al-Mitwalli, after a local 18th-century religious man who was said to perform miracles. People in need of baraka still sometimes hang a piece of clothing or hair on the bab, in the hopes that Mitwalli will help them.

This was not, however, always an uplifting spot. It was here that public hangings and beheadings took place. The last independent Mamluk sultan, Tumanbay II, was hanged from this gate by the conquering Turks in 1517. The unlucky man's agony was prolonged because the rope broke three times. Finally, fed up, the Ottomans had him beheaded.

Bab Zuwayla marks the southern end of the Fatimid city, as Bab al-Futuh marks the north. And al-Mu'iz, the central artery of medieval Cairo, runs from the latter through the former. Al-Mu'iz continues all the way to the Southern Cemeteries, but as is common with many older streets, the name keeps changing along the way as a way of describing the area it passes through, as when it passes through the Tent-maker's Bazaar. ⊠ *Bab Zuwayla, Shar'a al-Mu'iz.*

㉓ Mosque and Tomb of Qijmas al-Ishaqi. Carefully restored in the early part of this century, this complex is one of the jewels of Mamluk architecture. Qijmas, a pious and well-respected man of his time, served in the court of Qayt Bay until he took an appointment as viceroy of Damascus, where he died peacefully and was buried in 1487.

The triangular lot is mitigated by careful and elegant design, notably the immensely pleasing proportions of the building's facade and volume. Look for the corner pilasters, the recesses filled with long stalactites, and especially at the sabil's grilles for Qijmas' blazon (a napkin, two horns and a cup). By Mamluk standards the minaret is simply ornamented but nevertheless graceful. If you haven't tired of climbing, ascend the minaret's staircase for a view of Bab Zuwayla.

Despite its irregular footprint, the mosque is a perfect cruciform plan. And the quality of light is excellent, as it filters in through the *shukhshayhka* (lantern) of the central covered court. The marble inlay and stucco work along the walls is superb, as is the mosaic marble paving in the liwans. The tomb is simple but dignified, bare of any ornamentation save a single band of inscription along the wall and a beautiful blue tiled floor. Buried here is Abu Hurayba, a 19th-century holy man. The mosque is popularly known by his name. ⊠ *Shar'a Darb al-Ahmar,* ☎ *no phone.* ⊠ £e6.

㉔ Mosque of Mu'ayyad Shaykh. The Sultan Mu'ayyad chose this site because he was once imprisoned at this location. During his captivity, he swore that he would build a mosque here if he was ever freed. He made good on his promise in 1420 and tore down the infamous jails that once occupied the site.

The mosque's facade is remarkable only in that the ablaq is black and white, less common than the usual red and white. The high portal is inspired by the famous entrance of the Sultan Hassan Mosque below the Citadel (☞ The Citadel section, *below*). The beautiful bronze-plated door was a little more than inspired; Mu'ayyad had it lifted from the mosque of his better known predecessor.

The **qibla wall** is something to see: a spectacular combination of black and white marble, blue tiles, and stucco. Check out the ceiling as well. It is a restoration, done in a manner true to its original design of interweaving foliage, rather than the standard geometrical patterns.

The two elegant **identical minarets** rest against the towers of Bab Zuwayla, which makes them appear to be a part of the gate and not the mosque. A climb up one of these minarets is only for the strong of heart until the wooden railing is fixed—but the climb is well rewarded with a spectacular view of al-Mu'iz and its environs from the top of Bab Zuwayla. When you come down, relax in the garden courtyard. ⊠ *Gam'a al-Mu'ayyad Shaykh, Shar'a al-Mu'iz at Bab Zuwayla,* ☎ *no phone.* ⊠ £e6.

★ ㉔ Museum of Islamic Arts. Often overlooked, this is one of the finest museums in Cairo, and it possess the rarest and most extensive collection of Islamic art anywhere. The fact that this is so, in spite of its being out of the way and its sometimes shoddy displays, speaks to the quality of the pieces themselves.

The collection comes mainly from Egypt, but there are objects from elsewhere in the Islamic world as well. Part of the exhibit is arranged chronologically—moving from Ummayad to Abbasid, Fatimid, Ayyubid, and Mamluk works—to show the strengths of different eras. Particularly notable items include one of the earliest Muslim tombstones, which dates from 652, only 31 years after the Prophet returned to Mecca victorious; a bronze ewer from the time of the Abbasid caliph Marwan II that has a spout in the shape of a rooster; a series of Abbasid stucco panels from both Egypt and Iraq displaying the varied styles of the time; frescoes from a Fatimid bathhouse; wooden panels from the Western Palace; carved rock crystal; a wooden piece from the Ayyubid era covered with exquisite carved inscriptions and foliage; an excellent brass-plated Mamluk door, which looks at first glance like a standard arabesque decoration but is in fact interspersed with tiny animals and foliage; and a series of mosaics from various Mamluk mosques, some made with marble and mother of pearl inlay.

The rest of the museum is arranged by medium. You enter a set of halls displaying woodwork through the huge doors al-Hakim had commissioned for al-Azhar. This area has some of the finest mashrabiyya and minbars found anywhere. The metalwork section has the doors of the Mosque of al-Salih Tala'i. Metalwork inlaid with silver and gold includes incense burners, candlesticks and vases, some with Christian symbols. There is also a set of astronomical instruments. The armor and arms hall is still impressive despite the fact that Selim, the conquering Ottoman sultan of 1517, had much of this type of booty carried off to Istanbul, where it is now on display at Top Kapi Palace. The ceramics display is excellent, particularly pieces from the Fatimid era and Iran. A hall of glassware merits particular attention, especially the Mamluk mosque lamps. Also look for textiles—woven silk, appliqué, and printed cottons and linens—and a fine collection of Turkish carpets. And the collection of rare manuscripts and books is superb. ⊠ *Shar'a Bur Sa'id at Maydan Ahmad Maher,* ☎ *02/390–9930.* ▦ *£e16.* ☉ *Sat.–Thurs. 9–4, Fri. 9–11 and 2–4.*

㉒ Wazir al-Salih Tala'i Mosque. Built in 1160, this is one of the last Fatimid structures constructed outside the city walls. It is also one of the most elegant mosques in Cairo, in part because of its simplicity. Like many mosques in Cairo, the ground-floor level housed several shops, which allowed the authorities to pay for the upkeep. Today these shops are underground, because the street level has risen considerably over time.

The mosque has a standard, early Islamic, rectangular courtyard plan. The main facade consists of five keel arches on Greco-Roman columns taken from an earlier building that are linked by wooden tie beams. Between each arch, a set of long panels is topped with Fatimid shell niches. The most distinctive architectural feature of this mosque is the porch-like area, underneath the arches of the main facade, that creates an open, airy interior court. Inside, the columns are also taken from elsewhere: no two of their capitals are alike. ⊠ *Gam'a al-Salah Tala'i (Shar'a al-Mu'iz at Bab Zuwayla),* ☎ *no phone.* ▦ *£e6.*

⑱ Wikala of al-Ghuri. Built in 1504–1505 by Sultan Qansuh al-Ghuri, this classical Mamluk structure was constructed to accommodate visiting merchants. It went up, as fate would have it, at the end of a period of Mamluk prosperity, the result of their control of the spice trade between Asia and Europe. When Vasco da Gama discovered a path around Africa in 1495, the decline in Cairo's importance began. Sadly, while he was a prolific builder and a courageous soldier, al-Ghuri was a decade behind the curve. He died in 1516 staving off the Ottomans in Aleppo, Syria. His successor, Tumanbay II, was destined to last only a year before succumbing to the might of Istanbul.

Nevertheless, the building is in fairly good shape, and it provides an indication of how medieval Cairene commerce operated. Merchants would bring their horses and carts into the main courtyard, where they would be stabled, while the merchants would retire to the upper floors with their goods. This handsome building with its strong, square lines seems almost modern, save for the ablaq masonry, a clear indicator of its Mamluk origin.

Today the wikala's rooms are used as studios for traditional crafts, including carpet weaving, metalwork, and the making of mashrabiyya that are not so different from the ones that protrude from the upper floors into the courtyard. During the month of Ramadan, musical events are held here in the evenings. ✉ *Shar'a Muhammad 'Abdu,* ☎ *02/511–0472.* 🎫 *£e5.* ⏲ *8 AM–midnight. Studios close at 3 PM.*

The Citadel to the Mosque of Ibn Tulun

The third walk through Islamic Cairo covers a significant amount of territory, as well as the city's most outstanding medieval monuments. The Citadel, home to Egypt's rulers from the 12th to 19th centuries, houses a number of places of interest, including the Muhammad 'Ali Mosque, which dominates the Cairo skyline. It also provides some of the most comprehensive views of the city. In a square at the foot of the fortress complex stands the amazing Mosque and Madrasa of Sultan Hasan, universally acknowledged as the pinnacle of Mamluk architecture. A kilometer and a half toward the Nile, the Mosque of Ibn Tulun is a vast oasis of tranquillity in the midst of urban chaos.

The areas between these three mosques have been cut through with a series of main roads—including modern attempts to clear paths across the dense medieval urban fabric—and as a result, this part of the city lacks the coherence and charm of Coptic Cairo and in Islamic Cairo the Khan or the area around Bab Zuwayla. Nevertheless, the scale and quality of these monuments is so impressive that if you have time to see only a few of Cairo's Islamic treasures, the Citadel and the Sultan Hasan and Ibn Tulun mosques should be among them.

One way of getting to Ibn Tulun from Sultan Hasan is via Shar'a Saliba, an old thoroughfare that crosses Shar'a al-Mu'iz. At the intersection is the complex of Shaykhu, commander in chief of Sultan Hassan's army. Despite the buses and the billboards, there remains a medieval feel to this part of the road.

A Good Walk

The easiest way to reach the **Citadel** ㉕ is by cab via Shar'a Salah Salem (about £e7 from Maydan Tahrir). If you're feeling adventurous, take a bus or a minibus. Many lines stop at the square known as Maydan Salah al-Din: buses 174 (originating in Maydan Ramses), 173 (Maydan al-Falaki), 905 (the pyramids), 404 (Maydan Tahrir), and the number 54 minibus from Tahrir.

Enter the Citadel through the southeast gate below the Muqattam tower at the terminus of a long, ramped approach to the walled fortress. Take time to enjoy the cooling winds and to explore the complex, which includes three mosques, three museums, and the best views of the old city.

Exit through the Muqattam gates and descend to Salah Salem. Turn right, then right again onto Shar'a Salah al-Din and head to the square of the same name. Along the way on the left is the **Tomb and Museum of Mustafa Kamil,** a nationalist leader from the turn of the century.

Maydan Salah al-Din served as the site for tournaments, polo matches, and as the starting point for processions through the city. Around the square are several important monuments. Stand with your back to Mustafa Kamil. Then count clockwise around the square from the upper left. The **Mosque and Madrasa of Sultan Hassan** ㉖ is first; then comes the **al-Rifa'i Mosque** ㉗; then the **Madrasa of Qanibay al-Sayfi,** built by a powerful Mamluk amir whose political skills allowed him to maintain his position after the Ottomans took over; then the **Mahmud Pasha Mosque,** an Ottoman mosque built in the Mamluk style (except for its pencil-thin Ottoman minaret); and finally, to your right, the Ottoman gates to the Citadel's lower enclosure, **Bab al-'Azab,** modelled closely after Bab Zuwayla.

After touring Sultan Hassan and Rifa'i—and relaxing for a while, perhaps, in the café adjacent to the Sultan Hassan—return to the square and take a right onto a relatively major street, Shar'a Saliba. About 50 yards up the street on the left is the **Sabil-Kuttab of Qayt Bay.** Decorated in the highly ornate style of this famous Mamluk builder, it is significant in that it was the first time that a sabil-kuttab was concieved as an independent structure. Previously, water dispeners and schools for teaching Qur'an were attached to larger projects. It would later become a very popular building type, especially during the Ottoman and khedivial eras. Farther along the left side of the street, the **Mosque of Qanibay Muhammad** and the **House and Sabil of Amir Abdullah** were built in 1413 and 1719, respectively.

Immediately after these stands the impressive **Complex of Amir Shaykhu** ㉘, with a khanqah on the left side of the street and a mosque on the right. At the next intersection, to the right, is the **Sabil-Kuttab of Umm 'Abbas,** commisioned in 1867 by the mother of Khedive 'Abbas. It is at this point that Shar'a Saliba crosses the central artery, al-Mu'iz—it is called Shar'a al-Suyuiyya here because it was once the location of the swordsmiths' bazaar. In fact, *Shar'a Saliba*—Cross Street—derives its name from this intersection.

A short walk brings you to the **Madrasa and Mausoleum of Taghribardi** ㉙, a small but elegant Mamluk structure on the right side of the street. On the left, just after Taghribardi, stand the ruins of the **Palace of Sultan al-Ghuri.** Little remains of this once vast complex save the portal and a small section of the wall that still has some inscriptions on it. Two blocks down on the left, is the **Madrasa of Sarghatmish** ㉚; he was a Mamluk contemporary of Sultan Hassan. The madrasa is famous for its unusal domes.

Just before Sarghatmish on the same side of the street is a clearing in which stands one of the oldest and most beautiful pieces of arhictecture in Cairo, the **Mosque of Ibn Tulun** ㉛. To the north of its famous minaret is **Sayyida Zaynab Children's Park,** which won an Aga Khan architectural award in the early 1990s. Thanks to bureaucratic logic it's nearly impossible to get in without special permission. You can catch a glimpse of it from the minaret of Ibn Tulun. The **Gayer-Anderson Museum** ㉜, just beyond the entrance to Ibn Tulun, is more accessible.

Make your way back to Shar'a Saliba, turn left (west), and follow the road past the **Madrasa-Khanqah of Salar and Sangar,** an imposing-looking structure built on the face of a small hill, on your way to the **Mosque of Sayyida Zaynab.** The latter is the site of one of the most important mulids in the country. During the Muslim month of Ragab, the street is lined with lights and almost a million visitors who flock to the mosque from all over Egypt. It is currently being extended to accomodate the crowds. The square in front serves as a bus stop.

TIMING

This walk will take about five hours at a leisurely pace. Plan to spend at least an hour and a half at the Citadel, about 45 minutes between Sultan Hassan and al-Rifa'i, 20 minutes at Shaykhu, 15 apiece at Taghribardi and Sarghatmish, and about an hour and a quarter at Ibn Tulun and the Gayer-Anderson Museum.

There are alternative ways to do this walk: because it is somewhat removed from the city beneath it, you can take on the Citadel on its own, reserving the trek from Sultan Hassan to Ibn Tulun for another time. Or, hit only the big three, taking a cab or bus down Shar'a Saliba in between them.

For Islamic sights' hours and prayer times, *see* Timing *in* Islamic Cairo North, *above*.

Sights to See

㉗ Al-Rifa'i Mosque. Intended to compliment its neighbor, Sultan Hassan, al-Rifa'i is often confused with the great mosque. Although it appears neo-Mamluk in style, it was not commisioned until 1869, by the mother of Khedive Isma'il, the Princess Khushyar. The projected was completed in 1912.

The work here is not as fine as it is at Sultan Hassan, nor are the proportions. And true to the excessive khedivial tastes, the inside is markedly different from the other mosque: where Sultan Hassan is relatively unadorned, al-Rifa'i is overdecorated. Inside the mausoleum are the bodies of Khashyar, Khedive Fu'ad (father of the last king of Egypt), other members of the royal family, Sufi holy men of the Rifa'i order (hence the establishment's name), and the last shah of Iran. ✉ *Maydan Salah al-Din,* ☎ *no phone.* 🎫 *£e12.*

㉕ The Citadel. Until Salah al-Din al-Ayyubi arrived in Cairo in 1168, local rulers had overlooked the strategic value of the hill above the city. Within a few years he began making plans for the defense of the city with *al-Qala'a* (the fortress) being the key element. He and his successors built an impenetrable bastion, using the most advanced construction techniques of the age. For the next 700 years, Egypt was ruled from that hill. Nothing remains of the original complex except a part of the walls and Bir Yusuf, the well that supplied the Citadel with water. The Ayyubid walls that circle the northern enclosure are 33 feet high and 10 feet thick; they and their towers were built with the experience gleaned from the Crusader wars. Bir Yusuf is also an engineering marvel; dug 285 feet straight into solid rock to reach the water table, the well was powered by oxen who would walk in circles all day to draw water up to the level of the Citadel.

During the 1330s al-Nasir Muhammad tore down most of the Ayyubid buildings to make room for his own needs, which included several palaces and a mosque in addition to barracks for his army. These too were not to last, for when Muhammad 'Ali assumed power he had all the Mamluk buildings razed and the complex entirely rebuilt; only the green-domed mosque and a fragment of *al-Qasr al-Ablaq* (the striped palace) remain. The Citadel's appearance today is really the vision of Muhammad 'Ali, particularly the mosque that bears his name.

The **Muhammad 'Ali Mosque** is the most noticeable in all of Cairo. For over 150 years it has dominated the skyline, making it almost the symbol of the city. This is unfortunate, for it is at best a second-rate imitation of the graceful Ottoman mosques in Istanbul. The proportions are awkward, the alabaster facing on the outside is of poor quality, and the interior—well, the interior needs to be seen to be believed.

In an attempt to weld Middle Eastern and French rococo, it is finished with ornate lines of red, green and gold, the result being nothing short of gaudy. Nevertheless, there are interesting aspects to the place. Ottoman law prohibited anyone but the sultan from building a mosque with more than one minaret; note that this mosque has two. This was one of Muhammad 'Ali's first indications that he did not intend to remain submissive to Istanbul.

The courtyard within the mosque is rather spacious and comfortable. It is also has a gilded clock tower given to Muhammad 'Ali by the king Louis Philip in exchange for the obelisk that stands in the middle of Paris. It is fair to say that the French got the better end of the bargain: the clock has never worked.

Behind Muhammad 'Ali's gilded beast stands a far more elegant creature, the **Mosque of al-Nasir Muhammad.** The beautifully crafted masonry, the elegant proportions, the ornate but controlled work on the minarets all indicate that the building is a Mamluk work of art. Much of the original interior decoration was carried off to Istanbul by the conquering Ottomans, but the space is nevertheless impressive. The supporting columns around the courtyard were collected from various sources and are possibly pharaonic.

Directly across from the entrance of al-Nasir is the **National Police Museum.** A prison until 1985, this small structure is hardly worth the five minutes it will take to walk through it. Two things rescue it from complete dismissal: the exhibition on political assassinations in Egypt, and the spectacular view from the courtyard behind it. On a clear day, you can see both the Giza and Saqqara pyramids. On a regular day the city is fantastic from this height. Directly below is the lower enclosure gated by the Bab al-'Azab, the site where Muhammad 'Ali decisively wrested control from the unruly Mamluk warlords, who, while they had submitted to Ottoman rule for 300 years, had not really accepted it. In his capacity as Ottoman governor, Muhammad 'Ali invited all the powerful Mamluks up to the Citadel where they ate, drank and were merry. As they were making their way to the gate for their exit, the governor's men ambushed them, eliminating in a single stroke all internal opposition.

To the northwest of al-Nasir's mosque is the **Bab al-Qulla** which leads to the **Qasr al-Harem** (the Harem Palace), now the site of the **National Military Museum.** The brainchild of King Faruq, the exhibit was intended to chronicle the glories of his family but has been extended by the post-Revolution administrations to include the military glories of presidents Jamal 'Abd al-Nasir (Nasser), Anwar Sadat, and Hosni Mubarak. The display of uniforms and weaponry may be of some interest to historians and military aficionados. For those less taken with martial affairs, the building itself is another example of the bizarre eclectic taste that Muhammad 'Ali and his descendants appreciated.

Farther west, the **Carriage Museum** was the dining hall of the British officers stationed at the Citadel in the early 20th century. It now houses eight carriages used by Egypt's last royal dynasty (1805–1952).

In the northwest part of the Citadel is a rarely visited site, the **Mosque of Sulayman Pasha.** Built in 1528 by Egypt's Ottoman governor for his crack Janissary troops, this is a small but graceful mosque. While its plan is entirely a product of Istanbul, the sparse stone decoration shows traces of Mamluk influence. The tomb contains the remains of several prominent Janissary officers, as well as a Fatimid saint.

Before leaving the Citadel, pass by the **Qasr al-Gawhara** (the Jewel Palace), where Muhammad 'Ali received guests. When the khedives moved their residence down to 'Abdin Palace in the city, it was opened to the public, and after the revolution it was turned into a museum displaying the royal family's extravagance. Heavily influenced by the early 19th-century French style, the building is similar in taste to the Harem Palace. The painted murals on the walls and ceiling of the main Meeting Hall are worth the visit, as is the furniture in the model royal bedroom. ⊠ *al-Qala'a, Shar'a Salih Salem,* ☎ *no phone.* ▨ *£e 12.*

㉘ Complex of Amir Shaykhu. Flanking Shar'a Saliba, this mosque and khanqah were built by the commander-in-chief of Sultan Hassan's forces and form a well-integrated whole. The mosque was badly damaged by shelling during the Ottoman takeover because Tumanbay, the last Mamluk sultan, hid here. Nevertheless, the qibla liwan still has the original marble inlay work.

The khanqah, with its central courtyard surrounded by three floors of 150 rooms, once housed 700 Sufi adherents. As in the mosque, the ground floor arches are supported by classical pillars. To the left of the qibla wall are the tombs of Shaykhu and the first director of the school. ⊠ *Shar'a Saliba (just east of Shar'a al-Suyuiyya),* ☎ *no phone.* ▨ *£e6.*

★ ㉜ Gayer-Anderson Museum. Also known as Bayt al-Kiritliya, the museum consists of two Ottoman houses joined together, restored and furnished by Major Gayer-Anderson, a British member of the Egyptian civil service in the 1930s and '40s. It isn't the grandest of Ottoman buildings, but it is by far the best way to get a taste of what life in the house of a properous 18th-century merchant might have been like. Spend some time in the reception room, where a mosaic fountain lies at the center of an ornate marble floor. Above the liwans are mashrabiyya-covered mezzanines, where the women of the house could watch the proceedings below. ⊠ *4 Maydan Ibn Tulun,* ☎ *02/364–7822.* ▨ *£e 16.* ☉ *Daily 8 AM–5 PM; closed for Friday prayers.*

㉙ Madrasa and Mausoleum of Taghribardi. This small but impressive complex was built in 1440 by the executive secretary to Sultan Jaqmaq. Fitting the standard minaret, entrance portal, sabil-kuttab, and dome into a single ensemble required a talented architect—and it would seem that many existed in the time when the Taghribardi went up. Also interesting is the way in which the orientation toward Mecca (southeast) was meshed with that of the street: the difference is hidden through the thickening of certain walls. Much of the top part of the building is an Ottoman reconstruction, including the final tier of the minaret. The work is clearly of a lower standard, demonstrating architecturally the demotion in Cairo's status from the capital of an empire to that of a province within an empire. ⊠ *Saghri Wardi, Shar'a Saliba,* ☎ *no phone.* ▨ *£e6.*

㉚ Madrasa of Sarghatmish. Completed in 1356 by the amir who suceeded Shaykhu, Sarghatmish was probably designed by the same architect who designed Sultan Hassan. The layout is a cruciform plan—its innovative placement of the madrasa in the corners is identical to that of the great mosque—although smaller in scale. But far from being a diminutive copy of a masterpiece, Sarghatmish has several features that make it interesting in its own right, the first being a tall arched entrance that rises slightly above the facade. Most significant are the two domes, which are very unusual for Cairo. One has unfortunately been renovated with concrete, the other is sublime. Built in brick, it has a slight bulge reminscient of the Persian style domes of Iran and central Asia. The interior is stripped of its original finishings, but the space is pleasing nevertheless. ⊠ *Shar'a Saliba (just east of Shar'a Qadry),* ☎ *no phone.* ▨ *£e6.*

★ ❷ **Mosque and Madrasa of Sultan Hassan.** Built between 1356 and 1363 by the Mamluk ruler Sultan Hassan, this is one largest Islamic religious buildings in the world. Historians believe that its builders may have used stone from the pyramids at Giza. The scale of the masterpiece is so colossal that it nearly emptied the vast Mamluk Treasury.

You enter the complex at an angle, through a tall portal that is itself a work of art. Before going in, look at the carving on both sides of the entrance that culminates in a series of stalactites above. A dark and relatively low-ceilinged passageway to the left of the entrance leads to the brightly lit main area, a standard cruciform-plan open court.

What is different about this plan is the fact that between each of the four liwans is a madrasa, one for each of the four Sunni schools of jurisprudence, complete with its own courtyard and four stories of cells for students and teachers. Also unique is the location of the mausoleum behind the qibla liwan, which, in effect, forces people who are praying to bow before the tomb of the dead sultan—a fairly heretical idea to devout Muslims. Nevertheless, the mausoleum, facing the Maydan Salah al-Din, is quite a beautiful place, particularly in the morning when the rising sun filters through grilled windows.

Only one of the two tall minarets is structurally sound, the one to the left of the qibla liwan. Have the custodian take you up inside of it to get a view of the city, especially of the Citadel. In fact, this roof was used by several armies to shell the mountain fortress, Bonaparte's expedition included. ✉ *Maydan Salah al-Din,* ☎ *no phone.* 🎟 *£e 12.* ⏲ *8 AM to 5 PM, except during Friday prayers.*

★ ❸ **Mosque of Ibn Tulun.** This huge congregational mosque was built in 879 by Ahmad Ibn Tulun with the intention of accomodating his entire army during Friday prayers. Ahmad was sent to Egypt by the 'Abbasid caliph in Samarra to serve as its governor, but it seems that he had his own plans. Sensing weakness in Iraq, he declared his independence and began to build a new city, al-Qata'i, northwest of al-Fustat and al-'Askar, the Muslim towns that had grown up north of the Roman fortress of Babylon. Replete with numerous palaces, gardens, and even a hippodrome, al-Qata'i was not destined to survive. When the 'Abbasids reconquered Egypt in 970, they razed the entire city as a lesson to future rebels, sparing only the great Friday mosque but leaving it to wither on the outskirts of the city.

In 1293, the amir Lagin hid out in the derelict building for several months while a fugitive from the Mamluk sultan, vowing to restore it if he survived. Three years later, after being appointed sultan himself, he kept his word, repairing the minaret and adding a fountain in the courtyard, the mihrab, and the beautiful minbar. All of this background is secondary to the building itself—you can delight in this masterpiece without even the slightest knowledge of history. Its grandeur and simplicity set it apart from any other Islamic monument in Cairo.

The mosque is separated from the streets around it with a ziyada, in which the Friday market was once held, and where the famous minaret is located. At the top of the walls a strange crenellation pattern almost resembles the cut-out figures that children make with folded paper. In fact this pattern was never used again because it was seen to be too anthropomorphic for a mosque. Inside, the mosque itself is of the classic courtyard variety writ large, covering an area of more than 6 acres. The vast courtyard is surrounded by four arcaded aisles. The arches are covered in beautifully carved stucco, the first time this medium was used in Cairo. Look for the stucco grilles that cover the windows, especially those in the qibla wall. The minaret, the only one of its kind in Egypt, is modeled after the minarets of Samarra, with the ziggurat-like stairs spiralling on the outside of the tower. The view from the top, of both the city and the mosque, is remarkable. ⊠ *Shar'a Tulun Bay,* ☎ *no phone.* 🎫 *£e6.*

Coptic Cairo (Mari Girgis, or Misr al-Qadima)

Often mistranslated as Old Cairo, the area known as *Mari Girgis* (Coptic Cairo) is centuries older than the Islamic city of Cairo. But even calling it Coptic Cairo isn't entirely accurate, because it also includes an important synagogue and, nearby, some significant mosques. Known from the ancient historians as the town of Babylon, it was here that the Roman emperor Trajan (AD 88–117) decided to build a fortress around the settlement. At a time when the Nile flowed 1,300 feet east of its current course and was connected by way of canal to the Red Sea, the fortress occupied a strategic location.

The Christians of Egypt, the first in Africa to embrace the new faith, were far from welcome here. They were persecuted harshly, and many fled to the desert or south to the Upper Nile Valley. Under the Byzantine emperors, the local Christian population—known as Copts (a derivitive of the Greek word for Egypt)—came out of hiding and began building several churches within and around the town walls. But harmony within the church was not to last; serious theological disputes about the unity of God (the Coptic view) or the trinity of God (the Byzantine) arose between the Egyptians and Constantinople, and once again the Copts were threatened with persecution. So when the Arabs arrived across the desert, local Copts initially welcomed them as liberators from the tyranny of Byzantium, despite their different religion. Fustat, the encampment that the Arabs established just outside the walls of Babylon, quickly grew into a major city, leaving the older town as an enclave for Christians and Jews.

Thus Coptic Cairo encompasses elements from all these eras: portions of the Roman fortress survive; within the walled city stand four churches, a convent, a monastery, and a synagogue that was originally a church; and the oldest mosque in Africa is nearby. The Coptic Museum has a collection of local Christian art that displays pharaonic, Hellenistic and even Islamic influences. And there is a soothing quality to the neighborhood. In contrast to the big-city feel of downtown Cairo, or the hustle of the al-Husayn area, Coptic Cairo is relatively quiet and calm.

A Good Walk

Without a doubt the easiest way to get to Coptic Cairo is by metro. If you are coming from Downtown, take the southbound (Helwan) and detrain at the Mari Girgis Station. It is fairly comfortable, inexpensive—50 piastres from Maydan Tahrir (Liberation Square) or Sadat Station—and it takes less than a quarter of an hour. If you are feeling especially adventurous, you can take a bus and get off at the final stop in front of the mosque of Amr Ibn al-'Aas; buses 135, 431, and 814 go there from Tahrir. If you decide to take a taxi, just ask for Mari Girgis.

The main entrance to the complex is directly across from the metro station. On the left-hand side is the Greek Orthodox **Church of Mari**

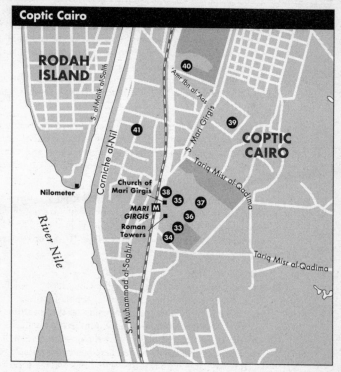

Girgis. Flanking the entrance are the remains of the the **Roman Towers of Babylon Fortress.** The south tower was once the riverside entrance to the fort; a descent well below the current street level into the south tower reveals an oil press used by the Romans. Inside the grounds you can find the ticket booth for the **Coptic Museum** ㉝, the location of the largest collection of Egyptian Christian art. South of the museum is the **Hanging Church** ㉞, so named because it rests upon two bastions of the old fortress.

Returning to the ticket office, you will see a flight of stairs to the right that lead to old alleyways, along which you'll find several houses of worship. The first is the **Church of St. Sergius** ㉟, on the right a few yards past the stairs. The first right after St. Sergius is a small alley that leads to a path upon which are the **Ben Ezra Synagogue** ㊱ on the right and the **Church of St. Barbara** ㊲ on the left. Retrace your steps back to St. Sergius and turn right, away from the stairs and the church. Take the first left to find the **Convent of St. George** ㊳. To get to the main street again, continue past the convent and through a small tunnel.

A left turn (away from the metro station) and a five-minute walk will lead you to the **Mosque of 'Amr Ibn al-'Aas** ㊴. 'Amr Ibn al-'Aas was the Muslim conqueror of Egypt and the founder of the city of Fustat. If you want to wander around the ruins of Fustat on your way back to the metro station, take a left directly across from the coffeehouse on Shar'a Mari Girgis. Along the half-kilometer (⅓-mile) walk are the kilns and workshops of Cairo's potters, well worth exploring.

Also outside the old fortress town of Babylon is the **Church of St. Mercurius** ㊵, better known in the area as Abu al-Sayfayn. To get here, walk back to the Mosque of 'Amr and turn right. Take the second left onto Shar'a 'Ali Salem. The church is at the end of the street on the right.

Return to the metro tracks and cross them on the footbridge. On the other side turn right (north) onto Shar'a Muhammad al-Saghir, which parallels the tracks. Heading north—with the tracks on your right—take the third street on the left to a small enclosure that houses the **Tomb of Sulayman al-Faransawi** ㊶, a French convert who trained Muhammad 'Ali's troops. You can retrace your steps to the station or continue heading west to the Nile and hail a cab back to your hotel.

TIMING

You could spend five or six hours here, but three would be enough—the ground to cover is by no means vast, but like the rest of the city there is so much to see. If you have only an hour and a half, go straight to the museum, then see the Roman towers, the Church of St. Sergius, and the Ben Ezra Synagogue.

The sites are generally open every day from 9 AM to 4 PM, although those that are still active places of worship are not open to the non-practicing during services: no mosque visits during Friday prayers, no church visits during Sunday services (7–10 AM) or Fridays (8–11 AM), and no temple visits Saturday.

Sights to See

㊱ **Ben Ezra Synagogue.** Originally the Church of St. Michael, the synagogue is named after the 12th-century rabbi of Jerusalem who obtained permission to build a temple of worship on this location. According to the local Jewish community, now numbering about 50 families, this was the site of the temple built by the prophet Jeremiah. Some claim that Jeremiah is actually buried here beneath a miracle rock. Another legend associated with the area is that this was the location of a spring where pharaoh's daughter found the baby Moses.

Little differentiates the synagogue's outside appearance from a church, save, of course, signs like the Star of David on the gate. Restoration has just been completed on the inside; a fine 12th-century *bimah* (pulpit in a synagogue), made of wood and mother-of-pearl remains.

During restoration, it was discovered that the site was used by medieval Jews as a *genizah* (storage) for any documents on which the name of God was written (it is against Jewish law to destroy any such papers). Thus, all contracts, bills of sale, marriage licenses and the like were placed in the genizah. Needless to say, this find was a treasure trove for medieval Middle Eastern historians. ⊠ *Hara al-Qadisa Burbara,* ☎ *No phone.* ⌕ *Free.* ☉ *Daily 9–4 (except during services).*

㊲ **Church of St. Barbara.** Named for the a young Nicodemian woman who was killed by her pagan father for converting, the church was originally dedicated to Saints Cyrus and John (in Arabic, Abu Qir and Yuhanna, respectively), two martyrs from the city of Damanhour. It is said that when they refused to renounce their Christianity, they were shot with arrows, burned, and drawn and quartered, but would not die until they were beheaded.

The church was first built in 684, destroyed in the great fire of Fustat in 750, and then restored in the 11th century. Further additions were made when the relics of St. Barbara were brought here. The church is one of the largest in Cairo. Replete with the standard division of narthex, nave and side aisles, and three sanctuaries, the church is also considered one of the city's finest.

The sanctuary screen currently in place is a 13th-century wooded piece inlaid with ivory—the original screen is in the Coptic museum. The icons above the church's screen include a newly restored Child Enthroned and a rare icon of St. Barbara. A domed apse behind the main altar has seven steps decorated in bands of black, red, and white marble. To the left of the sanctuary is the chapel dedicated to Saints Cyrus and John, a square structure with a nave, transcept, two sanctuaries (one for each saint), and a baptistry.

Access to Coptic Cairo's cemetery is through an iron gate to the left of the church. ⊠ *Hara al-Qadisa Burbara,* ☎ *no phone.* ⌨ *Free.* ⊙ *Daily 9–4 (except during services).*

40 **Church of St. Mercurius.** Yet another Roman legionary, Mercurius, or *Abu Sayfayn* (of the two swords) dreamed one night that an angel gave him a glowing sword and ordered him to use it to fight paganism. He converted to Christianity and was martyred in Palestine. His remains were brought to Cairo in the 15th century.

This site is of great importance to Coptic Christians. It was the cathedral church of Cairo, and when the seat of the Coptic Patriarch moved from Alexandria to Cairo, St. Mercurius was the chosen location. The complex actually contains three churches, a monastery, and a convent.

Abu Sayfayn is also special for the treasures it contains, including beautifully carved marble windows and exquisite wood and ivory work, particularly the domed altar canopy. The collection of icons of saints, martyrs, patriarchs, bishops, monks, and stories from the Old and New Testaments justify a visit. Additionally, careful cleaning has revealed rare paintings on the marble columns, a feature that has disappeared from most medieval churches. ⊠ *Shar'a 'Ali Salem,* ☎ *no phone.* ⌨ *Free.* ⊙ *Daily 9–4 (except during services).*

35 **Church of St. Sergius.** Known in Arabic as Abu Serga, this church is dedicated to two Roman officers, Sergius and Bacchus, who were martyred in Syria in 303. St. Sergius was a major pilgrimage destination for 19th-century European travelers because it was built over a cave where the Holy Family was said to have stayed the night during their flight from King Herod—a special ceremony is still held every year on June 1 to commemorate the event. Originally constructed in the 5th century, the church has been destroyed and rebuilt several times, including a major restoration during the Fatimid era. Reconstructions aside, it is considered to be the oldest church in Cairo and a model of early Coptic church design.

The entrance is down a flight of steps that leads to the side of the narthex, at the end of which is a baptistry. Look up at the ceiling of the nave; a series of arched timbers is supported by 24 marble pillars that were taken from an earlier site, possibly from the Ptolemaic era (304–30 BC). A 13th-century wall carving depicting the Last Supper is interesting for the similarity of the table shown to the offering tables represented in pharaonic bas-reliefs.

Most of the furniture in the church is modern replicas of older pieces. The originals can be found in the Coptic Museum, including pieces from a rosewood pulpit and the sanctuary canopy, considered to be one of the museum's prized possesions. To the left of the sanctuary is the crypt in which the Holy Family is believed to have hidden. ⊠ *Hara al-Qadis 'Abu Serga.* ⌨ *Free.* ⊙ *Daily 9–4 (except during services).*

38 **Convent of St. George.** This convent's namesake holds a special place in the hearts of Copts. The remains of this Roman legionary who was martyred in Asia were brought to Egypt in the 12th century. Images of St. George abound in Egyptian Christianity, and the most common depicts the saint on a steed crushing a dragon beneath him. So it should come as no surprise that within the walls of Babylon are a church, a monastery, and a convent dedicated to the dragon slayer.

The convent, while less impressive in its present-day form than in the past—medieval historians describe a huge complex; it now houses about 30 nuns—is still worth the visit. Off the internal courtyard on the left is a stairway leading to a structure that dates from the Fatimid era. Inside is a huge reception hall with a beautiful wooden door about 23 feet high. Behind the door, a shrine contains the icon of St. George and a set of chains used for the chain-wrapping ritual (still practiced), said to represent the sufferings of St. George at the hands of the Romans. ⊠ *Hara al-Qadis Girgis,* ☎ *no phone.* ☒ *Free (small donation to be wrapped in chains).* ☉ *Daily 9–4 (except during services).*

....
NEED A
BREAK?
Coffee House. A traditional *ahwa* (coffeehouse), this convenient stop between Babylon and Fustat is used to dealing with tourists, and it is still a favorite locale for the neighborhood. ⊠ *Shar'a Mari Girgis.*
....

★ ㉝ **Coptic Museum.** Housing the largest collection of Coptic Christian artwork, this museum provides a link between ancient and Islamic Egypt. Remember that Christianity was not just a flash in the Egyptian historical pan. St. Mark made his first convert in Alexandria in AD 61, and the majority of the city's population remained Christian until the 11th century, a full half millenium after the Arabs brought Islam to Egypt. This link can be seen stylistically as well, because the collection includes pieces with a late-pharaonic/Greco-Roman feel, as well as items that are identified as Islamic.

The museum is classified by medium: stonework, metalwork, tapestries, and manuscripts are found to the left of the entrance; woodwork, pottery, and glassware to the right. Chronological divisions are made within each grouping to show the evolution of the art form.

The collection includes many exquisite pieces, but several are noteworthy first for their quirkiness or their syncretic quality, rather than their beauty. Look, for example, at carvings and paintings that trace the transformations of the ancient key of life, the ankh, to the cross; or Christian scenes with Egyptian gods. The depictions of the baby Jesus suckling at his mother's breast are striking in their resemblance to pharaonic suckling representations, including one at Karnak in which the god Horus is being nursed by Mut. Such characteristics are unique to Egyptian Christianity and also to pieces in this museum. For a detailed guide of the Coptic Museum, look for Jill Kamil's *Coptic Egypt: History and Guide* (American University in Cairo Press). ⊠ *Shar'a Mari Girgis,* ☎ *02/841–766.* ☒ *£e8, £e10 camera fee.* ☉ *Sun.–Thurs. 9–4, Fri. 9– noon and 1–4.*

★ ㉞ **The Hanging Church.** Known in Arabic as al-Muallaqah, the church is consecrated to the Blessed Virgin. Originally built in the 9th century on top of a gatehouse of the Roman fortress, the Hanging Church has been rebuilt several times, like most of Cairo's churches. Only the section to the right of the sanctuary, above the southern bastion, is considered original. Nevertheless, it remains one of the most impressive churches in the city.

The entrance gates lead to a flight of stairs that opens onto a covered courtyard, the narthex, which is partially paved with glazed geometrical tiles that date from the 11th century. Beyond the narthex is the nave, the main section of the church, where services are held. This is divided into a central nave and two side aisles by eight Corinthian columns, a feature that suggests that they were taken from an earlier building. Most columns in Coptic churches were painted with pictures of saints, but few of the paintings survived. Those in the Hanging Church are no exception; only one column still has traces of a figure on it.

Perhaps the most impressive aspect of this space is the marble pulpit. Considered the oldest existing pulpit in the country, it was constructed in the 11th century, with some of its materials coming from earlier furniture. The pulpit is supported by a series of slender columns arranged in pairs of which no two are alike. Some say this represents the sacraments of the Church; others describe it as being symbolic of Christ and his disciples.

The sanctuary screen is also of exceptional quality. It is made of cedarwood and ivory cut in small segments then inlaid in wood to form a Coptic cross, which has arms of equal length and three points at the end of each arm. The top of the screen is covered with icons depicting Christ in the center; the Virgin, the archangel Gabriel, and St. Peter on the right; and St. John the Baptist, St. Paul, and the archangel Michael on the left. Behind the screen is the sanctuary dedicated to the Virgin Mary. Two side sanctuaries are dedicated to St. John the Baptist (right) and St. George (left), a very popular saint in Egypt.

To the right of St. George's sanctuary is another beautiful screen dating from the 13th century. Made of wood and mother-of-pearl, it glows dark pink when a candle is held behind it. Behind the screen is a small chapel attached to the Ethiopian St. Takla Hamanout Church. This chapel is worth visiting for its two wall paintings, one depicting the 24 Elders of the Apocalypse and the other of the Virgin and Child. A stairway leads from this chapel to one above it, dedicated to St. Mark. This area is probably the oldest part of the church, built in the 3rd century, when this was still a bastion of the old Roman fort. ⊠ *Shar'a Mari Girgis,* ☎ *no phone.* 🎫 *Free.* ⊙ *Daily 9–4 (except during services).*

❸❾ Mosque of 'Amr Ibn al-'Aas. Built in 642 following the conquest of Egypt, this was the first mosque on the African continent. Because the original structure probably had mud-brick walls and a palm-thatch roof, it did not survive for long. It was restored and expanded in 673 and again in 698, 710, 750, and 791. In 827, it was expanded twofold to its current size. It has since been renovated at least five times, most recently in the late 1980s, in an attempt to restore its interior to its 827 appearance. ⊠ *Shar'a Mari Girgis,* ☎ *no phone.* 🎫 *£e6.* ⊙ *Daily 9–4 (except during prayer).*

❹❶ Tomb of Sulayman al-Faransawi. Sulayman, a Frenchman, was born Octave de Sèves in Lyons, France. An officer in Napoléon's army, he came to Egypt when Muhammad 'Ali was in need of European trainers for his new army. After facing dissent among the ranks, he converted to Islam and took the name Sulayman. Popular with the khedieve Ibrahim for his role in victories in Arabia, Crete, Syria, and Anatolia, he died in 1860 a rich man. His tomb was designed by Karl von Diebitsch, the architect responsible for the palace that is now the Marriott Hotel in the suburb of Zamalek. Like the hotel, the cast-iron pavilion manages to combine Orientalist kitsch and elegance. ⊠ *Off Shar'a Muhammad al-Saghir,* ☎ *no phone.* 🎫 *£e6.* ⊙ *Daily 9–4.*

OFF THE
BEATEN PATH

Nilometer. After you exit Sulayman's tomb, head toward the Nile and walk north to the wooden footbridge. Cross it and make for the southern tip of Rodah Island. Here you will find *al-miqyas,* the nilometer used from pharaonic times until the completion of the Aswan Dam in the late 1950s to measure the height of the flood. If the Nile rose above 16 cubits (a cubit is about 2 feet), no flood tax would be levied that year. Needless to say, this was a ceremony that the populace followed with great interest—and if the floods were plentiful, with great celebration.

Built in 861 on the site of an earlier nilometer, the present structure is considered to be the oldest extant Islamic buidling (the conical dome is an 1895 restoration). Inside is a shaft that houses the graduated column that served as the measuring device. Outside the structure is a model explaining how it worked. ⊠ *Rodah Island.* 🎫 *£e6.* ⊙ *Daily 9–4.*

Downtown Cairo and the Egyptian Antiquities Museum

By Sean Rocha   In the middle of the 19th century, the slavishly Francophile Khedive Isma'il laid out this district on a Parisian plan across the old canal from Islamic Cairo, which until then had been the heart of the city. It quickly became the most fashionable commercial and residential district, lined with cafés and jewelers and settled by all the major department stores. In time, as new residential districts like Garden City and Zamalek opened up, Downtown lost favor as a place to live. But it was, above all else, a colonial city, standing in proximity to traditional Cairo but self-consciously apart from it.

With the rise of Egyptian nationalism in the early 20th century, that could not last. Much of Downtown was systematically torched in antiforeign riots on Black Saturday in January 1952, in a spasm of violence that shows how closely architecture was associated with colonial rule. The riots marked the beginning of the end for the foreign presence in Egypt: the revolution that overthrew the British-backed monarchy followed Black Saturday within months, and with it all the street names changed to reflect the new heroes. In some ways, it was the wave of nationalizations in the early 1960s that finally closed the colonial chapter Downtown, as those foreigners who had stayed on past the revolution lost their businesses, their way of life, and their place in a city that had never really belonged to them.

Downtown is still loved today, but more for its shoe stores and cinemas than for its architecture and the unique melding of cultures and influences that it once represented. Walking through the district one has a sense of infinite discovery, of little fragments of a time and place now lost that haven't quite been swept away by the changing politics. Although all the shops at street level have redecorated their own pieces of façade, look higher and the fin-de-siècle city comes alive. Sadly, most of the buildings are in an advanced state of decay, so you'll have to use a little imagination to recreate the neighborhood's former glory.

Quite apart from the experience of downtown Cairo, the Egyptian Antiquities Museum is a lens through which to see the ancient world. And it is essential to any trip to Egypt. Its vast stores of treasures from ancient Egypt are as astonishing as they are daunting to take in. Tour the museum in conjunction with a day in Giza, or before you head upriver to Luxor, Aswan, and beyond for the Nile Valley monuments.

A Good Walk

The **Egyptian Antiquities Museum** doesn't fit into this tour thematically, but there's no reason not to combine it with downtown explorations while you're in the neighborhood.

Before or after you see the museum, start at **Maydan Tala'at Harb** (Tala'at Harb Square), a circular square with streets radiating out like a star, easily the most majestic square in the city. An elaborate sign marks the site of the once-grand café **Groppi's.** A newsstand stacked with foreign periodicals runs along one wall. Across the street is the antiquarian bookseller **L'Orientaliste.** The **statue** at the center of the square is of Tala'at Harb, the founder of the first native Egyptian bank, Banque Misr, which became a symbol of nationalist pride despite being corrupted by its owners, who falsified accounts and drove it into bankruptcy. Before the revolution, the square was called Sulayman Pasha, after a French soldier, born Octave de Sèves, who organized the

Egyptian army under Muhammad 'Ali, converted to Islam, and fancied himself an honorary Egyptian.

Exit the square on **Shar'a Qasr al-Nil,** named for an old palace and lined with stylish buildings. The elaborately worked metal doors at #17 and the New Orleans–style filigree balconies at #19 are typical of the incredible craftsmanship of the time. The turn-of-the-century **Cosmopolitan Hotel** is down an alley to the right, but even more beautiful is the **Trieste**—look for the green AHMED DAOUD signs on the upper floors—which was built by Antoine Lasciac in an updated version of the Mamluk style of Islamic Cairo. Farther up, on the left, an alley leads to the Greek-owned **Catsaros Auction House,** followed at the next corner by the bookstore **Livres de France** that a Lebanese woman founded in 1947; it stands as a reminder of the city's Francophone past. As you approach the next square, the little **patisserie** on the left with a wooden facade serves delicious ice cream—try the burnt caramel.

The circular square with the vaguely Turkish buildings surrounding it is named for **Mustafa Kamil,** an early nationalist whose statue stands at the center. The square was previously called Maydan Suarès, after one of prerevolutionary Cairo's most prominent Jewish families. Jews once owned many businesses downtown, including major department stores, but nationalization and changing regional politics led most to leave by the early 1960s. The street cutting across Maydan Mustafa Kamil is **Shar'a Muhammad Farid.** Take it to the right and you'll come to the stunning old **Banque Misr,** another Antoine Lasciac building—this one in excellent condition—with the red-and-yellow-striped **St. Joseph's Church** opposite.

Walk back to Maydan Mustafa Kamil and continue up Shar'a Muhammad Farid. You'll pass on the right the striking **St. David Building** on the corner of Shar'a Khalek Sarwat. On the ground floor on one side is the antique **Stephenson Pharmacy,** on the other a much-loved bookstore, **the Anglo-Egyptian.** At the next corner, Shar'a Adly, turn left and you'll see the **Chaar-Hachamaim Synagogue,** one of Cairo's few Jewish temples, an unusual concrete building decorated with floral motifs and the Star of David. The interior offers an unexpected explosion of color from the many stained-glass windows, which makes trying to persuade the guards to let you in worthwhile.

Backtrack on Shar'a Adly, cross Muhammed Farid, and you'll arrive at **Opera Square.** Now devastatingly ugly, it is hard to believe that this was once the chic center of European Cairo. Behind the **Statue of Ibrahim Pascha** on horseback is a parking lot where the graceful wooden **Opera House** once stood. Built for the opening of the Suez Canal in 1869 and meant to be inaugurated with Verdi's *Aïda* (the composer finished it a year late), it burned to the ground after the revolution. The building under construction to the right of it is where the Black Saturday riots began, growing out of a fight at **Madame Badia's Casino.** Also in the streets to the right are many **jewelers** of long standing, their elegant storefronts defying the deterioration of the neighborhood.

The massive yellow building obscured by shops on the corner of Shar'a Adly is the old **Continental Hotel,** once the only rival to the legendary Shepheard's Hotel. The Continental is now largely abandoned, although you can still peek inside. Opposite the hotel are the **Ezbekiyya Gardens,** sited on an old lake. They were designed by the official gardener for the city of Paris and once overflowed with exotic plants. You can still enter the gardens, but only the southern part with the banyan trees is original. **Shepheard's Hotel** occupied an enormous tract of land a block farther north where the gas station now stands. It was the site of much colonial intrigue and seduction before it was destroyed in the riots. If you've read or seen *The English Patient,* several scenes were set at Shepheard's, although the film scenes were actually shot in Tunisia. The original **Thomas Cook** office was next door, where the first Nile cruises to Upper Egypt were organized. Cook's cruises made and sold Egypt as an accessible place to visit—until he inaugurated his cruises, it was a rather strenuous place to travel. His tours ushered in the present age of mass tourism.

On a back corner of Ezbekiyya near Ataba Square, **Sedanoui's** is a spectacular department-store building modeled on one in Paris. These days, most Cairenes have pretty much forgotten about it. The store was built in 1913 as the main branch of a chain owned by a pair of Levantine brothers, and it has some delightful architectural flourishes: a large greenhouse atrium, a swirling central staircase, and two priceless copper elevators that are worth a quick ride.

If you follow the northern edge of the Ezbekiyya Gardens, you'll come to the **old red-light district,** whose main thoroughfare, Shar'a Clot Bay, runs to Maydan Ramses, where the central train station is located. Our walk leads in the opposite directon, through the alleys that once ran behind Shepheard's Hotel. This was the **old theater and cabaret district,** which suffered extensive damage during Black Saturday. The real death blow came with the mass exodus of foreigners that followed the revolution and the consequent change in moral values. As a result the area is now almost eerily quiet—the bars and cabarets have closed—although you can still see some great old **movie palaces** (including the Diana), where Arabic films still run, as well as **portrait studios** like Studio Vart and the well-known Van Leo.

The recently pedestrianized street running west out of the theater district is **Shar'a Alfi Bay,** and the once-interesting buildings along it have all been covered in white paint in a failed attempt to lend a sense of unity to the area. Look for the **Windsor Hotel,** where you can stop in for a drink and a dose of English colonial decor.

The buildings at the **Maydan Orabi** end of Shar'a Alfi Bay are particularly stunning—look for the Art Deco angels on one of them—and there is a **midnight fruit and vegetable market** nearby. Also in the area are several **seedy bars,** euphemistically called cafeterias because of local sensitivity about alcohol, that have a certain spit-and-sawdust charm to them. On a similar theme, check out the endearingly misspelled labels on the locally made liquor bottles in the window of **Nicolakis & Fils,** after you turn left onto Shar'a Tala'at Harb at Maydan Orabi. Continue down Shar'a Tala'at Harb to get back to Maydan Tala'at Harb.

TIMING

The district is flat and compact and the streets are regular, which makes Downtown easy to walk. You could cover the entire area in an hour or two without stopping anywhere. There are few sights in the traditional sense, but you will undoubtedly find yourself tempted to spend three or four hours exploring. Most shops close Sundays (unless otherwise noted), and traffic, a major nuisance, is at its lightest on Friday. As you make your way around, notice that some of the cracks between buildings lead to hidden back alleys, which are also worth exploring.

Sights to See

Banque Misr. Colonial Cairo emulated the French, was run by the British, and was built largely by Italians, yet for all that colonial layering, its profoundly Middle Eastern cultural origins always won out in the end. Nothing symbolizes this strange synthesis better than the buildings of the Italian architect Antoine Lasciac, who worked in Cairo from

1882 to 1936 and served as the chief architect of the khedival palaces. Lasciac set out to reflect Egypt's emergent nationalism in a new architectural style, by updating the Mamluk decorative work so typical of Islamic Cairo and grafting it on to the technical innovations of his era. The result can be seen in his best-preserved building, the old Banque Misr building, dating from 1927. Its mosaics, sculptural work, and decorations all draw on a range of Middle Eastern influences, while the core of the building, in plan and scale, is distinctly Western. ⊠ *Shar'a Muhammad Farid south of Maydan Mustafa Kamil.*

★ **The Chaar-Hachamaim Synagogue.** This unusual concrete block with a subtle Art Nouveau floral motif is easily overlooked from the outside. Arrive early, passport in hand, act unthreatening—the security guards are touchy about letting people in—and one of Cairo's great hidden treasures awaits, with an interior of exquisite stained-glass windows and light fixtures rumored to be from Tiffany's. Erected in 1905 by the Mosseri family, the synagogue is seldom used now because there are too few remaining Jewish men to hold a service. This possible end masks a long and prosperous history for the Jewish community in Egypt. For the past 500 years, whenever Europe went through its regular waves of persecution and expulsion, Jews have sought refuge in Muslim lands like Egypt, where they were protected as People of the Book. It was only fairly recently, with colonialism and the emergence of Israel, that local sentiment turned against them. The synagogue has no fixed hours, but mornings (Sun.–Fri.) are best. ⊠ *Shar'a Adly (opposite Kodak Passage).*

NEED A BREAK?

A stroll through the alleys that once constituted Cairo's theater district will take you to the **Windsor Hotel,** which has an atmospheric bar tucked away on its second floor. The Windsor opened in 1901 as the royal baths. Some years later it became an adjunct to the legendary Shepheard's. When the Shepheard's burned, the Windsor survived, and the bar still retains a vaguely Anglicized air, with heavy colonial furniture that is ideal for reclining with a cold drink. The place draws a regular clientele, many of them aging members of Cairo's intellectual community. The sense of timelessness infects the staff as well, who appear to have worked here since the '30s and will never rush you out the door. ⊠ *19 Shar'a Alfi Bey,* ☎ *02/591–5277.*

OFF THE BEATEN PATH

The old red-light district. Although the area around Shar'a Clot Bey is now rather conservative, earlier this century it was lined with brothels and bars, and you can still see the arched walkways and hidden nooks that once sheltered unspeakable vices. Prostitution was not made illegal in Cairo until 1949, but the trade had one last great boom period during World War II when the nearby Shepheard's was commandeered as the British officers' base and the Ezbekiyya teemed with young men less interested in the pyramids than in more carnal pursuits. To them, this area was known simply as the Birka, after one of the adjoining alleys, and it offered them comforts of all sorts for just 10 piastres. The shuttered second-floor rooms see less traffic these days, reborn as cheap if largely respectable pensions, and the nearby **St. Mark's Cathedral,** once a source of succor for guilt-ridden consciences, now serves a more prosaic function for the local Christian community. Every once in a while the local newspapers will run interviews with elderly women professing to have been madams in their youth, although few other Egyptians lament the passing of the trade.

★ **The Egyptian Antiquities Museum.** On the north end of Maydan Tahrir is a huge neoclassical building that is home to the world's largest collection of ancient Egyptian artifacts. With more than 100,000 items in total, it is said that if you were to spend just one minute on each item, it would take over 9 months to complete the tour. Needless to say, you'll need to be selective, and it's a good idea to buy a guidebook or hire a museum guide. The most reasonable book, *A Guide to the Egyptian Museum* (£e 10), categorizes the exhibit by subject rather than location (which is not very useful) and is rather short on historical description. *The Egyptian Museum in Cairo: Official Catalogue* (£e100) is a far more comprehensive and practical guide. Official museum guides are available at £e40 for a two-hour guided tour, which is barely enough time to scratch the surface of the collections. Five to six hours will allow for a fair introduction to the museum.

Some of the museum's finest pieces are in the center of the ground floor, below the atrium and rotunda. The area makes a good place to start, acting as a preview for the rest of the museum. Among the prized possessions here are three colossi of the legendary New Kingdom pharaoh, Ramesses II (1290–1224 BC); a limestone statue of Djoser (around 2600 BC), the 2nd Dynasty pharaoh who built the Step Pyramid in Saqqara; several sarcophagi; and a floor from the destroyed palace of Akhenaten (1353–1335 BC), the heretic monotheist king. The Narmer Palette, a piece from about 3000 BC, is thought to document the first unification of northern and southern Egypt.

Rooms around the atrium are arranged chronologically, clockwise from the left (west) of the entrance: the Old Kingdom (2575–2134 BC) in Rooms 31, 32, 36, 37, 41, 42, 46, and 47; the Middle Kingdom (2040–1640 BC) in Rooms 11, 12, 16, 17, 21, 22, 26, and 27; the New Kingdom (1550–1070 BC) in Rooms 1–10, 14, 15, 19, and 20; Greco-Roman Egypt (332 BC–c. AD 395) in Rooms 34, 35, 39, and 40; and Nubian Exhibits in Rooms 44 and 45.

Among the most important Old Kingdom items are a superbly crafted statue of Khafre (2551–2528 BC), builder of the second Great Pyramid at Giza (Room 42), and the delightful, lifelike dual statues of Rahotep and Nofret (2500 BC, Room 42). The Middle Kingdom display includes several statues of Senwosret I (1971–1926 BC), responsible for the first major temple to Amun at Karnak (Room 22). The rich collection of New Kingdom artifacts includes an exquisite statue of Thutmose III (1479–1425 BC), Egypt's greatest empire builder, suckling at the teat of the cow-goddess (Room 12); artwork from Akhenaten's reign, the realistic style of which is markedly different from anything that came before or after it (Room 3); and several statues and parts of colossi from the time of Ramesses II (Room 20). The works in the Greco-Roman exhibit are not as impressive as those on display in the Greco-Roman Museum at Alexandria, but they are interesting nonetheless in their attempts to weld Hellenistic and pharaonic cultures. Pieces in the Nubian section include saddles, weapons, and a mummified horse skeleton (Room 42)—again, of lesser quality but still of interest.

On the museum's upper floor is the famous Tutankhamun collection. Look for its beautiful gold funerary mask and sarcophagus (Room 3), ancient trumpet (Room 30), thrones (Rooms 20 and 25), the four huge gilded boxes that fit one inside the other (7,8), and a royal toilet seat to boot (outside Room 30). Also upstairs is the royal Mummy Room, which houses 30 pharaonic dignitaries, including the body of Ramesses II (Room 52). If you are discouraged by the Mummy Room's steep entrance fee, don't miss the assortment of mummified animals and birds in the adjacent room (Room 53), which has no additional charge. Also on the upper floor is a series of specialized exhibits, including a collection of papyri and Middle Kingdom wooden models of daily life (Rooms 24 and 27). ⊠ *al-Mathaf al-Masri, Maydan Tahrir,* ☎ 02/754–

319. ▨ £e20; *Mummy Room £e60; still cameras £e10; video cameras £e100.* ⊘ *Daily 9–4.*

Groppi's. On the western edge of Maydan Tala'at Harb, recognizable by the gorgeous mosaic decorating the entrance, Groppi's was once the chocolatier to royalty. Founded in the 1930s by a Swiss native, this café and dance hall (along with its older branch on nearby Shar'a Adly) was the favorite meeting place for everyone from celebrities and the local aristocracy to political activists and British soldiers. Ravaged by four decades of socialism and several tasteless renovations, Groppi's can now barely manage a good coffee, although the elaborate metal lights in the rotunda are worth a look. ⊠ *Maydan Tala'at Harb,* ☎ *02/574–3244.* ⊘ *Daily 7 AM–10 PM.*

L'Orientaliste. This small, unostentatious bookstore is one of the world's premier (and most expensive) sources for antique maps and out-of-print books on a Middle Eastern theme. The store smells appropriately musty, and you might easily while away an afternoon looking through the old postcards, photographs, and assembled treasures. Ask a clerk to show you what Downtown, particularly Opera Square, used to look like—it will aid your imagination as you walk around. Don't leave without seeing the map room, up the stairs in the back. ⊠ *15 Shar'a Qasr al-Nil,* ☎ *02/575–3418.* ⊘ *Mon.–Sat. 10–7:30.*

St. David Building. Founded in the 1880s by a Welshman as the **Davies Bryan** department store—Cairo's largest at the time—this building has an odd, almost witty roofline reminiscent of a fortress. The facade retains the cursive *d* and *b* of its former owner who, patriot that he was, decorated it with Welsh symbols, to which later occupants have added about a hundred little Venus de Milos. The antique, ground-floor **Stephenson Pharmacy** (☎ 02/391–1482; ⊘ open Mon.–Sat. 9:30–9) is not to be missed. It was one of the best in the city (according to the 1929 Baedeker's guide) and still displays advertisements for ancient cure-alls. Also in the St. David is the beloved **Anglo-Egyptian Bookstore** (☎ 02/391–4337; ⊘ open Mon.–Sat. 9–1:30 and 4:30–8), which is run by a 90-plus-year-old intellectual and has a pleasant search-through-the-stacks ambience. ⊠ *Shar'a Muhammad Farid at Shar'a Khalek Sarwat.*

Trieste. In worse condition than Antoine Lasciac's **Banque Misr** (☞ *above*), but if anything even more intriguing, the architect's 1910 **Trieste** building is rich in Islamic sculptural elements now hidden by years of pollution and neglect. ⊠ *Turn off Shar'a Qasr al-Nil at 2nd block southwest of Shar'a Sherif and look on south side of street.*

DINING

By Sean Rocha

Egyptians eat late: lunch from 1 to 3 and dinner often starting at 9 or 10. In summer, this all shifts an hour or two later, and during Ramadan it goes absolutely haywire. Most restaurants are open daily for both lunch and dinner.

Dress by and large is smart casual, and reservations are rarely necessary, except at restaurants that double as popular nightspots or draw business meetings. In fact, don't be surprised if even very good restaurants, especially in hotels, are almost empty; Cairo is just like that.

Unless noted, all restaurants below serve alcohol—generally beer, liquor (especially whisky), and terrible local wine. Top-end restaurants have a list of drinkable imported wines, which cost between £e200 and £e300 a bottle, but don't expect much of distinction, because the tastes of the government supplier are rather limiting.

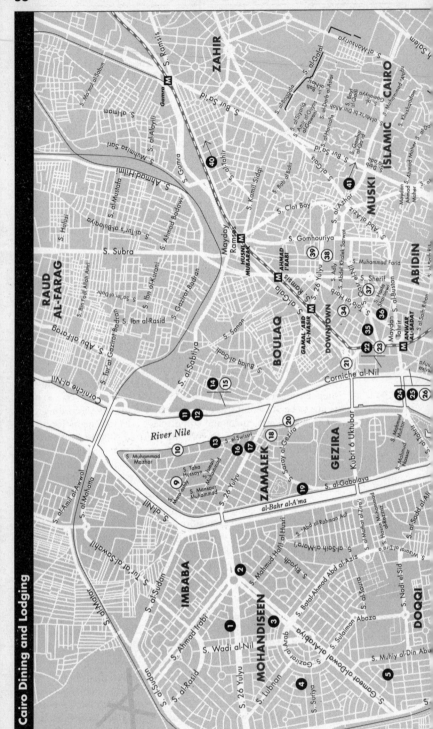

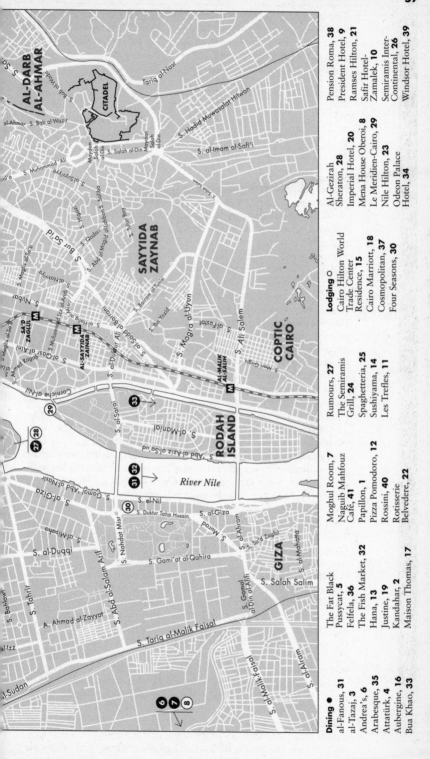

Dining ●
al-Fanous, **31**
al-Tazaj, **3**
Andrea's, **6**
Arabesque, **35**
Attatürk, **4**
Aubergine, **16**
Bua Khao, **33**

The Fat Black
Pussycat, **5**
Felfela, **36**
The Fish Market, **32**
Hana, **13**
Justine, **19**
Kandahar, **2**
Maison Thomas, **17**

Moghul Room, **7**
Naguib Mahfouz
Café, **41**
Papillon, **1**
Pizza Pomodoro, **12**
Rossini, **40**
Rotisserie
Belvedere, **22**

Rumours, **27**
The Semiramis
Grill, **24**
Spaghetteria, **25**
Sushiyama, **14**
Les Trefles, **11**

Lodging ○
Cairo Hilton World
Trade Center
Residence, **15**
Cairo Marriott, **18**
Cosmopolitan, **37**
Four Seasons, **30**

Al-Gezirah
Sheraton, **28**
Imperial Hotel, **20**
Mena House Oberoi, **8**
Le Meridien-Cairo, **29**
Nile Hilton, **23**
Odeon Palace
Hotel, **34**

Pension Roma, **38**
President Hotel, **9**
Ramses Hilton, **21**
Safir Hotel-
Zamalek, **10**
Semiramis Inter-
Continental, **26**
Windsor Hotel, **39**

Tipping is tricky, even for Cairenes. Although fancier places will levy a 12% service charge, it is customary to leave a tip in inverse relation to the size of the bill, ranging from, say, 8% at expensive places to 12%–14% at cheaper places. That said, if service is good, reward it handsomely—it is a rare thing in Cairo.

CATEGORY	COST*
$$$$	over £e150
$$$	£e100–£e150
$$	£e50–£e100
$	under £e50

Average cost of a three-course dinner, per person, excluding drinks, service, and 5% sales tax.

Middle Eastern

$$$ ✕ **Al-Fanous.** Colorful tilework and elaborate carvings cover every inch of this gorgeously decorated Moroccan restaurant. The food is uneven, but when the chef is in good form the *pastilla*, a flaky meat or chicken pastry, laced with spices and covered in a dusting of sugar and cinnamon, is out of this world. Likewise the chicken *tagine*, stewed with dates and served in a conical ceramic dish, can be outstanding. No alcohol is served. ⊠ *Riyadh Tower, 5 Shar'a Wissa Wassef, Giza,* ☎ *02/570–1226. Reservations essential. AE, MC, V.*

$$ ✕ **Andrea's.** Out by the pyramids down an unmarked canal off Shar'a King Faisal, Andrea's is hard to find—your taxi driver might know it, or ask pedestrians once you get out there—but it is absolutely worth the effort. Friday lunch in the gardens is an Egyptian family tradition. Chicken is grilled on beds of charcoal visible to the left as you walk in, and *warak einab* (stuffed grape leaves and chicken livers) are unequalled. At night the Byzantine interior becomes Cairo's most sophisticated nightclub—and getting in is almost as hard as finding the place. ⊠ *60 Maryotteya Canal, Shar'a Kerdessa, al-Haram,* ☎ *02/383–1133. Reservations essential. AE, MC, V. Nightclub closed Apr.–Oct.*

$$ ✕ **Arabesque.** Downtown, where most restaurants are much more casual, Arabesque is a common venue for business lunches, because the elegant *mashrabiyya* (screens) ensure privacy and the service is suitably discreet. Enter through a hidden passage that doubles as an art gallery. The Egyptian–Middle Eastern food is heavy on grilled meats—stick with local dishes like *bamia* (stewed okra) and *moussaka* (eggplant topped with béchamel sauce), or, if you want to venture further afield, try Tournedos Arabesque (north African beef fillets). ⊠ *6 Shar'a Qasr al-Nil, Downtown,* ☎ *02/574–7898. Reservations essential. AE, MC, V.*

$$ ✕ **Attatürk.** More Levantine than Turkish, despite the name and kitsch Ottoman decor, this restaurant serves delicious food that is a bit of a change from the routine. The *manakish* (flatbread) comes in a long flat loaf covered in black cumin and sesame seeds rather than the usual *za-atar* (sesame seeds mixed with powdered sumac and thyme), and the *börek peynir* (filo pastries stuffed with cheese) are spiced with a hint of nutmeg. Unfortunately, some of the other *mezze* (appetizers) disappoint by comparison. No doubt you'll feel stuffed even before the heavy main dishes arrive, but try to leave room for the *sharkassia*, a half-chicken in a mild walnut sauce. ⊠ *20 Shar'a Riyadh, Mohandiseen,* ☎ *02/347–5135. No credit cards.*

$$ ✕ **Papillon.** Beautifully remodeled to resemble a stone mansion, complete with a grand staircase at the entrance and a dining area that feels like a drawing room, Papillon serves superb Lebanese food. Although the menu is inevitably biased toward meat, including delicious lamb kebab and *kofta* (minced meat on kebabs), you can also fashion a vegetarian meal out of the substantial appetizers. Be sure to try fattoush

and the hummous, which comes with warm *'aish shami (*a puffy bread*)*. ⊠ *Tirsana Shopping Center (across from the Zamalek Sporting Club), Shar'a 26 Yulyu (26th of July St.), Mohandiseen,* ☎ *02/347–1672. Reservations essential. AE, MC, V.*

$–$$ ✕ **Naguib Mahfouz Café.** Named after Egypt's most famous novelist and run by the Oberoi Hotel Group, this is a haven of air-conditioned tranquillity in the midst of that sometimes chaotic medieval *souq,* the Khan al-Khalili. The restaurant serves variations on the usual Egyptian dishes, dressed up in historically resonant names to justify what, by the standards of the area, constitute exorbitant prices. That said, the food is a welcome reprieve from the informal, uninspiring kebab and kofta places that predominate nearby. The adjoining café serves lighter fare, consisting mostly of sandwiches, at a fraction of the price of the main dishes. ⊠ *5 al-Badestan Lane, Khan al-Khalili, Islamic Cairo North,* ☎ *02/590–3788. AE, MC, V.*

$ ✕ **Al-Tazaj.** When it comes to speedy service, McDonald's could learn a thing or two from the Saudis who own al-Tazaj. But in spite of its fast-food decor, this joint does some of Cairo's tastiest grilled chicken— and little else. The birds are small, so you might want two, and while you're at it, ask for an extra container of their deliciously garlicky tahina to use as a dip. Only the slightly soggy corn-on-the cob disappoints. ⊠ *16 Shar'a Gameat al-Dowal al-Arabiya, Mohandiseen,* ☎ *02/305– 0905. Reservations not accepted. No credit cards.*

$ ✕ **Felfela.** This Cairo institution is popular with both Egyptians and visitors. The main downtown branch has a pleasantly eclectic ambience that suggests the owner decorated it with little things she collected over the years. Felfela is a good place to taste Egyptian staples like *shorbat 'ads* (lentil soup), which is tasty with a squeeze of lemon in it; *taamiya* (the local version of falafel); and *ful* (stewed fava beans). The food is similar at the restaurant's other branches, with only the decor changing. Felfela serves beer. ⊠ *15 Shar'a Hoda Sharaawi, Downtown,* ☎ *02/392–2833. No credit cards.*

Asian

$$$$ ✕ **Moghul Room.** Any doubts you may have about the grandeur and
★ refinement of Indian cuisine won't survive a visit to the Moghul Room. The pyramids-view setting could hardly be more sublime, and the trio of Indian musicians who play during dinner create a seductive aural backdrop to a spectacular meal: luscious, yogurt-marinated tandoori (paste-rubbed, oven-cooked meats); rich, buttery *masala* (a classic blend of spices); tender *dal* (a lentil stew) cooked slowly over a flame; chicken or shrimp *biryani* (a baked rice dish)—all accompanied by delicious, fresh-baked breads. The best of the desserts are *kulfi* (a slightly grainy ice cream infused with pistachio and cardamom) and *gulab jamun* (fried milk balls). ⊠ *Mena House Oberoi Hotel, Shar'a al-Haram,* ☎ *02/383–3444. Reservations essential. AE, DC, MC, V.*

$$$ ✕ **Kandahar.** Overlooking Maydan Sphinx (Sphinx Square), Kandahar serves superb North Indian food in a tranquil environment. Because all dishes are excellent, consider ordering one of the set menus that include the highly seasoned mulligatawny soup, appetizers, a delicious stewed dal, a lamb or chicken curry, and rice and bread, as well as dessert. If you're only modestly hungry, one set meal is enough for two. If you like your food heavily spiced, make this known—the heat can be turned down for local tastes. This is not a sign of a lack of authenticity—chili pepper is only one of the spices in the Indian culinary palette. The service is some of the best in town. ⊠ *3 Shar'a Gameat al-Dowal al-Arabiya, Mohandiseen,* ☎ *02/303–0615. AE, MC, V.*

$$ ✕ **Bua Khao.** Run by a Thai woman who uses ingredients flown in from Bangkok, this restaurant manages mouthwateringly authentic food that has saved many an expatriate longing for *massaman* or *penang* curries. The Ma'adi branch is the original (avoid its Chinese food and steer for the Thai) and worth the trek because the Nile Hilton annex has an abbreviated menu. Start with a soup, perhaps *tom kar gai* (chicken and coconut milk), then move on to a delicious glass-noodle salad with shrimp, and end with a curry or two. ⊠ *#9 Road 151, Ma'adi,* ☏ *02/ 350–0126. Reservations essential. MC, V.*

$$ ✕ **Sushiyama.** It is always difficult to find reasonably priced Japanese food, but Sushiyama makes a good go of it. Lunch consists of set *bentō* boxes of tempura noodles or teriyaki, but at dinner a Japanese chef oversees freshly prepared sushi that can be ordered à la carte or from the endless list of combinations. If you prefer drama to authenticity, you can order *teppanyaki* and sit around the large grills while the cooks twirl their knives and toss ingredients over their shoulders (ask them to go light on the salt and soy). While the decor is a little too overtly Asian, the ceiling's elaborate latticework of air vents and natural wood has an ingeniously Japanese touch. Sushiyama serves sake, beer, and French wine. ⊠ *World Trade Center, Corniche al-Nil, Boulaq,* ☏ *02/ 578–5161. Reservations essential. AE, DC, MC, V.*

$ ✕ **Hana.** Although the kitchen can deliver any number of Chinese and Japanese dishes, the decorations on the wall, and its regular expatriate clientele, are a tip-off that this is really a Korean restaurant at heart. And true to form, it is the excellent Korean barbecue that makes Hana such a local favorite. Each large table has a built-in bed of charcoal over which you grill your own shrimp, squid, beef, pork, chicken, eel, tongue, liver—you name it—then dip the morsels in a delicious, slightly sweet soy sauce. Eight to ten spicy and mild *kimchi* (side dishes) are also set before you in tiny porcelain cups. The kitchen closes at 10:30. ⊠ *21 Shar'a Mahaad al-Swissri (enter on Shar'a Hassan Sabri), Zamalek,* ☏ *02/341–9734. No credit cards.*

Eclectic

$$$ ✕ **Rumours.** As much an evening's entertainment as a place to eat, this is probably the city's best piano bar—in this case quite literally, because one of the bars is a glass piano filled with lights. The singers are international acts, and the bar is the most impressive in Cairo, full of unusual liqueurs you won't find anywhere else. The atmosphere is enhanced by a panoramic view south over the Nile. The food competently ranges across Chinese, Italian, and French cuisines, although you can just as easily come here for a drink. There is a £e60 minimum charge; entertainment starts around 11 PM. ⊠ *al-Gezira Sheraton, al-Gezira Island,* ☏ *02/341–1333. Reservations essential. AE, MC, V. No lunch.*

$$ ✕ **Aubergine.** This casual vegetarian restaurant is a rare find, with an airy Mediterranean-style ground floor and darker, candle-lit upstairs. The always-innovative menu changes daily but usually consists of a soup, a couple of salads, half-a-dozen baked vegetable dishes, and four or five pastas—as well as a handful of meat and seafood specials. Some of the favorites include green salad with sautéed mushrooms and Parmesan shavings; baked avocado, mushroom, and eggplant lasagna; pan-fried halloumi cheese with grilled cherry tomatoes; and salmon ravioli in a creamy dill sauce. ⊠ *5 Shar'a Sayed al-Bakry, Zamalek,* ☏ *02/340–6550. Reservations essential. AE, MC.*

$$ ✕ **The Fat Black Pussycat.** Come for a drink—comfortable chairs and a well-stocked bar make it a good choice—or come for excellent pizzas and a 100-item (and ever-changing) menu of small dishes from around the world. The jazzy Pussycat also has theme nights that explore the cuisines of different countries. The owner is half-Croatian, and the selections with a Balkan or central European slant are always good. Occasionally there is live music. ⊠ *32 Shar'a Jeddah, Mohandiseen,* ☎ *02/361–6888. Reservations essential. AE, MC, V.*

French

$$$$ ✕ **Justine.** Established in the mid-1980s as Egypt's premier French restau-
★ rant, Justine has if anything improved with age. The executive chef, Vincent Guillou, is from Brittany, and the best way to experience his talents is to wander off the menu and ask him to prepare a few dishes from whatever is in season. A shipment of fresh mussels from Alexandria is given a light, delicious broth and placed over pasta; asparagus, harvested in the morning, is steamed and on your plate by evening; duck and goose liver paté, at its best for two weeks a year, is transformed into an array of delights. The à la carte menu is equally inspired. As the warm glow of ecstasy settles in, prepare yourself for one last indulgence, because Justine's is in a league of its own when it comes to dessert. Service is flawless, intuiting your needs before you've conceived them. ⊠ *4 Shar'a Hassan Sabri, Zamalek,* ☎ *02/341–2961. Reservations essential. AE, MC, V.*

$$$$ ✕ **Les Trefles.** With a sleek interior that would fly in New York or London and a uniquely Egyptian Nile-side terrace cleverly built into the branches of two trees, Les Trefles has the potential to be Cairo's most memorable dining experience. As it is, however, it misses the mark. The French chef manages tasty but undistinguished dishes such as *papillotte de saumon* (salmon with a thin herb-and-white wine sauce that is less than the sum of its parts) and sliced duck filet in a raisin sauce that is not quite as complex as you would hope. For dessert, the warm *pavé au chocolat* soaked in espresso is magnificently presented, even if it comes too late in the meal to redeem it. Service is also lackluster, but rumor has it that the quality might be on the rise (ask at your hotel). ⊠ *Corniche al-Nil (opposite the World Trade Center), Boulaq,* ☎ *02/ 579–6511. Reservations essential. AE, DC, MC, V.*

Grill

$$$$ ✕ **Rotisserie Belvedere.** On the top floor of the Nile Hilton (☞ *Lodging, below*), this eatery exudes ocean-liner opulence with alabaster lamps, an multilevel open-plan room, a piano tinkling in the background, and a small marble dance floor awaiting a twirl. The focal point is the panoramic view of the city, which, despite the wall of windows, you can only appreciate from up close. The specialty of the house is homemade foie gras, smooth and buttery, served with a mushroom bouquet or on a salad of warm quail breast. The extensive list of main courses leans toward seafood, some bearing hints of Asia. A mixed seafood grill provides a taste of everything. If you can manage the Grand Marnier soufflé for dessert, do so; the fine apple tart with cinnamon ice cream makes for a lighter finish. ⊠ *Nile Hilton, Maydan Tahrir, Downtown,* ☎ *02/578–0444. Reservations essential. AE, MC, V.*

$$$$ ✕ **The Semiramis Grill.** The trick to running a top-quality restaurant in a culinary environment as constrained as Cairo's is sourcing fresh ingredients, often from abroad. The Grill's talented German chef pulls it off, with simple, classic Continental dishes that show no signs of the long journey from field or farm to plate. As a starter, lobster and shrimp in a light saffron-butter sauce is superb, accented with shredded spring onions and cracked pepper. For main courses, the menu divides evenly between seafood and meat: highlights include the salmon roasted on its skin and the delectable beef au poivre. The extensive dessert menu is supplemented with a dozen or so daily specials, all of them enticing. The restaurant's green-and-gold gentleman's-club atmosphere is enhanced by waiters in tails who are engaged in a sedate bustle. ⊠ *Semiramis Inter-Continental, Corniche al-Nil, Downtown,* ☎ *02/ 355–7171. Reservations essential. AE, DC, MC, V. No lunch.*

Italian

$$ ✕ **Pizza Pomodoro.** Blessed with a charming Nile-side location—and cursed with a wall of tacky photos of the owner with various celebrities—Pizza Pomodoro has become one of Cairo's most popular nightspots. Go early or on a weeknight for surprisingly good, if basic, Italian food in a soothing setting. Penne alla vodka is delicious, as are the two dozen or so pizzas—the pizza bread with herbs makes an interesting change—but pass on the veal dishes. As the night goes on, a live singer takes over the small stage as the place turns into a club. ✉ *Corniche al-Nil (opposite the World Trade Center), Boulaq,* ☎ *02/579–6512. Reservations essential. AE, MC, V.*

$$ ✕ **Spaghetteria.** A great concept: build your own dish by choosing from five pastas, four or five sauces, and 30 or more items to put in it. The chefs cook it all right in front of you and—voilà—somehow it always turns out delicious. It's all-you-can-eat, so come with an appetite. There is also an antipasti buffet and a list of Italian à la carte options, but it's best to opt for pasta. The strolling guitar player is either a plus or a minus, depending on your mood. ✉ *Semiramis Intercontinental, Corniche al-Nil, Downtown,* ☎ *02/355–7171. Reservations essential. AE, MC, V.*

$ ✕ **Maison Thomas.** Famous among Cairenes for its pizza, Thomas also prepares smaller dishes to eat in or take out, including squid or mushroom salad and various sandwiches based on local and imported cheeses and cold cuts available in the deli section. The real treat is dessert: plain chocolate cake (ask to have it warmed) and chocolate mousse are heavenly. If you find yourself prowling around town at 4 AM, steer yourself to 26th of July Street in Zamalek, where Thomas never closes. Beer is sold to go only. ✉ *157 Shar'a 26 Yulyu, Zamalek,* ☎ *02/340–7057. Reservations not accepted. No credit cards.*

Seafood

$$$ ✕ **Rossini.** Housed in a renovated villa in Heliopolis, Rossini is a convenient choice for business that has plenty of romance as well. Forego the pleasant (if generic) interior and sit in the garden for one of Cairo's only alfresco dining places, with tables scattered among spotlit palm trees. Rossini is best known for its Italian-influenced seafood, including tender stuffed crab and a delicious shrimp-over-linguine dish. For a more local touch, whole fish baked in a casing of salt is a Coptic favorite, especially during the holidays. For dessert, this is probably the only restaurant in town that pulls off an authentic tiramisu. Service is excellent. ✉ *66 Shar'a Omar Ibn al-Khattab, Heliopolis,* ☎ *02/291–8282. Reservations essential. AE, DC, MC, V.*

$$–$$$ ✕ **The Fish Market.** This new chain helps plug a gap in the Cairo dining scene, where getting good, fresh seafood used to mean heading off on a three-hour trip to Alexandria. Situated on the upper deck of a boat permanently moored on the west bank of the Nile, the scene here is decidedly simple: there's no menu, just a display of unbelievably fresh fish, shrimp, crabs, calamari and shellfish on ice. Pick what appeals, pay by weight, and the kitchen will prepare it however you like, with a slew of Middle Eastern salads on the side. The delicious bread is baked on the premises in a *baladi* oven. ✉ *26 Shar'a al-Nil, Giza,* ☎ *02/570–9694. Reservations essential. AE, MC, V.*

LODGING

By Sean Rocha   It is rarely difficult to find a room in Cairo, but it is worth planning ahead because there is no set high season, rather a whole series of peaks and troughs. In general, August and September are crowded with Gulf Arab arrivals, December and January and Easter are peaks for Europeans, and the major Islamic holidays see a lot of local and regional guests. The government regulates prices, which means that off-season discounts are never officially available, but it is worth asking when you book.

Most hotels charge a slight premium for a Nile view, which, depending on your taste, is not always worth it. If you are in Cairo on business, ask where your meetings will be and choose a hotel by location: traffic can wreak havoc on travel times. And unless you're booked at the colonial-era Mena House, do not be duped into staying on Shar'a al-Haram (Pyramids Rd.)—the quality of its hotels does dishonor to its evocative name. Unless noted, all rooms have attached bathrooms.

CATEGORY	COST*
$$$$	over $160
$$$	$100–$160
$$	$40–$100
$	under $40

All prices are for a standard double room, excluding 19% tax.

Downtown and Bulaq

$$$$ 🏨 **Cairo Hilton World Trade Center Residence.** Cairo's best-kept lodg-
★   ing secret is that the palatial, fully furnished, 2000-square-foot apartments in this Hilton-managed luxury residential complex can be rented by the night or week, not just long-term—and for less than the cost of two hotel rooms, which makes it ideal for families. Each Royal apartment has two bedrooms, four bathrooms, a terrace (opt for the city view, better and cheaper), a large living room, a study, and a fully equipped kitchen. With these available, there is little reason to take a suite at more traditional hotels, especially because you'll have housekeeping and 24-hour room service here. And many of Cairo's best food and shopping options (☞ Sushiyama *in* Dining, *above*) are in the same building, just an elevator ride away. ⊠ *World Trade Center, Corniche al-Nil, Bulaq,* ☎ *02/580–2000,* FAX *02/579–0577. 104 apartments. Pool, health club, shops, nightclub, business services. AE, MC, V.*

$$$$ 🏨 **Nile Hilton.** As Cairo's first international chain hotel, the Nile Hilton's pharaonic-theme decor now has a slightly kitsch, 1960s airport-lounge feel. No matter: sandwiched between the Nile and the city's main square, and with an entrance that opens onto the Egyptian Museum and a reputation for service second to none, this is the hotel to choose for convenience. Rooms are spacious and have fantastic views—ask for a high floor, either city or Nile view—but bathrooms are small. The older section is preferable to the annex; if you want to indulge yourself, the Arabic Suite is more tasteful than the Thomas Cook Suite. Tennis fans love the red clay courts. ⊠ *Maydan Tahrir,* ☎ *02/578–0444,* FAX *02/578–0475. 431 rooms. 2 restaurants, no-smoking floors, pool, 2 tennis courts, health club, 2 squash courts, shops, nightclub, laundry service, business services, travel services. AE, MC, V.*

$$$$ 🏨 **Ramses Hilton.** Newer than its sister, the Nile Hilton, and geared toward tour groups and business clients (especially Japanese), this property's rooms are quite large and better decorated than most, albeit with miniscule balconies. But while some facilities, like the business center and health club, are among the best in town, others, like the small pool, seem insufficient. The main drawback is the location, which, while very close to downtown, is surrounded by major roads that make it almost impossible to wander around on foot. ⊠ *1115 Corniche al-Nil,* ☎ *02/575–8000,* FAX *02/575–7152. 900 rooms. 3 restaurants, lobby lounge, pool, health club, shops, business services, travel services. AE, MC, V.*

$$$$ 🏨 **Semiramis Inter-Continental.** This modern high-rise went up in 1987, and many of the rooms and corridors already look somewhat tired. The current three-year, full-scale renovation will undoubtedly raise the standard, if the excellent new health club is anything to go by. As it stands now, rooms are reasonably comfortable. Most of the suites are not worth the extra money, but the panoramic views from the Presidential Suite are breathtaking, taking in the Citadel on one side and the Nile and a sliver of the pyramids on the other. Even in a standard room, the views above the 20th floor are memorable. ⊠ *Corniche al-Nil,* ☎ *02/355–7171,* 𝖥𝖠𝖷 *02/356–3020. 840 rooms, 65 suites. 4 restaurants, café, no-smoking floor, pool, health club, shops, nightclub, laundry service, business services, travel services. AE, DC, MC, V.*

$$ 🏨 **Cosmopolitan.** This Art Nouveau hotel never quite lives up to the old-world grandeur of its entrance. As you walk in, the exquisite tilework, revolving wooden door, and glimpses of stained glass all prepare you for atmosphere that a tasteful but generic renovation swept out a while back. Still, the irregularly shaped rooms and dark-wooden furniture are pleasant, and the corner rooms with wraparound balconies give a nice vantage point on the city's colonial Downtown. Avoid the restaurant. ⊠ *1 Shar'a Ibn Talaab (off Shar'a Qasr al-Nil),* ☎ *02/392–3956,* 𝖥𝖠𝖷 *02/393–3531. 84 rooms. Restaurant, bar, café, business services, meeting room. AE, DC, MC, V.*

$$ 🏨 **Windsor Hotel.** Opened at the turn of the century as the khedivial bathhouse and converted to a hotel in the 1930s, the Windsor oozes atmosphere. The original fixtures have all been carefully preserved, including an antique elevator that operates by a hand crank. Rooms are comfortably fitted with heavy wooden period-piece furniture that gives the place the breezy, slightly creaky feel of a Somerset Maugham story about life in the colonies. Each room is different so ask to see a couple before you settle on one you like. ⊠ *19 Shar'a Alfi Bay,* ☎ *02/591–5277,* 𝖥𝖠𝖷 *02/592–1621. 45 rooms with full bath, 10 with shower. Restaurant, bar, roof garden, business services. AE, MC, V.*

$ 🏨 **Odeon Palace Hotel.** The name is a bit of a stretch for this serviceable—but not at all palatial—hotel on a relatively quiet side street downtown. Rooms are decorated in brown tones, which, combined with limited sunlight, make them feel slightly worn. They are, however, surprisingly large, with a small in-room reception area in addition to the bedroom. The bathrooms have been recently remodeled. Pass on the restaurant, but the 24-hour rooftop bar is one of downtown's hidden oases. ⊠ *6 Shar'a Abdel Hamid Said (off Shar'a Tala'at Harb),* ☎ *02/767–971,* 𝖥𝖠𝖷 *02/776–637. 30 rooms. Restaurant, bar. MC, V.*

$ 🏨 **Pension Roma.** Hidden away above the Gattegno department store, this small shoestring-budget pension is adored by students and backpackers. The high-ceilinged rooms are large—a few even have balconies—and beautifully appointed with 1930s-style furniture. The toilets and showers are communal but well kept—the owner, Mme. Cressaty, would tolerate nothing less—and the staff is more friendly and helpful than at most five-stars. The sunlit breakfast room is a great place to pick up tips on travel far afield. Downsides: the elevator is tempermental, guests often stay for months, making the best rooms difficult to get, so there are no guarantees as to what room will be available when you arrive. ⊠ *169 Shar'a Muhammad Farid,* ☎ *02/391–1088,* 𝖥𝖠𝖷 *02/579–6243. 32 rooms, 5 with bath. Restaurant, fans, library. No credit cards.*

Rodah Island

$$$$ 🏨 **Le Meridien–Cairo.** The best that can be said of the Meridien is that it occupies a majestic site on the Nile. Beyond that, the staff is clueless, the airy rooms are unattractively decorated, and the hotel faces two years of teeth-chattering noise from the 43-floor annex they're building next door. Do not expect a heavy French presence in the management either, because this hotel is now Saudi-owned and seems to operate under local civil-service rules, in which no one can be fired. ✉ *Corniche al-Nil, Garden City,* ☎ *02/362–1717,* ℻ *02/362–1927. 275 rooms. 2 restaurants, no-smoking floors, pool, health club, nightclub, laundry service, travel services. AE, DC, MC, V.*

The West Bank

$$$$ 🏨 **Four Seasons.** Currently under construction, with a scheduled opening in December 1999, this promises to be among Cairo's most luxurious hotels. It will occupy a tower in the new First Residence apartment and shopping complex—billed locally, for better or worse, as Trump standard—that will vie with the World Trade Center as the city's most exclusive address. Rumors swept through Cairo of solid-gold fixtures and other implausible extravagances, but the work finished so far suggests it will be a melange of textured marble and Greek-style columns. ✉ *36 Shar'a al-Nil, Doqqi,* ☎ *02/569–7581,* ℻ *02/569–7580. 265 rooms. 2 restaurants, food court, 3 bars, pool, health club, shops, business services, travel services. AE, MC, V.*

$$$$ 🏨 **Mena House Oberoi.** *The* great colonial-era hotel in Cairo began
★ life in the mid-19th century as a khedivial hunting lodge. After becoming a hotel, it hosted almost every politician, celebrity, and member of royalty ever to visit Egypt. There have been a number of expansions over the years (many of them unsuccessful), but the core of the hotel remains the Moorish fantasy lodge of old. Of course, it is the views of the pyramids, so close you can almost touch them, that will leave you gasping. The pyramids view is essential (there is a $15 charge per person just to guarantee one, plus the premium for the room), and the old section is a thousandfold more atmospheric than the new garden wing. If you're contemplating a splurge on a suite with a view, this is the place to do it, because they are the only rooms with period furniture. The downside to this dream is that the Mena House is at least 45 minutes from downtown, so you might consider a one-night stay for the day you visit the pyramids. There is a clear hierarchy of rooms here and the best of them go fast, so book six months or more in advance. ✉ *Shar'a al-Haram, Giza,* ☎ *02/383–3444,* ℻ *02/383–7777. 498 rooms. 5 restaurants, 2 bars, café, pool, health club, casino, dance club, nightclub, business services, travel services. AE, DC, MC, V.*

Zamalek and Gezira Island

$$$$ 🏨 **Cairo Marriott.** The centerpiece of this hotel, the largest in the Mid-
★ dle East, is a breathtaking palace built by Khedive Isma'il to give French Empress Eugénie a suitable place to stay on her visit for the opening of the Suez Canal in 1869. And it is fit for royalty: designed in a lush mix of European and Middle Eastern styles, it has ornately carved ceilings, marble staircases, and magnificent filigree lamps. Unfortunately you can't stay in the palace itself, because the Marriott's bright but comparatively undistinctive rooms are in two adjoining modern blocks. Still, the great joy of being a guest at the Marriott is that you can wander its gardens at all hours, and the stunning cast-iron Islamic arches lit up with spotlights are always nearby. ✉ *Shar'a Saray al-Gezira, Zamalek,* ☎ *02/340–8888,* ℻ *02/340–6667. 1,250 rooms, 115 suites. 5 restaurants, 3 cafés, bar, piano bar, no-smoking floors, pool, 3 tennis courts, health club, shops, laundry service, business services, travel services. AE, DC, MC, V.*

$$$$ ⊞ **Al-Gezira Sheraton.** The wedge-shaped rooms in this circular hotel are reasonably large and, at least in the upper-floor tower section, have all been recently renovated. Every one has an unobstructed view of the city and the Nile—on a clear day you can see the pyramids from the rooms that face southwest. But this is best seen as a comfortable back-up option when other five-stars are full. The isolated location at the tip of an island in the Nile is a mixed blessing: you're surrounded by greenery but also utterly dependent on the hotel's taxi mafia to get anywhere. If getting some excercise is important, note that facilities here are inadequate. On the plus side, the staff all come to seem like friends. ⊠ *al-Gezira Island (mailing address: Box 264, al-Orman, Giza),* ☎ *02/341–1333,* ℻ *02/340–5056. 477 rooms. 3 restaurants, 2 bars, piano bar, pool, business services, travel services. AE, MC, V.*

$$$ ⊞ **Safir Hotel–Zamalek.** This all-suites hotel is popular with long-staying guests, but you can also rent suites for shorter periods. The Safiri suites (two bedrooms) and the Emiri (three bedrooms) are both quite large, with kitchens and late-'70s white furniture. In the Emiri suites, the master bedroom has a walkaround balcony with views of the Nile. Somehow, these least expensive suites in town come to feel like home, locked in a time-warp: You find yourself swearing that one day you'll get around to remodelling the kitchen and living room. ⊠ *21 Shar'a Muhammad Mazhar, Zamalek,* ☎ *02/342–0055,* ℻ *02/342–1202. 104 suites. Bar, coffee shop. AE, MC, V.*

$$ ⊞ **Imperial Hotel.** If you're not doing a cruise in Upper Egypt but don't want to miss the life-on-the-Nile experience, then the Imperial makes an interesting option. This modern boat is permanently moored near the Marriott, and it operates as a full-service hotel, complete with a tiny disco. Three interior decks connect by a spiral staircase, with a small swimming pool and sundeck area on the top. Rooms are remarkably spacious for ship cabins, and the bathrooms are well-appointed. Riverview rooms put the Nile right at your feet, but views from land-view rooms are uninteresting. ⊠ *Shar'a Saray al-Gezira, Zamalek,* ☎ *02/ 341–4291. 42 rooms. 2 restaurants, bar, pool. AE, MC, V.*

$$ ⊞ **President Hotel.** Conveniently located in Cairo's finest residential quarter, the President has long been a moderately priced favorite. Too long, perhaps, because the bright green furnishings in the rooms now seem bizarre and out of date. The hotel is split between what they call large rooms—pleasant, sunlit rooms with balconies and nice views—and normal rooms—drab, dingy spaces without balconies. Make your preferences clear when you call to book. ⊠ *22 Shar'a Taha Husayn, Zamalek,* ☎ *02/341–6751,* ℻ *02/341–1752. 117 rooms. Restaurant, pub, business center. AE, DC, MC, V.*

NIGHTLIFE AND THE ARTS

The Cairo cultural scene defies preconceptions. You can go to a concert of classical Arabic music in a restored medieval house, watch dervishes whirl in an old palace, then take in a performance of *La Bohème* by the Cairo Opera Company, and end the night getting down in a disco. Although the traditional culture is more visible, a hip "global" scene thrives behind closed doors. Occasionally the two meet in a fusion style—a jazz concert of trumpet and *oud* (an Arabic stringed instrument) for example—that is unique to this city. For the latest listings and movies, check the English-language *al-Ahram Weekly, Middle East Times,* the fortnightly *Cairo Times,* or the monthly *Egypt Today.* Always call ahead to double-check perfomances.

The Arts

Art Galleries

Centre des Arts. This state-run gallery in an old villa hosts the annual Youth Salon, which gives a good survey (the work can be of mixed quality) of what is happening in the local art scene. ⊠ *1 Mahad al-Swissri, Zamalek,* ☎ *02/340–8211.*

Mashrabiyya Gallery. Shows of all the best contemporary artists in Egypt—including Adel al-Siwi, Muhammad Abla, Rehab al-Sadek, Hamdi Atteya, and Awad al-Shimy—change monthly, and there is a small shop in the back. ⊠ *8 Shar'a Champollion, downtown,* ☎ *02/578–4494.* ☉ *Sat.–Thurs. 11–8.*

Cinemas

Foreign films are subtitled in Arabic and usually start 30 minutes after the scheduled time (arriving 15 minutes after that time is usually fine). Theaters have reserved seating. Also note that most embassies have cultural centers that show original-language (and uncensored) movies—well worth looking into if you're in the mood to see a film.

Ramses Hilton. On the top floor in the shopping center next to the hotel, this has long been the best bet for (relatively) recent English-language films. ⊠ *Ramses Hilton Annex, 1115 Corniche al-Nil, Downtown,* ☎ *02/574-7436.*

Renaissance. This is the newest and best-equipped cinema in Cairo. ⊠ *World Trade Center Extension, Corniche al-Nil, Boulaq,* ☎ *02/580–4039.*

Dance, Opera, and Music

Al-Ghuri Palace. Regular whirling dervishes and Arabic music performances in a medieval mansion setting are free, so arrive early. ⊠ *Shar'a al-Azhar at Shar'a al-Mu'iz, Islamic Cairo,* ☎ *02/510–0823.*

Al-Hanager. Part of the Opera House complex, but intended as a space for experimental performing arts, the hall hosts some of Cairo's most interesting music and dance. With little cultural criticism in the local press to guide your decision, just take your chances; odds are the show will be worth seeing. There is also a café and gallery on-site. ⊠ *Shar'a Tahrir, Gezira,* ☎ *02/340–6861.*

Gomhouriya Theater. Many good visiting artists perform at this surprisingly elegant theater near Abdin Palace. ⊠ *12 Shar'a Gomhouriya, Abdin,* ☎ *02/390–7707.*

The Opera House. This tremendous, underused resource is one of the few places left on Earth where you can see things like the Bolshoi Ballet in stunning surroundings for as little as $8. There is a Cairo Opera Company that, while not quite of international standard, has an excellent soprano in Italian-trained Iman Mustafa. In addition there are resident Western and Arabic orchestras and a constant stream of visiting artists. Pick an event from the newspaper and go, but note that jacket and tie is compulsory in the Main Hall, but not in the others. ⊠ *Shar'a Tahrir, Gezira,* ☎ *02/342–0601.*

Nightlife

Bars

Absolute. Around the corner from Le Tabasco and under the same management, Absolute attracts wealthy Egyptians. If you're coming with a group, reserve a table. ⊠ *8 Maydan Amman, Mohandiseen,* ☎ *02/349–7326.* ☉ *Closes around 2 AM.*

Le Tabasco. With no sign or windows, the place is hard to find—look for the bouncer standing outside—but this seductively lit subterranean nightclub is easily Cairo's coolest bar scene. Look hip and go early if you want to eat dinner, because by 10 it starts to fill up with funky Egyptians and it doesn't empty until late. ⊠ *8 Amman Sq., Mohandiseen,* ☎ *02/336–5583.* ⊘ *Closes around 2 AM.*

Piano Piano. With subdued lighting and live music, this is the favorite piano bar of the Egyptian moneyed set. The food is fairly good, although almost everything is fried, but the bar scene in the back is the better option. ⊠ *World Trade Center, Corniche al-Nil, Boulaq,* ☎ *02/580–4575.* ⊘ *1–3 PM and 8 PM–2 AM.*

Windows on the World. The top floor of the Ramses Hilton draws a slightly older crowd for the late-night view and musicians playing softly in the background. ⊠ *Ramses Hilton, 1115 Corniche al-Nil, Downtown,* ☎ *02/575–8000.* ⊘ *Noon–1:30 AM.*

The Windsor Hotel. This quiet and comfortable downtown bar with a prerevolutionary style is better for a relaxing early evening beer than for late-nighters. ⊠ *19 Shar'a Alfi Bey, Downtown,* ☎ *02/591–5277.* ⊘ *10 AM–1 AM.*

Belly Dancing
Note: avoid the brothels and rip-off joints on Shar'a al-Haram (Pyramids Rd.) that masquerade as belly-dancing clubs.

Alhambra. Expect to stay up very late and spend a fortune watching an act of limited bawdiness (it's cheaper to crash a wedding and watch the belly dancing for free). The famous Dina is the resident dancer. ⊠ *Cairo Sheraton Hotel, Giza,* ☎ *02/336–9700. Closed Mon.*

Cafés
Café al-Horea. This haven for chess players has a pleasantly worn, wood-and-mirrors feel that evokes the 1930s. The café serves beer. ⊠ *Maydan Falaki, Bab al-Luq, Downtown,* ☎ *02/392–0397.* ⊘ *9 AM–midnight.*

Coffee Roastery. If you get a craving for real American coffee, this new chain, opened by a man who got his café start in northern California, is as close as Cairo gets. It's very comfortable, and often packed with students engaged in a low-key pickup scene. ⊠ *46 Shar'a Nadi al-Sid, Mohandiseen,* ☎ *02/349–8882.* ⊘ *8 AM–1 AM.*

Fishawy's. In the heart of the medieval marketplace, this is *the* great café in Cairo, beloved by tourists and locals alike. The chairs spill out into the alley, and the walls are hung with thick, old-style mirrors decorated with elaborate woodwork. Tea with fresh mint is the house specialty. ⊠ *Khan al-Khalili, Islamic Cairo.* ⊘ *24 hrs.*

The Promenade. The best way to spend a summer night is in the gardens flanked by the restored palace that serves as the lobby of the Marriott Hotel. The place is immensely popular with Gulf Arabs; it serves food and alcohol. ⊠ *Cairo Marriott, Shar'a Saray al-Gezira, Zamalek,* ☎ *02/340–8888.* ⊘ *Summer, 10 AM–2AM; winter, 10 AM–6 PM.*

Casinos
Most major five-star hotels have casinos that are open until sunrise, with all the usual games (roulette, blackjack, slot machines, and so forth), and horrifically poor odds. The best of them is the **Omar Khayyam** (⊠ Cairo Marriott, Shar'a Saray al-Gezira, Zamalek, ☎ 02/340–8888), which is open 24 hours and plies gamblers with free drinks as long as they're playing.

Discos

Jackie's Joint. Looser entry criteria (than Upstairs, *below*) and occasionally decent music are the primary advantages of this hotel disco. ⊠ *Nile Hilton, Maydan Tahrir, Downtown,* ☎ *02/578-0444.* ⊠ *£el.35.* ☉ *Closes around 3* AM.

Upstairs. When it comes to dancing in Cairo, this is the best of a bad lot. Modelled on Au Bar in New York, it draws a rich, overdressed Egyptian crowd. Although fairly strictly members only, they're less likely to turn away a group of foreigners, especially if there are women in the party. Men stand little chance on their own. ⊠ *World Trade Center, Corniche al-Nil, Boulaq,* ☎ *02/578–3334.* ☉ *Closes around 4* AM.

SHOPPING

Cairo has always been a great place to shop for traditional items because of its spectacular medieval marketplace, the Khan al-Khalili, where browsing and bargaining are half the fun. There is no tried and tested bargaining strategy; just shop around, decide how much something is worth to you, and start bargaining lower than that in order to end up at that point. In the Khan, the opening price is never the final price.

Not long ago Cairo had almost Soviet-style limitations when it came to shopping for modern or more practical items, but that has changed dramatically. There is no particular shopping district (although Mohandiseen comes close), but the World Trade Center in Boulaq, which has more than 100 shops, is perhaps the best single source. For luxury boutiques, try the First Residence shopping center in Giza. Stores open around 9 or 10 and close, depending on their location and trade, at anywhere from 6 to midnight. They generally close on Sunday if they close at all, but most are open seven days a week.

Antique Shops and Auction Houses

Although most of what you'll see are reproductions of varying quality, there is a long local tradition of connoisseurship in collectibles, which means that there is always the possibility of finding a real gem. Be prepared, however, for local tastes that favor ornate French-style furniture and antiques, not the Middle Eastern pieces you might be longing for. There are several nameless antiques shops along Shar'a Hoda Sharaawi (Downtown) that are worth looking into.

The best of the auction houses are **Catsaros** (⊠ 22 Shar'a Gawad Hosni, an unmarked alley off Shar'a Qasr al-Nil, Downtown) and **Osiris** (⊠ 17 Shar'a Sherif, look for the small blue sign on the second floor). Lots are shown for several days in advance of a two-day auction, which usually operates on a cash-only basis. Check the otherwise useless *Egyptian Gazette* for the latest auction schedules.

Art Gallery

Mashrabia Gallery. On the tree-lined Shar'a Champollion (the street named after the Frenchman who broke the hieroglyphic code), Mashrabia is Cairo's best contemporary art gallery. The space itself is not much to look at, but the quality of work is sometimes exceptional. Keep an eye out for exhibitions by Adel al-Siwi, Muhammad Abla, Rehab al-Sadek, Hamdi Atteya, or Awad al-Shimy. ⊠ *8 Shar'a Champollion,* ☎ *02/578–4494.* ☉ *Sat.–Thurs. 11–8.*

Department Stores

Sednaoui. This backstreet Downtown institution is worth a trip for its architecture more than its goods. Sadly, since Egypt's department stores were nationalized in the early 1960s, the original owners have long since left and there is little of interest to buy. ⊠ *3 Maydan Kazinder,* ☎ *02/590–3613.* ☉ *Mon.–Sat. 10–8.*

Markets

Cairo shopping starts at the **Khan al-Khalili,** the great medieval souq. Although it has been on every tourist's itinerary for centuries, and some of its more visible wares can seem awfully tacky, the Khan is where everyone—newcomer and age-old Cairene alike—goes to find traditional items: jewelry, lamps, spices, clothes, textiles, handicrafts, water pipes, metalwork, you name it. Whatever it is, you can find it somewhere in this skein of alleys or the streets around them. Every Khan veteran has the shops he or she swears by—ususally because of the fact (or illusion) she or he is known there personally and is thus less likely to be overcharged. Go, browse, and bargain hard. Once you buy something, don't ask how much it costs at the next shop; you'll be happier that way. Most shops close Sunday.

Specialty Stores

BOOKSTORES AND NEWSSTANDS

Anglo-Egyptian Bookstore. The selection of books here is excellent, especially nonfiction. ⊠ *165 Shar'a Muhammad Farid, Downtown,* ☎ *02/391–4337.* ☉ *Mon.–Sat. 9–1:30 and 4:30–8.*

The American University in Cairo (AUC) Bookshop. You'll find the widest range of foreign fiction here, as well as its books from the University Press—local and regional fiction and scholarly works—that are far more interesting than their covers. ⊠ *Hill House, 113 Shar'a Qasr al-Aini, AUC Campus, Downtown,* ☎ *02/357–5377.* ☉ *Sun.–Thurs. 8:30–4, Sat. 10–3.*

L'Orientaliste. This is the best source for old books, antique maps, and postcards. ⊠ *15 Shar'a Qasr al-Nil, Downtown,* ☎ *02/575–3418.* ☉ *Mon.–Sat. 10–7:30.*

Newsstands. For a surprisingly extensive selection of foreign-language newspapers and magazines, try any major hotel bookshop or the cluster of stands at the corner of Shar'a Hassan Sabri and 26th of July Street in Zamalek. Alternatively, try the stand downtown next to Groppi's on Maydan Tala'at Harb, or the one near the McDonald's across from the entrance to AUC.

CIGARS

La Casa del Habano. An unexpected gold mine for cigar lovers, this shop is stocked with all the cigars you can get back home and, if you're from the States, quite a few that you can't. ⊠ *Semiramis Inter-Continental, Downtown,* ☎ *02/357–1828.* ☉ *Daily 10 AM–11 PM.*

CLOTHES

International labels like Mexx, Daniel Hechter, Naf Naf, and Benetton manufacture in Egypt, so they have shops throughout the city; there is also a row of them downtown on Baehler Passage. You'll also find local brands like Mix & Match, On Safari, and Concrete. Generally, though, famous designer clothes are best purchased elsewhere.

Pandora's Box. As the name suggests, this is the exception to every Cairo rule: a funky Orientalist showroom for the latest club fashions for women from French labels like Plein Sud. Size up the clothes while lounging on antique and reproduction furniture (also on sale) from India and Syria. The owner, Alia, does custom-made haute couture dresses on request. ⊠ *Apt. #1, 4 Shar'a Isma'il Muhammad, Zamalek,* ☎ *02/ 341–2713.* ☉ *Mon.–Sat. 11–8:30.*

Youssef Spahi. Spahi is one of Egypt's most successful designers of evening wear. Designs are spare by local standards but more ornate than most others. ⊠ *20 Shar'a Mansour Muhammad, Zamalek,* ☎ *02/341–0976.* ◷ *Mon.–Sat. 10–7.*

FURNITURE

Al-Bustan. Come here for lamps, sofas, woodwork screens, textiles, and cushions, some of them hand-painted, some with more European style than you might be looking for. ⊠ *World Trade Center, Corniche al-Nil, Boulaq,* ☎ *02/574–8564.* ◷ *Daily 10–10.*

Mit Rehan. This is the best source for modern Egyptian furniture—which means Islamic or pharaonic motifs applied to traditional pieces, like mashrabiyya screens, or western-style pieces, like sofas. ⊠ *13 Shar'a Mara'ashly, Zamalek,* ☎ *02/340–4073.* ◷ *Mon.–Sat. 10–8.*

JEWELERY

Al-Ain Gallery. Stop here for furniture, lamps, and the work of Azza Fahmy, an internationally known jewelry designer who draws on traditional motifs for inspiration. ⊠ *73 Shar'a Husayn, Doqqi,* ☎ *02/349–3940.* ◷ *Sat.–Thurs. 10 AM–9 PM, Fri. 12–9.*

Nomad. Nomad sells relatively inexpensive, vaguely Bedouin-style jewelery along with some interesting textiles from Siwa Oasis and the Sinai. ⊠ *Cairo Marriott, Shar'a Saray al-Gezira, Zamalek,* ☎ *02/341–2132.* ◷ *10–9.*

SIDE TRIPS TO THE PYRAMIDS OF GIZA, MEMPHIS, ABU SIR, SAQQARA, AND DAHSHUR

By Salima
Ikram

In order that that the living could view the grandeur of the dead god-kings—and, in many cases, be buried alongside them—ancient Egyptians used the sites in the desert west of Memphis, one of the most enduring of ancient capitals, for their royal necropolises. These sites are filled with tombs from all periods of Egyptian history. And here, just outside Cairo proper on the Nile's West Bank, stand the monuments most closely identified with Egypt: the timeless Sphinx and the pyramids of Giza. Slightly farther away lie the pyramids of Abu Sir, Saqqara, Dahshur, and the site of Memphis. Most of the visitable pharaonic sites in the environs of Cairo date from the Old Kingdom (2575–2134 BC), although these sites also contain monuments and statuary from the Middle and New Kingdoms, and later.

It used to be that you approached Giza through green fields. Cairo's expansion means that now you'll have to run a gauntlet of raucously noisy city streets clogged wtih buses, vans, taxis, and the odd donkey cart. Unfortunately, the large concrete towers lining the road obscure the view of the Giza pyramids that loom at the desert's edge.

Giza is a suburb of Cairo, about a 45-minute taxi ride from downtown, depending on traffic. You should allow a minimum of two hours—more depending on your interests—for a very basic tour of the site. Driving to the various Memphite cemeteries from central Cairo takes one to two hours, depending on which places you decide to visit. Part of the road to Abu Sir, Saqqara, Dahshur, and Memphis follows a canal and passes through small villages, fields, and palm orchards, which is soothing compared to the drive to Giza. Seeing Abu Sir should take a leisurely 1½ hours; Saqqara can take from four hours to an entire day. For Memphis an hour is more than enough, but allow two for Dahshur. Taking in a combination of sites in one day can be very pleasant—Giza and Saqqara; Abu Sir, Saqqara, and Memphis; Dahshur and Saqqara, and so forth.

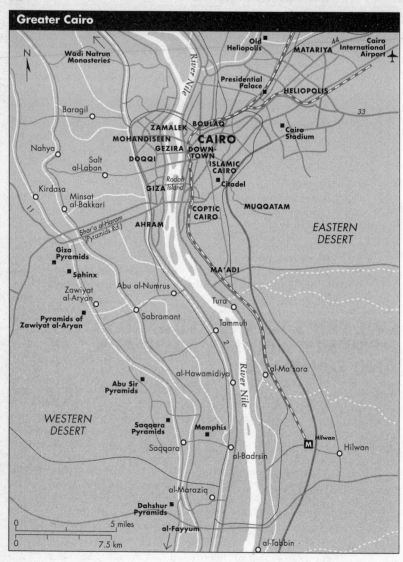

Greater Cairo

Giza

12 km (8 mi) southwest of Cairo.

The three pyramids of Khufu (Greek name: Cheops), Khafre (Cheph-ren), and Menkaure (Mycerinus) dominate the Giza plateau. Sur-rounding the father-son-grandson trio are smaller pyramids belonging to their female dependents, and the *mastabas* (large, trapezoid-shaped tombs) of their courtiers and relatives. The word mastaba comes from the Arabic word for bench, which these tombs resemble in shape, if not in scale, and the mastabas were often painted and-or decorated with reliefs inside, with the actual burial sites placed in shafts cut into the bedrock. The great Sphinx crouches at the eastern edge of the plateau, guarding the necropolis. And a museum south of the Great Pyramid contains one of the most extraordinary artifacts from ancient Egypt, Khufu's own royal boat. The pyramids, Sphinx, and some of the mastabas all date from the 4th Dynasty, while other mastabas date to the 5th and 6th Dynasties. South of the Sphinx and its adjacent temples, archaeologists have recently found the living and eating areas of the workmen who built the pyramids, as well as their cemeteries.

Several monuments on the plateau are open to visitors: a combination of pyramids, a mastaba, the boat museum, and the Sphinx will give you a taste of the site. Generally two of the three pyramids are open (this varies depending on restoration and conservation work), and recently the Queens' pyramids east of Khufu's pyramid have been opened to the public. If you chose one pyramid to go into, make it the Great Pyramid of Khufu. The sheer mass of it, pierced by the elegant Grand Gallery leading to the burial chamber, is one of the wonders of the world—ancient and modern. (Anyone suffering from heart disease, claustrophobia, and back strain should not enter any of the pyramids.)

Before you see the monuments, drive out to the viewing area beyond the third pyramid for a commanding view of the entire site—nine pyramids, one view, as the camel drivers will tell you. It is possible to ride around part of the site on rented horses and camels, which is picturesque and worth a try while in Egypt, and in carriages, which are ungainly. These are slowly being restricted to certain areas, the viewing area and environs remaining one of the unrestricted areas.

★ **Khufu's Pyramid (Great Pyramid).** The oldest and largest monument at the site, the Great Pyramid measures 753 feet square and 478 feet high, and it is the only remaining of the seven wonders of the ancient world. Its casing stones, once covered by graffiti dating from pharaonic times, were systematically stripped in the Middle Ages for a variety of Cairene building projects, leaving the structure as you see it today. The pyramid took some 20 years to build for the pharaoh Khufu, and it is one of two pyramids that contains the burial chamber within its body.

The surprisingly modest north entrance—this is not the ancient entrance, but one made in the 9th century when the Caliph Ma'mun blasted his way into the pyramid in search of buried treasure—leads through a curving passage and up to a long corridor that opens onto a small landing. From here, another passage leads to the so-called Queen's Chamber, which was probably for the pharaoh's grave goods rather than for the actual burial of a queen. The next stage from the landing is the magnificent Grand Gallery that soars up to the king's burial chamber. This contains a sarcophagus that was found empty, because it had been robbed in antiquity. Narrow air passages lead out of the burial chamber. Remains of the mortuary temple are on the east side, with the Queens' pyramids beyond.

Khufu's pyramid, more than any other, is the focus of several fanciful beliefs that hold that the pyramids are the site for the initiation for a secret priesthood, an ancient observatory or a landing device for extraterrestrials, or even a way of projecting oneself into space. In a similar vein are the ideas that, within the pyramid, dulled razor blades are sharpened, food and drink are preserved, people are healed, and meditation is enhanced. Experiments with foods, blades, and the rest have shown no supporting evidence for these beliefs, yet neither have the believers shown much interest in the experiments. New Age devotees continue to come to the Great Pyramid to meditate and seek miracles.

Five boat pits surround Khufu's Pyramid on the south and the east. Two of these, the southern ones, contain cedar boats that the pharaoh probably used during his lifetime. One of these is in the **Boat Museum,** and it may even have been used on the pharaoh's last voyage from the capital of Memphis to his tomb at Giza. When found in the 1960s, it lay dismantled in its limestone pit, sealed by 40 roofing slabs. Its 1,200

The Pyramids at Giza

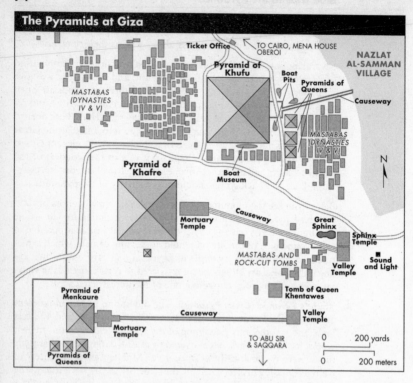

pieces were originally joined together by halfa-grass ropes and sycamore pegs. It was painstakingly restored by Hajj Ahmed Yusif over the course of 14 years.

★ **Khafre's Pyramid,** that of Khufu's son, is the second largest pyramid on the site. It measures 702 feet square and stands 470 feet high. It looks taller than Khufu's pyramid because it stands on a slightly higher part of the plateau, and it still retains part of its fine limestone casing—brought from the quarries at Tura on the cliffs on the eastern bank of the Nile—at its summit. Like Khufu's complex, Khafre's includes five boat pits (empty of boats), together with mortuary and valley temples and a connecting causeway some 430 yards long carved out of the living rock. The burial chamber, which is located underground, contains a red granite sarcophagus with its lid. Next to this is a square cavity that presumably once contained the canopic chest containing the pharaoh's viscera.

The pyramid has two entrances: one in the north face of the pyramid and another in the pavement on the north side. The latter is currently in use. Before reaching the burial chamber, the two entrance passages connect beneath the pyramid.

The pyramid was first entered in modern times by Giovanni Battista Belzoni—a colorful circus strongman, engineer, and archaeologist—in March 1818, an event he commemorated by scrawling his name in soot along the length of the burial chamber. The **valley temple**, near the Sphinx, is a massive building made of red granite, Egyptian alabaster, and limestone. It contains spaces for several statues—some of which are now in the Cairo Museum, notably the diorite piece showing a seated Khafre with a Horus falcon enfolding his head in its wings—and an area from which to view the Sphinx.

Menkaure's Pyramid is the smallest of the kings' pyramids at the site, measuring 215 feet square and 215 feet high. It is probable that Menkaure (2490–2472 BC) intended to cover his entire pyramid with a red granite casing, but only the bottom 16 courses of this were in place when he died. The completion of the casing in limestone may have been undertaken susequently only to be plundered. His successor, Shepseskaf, was responsible for finishing off his **mortuary temple,** a very pleasant place to wander about in, in mud brick.

On the left side, as you climb the ladder to enter the pyramid, is a carved inscription concerning the restoration and care of the pyramid subsequent to its construction. The subterranean granite burial chamber contained a sarcophagus that was lost at sea in the 19th century as it was being shipped to Britain. Another curious chamber containing several large niches adjoins the burial chamber; its use has yet to be determined. The pyramid and mortuary temple were refurbished in the 26th Dynasty (664–525 BC), when the king's cult enjoyed a renaissance. There are two queen's pyramids and a subsidiary pyramid associated with Menkaure's pyramid complex.

★ **Great Sphinx.** The "enigmatic" Sphinx is attached to Khafre's pyramid complex, just north of his valley temple, with a separate temple (now very much destroyed) of its own. The Egyptian Sphinx is related to the Greek Sphinx only in that both types are compound animals, part human and part feline. The figure of a recumbent lion with a man's face wearing the *nemes* (traditional headdress of the pharaoh), is thought to be Khafre in the guise of Re-Harakhte, a manifestation of the sun god, and, in this case, a guardian of the necropolis.

The Sphinx was carved from living rock, with additional details and the final casing made of limestone blocks. The monument used to sport a *uraeus* (the royal cobra) on its forehead and had a beard that has fallen off, bit by bit, through the ages. It is possible that the entire statue was painted; now only some traces of red ochre remain on the upper part of the cheeks. A stela stands between the Sphinx's paws, erected by Pharaoh Tuthmose IV (1401–1391 BC) to commemorate his coming to the throne and his clearing the Sphinx of encroaching desert sand.

The Sphinx is viewed by some as a guardian of hidden secret knowledge, with claims that a secret chamber underground beneath the Sphinx's paws contains this hidden knowledge. Various resistivity tests have been made and there is no evidence of any cavities. The Sphinx does have three openings in it: one behind its head (which contained nothing); the second, in the north side, contained a pair of old sandals; and the third, most fittingly, behind its tail. This opening led down to an area that contained some Late Period and Ptolemaic (712–30 BC) burials, but nothing else.

Mastabas. Several thousand mastabs and tombs are located on the Giza Plateau. Ask at the ticket booth for information and directions to the open ones. Most mastabas are decorated with scenes of daily life and offerings. The most beautiful mastabas are found at Saqqara, so it is not absolutely necessary to see the ones at Giza if you plan to continue to Saqqara.

Refreshments. Drinks and light snacks are available at the Sphinx, and small boys sell bottles of soda and water all over the site. For a real break, go for lunch or coffee to the **Mena House Hotel** at the foot of the pyramids, at the end of Shar'a al-Haram (Pyramids Rd.). Built in the 19th century as an opulent palace to celebrate the opening of the Suez Canal, it is now a five-star hotel. The coffee shop and the garden terrace both have views of the pyramids. Otherwise, try lunching at

Andrea's on the Kerdassa Road for grilled chicken, pigeons, or kebabs and mezze in a pleasant, garden atmosphere (☞ Dining and Lodging, *above*, for reviews of Andrea's and the Mena House).

✉ *Al-Haram, Giza,* ☎ *no phone.* ✉ *General admission (which includes the Sphinx) £e20; tickets for the Boat Museum and Great Pyramid £e20; tickets for the Khafre and Menkaure pyramids £e10 each; still camera ticket for Boat Museum £e10; video camera £e25; Sound-and-Light show in the evening (seating near the Sphinx, check timings and languages in* Egypt Today *or with a travel agent).* ☉ *Daily 8–4 (Fri. are most crowded).*

Getting Around

To get to the pyramids by bus, take a CTT bus from outside the muggama (passport office) on Tahrir Square for £e2; it will bring you to the foot of the Giza Plateau opposite the Mena House Hotel. Hiring a taxi for the day to take you to the pyramids and other ancient sites is by far the most convenient way to get to and from the site. Your hotel can arrange a taxi, or you can hail one in the street. A reasonable day-long taxi hire should cost £e80–£e100—if you bargain well.

Memphis

29 km (18 mi) southeast of Cairo.

Memphis was the first capital of unified Egypt, founded in 3100 BC by King Narmer. Little is visible of the grandeur of ancient Memphis, save for what is found in the museum and some recently excavated areas (not open to the public as yet), which proved to be the sites of temples to various gods and a curious embalming area used to mummify the sacred Apis bulls (☞ Serapeum *in* Saqqara, *below,* for more on the bulls). Most of the monuments of Memphis were robbed throughout history for their stone. This stone, together with that stripped from the casings of various pyramids, was used to build Cairo. Most of the other remains of the ancient city are covered by the modern village of Badrasheen, noted for its palm-rib furniture industry.

The **museum** enclosure encompasses all of what is viewable in Memphis. The most dramatic object is the colossal limestone statue of Ramesses II (1290–1224 BC) that lies within the museum proper. There is a viewing balcony that runs around the statue and provides good views of it from above. The statue shows fine details like finger- and toenails, as well as a very elaborately carved dagger at the pharaoh's waist. Outside the museum building, a sculpture garden contains a scattered assortment of statuary, coffins, and architectural fragments recovered from the area of Memphis. The Egyptian alabaster sphinx is one of the larger sphinxes found in Egypt, and there are several statues of Ramesses II in granite and limestone, including the one that traveled to Memphis, Tennessee. A curious sarcophagus carved upside down also lies in the garden, as well as columns decorated with textile motifs, dating to the later periods of Egyptian history. A series of stalls selling replicas of Egyptian artifacts is set up on one side of the garden. Quality varies, but on the whole you can find some attractive items here. ✉ *Memphis, Mit Rahineh, Badrasheen,* ☎ *no phone.* ✉ *£e20, still camera £e10, video camera £e25.* ☉ *Daily 8–4.*

Getting Around

The site of ancient Memphis is traversable by foot. The best way to get here is by hired car or with a tour. Combine it with Saqqara, or Giza and Saqqara—you needn't stop here for more than a half hour.

Abu Sir

23 km (14 mi) southwest of Cairo.

Abu Sir is the site of four pyramids—three of which are obvious, the fourth one less so—all dating to the 5th Dynasty (2465–2323 BC), as well as several mastabas and shaft tombs. The area has been the scene of much excitement because, in 1997–98, a Czech team of archaeologists came upon an intact shaft tomb of an official who lived sometime between 525 and 340 BC. This tomb is currently not open to the public, but plans are being made to make it visitable. Abu Sir itself has been sporadically open to the public, which means that the rather beautiful site nestled at the edge of the desert is rarely visited and free of tourists and touts. The site is scheduled to be opened to the public on a regular basis in late 1998.

The three pyramids that greet you when you arrive at Abu Sir are those of Sahure, Nyuserre, and Neferirkare. These, especially that of Sahure, are excellent pyramids to visit, because the whole complex of mortuary temples, valley temples, and a causeway are close together and easily visible.

Sahure's Pyramid, the northernmost of the three, is 257 feet square; its original height was 154 feet. This pyramid complex is typical of royal funerary complexes of the 5th Dynasty (Sahure ruled from 2458 to 2446 BC), and it contains all the elements of a pyramid complex, save boat pits. The pyramid itself is not too impressive, as its poor-quality core masonry collapsed after the Tura limestone casing stones were removed. It has been closed to visitors since a 1992 earthquake rendered its internal structure unstable.

The **mortuary temple** is very pleasant to wander through, with its granite pillars, stairs leading to a now nonexistent second floor, and fine basalt pavement. It is one of the few mortuary temples found in Egypt that retains a sense of its ancient grandeur. The **causeway** was decorated with finely carved scenes (now removed from the site) showing archery and fighting. There is much less left of the **valley temple**: a pavement, some doorways, and a scattering of fallen blocks. The area of the valley temple is wet, because it is close to the water table.

Nyuserre's Pyramid is 265 feet square, and it was originally 169 feet tall. Not much is left of this pyramid because the casing stones and part of the limestone core were removed and burned for lime in the 19th century. The builder of this pyramid complex, Nyuserre (2416–2392 BC), usurped the valley temple and causeway of Neferirkare Kakai's Pyramid, which are therefore not directly aligned to the east of this pyramid, but are at an angle out toward their original owner's pyramid.

Neferirkare's Pyramid is the largest on the site (344 feet square and originally 229 feet tall). The pyramid complex was meant to be larger than that of Sahure, but the pharaoh died prior to its completion. The pyramid itself, however, does dominate the site. Nyuserre usurped the causeway and valley temple, completed them, and appended them to his pyramid complex, leaving Neferirkare (2446–2426 BC) with only a pyramid and a mortuary temple that was completed after his death in cheap mud brick, rather than limestone or granite.

The very large **Mastaba of Ptahshepses** lies between Sahure and Nyuserre's pyramids. It is accessible only by climbing on a shaky ladder over the wall. The tomb is noted more for its size than for any remains of decoration. To the southwest is a double room that might have held boats, an unusual feature for a private tomb. ⊠ *Al-Haram al-Abu Sir,* ☏ *no phone.* ⌸ *Proposed ticket prices are £e20.* ☉ *Daily 8–4.*

It is best to visit Abu Sir in conjunction with some combination of Giza, Memphis, Saqqara, and Dahshur. Either go with a tour, or hire a taxi from your hotel or on the street (in the latter case, remember to bargain). To reach the site, go on the Saqqara Road, turn off for Saqqara, then turn right at the canal before reaching the Saqqara ticket booth, which is marked with a large blue and white sign. Continue down the road through the village, then follow the sign pointing left over a bridge that spans the canal. If you get lost, ask villagers for the *Athar wa Haram Abu Sir*. Walking is the best way to see the site itself.

Saqqara

25 km (16 mi) southwest of Cairo.

Approached through orchards of waving palm trees, Saqqara is best known for being the site of the earliest stone pyramid constructed in Egypt, the Step Pyramid of Djoser. The site encompasses at least four other pyramid complexes of different dates, countless tombs from all eras of Egyptian history, as well as several animal necropolises, the most notable of which is the Serapeum. Much active archaeological work is being done at Saqqara by both Egyptian and foreign teams. Recently a French team found the rock-cut tomb of Maya, the wet-nurse of Tutankhamun, at the edge of the plateau. This find complements the earlier finds of the tombs of Maya (the treasurer), Horemheb, and Aparel, all of whom were active during the reign of Tutankhamun.

Saqqara is large, sprawling, and best covered on foot and by car. A suggested route, which will depend somewhat on which tombs are open to the public, is to start at the Step Pyramid complex, which you can walk around. Ask at the ticket booth if the pyramid of Unas is open; if it is, go there next on foot. Then return to the car, drive to the Mastaba of Mereruka and the Pyramid of Teti, then drive to the Serapeum. If you have more time, visit the Tomb of Ti near the Serapeum. There are other mastabas open near the Step Pyramid, as well as the Mastaba of Ptahhotep near the Serapeum. See these if you have time, energy, and interest.

The **Step Pyramid** complex was built in the 3rd Dynasty (2649–2575 BC) for the pharaoh Djoser by his architect Imhotep, and it has been undergoing study and restoration for more than 70 years under the direction of J.-P. Lauer. This monument has earned Djoser, and more importantly Imhotep, everlasting fame—Imhotep was later deified and regarded as the patron god of architects and doctors. The base of the pyramid measures 459 feet by 386 feet, and the structure was originally 197 feet high.

The pyramid complex is completely unlike those of the 4th and 5th Dynasties. It is the first stone pyramid (and complex) to have been built in Egypt, and its form imitates wood, papyrus, mud brick, and matting in limestone. The Step Pyramid itself was begun as a mastaba tomb, but its design was modified six times before the final, six-stepped pyramid emerged. The structure was enlarged by accreting vertical faces, visible on the east side as you walk around the pyramid, rather than by stacking mastabas on top of one another.

You enter the complex from a small doorway that leads through a long passage flanked by columns that in turn leads to the vast open Heb-Sed court. The *Heb-Sed* was a race that the pharaoh had to run every 30 years, theoretically, in order to reaffirm his strength, power, and ability to rule—and to renew the favor of the gods. After he successfully completed the race, the pharaoh would officiate and participate in religous rituals that emphasized the support of the gods for his reign and the fealty of his nobles and governors. These ceremonies took place in the adjoining courtyard, which is flanked by shrines. The incorporation of a copy of the Heb-Sed court into the plan of the pyramid complex may have been an attempt to guarantee Djoser an eternal and successful reign in the afterlife.

The simple **mortuary temple** attached to the pyramid is to the north rather than to the east. Just before reaching it, you'll find a small structure, the *serdab* (a small room containing the statue of the deceased). It contains a statue of the pharaoh—a plaster cast; the original is in the Cairo Museum—that was placed there to receive offerings. The substructure is closed to the public because it is unstable.

The site of Djoser's Pyramid was a great attraction in antiquity: as the graffiti attests, people came here as tourists and seekers of blessings from at least as early as the Middle Kingdom (2040–1640 BC) onward. Portions of the pyramid were restored in the 26th Dynasty.

Unas' Pyramid was the last pyramid built in the 5th Dynasty, and was the first to contain a burial chamber decorated with the pyramid texts, which were a set of spells to ensure that the pharaoh had a successful afterlife. The pyramid occupies an area 188 feet square; its original height was 141 feet. The **mortuary temple** on the east side is ruined, save for the pavement, some column fragments, and a doorway leading to the causeway. The **causeway** is decorated in places with scenes of markets, transporting columns, wild animals, and so forth. To the south lie two empty boat pits. At the end of the causeway, near the ticket booth, stands the remains of the valley temple.

★ **Niankhkhnum and Khnumhotep's Mastaba** (5th Dynasty), also known as the Tomb of Two Brothers, or the Tomb of the Hairdressers, is noted for its fine colors, as well as the unusually intimate poses of the two tomb owners. These two individuals worked as the pharaoh's body servants, and they were buried together in this exquisitely decorated joint tomb. The scenes in the mastaba are fairly standard, showing everyday activities such as fishing, fowling, cooking, hunting, and the processing of foodstuffs. An unusual scene of the tomb owners on donkey back is carved on the second set of door jambs.

★ **Mereruka's Mastaba,** shared by his son and his wife, is the largest mastaba tomb in Saqqara. It dates to the 6th Dynasty (2323–2150 BC) and shows some of the finest scenes of fishing, fowling, hunting, metalworking (note the dwarfs), sailing, and force-feeding of animals, including a hyena in the statue chamber. A statue of Mereruka emerging from a niche marks the main offering spot for his cult.

★ **Kagemni's Mastaba** adjoins Mereruka's and is also well decorated. Presumably the artist or atelier responsible for decorating the mastabas in this area was the same, because certain scenes keep reappearing, such as the force-feeding, the poultry yards, and the tomb owner being carried about on a chair.

Teti's Pyramid (Teti ruled from 2323–2291 BC) measures 257 feet square and originally rose to 172 feet. Now one is hard pressed to recognize this as a pyramid, because the casing stones were stolen and the pyramid has been is reduced to a pile of rubble. The site has two queens' pyramids to the east and north, which are virtually indistinguishable from the sand, and a mortuary temple to the east. The burial chamber, with its pointed roof, is decorated with pyramid texts and contains a basalt sarcophagus.

The Serapeum is the site of the burials of the Apis Bulls. The Apis was a bull that was regarded as a manifestation of Ptah, a creator god. During its lifetime, the bull was worshipped, fed, washed, brushed, sung to, and generally made much of. When it died, it was elaborately mummified and buried, with golden grave goods, in a large basalt or granite sarcophagus that was placed in a chamber of the Serapeum. Then the priests embarked on a quest for a new bull, who took up the position of Apis. The dusty and gloomy Serapeum galleries stretch for miles under the bedrock; only a portion are open to the public.

Ti's Mastaba is architecturally different from Mereruka and Kagemni's in that it has a large courtyard that contains a stairway leading to Ti's burial chamber, which still contains his sarcophagus. The rest of the tomb is exquisitely decorated and painted, with the original roof preserved throughout much of the tomb. A statue—it is a reproduction—of Ti is visible in the serdab.

The ticket booth is at the main entrance to the site. Separate tickets required for the Mastaba of Niankhkhnum and Khnumhotep are available at the booth at the Step Pyramid. You must buy camera tickets from booths at each area. No flash photography is allowed inside the tombs. ⊠ *Athar Saqqara,* ☎ *no phone.* 🎫 *£e20, still cameras £e10, video cameras £e20.* ☉ *Daily 8–4.*

Getting Around

You can get to Saqqara either by signing up with a tour company or by hiring a taxi for the day from the hotel or the street (bargain hard). It is best to combine Saqqara with one or more sites, such as Memphis and Abu Sir, or with Giza. The site itself is best seen by a combination of walking and driving.

Dahshur

33 km (21 mi) southeast of Cairo.

Dahshur opened to the public recently, and it is one of the most tranquil and awe-inspiring pyramid sites. It contains five pyramids dating from the Old and Middle Kingdoms, of which three are obvious; only one can be entered. A suggested itinerary for the site is to drive to the first pyramid on the left of the entrance. After you take it in, drive over to the Bent Pyramid. You can walk around this, then over to the Black Pyramid (this is optional; it takes about half an hour or so), and then return to the car.

★ The **North Pyramid,** or Red Pyramid, named for the pinkish limestone that it is made of, belonged to the 4th-Dynasty pharaoh Sneferu (2575–2551 BC), father of Khufu. It is 721 feet square and was originally 341 feet tall—just a little smaller than Khufu's Great Pyramid. It marks the first successful attempt at building a true pyramid. This is the second of Sneferu's two pyramids. The other is the Bent Pyramid. Why he commissioned two pyramids is unknown; some scholars believe that Sneferu built this pyramid after the Bent Pyramid, because he feared the latter would collapse. As if in corroboration of this, the angle for this pyramid is identical to that of the second angle (of the point) of the Bent Pyramid. The North Pyramid contains three chambers with corbelled roofs and a plethora of 19th-century graffiti. The floor of the topmost chamber was battered by tomb robbers in search of treasure they never found.

★ **The Bent Pyramid,** built for Sneferu, is obviously named for its unique shape, which seems to demonstrate the transition between the step and the true pyramid. It is 599 feet square and its original height was 344 feet, although it was intended to be 421 feet. It retains much of its limestone cladding.

This was the first pyramid to have been planned as a true pyramid, as opposed to a step pyramid. Its unusual bent angle seems to have occurred because the builders felt that the initial angle was too steep, and that the pyramid would collapse if they did not adjust it. This pyramid is also unusual in having two entrances: the typical north face entrance, and a second in the west face that is just visible above the change in the angle.

Although the pyramid itself was undecorated, its valley temple is among the earliest to be adorned. (None of the decorated portions are at the site; the temple is a bit of a walk to the northeast, and it isn't very rewarding to visit.) The pyramid contains two chambers with corbelled ceilings. A passage from the north entrance leads to the chambers. To the south stands a subsidiary pyramid built of limestone, and on the east are the very ruined remains of a stone and mud brick mortuary temple.

The **Black Pyramid,** built for Amenemhet III (1844–1797 BC), was constructed out of mud brick and faced with limestone. The limestone was plundered, leaving only the black mud brick that gives the pyramid its modern name. The pyramid measures 344 feet square and originally rose to 265 feet. The entrance to the burial chamber was not in the north face, but outside the pyramid, in a courtyard opposite the southern corner of the east face. The top of the pyramid was crowned by a black basalt pyramidion, now in the Cairo Museum. Amenemhet, like Sneferu, had two pyramids; the other one is in Hawara in the Fayyum. The Black Pyramid is the southernmost of the Dahshur group of pyramids. ⊠ Al-Haram Dahshur, village of Menshat Dahshur, ☎ no phone. ☒ £e10, still camera £e10, video camera £e225. ۞ Daily 8–4.

Getting Around

Combine a trip to Dahshur with Saqqara and Memphis. A taxi or an organized tour are the best ways to get here. Drive down the Saqqara Road, past Saqqara and Memphis, and turn right at the sign for the Dahshur Antiquities. The road goes through the mainly mud-brick village of Dahshur straight into the site. You will need to drive around the site, as it is very large.

SIDE TRIP TO THE FAYYUM

100 km (62 mi) southwest of Cairo.

By Salima Ikram

The Fayyum is one of the largest and most fertile of all Egyptian oases, with an overall population of nearly 2 million people. Unlike the Western Desert oases, which are watered by artesian wells, the Fayyum is fed by a small river, the Bahr Yusuf (Joseph's River), which connects with the Nile. The rural Fayyum measures about 65 km (40 mi) from east to west, and the lake, Birket Qarun (which classical writers called Lake Moeris), is located in the northwest. The lake was much larger and richer in wildlife in antiquity, and it was the site of some of the earliest settlements (c. 6000 BC) in Egypt.

Sights in the Fayyum include the pyramids of al-Lahun and Hawara, the Greco-Roman site of Karanis, the large singing waterwheels, and some fine agricultural countryside that includes the lake, which is pleasant to visit on a warm day. The Fayyum was especially important during two periods of Egyptian history: the Middle Kingdom, when it began to be intensively exploited for agriculture, and the Greco-Roman Period (332 BC–AD 395), when it provided most of the grain for the Roman Empire.

There are two centers of activity in the area: one is the very salty Birket Qarun, the other Medinet Fayyum, the major city. The site of old Karanis is on the way in from Cairo, as is the lake. Medinet Fayyum is 20 km (12 mi) south of the lake, and the Hawara and Lahun pyramids are south of the city. The Fayyum is a day trip on its own from Cairo, because there are several things to see here in addition to the pharaonic antiquities.

Kom Aushim, the Greco-Roman town site of Karanis, is on the desert road on the way into the Fayyum, and it feels like a ghost town. It includes a temple dedicated to the local gods Petesuchs and Pnepheros, as well as the remains of houses, cooking installations, and bathrooms. Some of the latter are decorated with frescoes. A small museum at the entrance to the site contains some objects unearthed here and others found elsewhere in the Fayyum and around Egypt: mummies, statuary, relief fragments, a few objects of daily life, as well as Coptic and Islamic textiles and ceramics. The University of Michigan, Ann Arbor, excavated the site in the 1950s and '60s. ⊠ *Kom Aushim, Fayyum Desert Rd.,* ☏ *no phone.* ▣ *£e20, still camera £e10, video camera £e25 (separate tickets admit to the site and the museum).* ⊙ *Daily 8–4.*

Medinet Fayyum, the center city of the oases, is built around **waterwheels.** They are an icon of the Fayyum, and you'll hear them—the sound resembles the moaning of humpback whales—amid the honking of horns and the rush of traffic. There are four whaterwheels in the center of Medinet Fayyum near the information office, and many others are scattered throughout the oasis.

Al-Hawara Pyramid (393 feet square, original height 190 feet) is one of Amenemhet III's two pyramids; the other is at Dahshur. It, too, is built of mud brick with a limestone casing. The interior structure, entered from the south, is full of dead-ends and false passages and shafts, inaccessible now because of the high water table. In Classical times this pyramid was most famous for its **mortuary temple,** then known as the Labyrinth. It was located to the south rather than the east of the temple and was a very elaborate maze-like structure filled with riches, of which nothing remains today save some fragments of limestone chips and two rather pathetic carved limestone crocodiles, which are headless. To the east lies a Greco-Roman cemetery, where many of the celebrated Fayyum mummy portraits were found. There was also a cemetery of sacred crocodiles revered in this area. If you walk around the cemetery, you might well come upon mummy fragments. ⊠ *Haram al-Hawara,* ☏ *no phone.* ▣ *£e20.* ⊙ *Daily 8–4.*

Al-Lahun Pyramid, built by the Middle Kingdom pharaoh Senwosret II (1897–78 BC, also called Sesostris II), is another mud-brick pyramid whose outer casing was stolen in antiquity. (The pyramid is 347 feet square; original height 157 feet.) A natural knoll of rock was used as a central core for the pyramid, and stone walls were built radiating out from it; the interstices were filled with mud brick before finally being cased with fine limestone. This gives the illusion that this was a true pyramid completely built of stone. al-Lahun was the first pyramid to abandon a single northern entrance in favor of two entrances on the south side. Its underground chambers (inaccessible) contain dead-ends and twists and turns to disguise the whereabouts of the granite burial chamber, which when discovered in modern times contained an empty red granite sarcophagus and an alabaster offering table. The devious layout of the substructure, along with the transfer of the entrance from north to south, was perhaps the result of a quest for greater security for the place of burial. ⊠ *al-Haram al-Lahun,* ☏ *no phone.* ▣ *£e20.* ⊙ *Daily 8–4.*

Dining

$$ ✕ **Auberge du Lac.** The restaurant in this four-star hotel is known for its wild duck and game dishes, but its Lake Qarun views and the breezes are what make the Cairo-level prices worth considering. ⊠ *Birket Qarun,* ☎ *084/700–002. AE, MC, V.*

$ ✕ **Cafeteria al-Medina.** The location of the restaurant is lovely: it was built in a green spot around the waterwheels at the center of town. The wheels' eerie whining and the cool splashing of water make a lovely accompaniment to a relatively unexceptional meal. The fare is basic: shish-kebab, roast chicken, and the regular mezze (appetizers). Service is not exactly speedy, and prices might be considered a bit high for the food (a meal costs about £e30 per person). Beer is generally available, except during Ramadan. ⊠ *Medinet al-Fayyum, off Shar'a al-Gomhurriya,* ☎ *no phone. No credit cards.*

Getting Around

The best way to get to the Fayyum is by hiring a car (a taxi should cost between £e150 and £e200) or by taking a tour—a car is absolutely necessary to get around the area and between the sights. A tour might be better, because most Cairene taxi drivers don't know the geography of the Fayyum or its antiquities, and it can be difficult to navigate between sights. To get to the area, take Shar'a al-Haram and turn left just before the Mena House on the Alexandria Road, which is marked for Alexandria and the Fayyum. Then follow signs to the Fayyum. There are a few police checkpoints along the way, so bring your passport if you are not part of a tour group.

SIDE TRIP TO THE WADI NATRUN MONASTERIES

By Sean Rocha One of the many Egyptian contributions to Christianity was the idea of going off into the wilderness to subject yourself to all manner of deprivation as a means of devoting yourself to God. Monastic life began on the coast of the Red Sea with St. Anthony in the 4th century. Some of his earliest disciples migrated to the desert just west of the Delta and established monasteries in Wadi Natrun. At its peak in the centuries after the death of St. Anthony, the Natrun Valley hosted 50 monasteries and more than 5,000 monks. Since then it suffered almost uninterrupted decline until the 1970s, when the monasteries began to see something of a rebirth as educated, worldly Copts started taking their vows in record numbers.

Although the modern world encroaches on Wadi Natrun's earlier isolation, the monasteries still feel remote, huddled behind the high walls the monks built a millennium ago to protect themselves from Bedouin attacks. But make no mistake: these are some very hip monks. They speak countless foreign languages, run several successful businesses that include a large fruit and vegetable farm, and are clued into the ways of the world better than most young Cairenes. They are, as well, profoundly devout, and the monasteries maintain an air of spiritual calm no matter how many pilgrims are visiting. And when the winds sweep off the desert, rustling the tall, graceful tamarind trees that shade the sand-hued domes and smooth walls of the churches, you feel a long, long way from Cairo.

Monastic Life

Copts may elect to join a monastery after they have fulfilled some surprisingly unspiritual requirements. They need to be at least 25 years old, and they have to have finished university and national military service and held a job, because professional skills are needed to run the monastery. The primary criterion for entry, of course, is devotion to God, and monks must take vows of poverty and obediance.

The monastic day begins at 4 AM, when the monks gather in the church to pray and chant. At 6 AM the liturgy is recited, although monks may elect to pray privately. Then the work day begins: on the farm, in construction, guiding tourists, and so forth, until 4 PM (in winter) or 6 PM (in summer), with a break at 1 PM to eat in the refectory. A half-hour of prayer follows, and the monks are free to pray on their own until morning.

Fasting is an integral part of Coptic devotion, and it fills roughly two-thirds of the year. The comparison with Muslim fasting during Ramadan is interesting: Muslims do not eat, drink, smoke, or have sex during daylight hours, but Copts give up all animal products day and night for the duration of their fast. During fasts they eat nothing until early afternoon, when they eat a vegetarian meal. The fasting periods are usually broken with major holidays, such as Christmas or Easter.

Although Coptic monks may have retreated to the monasteries to forsake the world, they are very accustomed to having the world come to them. They run arguably the smoothest tour guide systems in Egypt, with a knowledgeable *abuna* (father) to walk you through the compound and tell you genuinely useful information about what you are seeing—even if their claims about the age of the buildings or the achievements of the Coptic community at times sound a bit grandiose. They do not charge admission, and the baksheesh customary elsewhere in Egypt is inappropriate here. The monasteries do welcome donations, for which there is usually a box near the reception areas.

Dress modestly—no shorts, and the less skin showing the better—but you needn't expect any fanaticism on the part of the monks. Copts can seem remarkably casual in their devotion: pilgrims sleep on the floors of the church, and children run and play in the middle of Sunday mass (the same is true in mosques, except at prayer time). Of course, you would do well not to take similar license. Be sure to remove your shoes before entering any of the churches.

The Monasteries

If only by virtue of its accessibility, **Deir Anba Bishoi** has become the busiest monastery in Wadi Natrun, but it remains one of the most charming. The monastery dates from the 4th century, as does its oldest church (one of five), which was built with domes and irregular stone-and-silt-mortar walls covered in smooth sand-hued plaster. It has been renovated and rebuilt several times; the most recent restoration revealed previously unknown Byzantine brick arches that have now been left visible. The interior consists of a high triple-vaulted main hall. Tiny apertures pierce the ceiling, admitting streams of brilliant sunlight that catch the plumes of incense that fill the air. To the left, through a spectacular 14th-century door is the *haykal* (sanctuary), where contemporary frescoes depict John the Baptist, St. Mark, and the 12 apostles, along with early monastic fathers. The carved wooden door (hidden behind a velvet curtain) was donated in the 7th century by the last Byzantine pope, just before the Arab invasion marked the emergence of Islam in Egypt. The coffin is that of St. Bishoi.

Elsewhere in the monastery, there is a workable (though unused) grain mill that looks every bit as old as the church itself. The monks live in cells known as *lauras*, and cells is exactly what they are: small boxes with a single window and few comforts. Near the entrance gate is the keep, a defensive tower with a drawbridge into which the monks could retreat in the event of attack. The Coptic Pope Shenouda III maintains a residence within the monastery, but it is not open to the public.

If you exit the grounds by a small door in the back wall, you will see the rolling fields of farmland that the monks reclaimed from the desert and now use to grow dates, grapes, olives, and vegetables for sale in markets throughout the country. If that's not worldy enough, the monks even have their own gas station and car-repair shop. The monks employ impoverished Egyptians, mostly from the Upper Nile Valley, and teach them skills for use when they return to their home villages.

When you exit Deir Anba Bishoi, turn left, and a 10-minute walk will bring you to **Deir al-Sourian.** Even if you have a car, it is worth walking: the approach gives you a powerful sense of the desert's small dunes with the lush foliage of the monastery just peeking over the high walls that shimmer in the haze of heat off the sands.

Deir al-Sourian was founded by a breakaway faction from Deir Anba Bishoi and dedicated to *Theotokos* (God's Mother). A later reconciliation made the new monastery redundant, so it was taken over by monks from Syria—hence its name *al-Sourian,* the Syrian. There is a tamarind tree in the rear of the monastery that supposedly grew out of the walking stick of the 4th-century Syrian St. Ephraem. Challenged by younger monks, who thought he carried the staff to look authoritative, Ephraem announced: "Were it used due to weakness, it will bud out," and he stuck his staff in the ground.

Many sections of Deir al-Sourian, including the 5th-century Roman-style keep established by King Zeno, are not open to the public, but the main church has a number of interesting sights. The most impressive is the ebony Door of Symbols, inlaid with ivory, in the haykal. Its seven panels represent what were thought of locally as the seven epochs of the Christian era. An inscription shows that it was installed in the church in the 10th century, when Gabriel I was the patriarch of Alexandria. On either side of the haykal are two half-domes decorated with frescoes, one showing the Annunciation to the Virgin and the other the Virgin's Dormition. Many other frescoes have been discovered throughout the church, and the monks are inordinately proud of them.

In the rear of the church is the Refectory, with a kitschy display of monastic eating habits, complete with plaster figures dressed up like monks. If you duck through a narrow passage to the left of the Refectory, you can find a stone cave that was St. Bishoi's private laura. According to legend, St. Bishoi tied his hair to a chain (now a rope) that hung from the ceiling to prevent himself from falling asleep during his marathon prayer sessions.

Deir Anba Baramus is thought to be the oldest monastic settlement in the wadi. Its Arabic name is derived from the Coptic word *Romeos* (meaning Roman), used in honor of Maximus and Domitius, sons of Emperor Valentinus who lived as monks in this area. It is impossible to access except by car and, despite its age, it is probably the least interesting of the three monasteries, because many of the buildings are of quite recent construction. The oldest church on the grounds is the restored 9th-century Church of *al-'Adhra'* (the Virgin). Work on the church in 1987 uncovered frescoes, in rather poor condition, long hidden by plaster. The coffins in the haykal are of St. Isadore and St. Moses the Black (a convert from Nubia). Adjacent to the coffins is a photograph of a T-shirt supposedly scrawled in blood during an exorcism. In the back corner of the church is a column, easily missed next to a wall, that is from the 4th century. It is the oldest part of the monastery.

Dining and Lodging

Bring food and water and plan to see the monasteries as a day trip. Wadi Natrun is mercifully free of tacky tourist facilities, but that means that the nearest restaurant is several miles away, and to put it generously, the meals are unrefined. Permission to stay overnight at the monasteries is granted only in writing to theological students or groups traveling with their priest.

Admissions and Hours

There are now four active monasteries: Deir Anba Bishoi, Deir al-Sourian, Deir Anba Baramus, and Deir Abu Maqar. Deir Abu Maqar has long been one of the most important Christian institutions in Egypt, and as a result, permission to visit is rarely granted without a very compelling devotional reason—even Copts find it almost impossible to get in. The first three are open to visitors—mostly Coptic pilgrims here to pay their respects or baptize children—roughly from 9 AM to 8 PM (6 PM in winter). It isn't necessary, as it has been in the past, to get advance permission from the **patriarchate in Cairo** (⌧ 222 Shar'a Ramses, next to the Cathedral of St. Mark, Abbasiya, ☎ 02/284–3159 or 02/285–7889). It is, however, still worth calling ahead to verify opening hours, because they vary based on the fasting schedule (devout Copts fast the majority of the year).

Getting Around

Wadi Natrun is 100 km (62 mi) from Cairo and 160 km (100 mi) from Alexandria, just off the Desert Road near the dreary planned satellite town of Sadat City.

Transportation to the monastery leaves much to be desired. The most painless option is to negotiate with a taxi driver from Ramses Square in Cairo to take you to each of the monasteries and back to the capital for around £e200–£e250, depending on your haggling skills and the number of people in your group. Be sure that the driver knows the way and understands the amount of waiting time involved—and pay once you're returned safely. The ride should take 1½–2 hours each way.

If you feel like taking the more challenging route, West Delta line buses leave every hour between 6:30 AM and 6:30 PM (excepting 11:30 and 2:30) from Abdel Monem Riyad Square in front of the Ramses Hilton hotel; tickets cost £e4.50. The trip takes at least two hours to meander its way to the Wadi Natrun Rest House along the Desert Road or, if you're lucky, the town itself. From there, you can catch a service taxi with other people (50p to £e1.25 per person) that will take you to Deir Anba Bishoi. It's an easy walk from there to Deir al-Sourian, but if you want to go on to Deir Anba Baramus, you'll have to rely on the kindness of your fellow pilgrims (which is abundant), because there is no established transportation system between the monasteries. To leave, hitch a ride to the Rest House, where the Cairo- and Alexandria-bound buses stop.

CAIRO A TO Z

Arriving and Departing

By Bus

Buses are an inexpensive means of traveling between cities. Generally they are safe, if not always relaxing. Most companies have installed videos to play Arabic and Indian movies at top volume, even on night buses. If this counts as local color rather than annoyance, take a bus.

Super Jet (☎ 02/772–663), relatively speaking, runs the most luxurious buses you'll find to Alexandria, to the Nile Valley, and to Red Sea,

Sinai Peninsula, and Suez Canal cities. Buses leave every half hour (between 5:30 AM and 10 PM) to Alexandria from Maydan Tahrir, Giza, the airport, and Almazah Station in Heliopolis. Tickets cost £e19 if you leave before 9 AM, £e21 if you depart after 9 AM, £e28 if you travel on the bus with phone access that departs from Almazah Station, and £e32 if you take the VIP bus from the airport. Buses to Sharm al-Sheikh leave once a day at 11 PM from Tahrir Square; return buses leave Sharm al-Sheikh for Cairo at 11 PM. A one-way ticket costs £e50. Buses to Hurghada depart from Maydan Abdel Moneim Riyadh at 8 AM and 2 PM; tickets cost £e45 each way. Buses return from Hurghada at noon and 5 PM. Buses to Bur Sa'id (Port Said, £e15) leave every half hour from Almazah Station.

To the Western Desert Oases, the **Upper Egyptian Bus Company** (☎ 02/260–9307) buses depart from El Azhar Street off Attaba Square. One bus departs for Bahariyya daily at 8 AM, for £e15–£e20; another leaves at noon, stopping first in Bahariyya and going on to Farafra, Kharga, and Dakhla, with tickets ranging from £e15 to £e40 depending on destination.

From Sinai Station in Abbasia, the **East Delta Bus Company** (☎ 02/482–4753) goes to Sharm al-Sheikh; tickets cost from £e50 to £e65 depending on when you leave (morning buses are cheaper). Buses leave every 45 minutes between 7 AM and 6:30 PM. There are also daily buses to Taba and Nuweyba (on the Sinai coast) at 8 AM for £e50 one way. Buses leave for Ismailiya, Suez, and Bur Sa'id every 45 minutes from 6:30 AM to 6 PM from Qulali Station off Ramses Square; tickets cost £e6 each way.

The **West Delta Bus Company** (☎ 02/245–1057) runs to Hurghada, Safaga, Qusayr, Luxor, and Aswan. Buses to Hurghada leave five times daily (9 AM, noon, 3 PM, 10:30 PM, and 11 PM) and one- way tickets cost £e30. Buses depart daily for Safaga and al-Qusayr at 9 AM and 3 PM, for Luxor at 9 AM, and for Aswan at 5 PM. Tickets to Safaga, al-Qusayr, and Luxor cost £e35 each way; tickets for Aswan cost £e50. Departures and arrivals are at Abdel Moneim Riyad Station by Maydan Tahrir and Almazah Station in Heliopolis.

By Plane

Cairo International Airport (☎ 02/291–4288 or 02/291–4299) lies on the northeastern outskirts of Heliopolis, about 30 km (19 mi) from downtown Cairo. International flights arrive and depart from Terminal 2. Domestic flights fly from of Terminal 1, Hall 2.

Egypt Air (☎ 02/390–2444) flies daily to Alexandria, Sharm al-Shaykh, Hurghada, Taba, Luxor, Aswan, and Abu Simbel.

BETWEEN THE AIRPORT AND CITY

Taxis and limousines are the best option for getting to and from the airport. The minute you exit the arrival hall, you will be inundated with offers from taxi drivers. The drive should prove to be good practice for bargaining—you should be able to bring the price down to around £e40. Keep in mind that most taxis do not use their fare meters. If you are too tired to go through the hassle, opt for one of the limousine companies located in the arrival hall for a flat fee of £e60–£e80. Cairo taxis are black and white or black and yellow; limousines are black, usually old-model Mercedes sedans. Going to the airport from the city is much easier, because you can have your hotel receptionist arrange your transportation.

By Train

All railway lines, from Cairo to all parts of the counrty that have service, depart from and arrive at **Ramses Station,** 3 km (2 mi) northeast of Maydan Tahrir. Trains traveling to and from Alexandria, the Nile Delta towns, and Suez Canal cities use Tracks 1–7 in the station's main hall. Trains to al-Minya, Luxor, and Aswan depart from Platforms 8, 9, 10, and 11 outside the main hall.

Torbini VIP trains, which are quite pleasant, run to Alexandria once a day at 8 AM (£e22–£e32); standard trains make the trip five times daily (£e17–22). Other lines such as the *Faransawi* depart every hour to Alexandria (£e17–22). *Espani* trains leave four times daily to Upper Egyptian cities. The most expensive and luxurious trains to Luxor and Aswan are the Wagonlits sleepers, with dining and lounge cars. One way tickets cost between £e400 and £e500, as opposed to £e200–£e300 on the less comfortable *Faransawi*.

For exact schedules and ticket prices, inquire and purchase tickets a few days before departing at the Egyptian Tourist Authority (⌧ Maydan Ramses, ☎ 02/764–214) or at your hotel reception desk.

Getting Around

By Bus
Using local buses in Cairo is probably an idea that most tourists will refrain from acting upon. But you can't come to Cairo and not experience at least one bus packed like a sardine can weaving its way through the streets of Cairo, letting off people in acrobatic movements all over the city. Buses are far and away the cheapest mode of transportation, with tickets costing a mere 10p–50p. Buses depart to and from the Maydan Tahrir, the Maydan Ataba and Opera Square, the Pyramids Road, Ramses Station, and the Citadel. Bus numbers are sometimes missing from the buses, so it is always best to ask where a bus is going before it lurches off with you on board.

Much less of an experience, and more reliable, are the orange-trimmed minibuses. They charge slightly more than the larger buses (25p–£e1), and they are usually much less crowded. Most importantly, if you decide to use either type of bus service, be very cautious. Especially on large buses, pickpockets are known to look for potential victims.

MAJOR BUS ROUTES

To and from Maydan Tahrir: #*400* for Heliopolis and Cairo International Airport (all terminals); #*815* for the Khan al-Khalili; #*174* for Ibn Tulun Mosque and the Citadel; #*913* for the pyramids in Giza; #*50* for Ramses Station. **To and from Maydan Ataba and Opera Square:** #*948* and #*410* for Cairo International Airport; #*65* for Khan al-Khalili; #*99* for Maydan Tahrir and Mohandiseen; #*93* for Fustat and the Mosque of 'Amr; #*81* for the Shrine of Imam Sahfe'i; #*48* for Zamalek. **To and from pyramids:** #*804* for Ramses Square and the Citadel; #*905* for Maydan Tahrir and the Citadel. **To and from Ramses Station:** #*65* for Khan al-Khalili, #*174* for the Citadel. **To and from the Citadel:** #*404* for Maydan Ataba and Maydan Tahrir; #*905* for Roda Island, Shar'a al-Haram, and the pyramids.

Another option is the **microbus,** or **service taxis.** These privately owned 12-seaters, newly painted blue and white, cost 60p and go from all the major terminals to just about anywhere you would want to go. They are unnumbered however, so ask the driver where he's headed.

By Car
If you manage to find (and fend) your way driving through the aggressive streets of Cairo, parking will prove to be an even greater challenge. Either you will spend half your day looking for a parking place or you will be ripped off by a *monadi* (one of the self-employed valet parking boys). Just do yourself a favor and forget about driving.

To get a real feel for the city, you really need to walk around. If walking is last on your list of priorities, take taxis, or hire a chauffer-driven car from any upscale hotel at a fixed flat rate. If you simply must rent a car and drive it yourself, you must be at least 25 years old, posses an international license, and have nerves of steel. *See* Driving *in* the Gold Guide for more information.

By Subway

By far the most efficient mode of public transportation, the metro is clean, reliable, and cheap. Tickets cost from 60p to £e1, with no multiday passes available to foreigners. Trains run from South Cairo (Helwan) to North Cairo (Heliopolis), with sub-lines to Shubra, Ataba, and Abdin. The system is constantly expanding, so inquire when you come about what stage the lines have reached. In winter, the metro runs from 5:30 AM to midnight, which extends to 1 AM in summer, with trains arriving every five to 10 minutes. The first car in every train is reserved for women. You are advised to use them, especially during rush hour travel, to avoid being hassled or groped.

By Taxi

The fact that meters are rarely used by Cairo taxi drivers makes life a bit more difficult for tourists, who are considered to be the best prey for the exorbitant fares that some drivers try to charge. The first rule is that you should not take any taxi parked in front of a hotel unless you bargain the price down before getting in. It is always better (cheaper) to hail a taxi off the street after walking a few meters away from the hotel.

Fares vary according to the time you are in the taxi and the distance you cover. Early in the morning and very late at night, fares are about 40%–50% higher than during daylight. During normal daylight hours and in the evening, a 20-minute cab ride from Maydan Tahrir to the pyramids should cost about £e20 one way; a five- to 10-minute ride should cost no more than £e5. If you are going a long distance, such as all the way to Saqqara, the ride should be about £e30 one way, and you should have the driver wait—it would be extremely difficult to get a cab back to the city from there.

Some drivers are extremely stubborn, so you must set a price before embarking on your ride to avoid unpleasent scenes once you arrive at your destination. When giving directions, name a major landmark near your destination, rather than a street address, such as Maydan Tahrir, or al-Azhar University. As you get closer to the destination, give more specifics; this will avoid confusion.

There is no cab company to call. Just go hail one on the street. There are always taxis in the streets of Cairo.

Contacts and Resources

Car Rentals

Car-rental operators with agencies in Cairo include the following; cars come with or without chauffeurs.

Hertz: Central Reservations Office (☎ 02/347–2238); Ramses Hilton Hotel (☎ 02/574–4400); Semiramis Intercontinental Hotel (☎ 02/354–3239 or 02/357–1874); Cairo International Airport (☎ 02/265–2430). **Budget Rent-a-Car:** Central Reservations Office (☎ 02/340–0070 or 02/340–9474 or 02/340–2565); Marriott Hotel (☎ 02/340–8888); Cairo International Airport (☎ 02/265–2395). **Europcar:** Head Office (☎ 02/347–4412 or 02/347–4713); Cairo International Airport (☎ 02/265–2212).

Doctors

Al-Salam International Hospital. ✉ *Ma'adi Corniche, Ma'adi,* ☎ *02/363–8050 or 02/362–3300.*

Anglo-American Hospital. ✉ *Shar'a al-Burg, Zamalek,* ☎ *02/340–6162 or 02/340–6165.*

Embassies

Australian Embassy. ✉ *World Trade Center, Corniche al-Nil, Bulaq,* ☎ *02/575–0444.*

British Embassy. ✉ *7 Shar'a Ahmed Ragab, Garden City,* ☎ *02/354–0850 or 02/354–0852.*

Canadian Embassy. ✉ *5 Maydan Saray Al-Kubra, Garden City,* ☎ *02/354–3110.*

U.S. Embassy. ✉ *5, Shar'a Amrika Al-Latinnya, Garden City,* ☎ *02/354–8211 or 02/355–7371.*

Emergencies

In case of an emergency, contact your embassy first for a physician referral, because hospital emergency rooms leave much to be desired.

Ambulance (☎ 123); **Fire Brigade** (☎ 125); **Police** (☎ 122 or 02/303–4122). **Tourist Police** (☎ 02/390–6028).

Cairo's major hospitals are **al-Salam International Hospital** (✉ Ma'adi Corniche, Ma'adi, ☎ 02/363–8050 or 02/362–3300); **Anglo-American Hospital** (✉ Shar'a al-Burg, Zamalek, ☎ 02/340–6162 or 02/340–6165); **Misr International Hospital** (✉ 12 Shar'a al-Saraya, Finny Square, Doqqi, ☎ 02/360–8261, 02/360–8270, or 02/713–388).

English-Language Bookstores

Zamalek Bookshop (✉ 19 Shar'a Shagaret al-Dor, Zamalek, ☎ 02/341–9197) is great source for books on Ancient Egypt, contemporary Egypt, and for Egyptian novels. It also sells an array of slides and albums.

AUC Bookstore (✉ 113, Shar'a Qasr al-'Ainy, ☎ 02/354–2969) is the main bookstore of the American University in Cairo. It carries an abundant range of books on Egypt, academic literature, and light reading material.

Guided Tours

If you are looking for a guided tour, your best bet is to try to set it up with a travel agent.

Late-Night Pharmacies

By law, every neighborhood is required to have at least one pharmacy open all night. Often pharmacies take turns. Check with your hotel staff about the open one nearest you. Two pharmacies that are permanently open 24 hours are **Seif** (✉ 76 Shari's Qasr Al-'Ainy, ☎ 02/354–2678) and **Issaf Pharmacy** (✉ Shar'a Ramses, at the corner of Shar'a 26 Yulyu (26th of July St.), ☎ 02/5743–369).

Travel Agencies

American Express Travel. ✉ *21 Shar'a al-Giza, Nile Tower, Giza,* ☎ *02/573–8465.*

Thomas Cook. ✉ *12 Maydan Sheikh Yusuf, Garden City, Cairo,* ☎ *02/356–4650.*

Misr Travel. ✉ *1 Shar'a Tala'at Harb, downtown,* ☎ *02/393–0010.*

Visitor Information

Egyptian Tourist Authority. ✉ *Misr Travel Tower, Abbasia, Cairo,* ☎ *02/285–4509.*

3 Alexandria

Home to polyglot communities in ancient and modern times alike, Alexandria embodies the Mediterranean side of Egypt's character: breezy, relaxed, oriented toward the sea. It is a city of cafés and late-night dinners, of horse-drawn carriages and long strolls along the Corniche. And it is a city of history—that is, of numerous overlapping histories.

THERE IS A WONDERFUL Italo Calvino story about a city so removed from its own history that it is as if the modern metropolis sits on the site of an unrelated ancient city that just happens to bear the same name. At times Alexandria, which Alexander the Great founded in the 4th century BC, feels like that.

By Sean Rocha

The fallen Alexandria of the ancient Greeks, of Cleopatra, Julius Caesar, and the Romans, and of pagan cults and the Great Library seems to have been a different place altogether: nearby, perhaps, but not underfoot. In fact, the discontinuity between past and present has grown so vast that some old guidebooks included a sketch of Pharos—the lost Alexandrian lighthouse that was one of the seven wonders of the ancient world—with instructions to stand on the Corniche looking out along the curving shoreline to Fort Qayt Bay, hold the book at arm's length, and squint. Only through this process of blocking out the current city with the pages of the book could you get a sense of that other city. It has come to that.

Yet that history *is* underfoot—all of modern Alexandria has been built over the ruins of the old city—even if little more than a glimmer of the old peeks through, at the excavations at Kom al-Dikka or the catacombs at Kom al-Shoqafa. Overlay a map of the contemporary city on one from antiquity and you would see that many of the streets have remained the same: Shar'a al-Horreya (Horreya Street) runs along the route of the ancient Canopic Way, and Shar'a Nabi Daniel is the old Street of the Soma. Near their intersection once stood the Mouseion, a Greek philosophic and scientific center that had at its heart the 500,000-volume collection of the Great Library. Today, eating pastry at the Vienous café that sits on that corner, you'll search in vain for any sign of the ancient world.

That doesn't mean Alexandria is bereft of history, for the city had another incarnation, more palpable than its ancient past but in some ways equally remote: that of a decadent, early 20th-century colonial enclave with a multicultural mix of Greeks and Arabs, Turks and Armenians, French and Levantines, Jews and Christians. This city started with an architecturally clean slate, given that much of downtown was destroyed in 1882 by British warships in an effort to put down an Egyptian nationalist rebellion. And it was this reborn, semi-new, semi-ancient city that belonged to Constantine Cavafy—a small, cerebral, intensely melancholy homosexual—who is now regarded as the greatest Greek poet of our century. It was the city to which the novelist E.M. Forster, who later wrote *Passage to India,* was posted during World War I. And it was the city that gave birth to Lawrence Durrell's *Alexandria Quartet,* which captivated a generation of American readers when the books were published in the late 1950s.

Despite the weight of this literary legacy, prerevolutionary Alexandria was above all a city of merchants, many of them fantastically rich. They were generally cosmopolitan without being intellectual, and they enjoyed the sort of idle existence that is born of privilege. The privilege in this case was not high birth but colonial rule, which shielded foreigners from Egyptian law and relied on them to serve as the nation's industrial class, a role for which they were handsomely rewarded. They lived in villas with extravagant gardens, frequented luxurious shops, gossiped in a jumble of languages over tea in grand cafés, lounged on the beach in private resorts along the coast, and went to concerts at the old San Stefano Hotel. Then quite suddenly they fled, driven out of Egypt by the nationalist revolution of the 1950s, the wars with Israel, and the nationalization of their businesses.

In the four decades since most of the foreigners left Alexandria—Greeks and Armenians are the majority among those who remained—the city has increased 8 or 10 times in size, in the process replacing many of the villas with giant apartment blocks. As a result, old-timers who return usually do so only once, too saddened by the changes to come again. But if you take Alexandria for what it is today and not as a lesser version of what it once was, none of this makes the city any less exhilarating, and Alex, as it's called, is an utterly charming place to explore. The Mediterranean laps at the seawall along the Corniche, and gentle sea breezes cool and refresh even in the dead of summer. Graceful old cafés continue to draw lovers and friends—Egyptians now, rather than foreigners—while the streets remain as lively and intriguing as ever. Alexandria is a great city, even shorn of its many pasts.

Pleasures and Pastimes

Café Life

The cafés in Alexandria are unlike any others in the rest of Egypt: grand, atmospheric, rich with history, and much closer to Europe than to the Middle East. Their heyday was at the beginning of this century when the city's diverse cocktail of nationalities used the cafés as common ground on which to meet. Some, like Pastroudis, became associated with literary figures; others, like Athineos, with a particular community. There are, as well, small stand-up espresso bars like the Brazilian Coffee Stores, where regulars stop in on their way to work. But the most majestic of all is the Grand Trianon, where young lovers court and old women gather in groups to keep up their French.

Dining

Alexandria's culinary gift is extraordinary seafood, drawing on the best of the Mediterranean and the Red Sea. The preparation tends to be simple: grilled or fried, perhaps laced with garlic, herbs or butter, typically served with *tahina* (sesame paste) and a couple of salads on the side. The ingredients are so fresh that anything more elaborate would obscure the flavor. Most places will arrange the fish, shrimp, crab, calamari, and mussels on ice, and you pay by weight. If you need help choosing, there will always be someone on hand to guide your selection.

If you tire of seafood, Alexandria has little to offer on the food front. Many restaurants manage a vaguely Continental menu with odd touches like Indian curry thrown in, but these dishes are generally uninspired. A few restaurants serve quite good pizza and there are even a few salad bars, but there is little distinctively Alexandrian about them.

There is, however, nothing more Mediterranean about Alexandria than the pace of dinner in the summer: after an evening siesta, have a *shisha* (water pipe) around 11, arrive at a waterfront restaurant after midnight, then wrap up the meal with an early morning espresso at an outdoor café nearby. You don't *have* to eat so late, but you'd be surprised how seductive it is.

People

Alexandrians like to think of themselves as calmer, more civilized, than their Cairo brethren. They could never imagine leaving their cool seaside city for that behemoth to the south. And every summer their partisanship is confirmed as the entire nation, including the government, migrates north to enjoy the pleasures that Alexandrians enjoy year-round.

Local attitudes mask the fact that the majority of Alexandrians have only been in the city a generation or two, having come in from the countryside after the revolution. The old-timers look on the new arrivals with dismay, concluding they lack the urban panache required to call oneself a true resident of this city. Fortunately the older generation is still here to insist, politely but firmly, that Alexandria remains the sophisticated, cosmopolitan city it once was.

EXPLORING ALEXANDRIA

Alexandria has grown so rapidly in the past 50 years that it now runs along the coastline from the Western Harbor all the way east to Montazah, a distance of more than 16 km (10 mi). The many seaside districts along the route—like Chatby, Rushdi, and Sidi Gabr—take their names from the adjacent beaches or tram lines. They are primarily residential areas of little interest, except perhaps for Rushdi, which is the city's most modern shopping district.

Alex is nonetheless a great walking city: the historic downtown occupies a compact area near the Eastern Harbor, and the ancient sights are a short taxi ride away. With breezes almost always coming off the sea, orientation is fairly easy—when in doubt, head into the wind.

Unfortunately, the string of once-elegant beaches that stretches along Alexandria's coastline is now polluted and unappealing—not that that stops locals from bathing there. If the sea beckons, better head to the Sinai or mainland coasts of the Red Sea, where fantastic coral reefs are an added attraction (☞ Chapter 6).

Numbers in the text correspond with numbers in the margin and on the Alexandria map.

Great Itineraries

Alexandria is an antidote to the rest of the country: cool when Egypt is hot, relaxed while Cairo is frenzied, and almost monument-free in a country with more ancient temples than it knows what to do with. It is the kind of place where one-day visits easily extend into weeks. If you like to check sights off a list, a day in Alex will do the trick; to get into the rhythm of a place, two days is a practical minimum.

IF YOU HAVE 1 DAY

With limited time, skip the ancient monuments, which pale in comparison to those elsewhere in Egypt. The most charming part of Alexandria is **downtown,** in the easily walkable area of the Eastern Harbor running from Raml tram station to Maydan Orabi (Orabi Square). There you will find Alex's many **classic cafés,** including the stunning Grand Trianon and Pastroudis of literary fame and the evocative **Cavafy Museum,** as well as the many churches, mosques, and synagogues that reflect the city's bygone diversity. This is also where the most elegant **colonial architecture** and old shops are to be found, along with the intriguing **Attarine Market.** If you do want the history, spend the afternoon at the **Greco-Roman Museum** or the **Roman Theater,** then end the day with a ride out to **Fort Qayt Bay,** site of the legendary lighthouse of **Pharos,** in a horse-drawn cart along the Corniche.

IF YOU HAVE 2 DAYS

With an extra day you can visit the past, taking in **Pompey's Pillar,** the **Anfushi tombs,** and the **catacombs** in a tour of the Western Harbor. The sites being small and relatively close to each other makes them easy to see in a morning. Spend the afternoon out at the **royal gardens** in Montazah and play on the rocks as the Mediterranean covers you in spray. Be sure not to miss the wild European/Middle Eastern **palace**

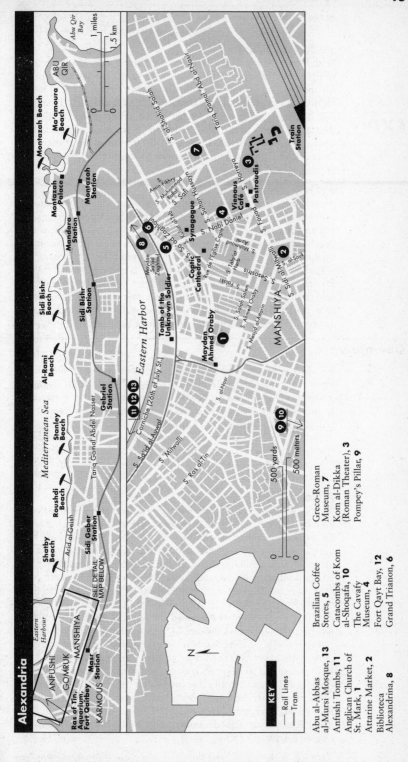

Alexandria

KEY

— Rail Lines
— Tram

Abu al-Abbas
al-Mursi Mosque, **13**

Anfushi Tombs, **11**

Anglican Church of
St. Mark, **1**

Attarine Market, **2**

Biblioteca
Alexandrina, **8**

Brazilian Coffee
Stores, **5**

Catacombs of Kom
al-Shoqafa, **10**

The Cavafy
Museum, **4**

Fort Qayt Bay, **12**

Grand Trianon, **6**

Greco-Roman
Museum, **7**

Kom al-Dikka
(Roman Theater), **3**

Pompey's Pillar, **9**

of the former khedive. Spend the evening out at **Abu Qir** (aboo-*eer*), at the far eastern end of Alexandria's waterfront, feasting on seafood.

IF YOU HAVE 4 DAYS

With four days you'll be able to see Alexandria at its best—not a city of sights, but a place for exploration that requires enough time to allow for spontaneity. Take another day downtown, which is full of hidden treasures. Linger over coffee at the Grand Trianon while watching Egyptian lovers engage in courtship. Set off on a nighttime stroll through the narrow alleys of the **Turkish Quarter,** a fragment of stained glass or the arch of a doorway lighting up the darkness. Scour the waterfront east of downtown for the **decaying villas** of the city's past glory. Or just wander and let your eyes guide you.

WHEN TO TOUR ALEXANDRIA

Alexandria's peak season is summer, when Egyptians flee the heat of Cairo and Upper Egypt for the refreshing Mediterranean breezes. Hotels are often booked long in advance, especially on weekends, and the beaches are packed. Few are here for culture, however, so the impact on downtown or the ancient sights is hardly noticable. Off-season, Alex is spectacular, as the city settles back into its natural, relaxed rhythm. It rains more here than elsewhere (which isn't saying much in such an arid country), and the presence of the sea means it is always a few degrees cooler. Winter is chilly and sometimes windy, which can be a pleasant break from Cairo's annual 360 days of sunshine.

Downtown

Nowhere is Alexandria's cosmopolitan past more evident than downtown, where its Italianate buildings house French cafés, Armenian jewelers, and Greek restaurants. Because so few buildings survived the British bombardment in 1882, it is no surprise that what stands today reflects the late-19th-century European city that rose from the rubble of the city's past. There are a few historical and cultural sights downtown, including the Roman Theater, the Greco-Roman Museum, and the resurrected Great Library, which are a bit of a side trip from the heart of downtown.

A Good Walk

Start on the Corniche in front of the neoclassical **Monument to the Unknown Soldier** at the bottom of **Maydan Ahmed Orabi,** which is named for the leader of the nationalist rebellion of 1882. This long square was once known as the French Gardens (a street called Shar'a Faransa runs off to the right), and it was the heart of the European city. These days it is somewhat congested, and the gardens have long since been paved over. As you walk to the south end, **Maydan Tahrir** abuts Maydan Orabi at a 90-degree angle. During World War I, E.M. Forster described Maydan Tahrir's **Statue of Muhammad 'Ali on Horseback** as "one of the few first-class objects in the city." Directly behind the statue is a long European-style building that was once the **Mixed Tribunals,** one of the most resented symbols of colonial privilege. Foreigners living in Egypt were not subject to Egyptian law in criminal cases—they came before the Mixed Tribunals in all other cases—but were tried instead in front of the notoriously generous "courts" of their own national consulates. As a result, foreigners were responsible for much of the illegal activity in Alexandria. This immunity came to an end with the Anglo-Egyptian Treaty of 1936.

Turn left at the statue, and the charming pseudo-Byzantine **Anglican Church of St. Mark** ① is on the left. It's worth stopping for a moment in its peaceful interior. Back outside, continue left, and you'll see a parking lot marking the end of Maydan Tahrir; this was the site of the famous **Bourse,** which, at cotton's peaks during the United States' Civil War and in the early 20th century, was one of the busiest in the world. It was torn down in the early 1980s, but you can still see its outline on the wall of the building to which it was once attached. Maydan Tahrir now splits into two streets running on either side of the parking lot; take the left-hand street, which is **Shar'a Salah Salem.** This was once Alexandria's most chic shopping street, and it is still blessed with a string of beautiful buildings and fancy shops. At Number 13, on the right, is **Joseph & Alfred Youssoufian,** an Armenian jeweler of long standing with a gorgeous black and gold sign over the door. The street running opposite is **Shar'a Falaki,** home to many shoemakers. Continuing on Salah Salem, Number 20 on the left is one of the city's antique **Brazilian Coffee Stores,** with bean stalks decorating the columns. Then come a series of Italianate palaces now taken over by banks, the nicest of which is on the corner at Number 30, on the left-hand side. This was once the Banco di Roma; you can still see a crest above the door with a relief of a she-wolf suckling Romulus and Remus—the symbol of Rome.

Turn left at this corner—when Lawrence Durrell worked here during World War II it was called Rue Toussoum Pacha; now it's Shar'a Mahmoud Azmi—and at the next corner you'll see the circular rotunda of the old **Credit Foncier Egyptien,** one of the European instutions that ran Egypt's finances in colonial days. Turn right there onto Shar'a Tala'at Harb, and at Number 11 you'll see the **Alexandria Stock Exchange** and at Number 9 the exquisite neo-Islamic **Banque Misr,** which is stylistically similar to the one in Cairo. Continue on Shar'a Tala'at Harb, and you'll run into a three-way intersection with Shar'a Nabi Daniel— the ancient Street of the Soma—and Shar'a al-Horreya—the ancient Canopic Way. **Vienous** café is on the corner. As near as can be approximated, this is the former site of the sprawling, ancient Mouseion, Alexandria's renowned academy and Great Library.

Take a detour by turning right down **Shar'a al-Horreya,** and within a couple of blocks you'll see the striped **Attarine Mosque** on a narrow, angular corner on the right. The mosque is fairly new and not terribly interesting, and non-Muslims are not allowed inside. But if you turn your back to it and look across Shar'a al-Horreya, you'll see the unmarked alley (between a café and a ball-bearings shop) that leads to the **Attarine Market** ②. The market runs several blocks back, with furniture and antiques on this alley and books on the slightly larger street that runs parallel to it on the left.

Return to the intersection with Shar'a Nabi Daniel and the Vienous café, and continue one block ahead to the Art Deco café **Pastroudis,** on the right. Turn up the curved street behind Pastroudis, and after a few minutes the **Kom al-Dikka** ③ excavations will appear on the right.

Make your way back to Shar'a Nabi Daniel and turn right. A block later, an alley on the right marked by Lasheen shoe store and Style locksmiths leads to a modest, rust-colored building with a sign in Greek by the entrance. On the second floor, the **Cavafy Museum** ④ resides in what was once the home of Alexandria's greatest poet.

Returning to Shar'a Nabi Daniel, turn right. On the right side you'll see the heavily guarded gates that shelter a **synagogue** (the facade looks churchlike, but the interior is interesting) that requires divine intervention (or being able to prove you're Jewish) to gain entrance. On the left is a **Coptic cathedral,** and soon after it you'll come to Shar'a Sa'd Zaghlul—the Street of Cafés. If your feet need a rest, turn left and visit the hidden garden at the **Baudrot** café. If all you need is a shot of caffeine, stop in at the espresso bar at the **Brazilian Coffee Stores** ⑤ in front of you, which is a must-see anyway for its timeless decor. Exit the café and turn left, past the overrenovated Delices patisserie and the entrance to the Metropole Hotel. The headquarters of the street of cafés' is ahead at the corner of Shar'a Safiya Zaghlul (Safiya was Sa'd's wife), the location of the **Grand Trianon** ⑥, the patisserie with Venetian paintings worthy of a museum.

If the tides of espresso from so many cafés have revived your feet, make your way to the **Greco-Roman Museum** ⑦, which is a 10-minute walk south on Shar'a Safiya Zaghlul, then left after the blue-and-white Elite restaurant. The modernist **Bibliotheca Alexandrina** ⑧, which is intended to resurrect the ancient Great Library, is about 15 minutes past the museum, easily reached by walking toward the water, then turning east along the harbor and walking in the direction of Montazah to the al-Silsileh Breakwater.

TIMING

This walk could take a morning or three days, depending on your sense of adventure. The actual distances are not far, even if you include the historical excursions, and could be walked in a couple of hours. Allocate a half hour or more for the Cavafy Museum, which is quite small, and from one to two for the Greco-Roman Museum; 30–45 minutes will do for the Roman Theater, likewise for the Bibliotheca Alexandrina. The cafés are seductive—the Grand Trianon alone might detain you for an afternoon.

Sights to See

❶ **Anglican Church of St. Mark.** St. Mark's odd mix of Western, Moorish, and Byzantine design elements somehow manages to blend together harmoniously. The soft yellow stone and colorful stained-glass windows are particularly exquisite in the early morning sun. The walls are lined with plaques, some of which date back almost a century, commemorating members of the Anglican community for their years of long service to the church. The 1855 church was one of the few buildings left undamaged by British warships in the shellings of 1882.

❷ **The Attarine Market.** This area acquired its reputation in the 1960s as the place where the high-quality antiques sold by fleeing foreigners resurfaced. Those days are long gone. There are now only a few true antiques stores left in the area, but it is fascinating nonetheless to see the tiny workshops where the reproduction French-style furniture so popular in Egypt originates. Almost all the workshops will be happy to sell direct if you find a piece that appeals to you, but consider the challenge of shipping it back before you give in to temptation. To find the market, stand on Shar'a al-Horreya with your back to the Attarine Mosque and make your way up the alley between the café and the ball-bearings store. The market actually consists of a series of alleyways, the sum of which feels less established—and far less touristy—than Cairo's Khan al-Khalili.

❽ **Bibliotheca Alexandrina.** This monumental, $180 million, UNESCO-sponsored project (scheduled to open in 1999) began with an instinctively appealing idea: to resurrect the Great Library of ancient Alexandria, founded in the 4th century BC, once one of the world's major centers of learning. The modernist Norwegian-designed building is in the form of an enormous multitiered cylinder with triangles and diamonds as recurrent elements throughout, including on the roof, which is meant to be transparent and open to the sky. Its location near the Silsileh Peninsula on the edge of the Eastern Harbor has tremendous symbolic resonance, having been the royal quarters in ancient times and one of several possible locations of the original library.

In case you want to be welcomed there.

We're here to see that you're always welcomed at establishments everywhere. That's why millions of people carry the American Express® Card – for peace of mind, confidence, and security, around the world or just around the corner.

do more®

Cards

In case you're running low.

We're here to help with more than 118,000 Express Cash locations around the world. In order to enroll, just call American Express before you start your vacation.

do more

Express Cash

And just in case.

We're here with American Express® Travelers Cheques and Cheques *for Two*.® They're the safest way to carry money on your vacation and the surest way to get a refund, practically anywhere, anytime.

Another way we help you...

do more

**Travelers
Cheques**

Relatively little is known about the ancient library itself, beyond reputation for scholarship. It was founded in the 4th century BC by Ptolemy I and is said to have held a collection of 500,000 volumes—all hand copied at a time when books were rare and costly commodities. Theories about its destruction abound, but most assume it stood for roughly 500 years before being consumed by fire. What is known is that the Great Library—and the complex of lecture halls, laboratories, and observatories called the Mouseion, of which it was part—was a source of literary and scientific wisdom that changed the world. It was here, for example, that Euclid set forth the elements of geometry still taught in schools today, and Eratosthenes measured the circumference of the Earth. And it was here that the conqueror Julius Caesar had a new, more accurate calendar drawn up—the Julian calendar—that became the framework for the measurement of time throughout the Western world.

Whether the new library turns out to be a triumph or a white elephant on an epic scale won't be known until it opens, but there are grounds for scepticism. In ancient times, the library stood as a repository of learning, much of it generated within the city. Alexandria today is a less productive, less innovative place. It is hoped that the new library will spark a renaissance of research and scholarship: a goal that anyone with an eye for history and an ounce of romanticism has to hope will be achieved. It will certainly be the greatest intellectual resource in the country after the National Library in Cairo. Call ahead for hours of service. ✉ 63 Shar'a Soter, Chatby, ☎ 03/422–5002.

❺ Brazilian Coffee Stores. Little has changed since this stand-up espresso bar opened in 1929, as you can see from the foot-traffic patterns worn into the tile floor. The ancient roasters are visible to the right—if you're lucky, they'll be roasting beans when you walk in, and the café will be filled with plumes of aromatic smoke. Lining the walls are the original stunningly painted mirrors showing a map of South America, along with population and coffee-production statistics for Brazil, now endearingly out of date. There's even an enormous Brazilian flag painted on the ceiling. ✉ 44 Shar'a Sa'd Zaghlul, ☎ 03/482–5059. ☉ Daily 7 AM–11 PM.

★ ❹ The Cavafy Museum. Constantine Cavafy was born in Alexandria in 1863 and began writing poetry at age 19. It wasn't until much later, as a result of the exposure that the novelist E.M. Forster's celebrated guidebook to Alexandria gave Cavafy, that he came to be regarded as the most accomplished Greek poet of our age. Jacqueline Kennedy Onassis left a request that Cavafy's poem "Ithaka," which describes life's beauty being in the journey and not in the destination, be read at her funeral.

Cavafy's poems—including "God Abandons Antony" and most famously "The City"—are suffused with melancholy, and with a sense of his alienation from the society around him. Ironically, considering his rejection during his lifetime, they give such a strong evocation of place that they define the cultural memory of Alexandria in his time. But Cavafy's despair was as much internal as external, a discomfort with himself as much as with the city. He used to visit the billiards hall on Rue Missala, which was then a red-light district of sorts and now is the very staid Shar'a Safiya Zaghlul, and pick up boys to bring back to his flat around the corner.

It is this flat, after serving an intervening stint as a cheap pension, that has been turned it into a museum. Half of it is given over to a recreation of his home, with a period-piece brass bed and a case of reputedly genuine Christian icons. On the walls is an endless collection of portraits and sketches of Cavafy that only the most vain of men could have hung in his own apartment. Despite these improbable touches, it does feel like you're in his space. Whether it was the space that shaped his work or his work that seeped into the walls and shaped the space is another question.

The other half of the museum houses newspaper clippings about the poet's life and a library of his works, in the many languages and permutations in which they were published after his death—a remarkable legacy for a man who lived so quietly. There is, as well, a room dedicated to a student of Cavafy named Stratis Tsirkas, who lived in Upper Egypt and wrote a massive trilogy set in the Middle East. And there is one last curiosity: a cast of Cavafy's death mask, serene but disfigured, lying cushioned on a purple pillow. ⊠ *4 Shar'a Sharm al-Sheikh,* ☎ *03/482–5205.* 🎟 *£e8.* ◷ *Tues.–Sun. 10 AM–3 PM.*

NEED A BREAK?	Even if your body can't handle any more caffeine, it's worth stopping at **Baudrot,** one of downtown's easily overlooked oases, for a soda. The plain white facade and empty display cases in the window seem purpose-built to put off customers, but if you walk straight through the drab patisserie, there's a peaceful vine-covered garden café in back. The plastic chairs and tables aren't exactly luxurious, but in this little sliver of tranquillity the only noises are made by birds chirping in the trees overhead. ⊠ *23 Shar'a Sa'd Zaghlul,* ☎ *no phone.*

★ ❻ **Grand Trianon.** One of Alexandria's most stylish institutions since it opened in the 1920s, the Grand Trianon remains a forum for courtship, gossip, and rediscovery. The most popular area is the café, which has a certain Old World grandeur, despite being the least decorated part of the place. The adjacent restaurant is an extravagant Art Nouveau jewel, with colorful murals on the wall and a spectacular stained-glass window over the entrance to the kitchen. But the pièce de résistance is in the patisserie around the corner. There, behind elaborately carved wooden cabinets, a series of Venetian wood-panel paintings of sensual water nymphs will take your breath away. The colors are muted, but as your eyes adjust the images will start to shimmer like a Gustav Klimt kiss. The café and restaurant close at midnight; the patisserie at 8 PM. ⊠ *Maydan Sa'd Zaghlul,* ☎ *03/482–0986.*

❼ **Greco-Roman Museum.** This museum was founded in 1895 and contains the best of the pieces found at Pompey's Pillar—including a statue of the Apis Bull—and two statues from the catacombs at Kom al-Shoqafa (☞ *Historical Alexandria, below*). In spite of some uninteresting pieces, this is Egypt's finest museum covering the period of Egyptian history from Alexander the Great's conquest in 332 BC to the third Persian occupation in AD 619. There are a great many pharaonic pieces here as well—indeed, the most impressive thing about the museum is that it shows the scale of cross-fertilization between pharaonic culture and the Greek and Roman cultures that followed. Highlights of the collection include its early Christian mummies, remnants of a temple to the crocodile god Sobek, and courtyard full of sun-drenched statuary. ⊠ *5 Shar'a al-Mathaf, Raml Station,* ☎ *03/483–6434.* 🎟 *£e12.* ◷ *Daily 9 AM–5 PM.*

❽ **Kom al-Dikka (Roman Theater).** A Polish team has been excavating the site since 1960 (and work continues), and a recent sprucing-up makes this a quiet retreat in the middle of the city. The focal point is a well-preserved amphitheater—the only one of its kind in Egypt—originally constructed in the 4th century AD, then rebuilt in the 6th century, following an earthquake. At that time a large dome was added (only its supporting columns still stand), and the theater went from being a cultural venue to a forum for public meetings of the City Council—a change deduced from ancient graffiti promoting various political parties.

The other half of the site is technically off-limits (although judiciously placed *baksheesh* might get you in) because of ongoing excavations of the ancient baths and living quarters. This area, in fact, is best seen through the fence from the side near Pastroudis café, where the cisterns and walls are clearly visible. The red bricks mark the location of the heated baths—warmed by an elaborate underground system—which complemented the adjacent cold and steam baths. The whole area fell into disuse after the 7th-century Persian conquest of Egypt. ✉ *Downtown (opposite the Misr train station),* ☎ *03/490–2904.* ✉ *£e6.* ⊙ *Daily 9 AM–5 PM.*

Historical Alexandria

Somewhere—everywhere—underground lies a wealth of archaeological remains, but little of it has been excavated. As a result, Alexandria's ancient and medieval remnants exist in scattered pockets. The most central sights are the Greco-Roman Museum and the Roman Theater (☞ Downtown Alexandria, *above*), but none of the rest are more than a 15-minute taxi ride from Raml Station.

A Good Tour

Start at **Pompey's Pillar** ⑨ in the southwest of the city, reached by taxi or yellow Tram 16. The site is not the most impressive in the city, but it has been adopted as Alexandria's unofficial symbol and is worth a look, as much for the view from the hill as for the pillar itself. You can then walk to the fascinating **Catacombs of Kom al-Shoqafa** ⑩ by turning right outside the gate and following the wall to the next right. It's then a straight 10-minute walk up a slight hill to the catacombs, which are on the left. The neighborhood is poor but completely safe, and locals are used to directing foreigners who lose their way. The catacombs are on a scale you don't expect from your first glance as you pass the ticket window. The main hall is reached by a spiral staircase—look for the greenhouse roof that protects the entrance.

After the catacombs, if you still crave more burial grounds, take a taxi to the smaller **Anfushi Tombs** ⑪; otherwise, take one to **Fort Qayt Bay** ⑫ at the tip of the Corniche. This was the site of **Pharos,** the ancient lighthouse, and while the interior of the fort is not especially compelling, the ramparts walk justifies the unusually steep ticket price. The view from the fortress wall is unbroken all the way to Montazah. From the fort it's a 10-minute walk down the Corniche to the attractive **Abu al-Abbas al-Mursi Mosque** ⑬.

The most charming way to return to downtown is to hail a horse-drawn calèche, which can also take you to the **Roman Theater,** the **Greco-Roman Museum,** or the **Bibliotheca Alexandrina,** if you missed any of them while making your way around colonial Alexandria.

TIMING

Because the most convenient way to link up the sights is by taxi, there is only 30 to 45 minutes of walking around these sights. Even including the time at the sights themselves, you can easily get to all of them in a day, as long as you can tear yourself away from the ramparts of Fort Qayt Bay.

Sights to See

⑬ **Abu al-Abbas al-Mursi Mosque.** This attractive mosque was built during World War II over the tomb of a 13th-century holy man, who is the patron saint of the city's fishermen. Until recently, the mosque looked suitably old and traditional, but it has been restored to its original gleaming-white condition and is less charming for it—although a few details, such as the wood-and-metalwork doors, are still stunning. The area surrounding it has been turned into Egypt's largest and most bizarre religious/retail complex, with four mosques (one of them built on an inhuman scale) sharing a terrace that hides an underground shopping center. Intruding on the space is a horrific modernism-on-the-cheap office building (with more shops) that is pointed and angular where the mosques are smooth and curved. If you are dressed modestly and the mosque is open, you should be able to get inside. If so, remove your shoes and refrain from taking photos. ⊠ *Corniche, al-Anfushi.*

⑪ Anfushi Tombs. You need to have a fairly serious death fetish to make the effort to see these 3rd century BC Ptolemaic tombs. Although on a smaller scale than the Catacombs at Kom al-Shoqafa, this necropolis has more extant decoration, including paintings on the limestone walls to simulate marble and various images from the pantheon of pharaonic gods. The tombs are on the spit of land (which at one time was an island) separating the Western and Eastern harbors, roughly a third of the way between the Palace of Ras al-Tin on the western point and Fort Qayt Bay on the east point. ⊠ *El Anfushi,* ☎ *no phone.* ⊡ *£e6.* ⊙ *Daily 9 AM–5 PM.*

★ ⑩ Catacombs of Kom al-Shoqafa. This is the most impressive of Alexandria's ancient remains, dating from the 2nd century AD. Excavation started in 1892, and the catacombs were discovered accidentally eight years later when a donkey fell through a chamber ceiling. A long spiral staircase leads to the main hall. The stairs run down the outside of a shaft, which excavators used to transport the bodies of the dead. The staircase leads to the rotunda, which, like all but the lowest chamber, is undecorated but striking for the sheer scale of the underground space, supported by giant columns carved out of the bedrock.

A few rooms branch off from the rotunda: the Triclinium was a banquet hall where relatives and friends toasted the deceased, and the Caracalla Hall has four lightly painted tombs and a case of bones. The next level down contains a labyrinth of smaller nooks for storing bodies and leads to the lowest excavated room, which is framed by columns and sculpted snakes. Casts of two statues stand here—the originals are in the Greco-Roman Museum—and three tombs are of interest for their mix of pharaonic and Greek imagery. ⊠ *Karmouz,* ☎ *03/482–5800.* ⊡ *£e12.* ⊙ *Daily 9 AM–5 PM.*

⑫ Fort Qayt Bay (Pharos). This sandstone fort lies on the very tip of the Corniche, dominating the view of the Eastern Harbor. It was built on the site of the Pharos lighthouse, one of the seven wonders of the ancient world, and incorporates its remains, much of which is still visible, into the foundation. The lighthouse was constructed under the Ptolemies by a Greek named Sostratus in the 3rd century BC. Standing about 400 feet high and capable of projecting a light that could be seen 53 km (35 mi) out to sea, it was one of the most awesome structures created by ancients. The base of the four-tier Pharos was thought to have contained some 300 rooms, as well as a hydraulic system for lifting fuel to the top of the tower.

In the centuries that followed, the Pharos was damaged and rebuilt several times, until it was finally destroyed in the great earthquake of 1307. It lay in ruins for two centuries until the Mamluk Sultan Qayt Bay had the current fortress constructed in 1479.

The outer walls of the fort enclose a large open space, and the ramparts' walk affords magnificent views of miles and miles of coastline. The fort also encourages romance—the arrow slits built into the ramparts that were once used to defend the fort now shelter Egyptian couples enjoying the chance to court each other in semiprivacy. The interior of the building within the fort, by comparison, is exceptionally dull, housing an undecorated mosque, a patriotic mural of President Gamal Abdel Nasser reviewing a fantastically outfitted Egyptian navy, and a kitsch historical model of "the fleet of Senefroo." Upstairs are the iron bullets, swords, bombs, and shards of pottery recovered from Napoléon's ship *l'Orient,* which the British sank off Abu Qir, several miles east. ⊠ *Corniche,* ☎ *03/480–9144.* 🎟 *£e20.* ☉ *Daily 9 AM–5:30 PM.*

NEED A BREAK?	There are any number of cafés along the Corniche, but the one with the best view is **inside Fort Qayt Bay,** to the right of the main building within the walls. They have the usual sodas, tea, and Turkish coffee, but you can sit at their little tables or, better yet, take the drinks up to the ramparts. Just be sure to tell them you'll return the empty bottles, because they'll have to pay a replacement fee if you don't.

❾ Pompey's Pillar (Serapium Oracle). Despite being Alexandria's most famous tourist sight, Pompey's Pillar is a disappointment. After all it's just a granite pillar—albeit at 88 ft a very tall one—placed on a hill surrounded by ruins. Known in Arabic as *al-'Amud al-Sawiri* (Column of the Horseman), the pillar was misnamed after Pompeius (106–48 BC) by the Crusaders. In fact it dates to the 3rd century AD, when it was erected in honor of the emperor Diocletian on the site of a Ptolemaic temple to Serapis.

Helpful signs on the ruins name each virtually empty spot as a "pool" or "bath," which to the untrained eye look like indistinguishable rocks. The late-model sphinxes lying around on pedestals add a little character. The most interesting element, ironically, is that from the hill you can get a glimpse inside the walled cemetery next door, as well as a view of a long and busy market street. ⊠ *Karmouz,* ☎ *03/482–5800.* 🎟 *£e6.* ☉ *Daily 9 AM–5 PM.*

DINING

Off-season, Alexandrians eat meals at standard times: 1 to 3 for lunch and 8 to 11 for dinner. But in summer, dinner often begins after midnight. Because the focus is on fresh seafood, restaurants in Alexandria (especially the good ones) tend to be informal and quite inexpensive for the quality of what they serve. Naturally, many are near the water, some of them appropriately weathered, while others consist of no more than a few tables in an alley. Either way, the system is the same: there's no menu, the seafood is arranged on ice, and you pick what appeals and pay by weight. The price includes preparation, garnishes, tahina, and a couple of salads—there are no hidden costs. The prices for seafood listed below exclude shrimp, which can add an extra £e20 or £e30 to the bill. A few places will levy a service charge but most will not. In all places a tip of 8%–10% is appropriate. Do not expect alcohol to be served in most restaurants.

CATEGORY	COST*
$$$$	over £e 65
$$$	£e50–£e65
$$	£e35–£e50
$	under £e35

per person for a three-course meal, excluding drinks and service.

$$$$ ✕ **Al-Saraya.** Located on the top floor of a small citadel on the Mediter-
★ ranean end of the Corniche just past Stanley Beach, this superb restaurant has a curved, nautical-theme dining room that looks out on an

unbroken sweep of water. If you sit close to the windows, you can hear the waves crashing against the rocks as you eat—it's perfect. The menu (there is also the usual fish-on-ice display as well) goes a step beyond the standard offerings with specialties like an extraordinary, rich and complex shrimp bisque. Service is smooth and efficient, and the bar exceptionally well-stocked by Alexandrian standards. Note that al-Fayrouz is the actual name of the place, but al-Saraya is on the sign outside. ⊠ *205 Tariq al-Geish, Stanley,* ☎ *03/546–7773. MC, V.*

$$$$ ╳ **Grand Trianon.** This is Alexandria's most gorgeous restaurant: high ceilings, elaborate carved wooden chandeliers, and swirling Art Nouveau murals decorating the walls. Nothing else in the city is quite as evocative of the elegance of the 1920s, an atmosphere enhanced by the pianist who plays quietly off to one side. Some day, no doubt, the kitchen will be taken over by a master chef equal to the decor, but for now the food remains enjoyable but unspectacular. The overly ambitious menu ranges across continents, but if you stick close to home, you'll play to their strengths. As appetizers the *sambousik* (phyllo pastries stuffed with cheese or meat) and French onion soup are quite good, and the entrecôte of beef makes an excellent main course. For dessert, you can linger at your table or relocate to the adjoining café. ⊠ *Maydan Sa'd Zaghlul, Raml Station,* ☎ *03/482–0986. AE, MC, V.*

$$$ ╳ **Samakmak.** Owned by a belly dancer—but don't expect any impromptu performances—this seafood restaurant is located in a suitably rundown area near the port where the fishing boats dock. Inside, the place has a slightly more formal atmosphere than most and serves exquisitely fresh seafood that benefits from the short walk from boat to plate. The staff is friendly and helpful. ⊠ *42 Shar'a Ras al-Tin, Gomrouk,* ☎ *03/481–1560. Reservations essential. No credit cards.*

$$–$$$ ╳ **Zephyrion.** Established in 1929 beside a small proletarian beach in the dusty village of Abu Qir east of Montazah, Zephyrion has been synonymous with good seafood for three generations. The restaurant could seat 400 without effort—more in the summer when the veranda is opened up—so it always feels empty, but the seafood is as fresh as it gets. Old men wander in from the beach with plates of shellfish trying to tempt you, but Zephyrion's own offerings are in the iceboxes in the back. The restaurant is at its most peaceful in the late-afternoon sun. It has no address, but everyone in Abu Qir knows where it is. Since it is 20 minutes from Montazah (and 40 from downtown), the big question is whether it is worth the trip. The answer: yes, if you see the trip itself as part of the adventure. The kitchen closes by 10:30 PM. ⊠ *Abu Qir,* ☎ *03/560–1319. No credit cards.*

$$ ╳ **Abu Ashraf.** This is what a hole-in-the-wall—or in this case a chairs-
★ in-the-alley—fish restaurant should look like: makeshift tables, butcher paper, open-air grills, and a market street nearby. Despite its casual appearance, Abu Ashraf is a legend among locals for its fresh seafood and reasonable prices. It certainly delivers on the succulent grilled prawns and melt-in-your-mouth crabs, although afficionados might contend that the sauce for the fish is a bit salty. Still, this a great setting for a feast, and the piping hot *shami* bread (flat and made from white flour) is delicious. Don't try to find this place based on the address, just take a taxi and rely on your driver. ⊠ *28 Shar'a Safr Basha, Zawit Khattub, Gomrouk (near the Western Harbor),* ☎ *03/481–6597. Reservations not accepted. AE, MC, V.*

$$ ╳ **Far 'n' Away (Au Privé).** For licensing reasons, the old Au Privé name still stands, but the wide-ranging restaurant/bar is now called Far 'n' Away. The theme of the place is American Old West, with wooden barrels and shotguns at the entrance and license plates on the wall, but the cozily lighted, wood-paneled dining room is unexpectedly inviting. The menu is essentially Egyptian and Continental, with a few appropriately inauthentic Tex-Mex dishes thrown in. While no Mexican would recognize the sizzling fajitas, they are pretty tasty, if not at all spicy. The real surprise is the long bar, which has the widest range of drinks in the city. The place is a little tricky to find: it's down an alley off Shar'a al-Horreya and not far from Vienous café (look for the AU PRIVÉ/L'EXTRA sign overhead). Entrance is theoretically restricted to those over 25 years old. ✉ *14 Shar'a Fu'ad (a.k.a. Shar'a al-Horreya), Manshiya,* ☎ *03/483–1881. Reservations essential. AE, V.*

$$ ✕ **Elite.** This Alexandrian institution occupies a prime corner on busy Shar'a Safiya Zaghlul, with a breezy glassed-in front where booths and sliding windows make people-watching easier. The darker back area is covered in art posters from around the world and has colorful Japanese paper fish lanterns hanging from the ceiling. Alas, Elite's range of fish kebabs to standard Egyptian fare is decent, but not exceptional. More remarkable is the ageless Greek owner, Christina Constantinou, who speaks every known language and keeps an eye on the place from a permanent table by the door. Beer is available. ✉ *43 Shar'a Safiya Zaghlul,* ☎ *03/482–3592. No credit cards.*

$$ ✕ **Grand Café.** Adjacent to the Tikka Grill (☞ *below*) and under the same management, this outdoor restaurant is one of the coziest, most romantic places in Alexandria. Tables are scattered throughout a lush garden, amid palm fronds lit against the night sky and small wooden bridges leading to private corners. The menu offers the standard Egyptian dishes—kebabs, *shish taouk* (chicken kebabs), *kofta* (minced lamb on a skewer), and so forth—but it is the setting that should bring you here. The £e23 minimum charge is no obstacle if you're eating but discouraging if you only want to linger over a cup of tea. ✉ *Corniche (near the Abu al-Abbas al-Mursi Mosque),* ☎ *03/480–5114. Reservations essential. MC, V. No lunch.*

$$ ✕ **Kadoura.** Granted, it looks unpromising: not shabby enough to feel authentic, not stylish enough to feel elegant. So close your eyes. Kadoura is famous throughout Egypt, and it is every bit as good as its reputation. Fish is grilled with a fresh tomato, garlic, and herb purée that is out of this world; calamari comes lightly fried, tender, and tasty. Pick your seafood downstairs, grab a wood-block number, and sit upstairs. Everything else that comes to you—salads, tahina, drinks—is included in the price. It is very popular for lunch, especially on Fridays, when space is at a premium. ✉ *48, 26th of July St. (a.k.a. the Corniche),* ☎ *03/480–0967. Reservations not accepted. No credit cards.*

$$ ✕ **Pastroudis.** Known primarily as an old-world patisserie and literary café, Pastroudis also has a dark, vaguely Art Deco restaurant in back. In truth, the Continental food is not fantastic—although the house-specialty paella is tasty if you ask them to hold off on the salt—but the atmosphere is charming, and there are few good restaurants as close as this to the city center. There are tables lining the sidewalk, looking out toward the Roman Theater, but the policy on whether you have to order a meal or can just have a coffee depends on the mood of the staff. Ask nicely and they're sure to acquiesce. ✉ *39 Shar'a al-Horreya, Manshiya,* ☎ *03/492–9609. No credit cards.*

$$ ✕ **Tikka Grill.** Although Alexandrians swear by this place, it seems to have a bit of an identity problem. On one hand, it's a Kentucky Fried Chicken-affiliated chain restaurant: there's a KFC staffed entirely by the deaf in the same complex. On the other hand, it has surprisingly elegant decor and a magnificent setting next to the water—the only Eastern Harbor restaurant to have one. It also has the best salad bar in the country—even though there's little competition for the title—and very good Egyptian food. Ironically, the eponymous Chicken Tikka is disappointing (not at all Indian, as it claims to be), while the "spaggati pelognese" is dubious on linguistic grounds alone. Stick with food from the Middle East. ⊠ *Corniche (near Abu al-Abbas al-Mursi Mosque)*, ☎ *03/480–5114. Reservations essential. MC, V.*

$ ✕ **Taverna.** This is more a pizza place than a real Greek taverna, but its convenient location makes it an attractive option. The pizza is delicious, assembled in front of you, and baked in an oven to the left of the entrance. The baladi oven to the right is used for *fatir,* a kind of Egyptian pizza than can be sweet or savory, and often fairly oily—ask them to go light on the *ghee* (clarified butter), a heart-stopping toxin in liquid form. They also serve some fish and shrimp dishes. The proper seating area is upstairs, but it's even cheaper if you eat at the informal area downstairs, where a *shawerma* (pressed lamb carved from a vertical rotisserie) sandwich makes a nice midday snack. ⊠ *1 Maydan Sa'd Zaghlul, Raml Station,* ☎ *03/482–8189. AE, MC, V.*

LODGING

Hotels in Alexandria are located in two clusters roughly 30 minutes apart: the five-stars are all out along the eastern shoreline in Montazah, close to or even within the manicured khedival palace gardens—but not convenient to the city or the historical sights. Lower-budget hotels are much more convenient, but less tranquil. In truth, with the exception of the Salamlek Palace, the luxury hotels in Alexandria are drab, generic places not worth what they charge. Fortunately, a couple of midrange hotels, like the surprisingly elegant Metropole and the historic Cecil, make attractive alternatives right in the city center. If you're looking for a comfortable but inexpensive place to sleep, Alexandria is one of the few cities on the Mediterranean where a cozy double with a panoramic view of the sea goes for less than £e70 ($21). Outside the peak summer season, discounts at most hotels are 30% to 40%.

CATEGORY	COST*
$$$$	over $150
$$$	$75–$150
$$	$25–$75
$	under $25

All prices are for a standard double room in high season.

City-Center Hotels

$$$–$$$$ ▥ **Sofitel Alexandria Cecil.** With the Cecil, you're paying for history. Built in 1930, and immortalized as one of Justine's haunts in Lawrence Durrell's *Alexandria Quartet,* it actually retains few reminders of that era—its elegant revolving door at the main entrance and two gorgeous old wooden elevators. Most rooms are painted in vibrant pastels more evocative of Miami in the late 1980s than Alexandria before the revolution, and the simple wooden furniture seems a bit modest for a hotel of this stature. Proximity to a major square and the Corniche make street noise an issue. And although it's under French management, there is a sense of disarray among the staff, with supposedly full-time facilities rendered inaccessible because the employee with the key might be eating lunch. ⊠ *Maydan Sa'd Zaghlul,* ☎ *03/483–7173,* 𝔽𝔸𝕏 *03/483-6401. 86 rooms. 2 restaurants, bar, excercise room, sauna, casino, nightclub, cigar shop, business services. AE, MC, V.*

$$$ ▥ **Paradise Inn–Metropole.** The best value in Alexandria, hands down, ★ is in a turn-of-the-century building on Maydan Sa'd Zaghlul, right above the Grand Trianon café. The Metropole has an elegance few others can match. You'll fear the worst as you step into the overdone lobby, because the gilt, mirrors, Flemish tapestries, and bas-relief moldings cry out for a restraining hand, but the large rooms come as a pleasant surprise. The 20-ft ceilings, simple antique furniture, and flowing velvet

drapes add a luxurious touch, as do the whirlpools in the suites. Tram noise, which has been a slight problem, should end with the imminent relocation of the tram station. The hotel serves no alcohol. ⊠ *52 Shar'a Sa'd Zaghlul, Raml Station,* ☎ *03/482–1467,* FAX *03/482– 2040. 66 rooms. Restaurant, café, business services. AE, MC, V.*

$$$ ⊞ **Windsor Palace.** This 1920s-style hotel on the Corniche has seen its charm fade over the years. The rooms have tall ceilings and great potential, but the decorations are lackluster. Corner rooms are the most desirable, with undulating walls that overwhelm other attempts to make the space feel generic. Management is adamant that only the renovated (and higher-priced) first floor is "suitable for foreigners," but noise from the Corniche road means that upper-floor rooms do have their advantages. The hotel serves no alcohol. ⊠ *17 Shar'a al-Shohada, Raml Station,* ☎ *03/480–8123,* FAX *03/480–9090. 81 rooms with bath. Restaurant, coffee shop, business services. AE, V.*

$$ ⊞ **Hotel Alex.** Inside a modern building on the south side of Maydan Nasser, a busy commercial area near the port, velour couches and brown carpets are the tip-off that little has changed since this hotel opened in the early 1980s. Still, rooms are spacious and comfortable, with very clean canary-yellow bathrooms. The massive common space on each floor is wood-paneled and soothingly lit, almost with the feel of a gentleman's club. The building is triangular, so the rooms that end with the number 7 are smaller wedges, while room numbers that end with 5 or 9 lie in between on the sides. Recent construction has hemmed in the building on all sides, leaving only the suites (rooms numbers that end in 1 or and 2) with views of the square—and significant sunlight. ⊠ *23 Shar'a al-Nasr, Manshiya,* ☎ *03/483–7694,* FAX *03/482–3113. 80 rooms with bath. Restaurant, bar, billiards, nightclub. MC, V.*

$$ ⊞ **Hotel Amoun.** The Amoun curves around one side of Maydan Nasser, opposite the more congenial Hotel Alex. The functional rooms here are reasonably large, with funky green velour curtains and very basic furniture. All overlook the square, which makes street noise less of an issue on higher floors. The main drawback is the late-night "disco," which, given the proximity to the port, may be a euphemism for other more basic (sleazy but not threatening) activities. The hotel's clientele is almost exclusively Russian. ⊠ *32 Shar'a al-Nasr, Manshiya,* ☎ *03/481–8239,* FAX *03/480–7131. 86 rooms. Restaurant, café, billiards, dance club. No credit cards.*

$$ ⊞ **Petit Coin.** The name (Little Corner in French) fits this cozy hotel, just off Maydan Ahmed Orabi. There's nothing complicated about the Petit Coin—the spare rooms are clean, comfy, freshly painted, and air-conditioned, which makes it an inviting choice if you want a convenient place to stay right in the city. Rooms look out over the busy square, and down to the water, but you're high enough that noise is not an issue. The best views are at the hotel's café, which is a fine place to watch the sun set over the rooftops. The hotel serves no alcohol, and it's a good idea to pass on the restaurant. ⊠ *5 Shar'a Ahmed Orabi, Manshiya,* ☎ *03/483–1503,* FAX *03/483–1505. 52 rooms. Restaurant, café, billiards. No credit cards.*

$ ⊞ **Marhaba.** Once you get past the lobby, this hotel feels like a slightly eccentric grandmother's house: flowery wallpaper covers every inch of space both in the rooms and in the corridors, and the super-kitsch Louis-Faruq mirrors and creaky furniture create a sense of clutter. But for all that, the worn, uncomfortable rooms could be nicer and the cramped bathrooms might create logistical difficulties. Some rooms look out onto the square, which affords light and a view at the cost of traffic noise. All in all, the similarly priced Sea Star and Union (☞ *below*) are more appealing. ⊠ *10 Maydan Ahmed Orabi, Manshiya,* ☎ *03/*

480–0957, FAX 03/480–9510. 33 rooms, 22 with bath. Restaurant, coffee shop. No credit cards.

$ ⛱ **Sea Star.** Although the lobby suggests a slightly more formal hotel than the upper-floor rooms deliver, the Sea Star has a pleasantly beach-weathered feel—one of the few reminders that Alexandria was once seen primarily as a summer resort. The whitewashed walls and breezy stairwell between the two wings of the hotel give way to small but comfortable rooms with balconies that look out on the square Venetian-style apartment buildings near Raml Station. The so-called suites offer more space but are less enticing. ⊠ 24 Shar'a Amin Fikhry, Raml Station, ☎ 03/483–1787, FAX 03/480–5343. 49 rooms, 14 suites. Restaurant, café. No credit cards.

$ ⛱ **Hotel Union.** Don't be misled by the dingy entrance and modest common area: this is the best inexpensive hotel in the city. The upstairs rooms with baths all have crisp white walls, stylish hand-blown glass lamps suspended in the middle of the room, and splendid bathrooms. But it is the balconies, which appear to hang over the Mediterranean, that make the place feel like such a steal at this price. The rooms without bath (downstairs) are in much worse shape. There are signs advertising a Belvedere disco on the sixth floor, but have no fear: the disco is long gone. ⊠ 164 Corniche, Raml Station, ☎ 03/480–7312, FAX 03/480–7350. 37 rooms, 26 with bath. Coffee shop. No credit cards.

Eastern Shoreline Hotels

$$$$ ⛱ **Helnan Palestine.** In a magnificent setting in the royal gardens between the old palace and a private cove, the fan-shaped concrete dreariness of the Palestine is an example of modernism gone very wrong. Built in 1964 to house visiting heads of state attending an Arab summit, this hotel is still fondly remembered by old-timers as a symbol of the progressive, forward-looking promise of that era. Newer arrivals with less of an eye for symbolism are more likely to notice the aging plastic icycle chandeliers in the dim lobby and the dated furniture in the rooms. Outside, the tiny cove and artificial sandlot hardly justify the beachside sales pitch. ⊠ Montazah Palace grounds, Montazah, ☎ 03/547–4033, FAX 03/547–3378. 209 rooms. 2 restaurants, beach, nightclub. AE, DC, MC, V.

$$$$ ⛱ **Ramada Renaissance.** Despite its five-star rating, the Ramada has just as many strikes against it. An air of chaos reigns in the lobby, and the intercom system sounds like it's issuing air-raid warnings. Service is slow, and the rooms are the standard-issue found in chain hotels worldwide. The view of the churning sea and nearby beach is attractive; the ongoing construction work to enlarge the Corniche road by two lanes is less so. And it's a good thing the hotel has a full range of facilities in-house, because there is nothing else to do within a 15-minute walk in any direction. ⊠ 544 Tariq al-Geish, Sidi Bishr, ☎ 03/549–0935, FAX 03/549–7690. 171 rooms. 3 restaurants, 2 bars, coffee shop, no-smoking rooms, pool, sauna, excercise room, dance club, business services, travel services. AE, DC, MC, V.

$$$$ ⛱ **El-Salamlek Palace.** Built in the late 19th century by the khedive as
★   a lodge for his Austrian mistress, the Salamlek is Alexandria's most luxurious hotel. Each suite is a unique, charming space, with sloping wood ceilings or arched windows. The furnishings are contemporary, and the canopy beds and glittering gold can sometimes feel a touch nouveau riche. The heart-stoppers are the gorgeous tiled terraces in three of the suites: overlooking the royal gardens and the nearby cove, they have wicker furniture practically begging you to lounge, drink in hand, in the late-afternoon sun. Compared to the suites, the handful of standard rooms and studios feel like an afterthought. ⊠ Montazah Palace

grounds, ☎ *03/547–7999,* FAX *03/547–3585. 14 suites, 4 rooms, 2 studios. 2 restaurants, café, bar, casino, business services, travel services. DC, MC, V.*

$$$$ 🏨 **Sheraton Montazah.** Outside the main entrance to the royal gardens, the Sheraton is a generic modern hotel with little going for it except reliability. Rooms are pleasant in an interchangable international hotel fashion, but the bathrooms are modest even by chain standards. The view of the sea is good, especially at sunset, but it won't take your breath away. Because it's not actually in the royal gardens, the Sheraton has Montazah's disadvantage of distance from the major sights without the advantage of being surrounded by greenery and silence. ⊠ *Corniche, Montazah,* ☎ *03/548–0550,* FAX *03/540–1331. 269 rooms. 2 restaurants, café, pool, sauna, dance club, nightclub, business services, travel services. AE, DC, MC, V.*

NIGHTLIFE AND THE ARTS

The Arts

Most of Egypt's national cultural institutions are in Cairo. In Alexandria, the main venues for music, theater, and exhibitions are the cultural centers attached to foreign consulates. Their programs are often very interesting, particularly at the Cervantes Institute and French center, and they connect you with the cosmopolitan side of Alex that is often invisible in the city at large. To find out what is happening, call consulates for their schedules, pick up *Egypt Today* (which occasionally lists events), or look for advertisements at expatriate hangouts like Elite restaurant (☞ Dining, *above*).

American Cultural Center. ⊠ *12 Shar'a Pharana,* ☎ *03/481–4305.*
British Cultural Center. ⊠ *9 Shar'a Batalsa,* ☎ *03/481–0199.*
Cervantes Institute. ⊠ *101 Shar'a al-Horreya,* ☎ *03/492–0214.*
French Cultural Center. ⊠ *30 Shar'a Nabi Daniel,* ☎ *03/492–0804.*
German Cultural Center. ⊠ *10 Shar'a Batalsa,* ☎ *03/483–9870.*
Greek Cultural Center. ⊠ *18 Shar'a Sidi al-Metwalli,* ☎ *03/482–1598.*
Italian Cultural Center. ⊠ *52 Shar'a al-Horreya,* ☎ *03/482–0258.*
Russian Cultural Center. ⊠ *5 Shar'a Batalsa,* ☎ *03/482–5645.*

There are a couple of annual or biennial festivals that don't on their merits alone warrant a trip to Alex but are worth a visit if you're in town when they're on. The **Alexandria Biennial** is a festival of international and local artists held in October in even-numbered years at the Museum of Fine Arts, which has been renamed in honor of Husayn Sobhi. The **International Film Festival** is held every September at local theaters. Chaotically organized, it is regarded mainly as a chance to see fleeting nudity on screen (there is censorship the rest of the year). The festival occasionally brings interesting art films.

Nightlife

The joke among foreign residents in Alex is that if you want nightlife, go to Cairo. In fact, things aren't quite that dire, but you'll still find that your nocturnal activities lean toward the wholesome, rather than the iniquitous. Some top-end hotels have what pass for discos, and the Salamlek and Cecil have casinos, but the city as a whole is definitely quieter than the capital.

Bars

Alexandria is a conservative town, so drinking here feels a bit like a return to the days of the speakeasy, with tiny, hidden-away bars that work hard to keep a low profile. Of course, getting into the sense you're doing something illicit can make it more fun. If that doesn't appeal, stick to the five-star hotels, which have a better selection of drinks, albeit in generic surroundings.

Far 'n' Away (Au Privé). No speakeasy feel here: this Old West–theme place has two restaurants (☞ Dining, *above*) and a comfortable and well-stocked bar. They even have two-for-one happy hours. ⊠ *14 Shar'a Fu'ad (a.k.a. Shar'a al-Horreya) east of Nabi Daniel, Manshiya,* ☎ *03/483–1881. AE, V.*

Cap d'Or (a.k.a. Sheikh 'Ali). This modest place is blessed with a gorgeous old Art Nouveau bar, and it serves a range of Stellas (beers) along with some cognacs. Beware: the management tries to ply you with supposedly free snacks that aren't free and gives a commission to any of the small-time agents who escort you through the door. Ascertain the price of everything before you accept it, and turn down anything you didn't order—the bar is beautiful enough to be worth the hassle. It's on the small street that runs south from Sa'd Zaghlul next to the Sofianopoulo café. ⊠ *4 Shar'a Adib, Manshiya,* ☎ *03/483–5177. No credit cards. Closes around 3 AM.*

Centro do Portugal. The Centro feels more like the British Isles than Iberia. No matter, it's a central element in expatriate life. The place uses a card system for its fairly pricey drinks, which means that there is effectively a £e45 minimum charge, spread out over however many times you visit. Add to that a £e5 ticket per person to get in and a £e5 cover charge if you eat, and the bottom line is that talking to Westerners is the only real appeal here. The food, whatever local partisans may tell you, is mediocre. ⊠ *42 Shar'a Abdel Kader (next to Dr. Ragab's Papyrus Museum), Roushdi,* ☎ *03/847–599. No credit cards.* ☉ *3 PM–midnight, later on Thurs.*

Spitfire Bar. This is a real sailor's bar: banknotes and bumper stickers from all over the world cover the walls, and there's a yellowing advertisement for the marines by the cash register, a fairly tame poster of a woman in a wet T-shirt, and the inevitable dogs-playing-pool carpet. But the atmosphere could not be more congenial—it's almost sedate—and there isn't a hint of sleaze to be found anywhere. The Spitfire is just north of Shar'a Sa'd Zaghlul on Shar'a Ancienne Bourse. ⊠ *7 Shar'a Ancienne Bourse, Manshiya,* ☎ *03/480–6503. No credit cards.* ☉ *Daily about noon–midnight.*

SHOPPING

Alexandria is not a shopping city. There is little to buy here that you can't do better finding in Cairo, where the selection is much greater. If you're looking for chain stores, try Shar'a Suriya in Roushdi, Alexandria's most upscale neighborhood, 15 minutes east of downtown by taxi. But even there the options are limited.

Markets

The **Attarine Market** is the best, if slightly informal, source for reproduction furniture, old books, and antiques (☞ Downtown Alexandria, *above*). The other markets in Alexandria tend to be more basic and practical, selling kitchen items or cheap clothes. There is a **flea market** at the back end of the Attarine Market, and clothes are sold in the streets west of Maydan Orabi. Perhaps the most visually interesting is the **produce market,** which begins at Maydan al-Gumhorreya in front of the main train station and runs west for a mile.

Shoes

Downtown has a breathtaking number of shoe stores, but most of shoes are of poor quality. The best are on Falaki Street (try the Armenian-owned **Gregoire** or **Fortis**) where, given enough time, the *chaussuriers* can produce custom-made shoes at a fraction of the price they would be in Europe or the United States.

ALEXANDRIA A TO Z

Arriving and Departing

By Bus

Superjet (☎ 02/482–4391 in Cairo) and **West Delta Bus Company** (☎ 02/765–582 in Cairo) run air-conditioned deluxe buses to Alexandria from Cairo every half hour from around 5 AM to midnight. Tickets cost £e20. Buses depart Cairo from Maydan Abdel Monem Riyad under the overpasses in front of the Ramses Hilton and take up to three hours, depending on traffic. They drop you off behind Sidi Gabr railway station, where they in turn depart for Cairo. The railway station is between downtown and Montazah, so you need to take a taxi from the station to get to either place.

By Car

Unless you plan to continue on to remote areas of the Mediterranean coast west of Alex, there is little reason to come by car. Taxis within the city are inexpensive, and parking is so difficult that a car is more trouble than it's worth. On top of that, the two highways connecting Cairo and Alexandria—the Delta and Desert roads—are both plagued by fatal car crashes. If you still want to come by car, the Desert Road, which starts near the pyramids in Giza, is the faster, taking roughly three hours. If you do come by car, avoid driving at night.

By Plane

Flying to Alex from Cairo will end up taking longer than catching a train, which is why so few people do it. Taking into account ground transport to and from the airports, frequent delays of flights, and having to get to the airport an hour before your flight, the half-hour flight doesn't save any time.

By Train

Trains are by far the most comfortable and convenient option for getting to and from Alexandria, and the schedule and ticket prices are the same in either direction. There are three trains: the *Torbini* (£e22–£e32; departs at 8 AM, 2 PM, and 7 PM; and takes 2¼ hours), the *Spanish* (£e17–£e22; departs at 9 AM, noon, 3 PM, and 6 PM; takes 2¼ hours), and the *French* (£e17–£e22; eight per day; takes 3 hours). The *Torbini* and *Spanish* are both modern and well-maintained, but even the *French* is comfortable. Seats are reserved, and tickets are best bought a day in advance—a laborious process that requires a trip to the station. If you take your chances, there are almost always seats available for same-day travel, except on the morning Torbini.

In Cairo station, the first-class ticket windows are in the back corner (look for the Misr Insurance ad above the entrance); the second-class windows are in another room, down three steps to the left. In Misr Station in Alexandria, a sign in English shows where to purchase first- and second-class tickets.

When arriving in Alex, do not get off at the first station in the city, Sidi Gabr. The main station is Misr Station, at the end of the line.

Getting Around

By Car

If you are reckless enough to elect to drive to Alex, you'll find traffic relatively orderly compared to that of Cairo. Streets are less crowded, and drivers are better about obeying traffic regulations. The governor has even instituted a no-horns policy, complete with wooden cut-out policemen at intersections to remind drivers.

The main road in Alexandria is the Corniche—technically 26th of July Street, but no one calls it that—which runs along the waterfront from Qayt Bay Fort all the way to Montazah. East of Eastern Harbor, the Corniche is mostly called Tariq al-Geish. Unless you park on a hill, be sure to leave the your car in neutral, because people will want to push it around a bit to maximize parking space.

By Minibus

Although most bus routes are too convoluted to bother with, a constant stream of minibuses make the Corniche run night and day. Flag them down anywhere, using a hand signal to point the direction you want to go, then pile in. They are are shockingly cheap (25p to Stanley, say, and 50p to Montazah) and, if anything, too fast. There are two catches to minibus travel: first, you have to know the name of the district (Manshiya, Sporting, Montazah, and so forth) you want to go to, because you will need to shout it in the window to the driver, who will let you know if he goes there. Second, you have to know what your destination looks like so you can tell the driver to stop. It's easier than it sounds and your fellow passengers will always help you out.

By Taxi

Taxis are the best way to get around. They are very inexpensive, and you can flag them down almost anywhere. If you're alone and male, you're generally expected to sit in the front; women and couples can sit in the back. The reason for the men-in-front rule is that the driver might try to pick up another passenger en route—it's standard practice, so don't be surprised.

Drivers don't use their meters, so you will have to guess at the appropriate fare. A ride within downtown should be £e2 to £e3; from downtown to Montazah (15–30 minutes), roughly 6 km (10 mi) about £e8 to £e10. If you look rich, expect to pay a bit more—this is a progressive system: elderly widows often pay nothing—and prices double, at a minimum, if a driver picks you up at a five-star hotel. There are no call services, but major hotels will always have taxis waiting.

By Tram

Picturesque and cheap, trams are likely to take four to five times longer to get where you're going than a taxi would. The main station is Raml, near Maydan Sa'd Zaghlul (officials are considering moving the station a block or two east). Buy tickets on board.

Numbers are marked in Arabic on cards in the front windows. Blue trams (20p) run east: numbers 1, 2, 6, and 8 terminate at al-Nasser (formerly Victoria) College, Tram 3 at Sidi Gabr (by the sea; a 2hr trip), Tram 4 at Sidi Gabr Station, and Tram 5 at San Stefano. Yellow trams (15p) run west: Tram 16 goes to Pompey's Pillar (a 40-min trip), Tram 11 to the Nouzha Gardens, and Tram 15 to Ras al-Tin.

Contacts and Resources

Car Rentals

You can rent a car without a driver from **Avis** (⊠ Cecil Hotel, Maydan Sa'd Zaghlul, Raml Station, ☎ 03/480–7055) or with a driver from **Alexandria Limousine** (⊠ 5 Albert Shar'a al-Awal, Smouha, ☎ 03/422–2999).

Consulates

British Consulate. ⊠ *3 Shar'a Mina, Roushdi,* ☎ *03/546–7001.*
U.S. Consulate. ⊠ *110 Shar'a al-Horreya,* ☎ *03/482–1911.*

Emergencies

Ambulance (☎ 123); **fire brigade** (☎ 180); **police** (☎ 122).

There are three major **hospitals** in Alexandria: **German Hospital** (⊠ 56 Shar'a Abdel Salam Aref, Saba Basha, ☎ 03/588–1806); **Smouha Medical Centre** (⊠ 14 Shar'a May, Smouha, ☎ 03/420–2652); **El-Medina al-Tebbaya Hospital** (⊠ Shar'a Ahmed Shawky, Mustafa Kamel, ☎ 03/852–150). Their emergency rooms do not have separate phone numbers.

English-Language Bookstores

Dar al-Maaref. (⊠ 42 Shar'a Sa'd Zaghlul, Raml Station, ☎ 03/480–7644). This bookstore has a few reference texts, Western classics, and used books upstairs.

El-Maaref. (⊠ 44 Shar'a Sa'd Zaghlul, Raml Station, ☎ 03/483–3303). The best of a limited set of options, al-Maaref has a small selection of foreign-language (particularly French) novels and guidebooks in the back.

For **newspapers and magazines,** there is a very good newsstand in front of the post office at Raml Station—which could be forced to move pending the reorganization of the tram system—and a smaller one near the entrance to the Metropole Hotel.

Guided Tours

There is little reason to take a guided tour in Alex, given the limited historical remains and easy transportation. If you do want a guide, make arrangements through your hotel (or any top-end hotel, if you're staying elsewhere), which will have special relationships with particular companies. This should offer a modest guarantee of quality in a market saturated with imposters.

Late-Night Pharmacies

Alexandria has no shortage of pharmacies, most of which are open until 11 PM. In addition, a couple are open until about 1 AM: **Roushdi** (⊠ 423 Shar'a al-Horreya, Roushdi, ☎ 03/542–8018); **Essaf** (⊠ 155 Shar'a Muhammad Karim, Manshiya, ☎ 03/480–0772). **Oxford** (⊠ 10 Kuliat al-Teb, Raml Station, ☎ 03/483–6720) is a 24-hour pharmacy.

Travel Agencies

Bon Voyage. ⊠ *12 Shar'a Salah Salem, Manshiya,* ☎ *03/480–9043.*
De Castro. ⊠ *33 Shar'a Salah Salem, Manshiya,* ☎ *03/483–5779.*
Thomas Cook. ⊠ *15 Maydan Sa'd Zaghlul, Raml Station,* ☎ *03/484–7830.*

Visitor Information

Tourist Information Center. The maps and brochures here are of poor quality, but the multilingual staff is easily the most helpful of any government office in the country. ⊠ *Maydan Sa'd Zaghlul, Raml Station,* ☎ *03/484–3380.* ☉ *Daily 8–6.*

4 The Nile Valley and Lake Nasser

From the implacable nobility of its pharaonic monuments to the raw strength of the Aswan High Dam, the Nile Valley is arguably the world's most enduring nexus of human striving for greatness. Natural beauty is fused with historic destiny as nowhere else on the planet. Stark desert borders verdant fields and silvery palm groves, and the diamond gleam of the late afternoon sun plays on the mighty river. Prepare yourself for a dose of pure iconography.

We made from water every living thing.
–Koranic verse

It flows through old hushed Egypt and its sands,
Like some grave mighty thought threading a dream.
–Leigh Hunt

By Maria
Golia, Salima
Ikram, and
Nathalie
Walschaerts

THE **ULTIMATE PROOF** of Herodotus's claim that "Egypt is a gift of the Nile" is visible on a flight from Cairo to Upper Egypt. From the air the Nile is a thin blue line, fringed with green, wending its way through a limitless horizon of sand. You realize that this is the Sahara, and that here, on the edge of the world's harshest desert, Africa's greatest city and Egypt's 62 million souls rely on one river's undiminished bounty.

Until very recently, the Nile was a principle trade route between the interior and the Mediterranean. And Upper Egypt, the Nile Valley south of Abydos, was a gateway to Africa. Because of the ease of access it afforded, the river shaped destinies: Nubia, Sudan, and Ethiopia alternately benefited from trade and suffered the predations of pharaohs. Now, perhaps more than ever, the 6,650 km (4,160 mi) of the world's longest river bind the fates of nine countries—Burundi, Ethiopia, Egypt, Kenya, Rwanda, Sudan, Tanzania, Uganda, and Zaire—by the common need to share this precious resource.

Cairenes take for granted modern control of the Nile—they open their faucets complacently even if they don't *always* obtain the desired results—but in antiquity the river and its capricious annual floods were endowed with divinity and honored with all the force of empire. The flood waters acted as god and teacher, as the ancients learned the movements of the stars and devised calendars in order to predict the arrival of the inundation.

The Nile was the pharaohs' vehicle for empire building. It was the carriage road for troops, trade, and the massive granite blocks quarried in Aswan—the temples that line its banks from al-Minya to Abu Simbel glorify both the ancient gods and the Egyptians' ingenuity in putting the river's power and wealth to work. The river also made agriculture and the feeding of the population—the work force—so easy: Herodotus noted in 460 BC that the Egyptians "gather in the fruits of the earth with less labor than any other people." Having mastered several straightforward irrigation techniques still in use today, farmers sowed their seeds and harvested two annual crops from the rich silt that the floods left behind.

No other river and no other ancient civilization has so fired the imagination of the modern West. But, aside from the works of ancient Greek, Roman, and Arab historians, and an antagonistic contact during the Crusades, the West remained essentially ignorant of Islamic culture and the marvels of the pharaohs until the late 1700s. At that time, Egypt's population was nearing 2.5 million, a mere third of what it had been at the time of the pharaohs. Alexandria's ancient glory had faded to ruin. Cairo later thrived under the Mamluks (1250–1517). And the people of the Upper Nile lived in relative isolation, working the land as they had for millennia.

The colonial predations of the West would bring this "long Egyptian night"—the phrase belongs to historian Alan Moorehead—to an end. In 1798, Napoléon looted his way across the Mediterranean, occupied Egypt, and briefly cut off the British trade route to India. He brought with him a group of savants who meticulously recorded everything they saw. Their images enthralled the West and inspired a fascination with the Nile and Egypt—not to mention wanderlust—that is still strong.

While other valiant travelers made it here well before Napoléon, his exploits heralded an age of African exploration. An urge to find the Nile's sources swept the world with a fever rivaled only by the space race of the 1950s and '60s. Back in the days of ancient Egypt, in AD 150, Ptolemy the geographer drew a map attributing the origins of the river to a place called the Mountains of the Moon. As it happens, he wasn't too far off. British explorer John Speke identified the source in 1862 as the vast Lake Victoria, which straddles the borders of Uganda, Kenya, and Tanzania. This is the headwater reservoir of the White Nile—the longer western branch of the river above its fork at Khartoum, in Sudan. That of the Blue Nile—the eastern branch above Khartoum—was later determined to be Ethiopia's Lake Tana, and for the rest of the 19th century, the river flowed on, "impervious to time," as Moorehead put it.

In 1902 the British built the first Aswan dam to conserve late-summer flood waters for the low-water season and increase agricultural output. As the population grew, these reserves were no longer sufficient. The building of the Aswan High Dam in the 1960s altered the river's character dramatically, putting an end to the seemingly eternal and sometimes devastating annual floods. But the dams were just technological updates on what men have been doing for ages: tapping the river's power.

That power lies at the heart of the current administration's plans to expand Egypt's arable land. Today, the population is crammed into 4 percent of the country's total area. If present land reclamation schemes are realized, that could grow to more than 20 percent over the next few decades. Canals are under construction in the northern Sinai near the Nile Delta, likewise in the southern part of the Western Desert, where the Lake Nasser reservoir will sustain new agricultural communities.

The construction of the massive Aswan High Dam was a blessing and a curse for the varied populaces living on the banks of the Nile. For although the dam generates electricity and ensures a water supply, the birth of Lake Nasser was a death sentence for the region that it flooded: Nubia, which extends from the river's First Cataract (rapids), near Aswan, to the Fourth Cataract, more than 750 km (500 mi) south in Sudan. The region's name is said to come from the pharaonic word *nub* (gold), although Nubia itself was referred to in texts as "Ta-Seti," the "land of the bow." Established in prehistoric times, this agriculture- and trade-based civilization flourished under pharaonic domination. Then around 760 BC, Nubian kings of the "Kushite" 25th Dynasty (760–656 BC) gained ascendancy in Egypt and ruled as pharaohs for 100 years.

It is a paradox that Nubia's inundation resulted in a greater knowledge of its civilization than we would have if it had been left to bake in the desert heat. UNESCO's Nubian campaign performed an archaeological survey of the area that shed much light on the region's role throughout the pharaonic age and into the Greco-Roman, Christian, and Islamic periods. It also carried out the prodigious task of salvaging the ancient monuments that Lake Nasser would have submerged had they been left in place.

The creation of Lake Nasser is the latest example of Egypt's seemingly inexhaustible ability to transform and renew itself. It is a country that

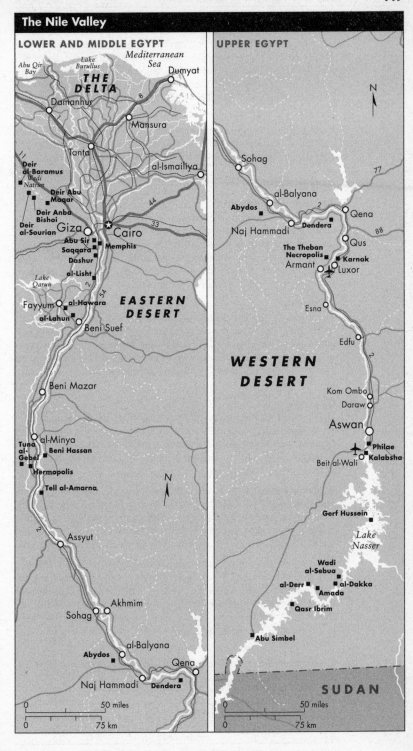

The Nile Valley

LOWER AND MIDDLE EGYPT

UPPER EGYPT

has submitted to the incursions of empire after empire, each of which made its contributions. From the brilliance of the pharaohs to the intellectual transfusions of the Persians and the Greeks, the stringent order of the Romans, the modernizing colonialist machinations of the French and the British, and the current U.S. cultural invasion, Egypt has always known how to absorb without being absorbed. It is a nation whose character remains ineluctably intact, and at the heart of this unique persona lies the Nile.

Note: For information on multiday trips on the Nile or Lake Nasser and individual reviews of boats, *see* Chapter 5. And for fuller descriptions of ancient Egyptian gods and rulers, *see* Chapter 8.

Pleasures and Pastimes

Ancient Monuments

The Nile Valley south of al-Minya is virtually an open-air museum, and it is the reason that most people travel to Egypt. Paintings, relief carvings, monumental statuary, dazzling tombs cut into mountainsides, and some of the finest architecture ever built—the ancient wonders of the valley never cease. And with archaeologists continuing to search for antiquities, the discoveries, too, never cease.

Bicycling

The Luxor Corniche is a great place to cycle, especially when you get off the main drag and into the rural area to the south. The West Bank landscape is also good for biking. The new bridge allows you to cross to it if you want to go the long way, or take your bike across on a ferry. Many hotels rent bicycles for the day, and bike stands sprout seasonally on the Corniche.

Dining

Upper Egypt may not be an epicurean paradise, but the standard fare of soups, salads, *mezze* (hot and cold appetizers), grilled meats, and *tagines* (earthenware-baked vegetables, meat, or chicken in a tomato-based sauce, variously spiced) can be perfectly satisfying when well prepared.

Alcohol is served except where mentioned. Egyptian Stella beer is quite good, and wine is reasonably priced. Be sure to taste wines carefully, however, because some producers overuse methane in the fermentation process. If you get a bad bottle—which would have a telltale tang of methane—drink no further. The effects of the toxin can be quite harmful.

The variable city tax on restaurants, combined with service charges, can total as much as 26%. Check menus to verify how each restaurant operates. Unless you are in a major hotel, consider tipping even if a service charge is included in the bill: waiters are not well paid, and the courtesy will be appreciated. If service is not charged, 10%–15% is a reasonable tip. As a rule, most hotel restaurants are open to the general public.

Reservations are recommended at all hotel restaurants.

CATEGORY	COST*
$$$$	over £e120
$$$	£e65–£e120
$$	£e35–£e65
$	under £e35

per person including the variable city tax and service charge.

Lodging

In Luxor and Aswan, hotel standards have little to do with the star rating you'll see in the lobbies. They usually fall into three categories, which rise and fall according to room rates: the luxurious, the mediocre, and the decrepit. We include only the best in each category. Remember that rates are cheapest in summer—late April to the end of September—sometimes dramatically so, and many hotels will offer discounted rates in times of low occupancy regardless of the season.

It's best to ask for a Nile view, slightly more pricey than a garden view, and specify the bed size you want when making reservations, because many double rooms come with twin beds. Half- and full-board supplements are usually available, and you may want to take advantage of them if you stay at a hotel with good restaurants. Most hotels arrange transportation from airport to hotel if requested.

If you choose to stay at a place that has no pool, be aware that many hotels open their pools to nonguests for a small fee (around $6). In Luxor, the splendid Club Med includes a beverage in its pool fee, the Sheraton is on a peninsula extending into the Nile, and the Hilton has a peaceful Nile-side garden and pool. In Aswan, the Basma Hotel and the Isis have good pools.

In both Luxor and Aswan, you can consult hotel staff on taxi and felucca rates, which are fixed either by the hour or the length of your trip. Most hotels can also arrange sightseeing excursions.

Several Aswan hotels are located on islands with regular ferry services to the town.

CATEGORY	COST*
$$$$	over $150
$$$	$100–$150
$$	$40–$100
$	under $40

All prices are for a double room in high season, tax and breakfast included.

Felucca Sailing

Moving at the speed of the wind on one of the traditionally-rigged sailboats that ply the waters of the Nile is a sure way to turn back the clock. You can find one anywhere on the Corniche (riverside road) in Luxor or Aswan. The price of a ride is $7 per hour (this is negotiable). Sunset and sunrise are the most exquisite times to set sail. The Luxor Hilton has beautifully presented felucca breakfasts, lunches, and dinners on one of their own boats for about $30 per person. Other riverside hotels in Luxor and Aswan have feluccas moored beside them as well, and picnics might be available.

Exploring the Nile Valley and Lake Nasser

If you are just getting to know Egypt, sifting through all the sight names—not to mention the ancient gods and rulers—can make your head spin. First, spend plenty of time looking at maps to locate the sights. Also refer to Nile Valley Monuments at a Glance, *below,* for a quick rundown on the monuments by name, location, and importance.

Most Upper Nile sights lie near the towns of Luxor and Aswan, and private taxis are by far the easiest way to get around. You can get to the more out-of-the-way monuments at Abydos (which is not always open; check before you go) and Dendera, both north of Luxor, on day trips. The temples at Esna, Edfu, and Kom Ombo and the Daraw Camel Market can also be taken on in a day, en route from Luxor to Aswan, or vice versa. From Aswan, you can take a day trip to Kom

Ombo and the camel market. The Aswan High Dam and the point of departure for Lake Nasser cruises is just a short distance from town, as are the docks for boats going to the island temples of Philae and Kalabsha. Abu Simbel, south of Aswan on Lake Nasser, is either a short flight or a grueling full-day trip involving three-hour drives each way through the desert. Bear in mind that the road from Aswan to Abu Simbel is undergoing repairs, and security checkpoints are being installed.

Because of the tragic incident in November 1997 at Deir al-Bahri, where terrorists killed 68 tourists, there is a much more noticeable presence of security personnel in Upper Egypt. As part of increased security measures, travel between Luxor and Aswan by road is done in police-accompanied convoys that leave early in the morning and stop together at the temples along the way. This limits your freedom of movement, but it also provides for your safety. Always travel with your passport; you'll need to present it at checkpoints.

Aside from these understandable inconveniences, it must be said that Egypt is a remarkably safe country, with one of the lowest crime rates in the world (commonly estimated as second to Japan). The massacre at Luxor was abhorred by Egyptians, a peaceful and hospitable people whose kindness you will doubtless find numerous occasions to enjoy.

Nile Valley Monuments at a Glance

Abu Simbel, Temples of Ramesses II and Nefertari (western shore of Lake Nasser, 280 km [175 mi] south of Aswan): Ramesses II's most awesome work, originally carved out of a cliff face; its relocation, to prevent its being submerged by Lake Nasser, was a tremendous feat of engineering.

Abydos, Temple of Osiris (West Bank, 150 km [95 mi] northwest of Luxor): Seti I's New Kingdom monument with refined relief carvings and paintings; an artistic high point in Egyptian history.

Beit al-Wali, Temple of Amun-Re (New Kalabsha Island, Lake Nasser): a small temple to the sun god, with bright paintings and an atmospheric island setting.

Deir al-Bahri, Mortuary Temple of Hatshepsut (West Bank, Theban Necropolis): one of the world's most inspired works of architecture, set into a cliff, with fine paintings and relief work and a delightful chapel to the goddess Hathor.

Deir al-Medina, the Workers' Village (West Bank, Theban Necropolis): jewel-box-like tombs with paintings of daily life made by and for the artisans who decorated the Theban Necropolis.

Dendera, Temple of Hathor (West Bank, 65 km [40 mi] north of Luxor): one of two examples of a complete ancient Egyptian temple, with roof; unique for its Hathor-head columns and relief of Cleopatra on its back wall.

Edfu, Temple of Horus (West Bank, 115 km [72 mi] south of Luxor): for its riverside location and its scale, *the* Greco-Roman temple to see; like Dendera, a complete temple, but far more impressive.

Kalabsha, Temple of Osiris, Isis, and Madulis (New Kalabsha Island, Lake Nasser): atmospheric for its island setting, and rarely crowded; built by Augustus Caesar.

Kom Ombo, Temple of Haroeris and Sobek (East Bank, 40 km [25 mi] north of Aswan): sited on a bend in the Nile, the only double temple (dedicated to two gods) extant.

Medinet Habu, Temple of Ramesses III (West Bank, Theban Necropolis): Built as a fortress and noted for its Migdol (Palestinian-style) gate; site of the first sit-in labor strike.

Philae Island, Temple of Isis (8 km [5 mi] south of Aswan): the most romantic island-in-the-Nile temple site; the last bastion of ancient Egyptian religious practice before Christianity eclipsed paganism.

Ramesseum (West Bank, Theban Necropolis): Ramesses II's mortuary temple; its fallen colossi indirectly inspired Shelley's poem "Ozymandias."

Tell al-Amarna (East Bank, Middle Egypt): site of the capital of the protomonotheistic (to ancient Egyptians heretical) pharaoh Amenhotep IV, later called Akhenaten.

Temple of Karnak (East Bank, Luxor): the world's largest stone religious monument.

Temple of Luxor (East Bank, Luxor): Elegant and comprehensible where Karnak is massive; the obelisk and colossi of its riverside facade convey the proper sense of what approaching an Egyptian temple was like in ancient times.

Tombs of Beni Hasan (East Bank, Middle Egypt): Middle Kingdom tombs of the nobility; lively paintings with entertaining scenes of daily life.

Tombs of the Nobles (West Bank, Theban Necropolis): extraordinarily detailed and beautifully rendered and colored paintings of scenes from daily life.

Valley of the Kings (West Bank, Theban Necropolis): famous royal burial places painted and carved with scenes from the *Book of the Dead* and other instructions for the afterlife.

Valley of the Queens (West Bank, Theban Necropolis): tomb of Nefertari and princes; superbly painted images of the ancient gods.

Great Itineraries

There are two questions to answer when you approach a trip to the Nile Valley: How serious are you about seeing ancient monuments and art? And do you want to take a Nile or a Lake Nasser cruise? If you want to see only the major monuments, your travel plans will be much simpler. You can confine yourself to Luxor, Aswan, and Abu Simbel, and you won't need any more than three to five days—five minimum if you decide to take a cruise. If, on the other hand, you want to see a fully representative group of ancient sights, you will need to arrange more time-consuming trips north of Luxor to Abydos and/or Dendera, between Luxor and Aswan to Edfu and Kom Ombo, and possibly even farther north of Luxor to Middle Nile Valley sights like Tell al-Amarna and the Tombs of Beni Hasan. The rewards for these longer trips can be tremendous, in part because you will be departing somewhat from the beaten path, and can include local events like the Daraw camel market.

If you decide to take a three- or four-day cruise, you will be able to see some of the in-between sights, like Edfu and Kom Ombo, or lakeside temples that you can only get to on a Lake Nasser cruise. Cruises skimp on Luxor sights, however, and don't include sights in Aswan, so you will need to allow a day or more on both ends to see the monuments in and around both towns. Longer seven-day cruises on the Nile continue north of Luxor to the Temple of Hathor at Dendera. (☞ Chapter 5.)

IF YOU HAVE 3 DAYS

On the morning of the first day, fly from Cairo to **Abu Simbel** to see Ramesses II's colossal monument; the plane will then take you to 🎦 **Aswan** for lunch. In the afternoon make your way to the **Aswan High Dam** and an island: either **Philae** for its Temple of Isis, **Elephantine** for its ancient temples, or **Kitchener's Island** for a walk through its sensational gardens. The **Nubia Museum** is open in the evening, and after dinner you can hit the **souk** to shop for souvenirs. Overnight in Aswan. In the morning take an early (7 AM) jaunt to the **Unfinished Obelisk,** then fly to 🎦 **Luxor.** After you check into your hotel, cross the Nile to the West Bank and take on two of the **Tombs of the Nobles** and either **Medinet Habu** or the **Ramesseum.** End the afternoon, when the light is best, at the **Temple of Luxor.** After dinner, go to the **Temple of Kar-**

nak for its sound-and-light show, or save it for the third night; on the off night go the **Luxor Museum,** or stroll through town and stop at the **souk** if you missed Aswan's. Start early on the third morning at Queen Hatshepsut's temple, **Deir al-Bahri,** to see the morning light raking across its courts and colonnades, then head for the **Valley of the Kings.** See two tombs, then make your way to the **Valley of the Queens** either before or after lunch, depending on how the time goes. Cross back to the East Bank to give yourself the afternoon at the **Temple of Karnak,** when the slanting light brings the heiroglyphs into sharp focus.

IF YOU HAVE 5 DAYS

Depending on your interests, you can expand on the three-day itinerary in a few ways. Start in ☒ **Luxor** and allow three days in and around town. Add **Deir al-Medina** (the town of the artisans who built the West Bank monuments) to your itinerary, and space your visits to the West Bank necropolis sights and the East Bank temples so you have more time in each place. Give yourself time for an afternoon swim or tea at the **Winter Palace,** and spend a few hours on a felucca in the Nile. On the fourth morning, take a flight to **Abu Simbel** and get to ☒ **Aswan** by lunchtime. With the remaining day and a half, allow time to see more Nile islands—sailing in the cataract is one of the town's delights. On the fifth morning, you could take a camel trip to the ancient tombs and the abandoned **St. Simeon's Monastery** on the West Bank. Or if you're in town on a Tuesday, take a taxi downriver for a slice of local life at the early morning **Daraw Camel Market.** Or you could spend two days in Luxor and two in Aswan, taking the day in between to drive through **Edfu** and **Kom Ombo** to see the most interesting Ptolomaic temples on the river.

IF YOU HAVE 7 DAYS

If you are staying this long and not taking a cruise, your interests will very likely draw you to Seti I's New Kingdom temple at **Abydos,** north of Luxor, which you should combine with **Dendera**'s Greco-Roman Temple of Hathor. Make the trip between Luxor and Aswan to see **Edfu** and **Kom Ombo.** Spend three of the remaining five days in Luxor and two in Aswan, or reverse that if you would rather have more time to relax by the Nile in Luxor. If you can't resist the off-the-beaten-path allure of the stylized art of Akhenaten's Middle Nile capital, **Tell al-Amarna,** and the Middle Kingdom **Tombs of Beni Hasan,** plan two days around the Middle Nile town of **al-Minya** to see them. Allow for travel time by train, because it is the best way to get to Cairo from al-Minya and from al-Minya on to Luxor.

WHEN TO TOUR THE UPPER NILE

Traditionally, high season begins at the end of September, peaks around Christmas, and lasts until April. To avoid crowds, stay away at these times. But tourism slackened following the terrorist attack, and as a result prices dropped, so even the high-season hordes have thinned out. The heat kicks in as early as March in Upper Egypt—a dry, pollution-free heat that you can get used to. Evenings are always cool in the desert.

A season of *mulids* (religious feasts) occurs about a month before Ramadan, the Islamic month of fasting. Mulids are wonderful celebrations with music, dancing, and exotica, and in Luxor, the mulid of Abu Haggag is a much-anticipated event. Generally speaking, feast dates are not fixed, so inquire locally when they are scheduled. Remember that if you do travel during Ramadan—which will fall between January and March for the next few years—many people neither eat nor drink from sunrise until sunset, and life slows down considerably, especially in Upper Egypt.

THE MIDDLE NILE VALLEY: AL-MINYA TO TELL AL-AMARNA

Middle Egypt has a slew of extremely interesting monuments dating from all periods of Egyptian history. The major sites in the area that are easily accessible are the Middle Kingdom tombs of Beni Hasan, the New Kingdom town-site and tombs at Tell al-Amarna, the Greco-Roman tombs and catacombs at Tuna al-Gebel, and the Greco-Roman remains of al-Ashmunayn. Beni Hasan, Amarna, and Tuna al-Gebel are the most worthwhile sites, though al-Ashmunayn is intriguing if you are interested in more Classical-style remains.

You can visit almost all the Middle Valley sites in one to two days. Amarna is best done on its own, and Beni Hasan and Tuna al-Gebel are easily combined if you rent a taxi for the day. You could also combine Amarna and Beni Hasan in a day if pressed for time. Take plenty of food and water with you, as, for the most part, there is none at the sites.

al-Minya

260 km (160 mi) south of Cairo; 450 km (280 mi) north of Luxor.

The best place for a base in Middle Egypt is the bustling town of al-Minya, which the Italians developed. The town has several pleasant piazzas, gardens, and fine buildings, which, alas, are rapidly being knocked down and replaced by modern Egyptian concrete boxes.

Among the scattering of hotels in al-Minya, the **Akhenaten** (✉ Corniche al-Nil, ☎ 086/325–917, FAX 086/326–966, $) is a modern building on the Corniche—a three-star, and the best value by far. The **Lotus** (✉ 1 Shar'a Bur Sa'id, ☎ 086/324–500, FAX 086/324–576, $), a tall modern building on the north side of the town, has reasonable rooms and rates, two to three stars, and a good view from the rooftop restaurant. Food, generally European style, can be had in these hotels or at small local hostelries. The ubiquitous ful, tammia, and cushari are easily available, as are roasted chickens or kebabs with bread and salad.

Beni Hasan

25 km (15 mi) south of al-Minya.

This magnificent cemetery site is located on the east bank of the Nile. Beni Hasan is generally approached from the west bank by ferry, which shows the site to its best advantage: a narrow, vibrant strip of green bordering the river that suddenly ends in dramatically sloping limestone cliffs that stand out starkly against an intense blue sky. The cliffs are pierced by tombs (39) of local rulers that date to the Middle Kingdom (c. 2040–1640 BC). Generally only three or four are open to visitors.

From the ferry landing proceed by microbus (erratic) or walk (a 10-minute walk if one is slow) to the base of the cliffs and the ticket booth. From there it is a stiff climb up modern concrete stairs to the top of the cliff and the tombs. Along the way you pass shaft tombs (closed) for the less important people. The tombs of the wealthy and more important folk are in the upper portions of the cliff. There are three basic tomb types on the cliff, aside from the shaft tombs. The first has a plain facade and is single-chambered (11th Dynasty), the second is plain on the outside, but its chamber is columned, and the third type (12th Dynasty) has a portico in front and a columned chamber.

One is never sure which tombs are open, but generally the ones listed here are accessible. The lighting in the tombs is erratic, so bring a flashlight. A café at the base of the cliff provides cold drinks; plan to bring your own packed lunch.

Tomb of Kheti (No. 17), 11th Dynasty. Kheti was the governor of the Oryx Nome. Scenes on the walls show hunting, offerings, scenes of daily life, and the wrestlers that are typical of Beni Hasan. An attack on a fortress is also shown.

Tomb of Bakht III (No. 15), 11th Dynasty. Built for another governor of the Oryx Nome, this tomb contains seven shafts, which suggests that members of his family were buried with him. The wall paintings show hunting in the marshes and desert, weavers, counting livestock, potters, metal workers, wrestlers, and offering bearers. The desert hunt scenes are particularly interesting because they show some very bizarre mythological animals.

Tomb of Khnumhotep (No. 3), 12th Dynasty. This large tomb, entered between two proto-Doric columns, belonged to Khnumhotep, governor of the Oryx Nome and a prince besides. This tomb contains a statue of the deceased carved in the back wall, and the color of the paintings is much better preserved than in any of the other tombs. It is famous for its hunt scenes and scenes of foreign visitors to Egypt.

Tomb of Amenemhat (No. 2), 12th Dynasty. Not only was the tomb owner a nomarch, or governor, but he was also the military commander-in-chief of the area. This tomb has some entertaining scenes of musicians, knife-makers, and leather workers in addition to the usual daily-life scenes. ⊠ *Beni Hasan,* ☏ *no phone.* ▦ *£e12, £e5 for camera (without flash) per tomb.* ☉ *Daily 7–5*

Getting Around

Take a taxi from al-Minya to the ferry, and be sure to bargain. Then cross the Nile to the site. Have your taxi wait while you visit the site, then take you on to other sites in the area.

Tell al-Amarna

40 km (25 mi) south of Beni Hasan.

Little remains of the magnificent town of Akhetaten (horizon of the Sun Disk), which was founded by the apparently monotheist pharaoh Akhenaten in the late 18th Dynasty. Akhenaten is most famous for adjusting the focus of Egyptian religion from the cult of Amun to that of Aten, a solar deity depicted as a sun disk whose rays ended in hands. The pharaoh was the only person allowed to have close contact with the god, a regulation that highlighted the pharaoh's divinity and reduced the power of the priesthoods. Whether the change to Atenism was inspired by faith or by political acumen, or a combination of the two, is unclear. In addition to changing the state god, Akhenaten moved the royal residence and capital of Egypt to the brand-new city al-Amarna (Akhetaten), thus effectively crippling the towns of Memphis and Thebes. Akhetaten was quite an impressive city, but it has almost completely vanished. Indeed, it is hard to imagine this large expanse of barren desert as a bustling town busy with government workers, commerce, and artisans. The few visible remains include the foundations of the North Palace and the Small Aten Temple and one restored pillar.

The Northern Tombs are more easily visited than their southern counterparts and are quite interesting, although somewhat ruined. Not all the tombs are open, but they are all relatively similar in design and decoration. Most of the tombs consist of an outer court, a long hall and a broad hall, sometimes columned, and a statue niche. The tombs are decorated in the typical "Amarna" style, with depictions of the town and architecture and depictions of the pharaoh and his family rather than the tomb-owner. People tend to be shown with sharp chins, slightly distended bellies, large hips and thighs. Some tombs show evidence of being reused in the Coptic period, so watch out for crosses, niches, and fonts (Tomb 6). ⊠ *Tell al-Amarna,* ☎ *no phone.* 🎫 *£e12, £e5 for camera (without flash) per tomb; tractor prices range from £e5 to £e12.* ☼ *Daily 7–5*

Getting There

Hire a taxi and either cross the river at al-Minya and take the desert road to the site (not always easy), or, more traditionally, drive down to Deir Mawass and cross over by ferry. Purchase tickets on the east bank for the site as well as for the (relatively) ancient tractor that takes one around.

al-Ashmunayn (Hermopolis)

30 km (19 mi) south of al-Minya.

The site features a late Roman basilica, the only surviving large building of its kind in Egypt, as well as a giant statue of the god Thoth in the guise of a baboon. A large temple to Thoth, god of Ashmunayn, used to stand at the site, but is pretty much invisible today. ⊠ *al-Ashmunayn,* ☎ *no phone.* 🎫 *£e12, £e5 for camera (without flash) per tomb.* ☼ *Daily 7–5*

Tuna al-Gebel

10 km (6 mi) southwest of al-Ashmunayn.

Tuna al-Gebel was the necropolis of Hermopolis—a large and scattered site, its focal point being a cluster of Greco-Roman tombs. These tombs, built literally as houses for the dead, show an entertaining blending of Classical and Egyptian styles of art. The tomb of Petosiris is one of the best-preserved and is open to the public.

The mummy of Isadora, a woman drowned in the Nile in the second century AD, is on display in a nearby building; baksheesh the guard. The other major attraction of the site is the elaborate catacombs containing burials of ibis and baboons, animals sacred to the god Thoth. These date to the late Persian and Greco-Roman periods, and one can see some animal burials in situ. An embalming workshop is also visible at the entrance to the rather smelly catacombs. ⊠ *Tuna al-Gebel,* ☎ *no phone.* 🎫 *£e12, £e5 for camera (without flash) per tomb.* ☼ *Daily 7–5.*

THE UPPER NILE VALLEY: ABYDOS TO ASWAN

Traveling along the Nile takes you through both space and time. Ancient Egyptian civilization as we know it came alive around 3100 BC, when Narmer united Lower and Upper Egypt, and breathed its last in the 4th century AD during the simultaneous rise of Christianity and collapse of both paganism and the Roman empire. The monuments that you see are the accretions of centuries of dynastic power, ritual practice, artistic expression, and foreign interference that continually adapted and renewed an inspiring system of beliefs.

You don't need to know any of this to appreciate the beauty and refinement of the paintings in Seti I's temple at Abydos or the majesty of the temples at Karnak and Abu Simbel. Just consider the high level of societal organization that it took to conceive and create what the ancient Egyptians left behind. Looking back at their civilization from the second millennium of the Christian era, we are gazing eye-to-eye with our equals in ambition, achievement, and, in many ways, technology.

Abydos

150 km (94 mi) north of Luxor.

The drive to Abydos takes you through lush fields of sugarcane, waving palm trees, and picturesque mud-brick villages dotted with pigeon towers. At the end of the trip, the temple appears rather surprisingly amid a cluster of houses and shops, the desert stretching out behind them. Groups are not allowed to visit the temples here, so Abydos is a good place to break away from whatever crowds there might be farther upriver.

Abydos was one of the most sacred sites in ancient Egypt, because it was the supposed burial place of Osiris, god of the netherworld. The complex includes several temples, tombs, and sacred animal burials dating from the predynastic period onward. Now the only parts of the site accessible to visitors are the Osireion—the temple to Osiris—erected by Seti I (19th Dynasty, 1290–1279 BC) and the temple erected by his son, Ramesses II.

Admission fees cover both the Temple of Seti I and the Temple of Ramesses II. A café at the front of the temple provides cold drinks and light snacks. ⊠ *Mabed Seti,* ☎ *no phone.* 🎫 *£e12, cameras free.* ☉ *Oct.–May, daily 7–5; Sept.–June, daily 7–6.*

Seti I's Temple to Osiris (1306–1290 BC)

★ This low-lying temple, modestly stretching across the desert between a series of shops and houses, is one of the jewels of ancient Egypt. Less visited by groups than temples farther south, it is filled with exquisitely carved and colored reliefs that delight the eye and stir the soul. Seti I initiated construction of the temple complex, but he died before its completion, which left Ramesses II to finish it.

After passing the ticket booth, walk up to the ruined first pylon, which leads into the almost completely destroyed first courtyard built by Ramesses II. This first court contains two wells, and only the lower level of the court's enclosure wall survives. These remaining walls are decorated with scenes of Ramesses killing the enemies of Egypt and offering to the gods. The second court is similarly decorated. Beyond this are a portico and the entrance to the temple proper. The portico is carved and painted with scenes of Ramesses II offering to the gods and being granted a very long and prosperous reign in exchange.

From the portico, enter the **First Hypostyle Hall**, begun by Seti I and completed by Ramesses II. (A hypostyle hall is one in which interior columns support a roof; in most temples the ancient roofs caved in long ago.) This hall consists of 12 pairs of papyrus-style columns aligned to create seven aisles that lead to seven chapels set in the back wall of the Second Hypostyle Hall. The walls are decorated with scenes showing the pharaoh offering to Amun-Re (the sun god), preparing and dedicating the temple building, and offering to Thoth (god of writing and knowledge).

The next room is the **Second Hypostyle Hall**, built and decorated—with its decoration scheme *almost* completed—by Seti I. The exquisite

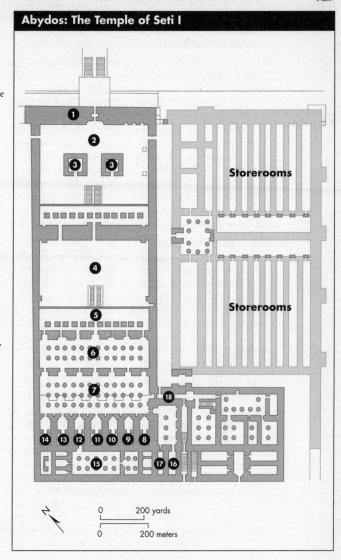

Abydos: The Temple of Seti I

quality of the relief carvings here stand in stark contrast to the cruder work commissioned by Ramesses II. Scenes include dedicatory texts of Seti I and show the pharaoh making offerings before various gods and receiving their blessings. A continuous row of fertility figures with *nome* (provinces of ancient Egypt) standards above their heads runs along below the main scenes.

The seven **chapels** off the rear wall are dedicated to various deities and are a rare feature in Egyptian temples. From left to right (east to west), they are dedicated to Seti I, Ptah (a creator god), Re Harakhte, Amun-Re, Osiris, Isis (goddess of magic), Horus (the god associated with kingship), Nefertum (a deity involved with creation), and Ptah-Sokar (a netherworld deity). Each chapel is decorated with scenes showing the daily temple ritual, which involved offerings, libations, and censing. The Osiris chapel leads to the Osiris complex, which shows Seti making offerings of wine, bread, incense, vases, and so forth, to various deities. The last rooms in the Osiris complex are mostly reconstructed.

This is where the mysteries of Osiris were performed; their exact nature remains, of course, mysterious—in other words, unknown to modern scholarship.

Beyond the chapels is a **hall** with two back rooms dedicated to Nefertum and Ptah-Sokar. The one on the right (west) is remarkable for its scenes showing the conception of Horus: as the story goes, Seth (who became the god of storms and deserts) had his brother Osiris, the king, killed and chopped up into pieces. Isis, Osiris's wife and a great magician, traveled throughout Egypt gathering the bits of her husband to remake him with magic. She found and reconstructed all of him, save his genitalia. These she fashioned out of mud, stuck them onto him, made them viable with magic, and, changing herself into a kite—no one is absolutely certain why this bird is her animal counterpart—placed herself on his member and thus conceived Horus. Later, Horus avenged his father's death and became king, and Osiris became king of the netherworld. Seth was exiled to distant places (☞ Edfu, *below*).

The **Gallery of Lists** leads left from the portico before the seven chapels out to the Osireion. On its walls is a list of gods and kings that is one of the cornerstones of Egyptian history. This king list notes the divine and semidivine (i.e., pharaonic) Egyptian rulers in the order of their reigns. Other rooms (a sacrificial butchery court, a hall of ritual barques), all of which are closed, lead off this passage. Another corridor, known as the corridor of the bulls, was named for a scene showing Ramesses II and one of his sons lassoing a bull before a god. A curious boat associated with Sokar, a god of the dead, is also carved on the wall.

Directly behind the temple lies the **Osireion**. Some scholars date the construction of this structure to the reign of Seti I, but the architectural style and massive quality of the building suggest that it is of an earlier, Old Kingdom (2625–2134 BC) date. It is built of quartzitic sandstone and granite, and only a portion of it bears inscriptions of Seti I, which are thought to have been added to the building long after it was constructed. The rest of the edifice is devoid of decoration. The Osireion includes built-in pools of different shapes—an unusual feature—that might represent the primeval chaotic ocean of Nun. Most of the chambers off the central courtyard are inaccessible because they are filled with water (a little poetic irony). South of the Osireion is an extension, the **long passage**, added by Merneptah, Ramesses II's successor. This is decorated with scenes from various books containing spells to ensure a safe passage to the afterworld.

Temple of Ramesses II (1290–1224 BC)

Some 300 yards northwest of the Seti I temple lies the Temple of Ramesses II. Its roof and most of the upper portions of its walls of are missing, but enough of it remains to give you a feeling for its layout and decoration. What remains of the decoration shows that this temple—unlike the inferior work that Ramesses commissioned to complete Seti I's temple—is close in style and quality to what was done during the reign of Seti I. And the vibrant reds, yellows, and bright green here are a joy to behold.

The first pylon and court are no longer in existence; instead, the entrance is through the semipreserved second pylon, which leads to a court surrounded by pillars decorated with the figure of Ramesses in an Osirid pose (as a mummy with arms crossed in front of his breast). The walls are carved and painted with scenes of Ramesses offering to various deities, animals being taken for sacrifice, and prisoners of war.

From the court, walk up to the portico leading to two pillared halls with chapels off of them. Scenes of captives, religious processions, and offerings made by the king to the various gods adorn the walls.

Dendera

65 km (40 mi) north of Luxor.

Dendera is a small village north of Luxor whose prime point of interest is its Temple of Hathor. The area is pleasantly green, and the drive provides an agreeable view of rural life in Egypt. The site of Dendera was occupied at least from the Old Kingdom onward, but it is the remains of the Late Period and Greco-Roman structures that are of interest. The site includes the main **Temple of Hathor,** two *mammisi* (gods' birth houses), a Coptic church, an asklepion (sanitorium), the remains of a sacred lake, and a small temple to Isis, as well as some other less visible monuments.

A café outside the temple offers snacks, cold drinks, and some very nice scarves. Admission includes all sights in the Temple of Hathor complex (☞ *below*). ⊠ *Mabed Denderah,* ☎ *no phone.* 🎫 *£e8, cameras free.* ☉ *Oct.–May, daily 7–5; June–Sept., daily 7–6.*

Temple of Hathor (4th Century BC–1st Century AD)

Hathor of Dendera was the goddess of love, beauty, music, and birth. She was often depicted as a cow, and in later periods of Egyptian history was syncretized with Isis. She was married to Horus of Edfu, and the two temples celebrated an annual festival, lasting about two weeks, when the statue of Hathor sailed upriver to Edfu to celebrate the divine marriage.

As you enter the temple grounds through stone portals, there is a dramatic view of the temple facade fronted by a row of Hathor-head columns and a decorated screen wall. The exterior of the temple is carved in relief with scenes of the pharaoh and divinities being suckled by goddesses, and of the pharaoh making offerings to various gods.

The portal leads into the **Outer Hypostyle Hall**, which consists of 24 tall columns (including the facade columns), all with Hathor-head capitals. The ceiling is carved and painted with a depiction of the night sky. The columns themselvs are densely decorated with scenes of the pharaoh making offerings to the gods and receiving their blessings in return. This very crowded, *horror vacui* (fear of blank spaces) decoration is typical of the Greco-Roman period.

The next room is the **Inner Hypostyle Hall,** with its six columns. Six small rooms open off this hall. These rooms are decorated with different scenes that supposedly illustrate what went on in them, or, more likely, what was stored in them. The first room on the left is the most interesting. Known as the **Laboratory,** it is where ritual perfumes and essences were prepared. The other rooms include a **Harvest Room, the Room of Libations,** and the **Treasury,** which is illustrated with carvings of jewelry and boxes containing precious metals.

This hall leads to the **First Vestibule,** where many of the daily offerings to Hathor would have been placed. Gifts included all kinds of food and drink: breads, fresh vegetables, joints of meat and poultry, beer, and wine. Staircases lead up to the **roof** (☞ *below*) from either side of the First Vestibule.

The **Second Vestibule** follows the first as a transitional area between the sanctuary and the rest of the temple. The **Sanctuary** was the most sacred spot in the temple and in antiquity would have contained an altar and a plinth supporting a *naos* (shrine) containing the sacred image of the goddess, probably either made of gold or gilded. The sanctuary is surrounded by a corridor, and several chapels lead off from it. The best of the chapels is the one immediately behind the sanctuary, because it contains a raised shrine reached by a ladder.

Dendera also has at least 32 **crypts** built into the walls and under the floor of the temple, hiding places for temple plates, jewelry, and statues. Some of the wall crypts would have permitted priests to hide behind different images of the gods and act as oracles. One of these, behind and to the right of the sanctuary, is open to the public. It is beautifully carved with scenes showing divinities. Look for the exquisite relief showing the god Horus in his falcon form.

On the right side of the temple's ground floor is another small and beautifully carved **chapel**. The roof shows the sky goddess, Nut, swallowing the sun and giving birth to it the next day, with Hathor emerging from the horizon.

Stairways, carved with priestly processions wending their way up the sides, lead from both sides of the First Vestibule to the **roof**, on which there are three chapels. An open chapel with Hathor-head columns (their capitals carved with reliefs of the face of the goddess) was used for solar rituals; the two closed chapels were used for the cult of Osiris. The eastern one of these, on the right as you face the temple, contains the cast of a famous zodiac ceiling—the most complete early zodiac, the original of which is in the Louvre in Paris. A metal staircase leads to the highest part of the roof, from which you can enjoy a wonderful panorama of the temple precincts and the surrounding landscape. Note the sacred lake enclosure (now dry) on the west side of the temple. The **temple exterior** is decorated with scenes of pharaohs and gods. The rear wall is particularly interesting, because it shows Queen Cleopatra VII—yes, the famous one, who was involved with Julius Caesar and Mark Antony, and Egypt's last pharaoh—presenting her son Caesarion to the gods as the next ruler of Egypt.

In an ancient Egyptian temple context, mammisi depict the birth of a god and are often concerned with the divinity of the king. The **mammisi** on the right side of the Temple of Hathor entrance is of the Roman period (built mainly by Trajan, who ruled from AD 98 to 117). It celebrates the birth of the god Ihi, son of Horus and Isis, as well as the divinity of the pharaoh. Ascend a short flight of stairs into a court; beyond it lies another courtyard with columns at the side. Two rooms then lead to the mammisi's **sanctuary**, which is illustrated with scenes of the divine birth and the suckling of the divine child by various divinities. The sanctuary is surrounded by an ambulatory, the outer portion of which is incompletely decorated.

Next to the Roman mammisi at the entrance to the Temple of Hathor lies a **Christian basilica** probably dating from the 5th century AD, making it one of the earliest intact Coptic buildings in Egypt. There is no roof, but the trefoil apse and basilical hall and several shell niches are still visible.

Next to the Coptic basilica are the ruins of an earlier **mammisi**—from the 30th Dynasty (381–343 BC) and later Ptolemaic period. Its decorative scheme is similar to that of the later, more intact mammisi.

Next in line stand the mud-brick remains of the temple's **sanitorium**, consisting of several small rooms and bathing areas for pilgrims. The pilgrims came to be healed by what we would now call dream therapy. They would sleep in the temple precincts and have dreams in which the gods came to them and cured them or told them what to do to be

Flying to France on Friday? Get Francs from Chase on Thursday. Call Currency To Go at 935-9935 for overnight delivery.

CHASE CURRENCY TO GO
935-9935

*O*r pounds for London. Or Deutschmarks for Düsseldorf. Or any of 75 foreign currencies. Call **Chase Currency To Go**^{SM} at **935-9935** in area codes 212, 718, 914, 516 and Rochester, N.Y.; all other area codes call 1-800-935-9935. We'll deliver directly to your door.* Overnight. And there are no exchange fees. Let Chase make your trip an easier one.

CHASE. The right relationship is everything.^{SM}

BONUS MILES MAKE GREAT SOUVENIRS.

Earn Miles With Your MCI Card.

Take the MCI Card along on this trip and start earning miles for the next one. You'll earn frequent flyer miles on all your calls and save with the low rates you've come to expect from MCI. Before you know it, you'll be on your way to some other international destination.

Sign up for MCI by calling 1-800-FLY-FREE

Earn Frequent Flyer Miles.

Is this a great time, or what? :-)

Easy To Call Home.

1. To use your MCI Card, just dial the WorldPhone access number of the country you're calling from.
2. Dial or give the operator your MCI Card number.
3. Dial or give the number you're calling.

# Bahrain	800-002
# Brunei	800-011
# China ✣	108-12
For a Mandarin-speaking operator	108-17
# Cyprus ♦	080-90000
# Egypt (CC) ♦ (Outside of Cairo, dial 02 first)	355-5770
# Federated States of Micronesia	624
# Fiji	004-890-1002
# Guam (CC)	1-800-888-8000
# Hong Kong (CC)	800-96-1121
# India (CC) ✣	000-127
# Indonesia (CC) ♦	001-801-11
Iran ÷	(Special Phones Only)
# Israel (CC)	1-800-940-2727
# Japan (CC) ♦	
To call using KDD ■	00539-121▶
To call using IDC ■	0066-55-121
To call using ITJ ■	0044-11-121
# Jordan	18-800-001
# Korea (CC)	
To call using KT ■	009-14
To call using DACOM ■	00309-12
Phone Booths ÷ Red Button 03, then press ★	
Military Bases	550-2255
# Kuwait	800-MCI (800-624)
Lebanon ÷ Collect Access	600-MCI (600-624)
# Macao	0800-131
# Malaysia (CC) ♦	1-800-80-0012
# Philippines (CC) ♦	
To call using PLDT ■	105-14
Collect access via PLDT in Filipino ■	105-15
Collect access via ICC in Filipino ■	1237-77
# Qatar ★	0800-012-77
# Saipan (CC) ÷	950-1022
# Saudi Arabia (CC) ÷	1-800-11
# Singapore	8000-112-112
# Sri Lanka (Outside of Colombo, dial 01 first)	440-100
# Syria	0800
# Taiwan (CC) ♦	0080-13-4567
# Thailand ★	001-999-1-2001
# United Arab Emirates ♦	800-111
Vietnam ●	1201-1022
Yemen	008-00-102

cured. The sanitorium contained several bathing areas lined with stones that were carved with spells and incantations. The water would run over the stones, taking the magic of the texts with it, and into the baths where pilgrims sat and received the magical waters' cures.

Behind the main temple is a small **Temple of Isis**, which has a strange, dual orientation: east–west as well as north–south. It contains scenes of Isis's divine birth and consists of a court, a small hypostyle hall, another columned hall, two chapels, and the sanctuary. Here, as in the main temple, a number of the images of the "pagan" gods were methodically defaced by the pious Copts.

Luxor and the Temple of Karnak: The East Bank

670 km (420 mi) south of Cairo; 210 (130 mi) north of Aswan.

Royal Thebes, Egyptian treasure-house of countless wealth, who boasts
her hundred gates . . .
–*The Iliad*

Poor Luxor! Along the banks is a row of tourist boats which nowadays infest the Nile from Cairo to the cataracts.
–*Pierre Loti, 1910*

Known in antiquity as Thebes, Luxor takes its name from the Arabic *Al Uqsur* (the palaces). It is a town that merits both poetry and a grain of pragmatism. One of the world's most popular destinations, Luxor lives (or dies) from tourism. But if a well-worn path has been trod to every site you'll see, Luxor's universal value in terms of art, natural beauty, and historic monuments is undeniable.

During the Old Kingdom—Egypt's first 1,000 years of history—Thebes was little more than a provincial capital. Around 2000 BC, a prominent Theban family won the struggle to unite Lower Egypt with Upper Egypt. Thebes enjoyed a period of prominence, and Egypt two centuries of peace. This was the Middle Kingdom (2040–1640 BC), the period when the sun god Amun-Re made his first appearance as the local deity.

The Hyksos invasion from the east ended this moment of stability, and the foreign rulers dominated the country for the next two centuries. After a series of battles, Thebans freed the nation from its oppressors, and an age of conquest and expansion began that extended Egypt's power as far east as the Euphrates River and as far south as Kush in Nubia.

This was the New Kingdom (1550–1070 BC), when Thebes was a center of trade, and the spoils of war passed through the hands of the newly empowered priests of Amun-Re, the deity who now became supreme among the gods. It was the priests' greed that brought about their downfall when the Kushite kings of Ethiopia came to conquer a capital weakened by corruption. They in turn struggled with the Assyrians, from Mesopotamia to the northeast, who plundered Thebes during the 7th century BC. But the Assyrians were fighting on too many fronts. The Kushites regained dominance, then native Egyptian rulers, and two more centuries of stability followed. Temples were restored, as was the order of the realm.

In 525 BC, the Persian ruler Cambyses II led his troops into Egypt and claimed it as a province. Alexander the Great expelled the Persians in 323 BC and established the rule of the Ptolomies, who embellished the city with monuments once again. Their reign was a brief but brilliant one, combining Greek and Egyptian theologies. As they declined, Rome had its eye on Egypt, and took it as a province, albeit with regional rule, through a series of political maneuvers. Meanwhile, downriver in Alexandria, Cleopatra VII's dalliance with Mark Antony made him an enemy of the state and served as an excuse for the Battle of Actium in 30 BC, when Egypt was seized and placed under direct control of Rome.

Heavy-handed Roman tax policies led to a revolt in Upper Egypt that was quelled harshly: Thebes was smashed to bits. As centuries passed, tomb and temple ruins served as quarries for locals, who took hewn blocks to build elsewhere. Some monuments were converted into Christian churches, others became peasant dwellings. The annual floods and the passage of time all but obliterated the glory that was once Thebes. It wasn't until the early 18th century that a Jesuit priest, Father Claude Sicard, "discovered" Luxor, correctly identifying a mass of sand-covered ruins as the site of the ancient capital. The intrepid priest was responsible for drawing maps subsequently used by Napoléon.

The Theban hills, with their tomb and temple openings gaping black in the beige stone, are a constant presence in Luxor, as are the clip-clop and jangle of horse-drawn caleches and the twittering of birds. Along the tree-lined Corniche, clusters of tall felucca masts hem the shore, and the boat captains approach and ask: "Other side?" When you cross the Nile to the West Bank you enter another world. There, against a background of modest mud-brick dwellings and pastoral calm, lie the Valley of the Kings and Valley of the Queens, awesome rock-hewn demonstrations of political muscle.

Sunset in Luxor has a transcendent beauty. As the red orb returns to the Western Lands, setting the landscape ablaze, consider the fact that this civilization was already ancient in antiquity. Egyptians who witnessed the erection of Abu Simbel, for example, knew even then that the pyramids were at least 2,000 years old.

Temple of Luxor (1390–323 BC). Far easier to explore and digest than the sprawling Temple of Karnak just down river, the Luxor temple stands near the edge of the Nile surrounded by modern buildings in the city center. The temple was dedicated to the Theban Triad, the gods Amun-Re, Mut (goddess of queenship), and Khonsu (moon god), as well as to the cult of Ka (the royal spirit). The ancient name of the 285-yard-long temple was Ipet-resyt (Southern Harem), the southern partner of Karnak, which was the starting point of the late-summer Opet festival. This feast involved a great procession of priests bringing the ceremonial barque of Amun-Re from Karnak to Luxor, where the god would be united with Mut.

It is likely that the largely 18th Dynasty (1539–1292 BC) temple was built over a Middle Kingdom predecessor. Amenhotep III (1390–1353 BC) started to develop the temple, then Ramesses II added to it a century later. Ruins from later periods also surround the main temple. The Avenue of Sphinxes was the creation of Nectanebo I (381–362 BC), almost 1,000 years later. The next considerable work was accomplished relatively soon thereafter, during the reign of Alexander the Great, who built, in the heart of the temple, a sanctuary for Amun-Re's sacred barque.

During the Roman period, the temple was transformed into a fortified camp. Following the 4th-century AD (i.e., Christian) ban on pagan cults, several churches were built inside the temple. One of them, in the northeast corner of the court of Ramesses II (19th Dynasty), was superseded by the **Abu al-Haggag** mosque during the 12th century AD, and locals refused to allow it to be torn down to complete the excavation of the Luxor temple.

Enter the temple compound through the modern gate on the Corniche, north of the Winter Palace Hotel. Go down the stairs, which lead to

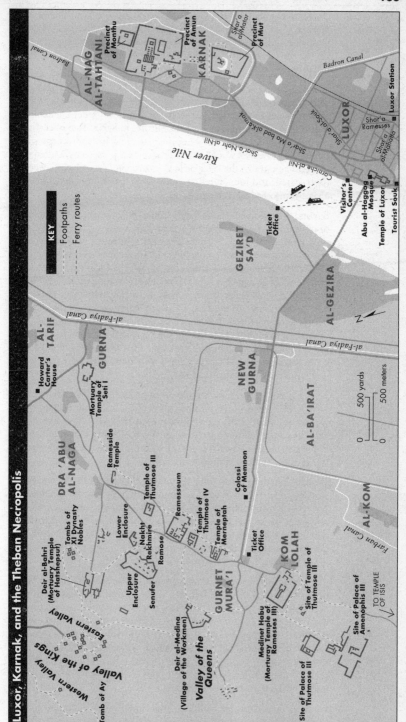

Luxor, Karnak, and the Theban Necropolis

the temple esplanade and the south end of the 3-km (2-mi) **Avenue of Sphinxes**, which is lined with 70 human-headed sphinxes, 34 on the west side and 36 on the east. The 6-yard-wide avenue at one time connected the Luxor and Karnak temples. Only part of the Luxor end of it has been cleared.

The Temple of Luxor's massive **First Pylon** (58 yards wide) is the work of that tireless builder, Ramesses II—ample evidence of whom you'll find in its decoration with scenes of the Battle of Qadesh, a campaign that Ramesses II waged against the Hittites in Syria. Two obelisks and six colossi representing the king used to stand in front of the pylon. One of the obelisks was given to France as a present by Muhammed 'Ali Pasha; it graces the Place de la Concorde in Paris. Of the six colossi (two seated, and four standing), only three are still on site. Two were also given to France and can be seen in the Louvre.

Beyond the pylon lies the **Peristyle Court of Ramesses II**, a double row of papyrus-bud columns interspersed with a series of standing colossi representing the king. To the right of the entrance is a triple shrine, also called a way station, originally built by the queen Hatshepsut (18th Dynasty). Her successor, Thutmose III, usurped it—a relatively common practice by which a later ruler took credit for a monument by excising the original builder's cartouches and writing in his own. The shrines here are dedicated to the Theban Triad: Amun-Re in the middle, Mut on the left, and Khonsu on the right. The shrines' purpose was to receive their sacred barques during the Opet processions. To the left of the entrance to the court is the **Mosque of Abd al-Haggag**, built atop a Christian church. Al-Haggag was a holy man, originally from Baghdad, who died in Luxor in 1244 AD.

Near the entry to the colonnade on the western half of the southern wall, a relief scene shows the dedication of Ramesses II's **Second Pylon**. It provides an accurate view of what the pylon must have looked like after its construction. In front of the Second Pylon, two colossal statues represent Ramesses II seated on a throne. His wife, Nefertari, as the goddess Hathor, stands at his side.

The **Colonnade of Amenhotep III**, on the other side of the Second Pylon, consists of two rows of seven columns with papyrus-bud capitals. The wall decoration, completed by Amenhotep's successors, illustrates the voyage of the statue of the god Amun-Re from Karnak to Luxor Temple during the Opet festival. On each side of the central alley are statues of Amun-Re and Mut, carved during the reign of Tutankhamun (18th Dynasty), which Ramesses II later usurped.

The Colonnade of Amenhotep III leads to the **Solar Court of Amenhotep III**, where 25 18th-Dynasty superbly executed statues of gods and kings were found in 1989. This peristyle court is surrounded on three sides with a double row of columns with papyrus-bud capitals of remarkable elegance. At the far side of the solar court is a direct access to the **Hypostyle Hall of Amenhotep III**, which consisted of eight rows of four papyrus-bud columns. Between the last two columns on the left as you keep walking into the temple there is a Roman altar dedicated to the emperor Constantine.

South of the Hypostyle Hall are **three chapels**: one dedicated to Mut (east side) and two to Khonsu (on each side of the central doorway). The first antechamber originally had eight columns, which were removed during the 4th century AD to convert the chamber into a Christian church, with an aspidal recess, flanked on both sides by granite columns in the Corinthian style. The ancient Egyptian scenes were covered with Christian paintings, which have been almost completely destroyed.

The second antechamber, known as the **Offering Chapel**, has four columns and leads to the inner sanctuary of the sacred barques. The chamber had the same divisions as the previous chapels, but Alexander the Great removed the four columns and replaced them with a chapel. This sanctuary received the sacred barque of Amun-Re during the Opet celebrations.

On the east side of the Offering Chapel, a doorway leads to the **Birth Chamber**, dedicated to the divine conception of the pharaoh. The purpose of the scenes in the Birth Chamber was to prove that Amenhotep III was, indeed, the son of the god Amun-Re, to strengthen the pharoah's position as absolute ruler. On the left wall, birth scenes spread over three registers. In the first one, look for the goddess Selkis, the Queen Mutemwia, and two goddesses suckling children, with two cows suckling children below it. In the second register, the third scene is the pharoah's actual birth, in front of several divinities. In the fourth scene, Hathor presents the infant to Amun-Re. The third register's fourth scene represents the conception of the royal child. The queen and Amun-Re face each other, supported by Selkis and Neith. ☒ *Corniche, Luxor center,* ☎ *no phone.* 🎫 *£e20.* ☉ *Oct.–May, daily 6–9; June–Sept., daily 6–10.*

★ **Luxor Museum.** The Luxor Museum contains, without a doubt, the crème de la crème of New Kingdom sculpture. On three floors, objects ranging from the Predynastic to Coptic periods are displayed in a soothing atmosphere. Each object has its own space, affording it the attention it deserves. Descriptions of artifacts are thorough and accurate.

There are several masterpieces on the ground level. The statue of Thutmose III (18th Dynasty) in green schist of rare quality emits pharaonic inner peace and transcendence. The calcite statue of Sobek with Amenhotep III (18th Dynasty) is also exceptional, both for its workmanship and its rather unusual subject—there are very few representations of the god Sobek offering life to a pharaoh. Colored reliefs, a sphinx, a scribe, and other royal statues are also superb.

On the first floor are Greco-Roman bronzes, a wooden maquette of a boat of Tutankhamun (18th Dynasty), papyri, royal statues, a sarcophagus, and other objects. At the end of the hall, in the first part of the first floor, is a statue of the famous architect Amenhotep, son of Hapu, who served under Amenhotep III and had his own funerary temple in the West Bank. A little variation in style is offered with the two sculptures representing the head of the heretic pharaoh Akhenaten (18th Dynasty), which are a good example of the Amarna style (Akhenaten ruled from Tell al-Amarna).

Back on the ground floor, a new room to the left of the entrance is dedicated to the 16 New Kingdom statues found in 1989 in the cachette of the Solar Court of Amenhotep III in Luxor Temple. These were hidden to protect them from destruction by later rulers. ☒ *Corniche (1 km [.6 mi] north of the Luxor Temple),* ☎ *no phone.* 🎫 *£e30* ☉ *Oct.– May, daily 9–1 (last ticket at 12:30) and 4–9 (last ticket at 8:30); June– Sept., daily 9–1 (last ticket at 12:30) and 5–10 (last ticket at 9:30).*

Mummification Museum. Considering that the Egyptian Museum in Cairo has an entire section dedicated to mummification, the admission price here is high for the small number of objects on display. That said, exhibits here are intelligently designed and include the most important elements of the mummification rituals. And the slightly macabre atmosphere is perfect for the subject.

The museum is divided into two parts: the first one explains, with modern drawings based on ancient Egyptian reliefs and wall paintings, the stages the deceased goes through during mummification, as well as his journey toward heaven. To complement the scenes, a mummy is exposed at the end of the first section. After this introduction, the actual display of artifacts begins. There are tools, canopic jars, painted sarcophagi, and products used during the mummification process. There are also mummified animals, among them a baboon, a crocodile, a ram, a cat, and an ibis. The thrill here, of course, comes from the mummified animals—and the split human head, post-mummification. The museum is 200 yards north of the Temple of Luxor, on the other side of the road, and is badly signed. ⊠ *Shar'a Al-Bahir,* ☏ *no phone.* 🎟 *£e20* ⊙ *Oct.–May, daily 9–1; June–Sept., daily 9–1 and 5–10.*

NEED A BREAK?

Tea in the Sofitel Winter Palace Victorian Lounge. This venerable drawing room, lined with richly upholstered divans and armchairs and hung with Oriental-style paintings of turbaned men wielding sabers, is a wonderful place to decompress after a day of temple stomping. Afternoon light filters through tall windows, birds twitter in the garden, and an ancient air conditioner rumbles while you whittle away at a plateful of sandwiches, pastry, and fresh-baked scones. The tea is served in heavy silver pots, and with porcelain cups and—alas—paper napkins. ⊠ *Corniche al-Nil,* ☏ *095/380-422.* 🎟 *$8* ⊙ *Daily 4–7.*

Karnak Temple. Karnak is, without a doubt, the most complex and impressive assemblage of ancient Egyptian religious monuments. The site is divided into three major precincts, dedicated respectively to the divinities Amun-Re (the central complex), Mut (south of the central complex), and Montu (north). Inside the temple precinct, as in the Temple of Luxor, the Theban Triad of Amun-Re, Mut, and Khonsu were the deities worshipped. The enclosure also comprises smaller sanctuaries dedicated to Khonsu, Ptah, and Opet. The various temples were continuously enlarged and restored from at least the time of the Middle Kingdom down to the Roman period. We owe the most immense and enduring structures to the pharaohs of the New Kingdom.

The 660-yard-long **main axis** of Karnak proceeds from west to east, oriented toward the Nile. Another axis extends south toward Luxor from the midpoint of the main axis.

An **avenue of ram-headed sphinxes,** protecting statuettes of Pinudjem I between their front legs, opens the way to the entrance of the **First Pylon.** This pylon was left unfinished by the kings of the 30th Dynasty. It is the most recent of all the pylons of Karnak, as well as being the most monumental on site.

Against the pylon, on the right side of Karnak's first **forecourt,** are the remains of ancient **mud-brick scaffolding,** used for the erection of the pylon. In the center of the court, a single open-papyrus column remains of what once was the 10-columned kiosk of Taharqa (690–664 BC), an Ethiopian pharaoh of the 25th Dynasty.

The small temple on the left side of the forecourt entrance is the **Shrine of Seti II** (19th Dynasty), some 1,000 years older than the First Pylon. Seti II built this building, with its three small chapels, to receive the sacred barques of the Theban Triad (Amun-Re in the center, Mut on the left, and Khonsu on the right) during the Opet processions. The barques are depicted on the walls of each chapel.

In the southeast angle of the forecourt, the **Temple of Ramesses III** (20th Dynasty) is fronted by two colossi representing the king. It has the same structure as most New Kingdom temples: a pylon, a court with 20 Osirid statues of the king (Ramesses III in the form of Osiris), and a hypostyle

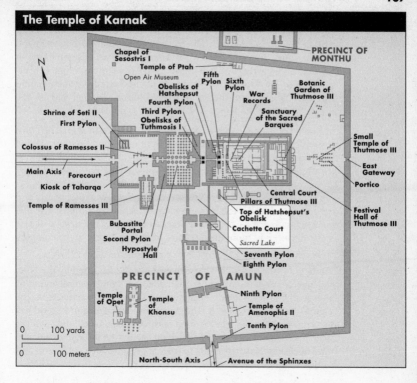

The Temple of Karnak

Chapel of Sesostris I
Temple of Ptah
Open Air Museum
Obelisks of Hatshepsut
Fourth Pylon
Third Pylon
Obelisks of Tuthmosis I
Shrine of Seti II
First Pylon
Colossus of Ramesses II
Main Axis
Forecourt
Kiosk of Taharqa
Temple of Ramesses III
Bubastite Portal
Second Pylon
Hypostyle Hall
Fifth Pylon
Sixth Pylon
War Records
Sanctuary of the Sacred Barques
PRECINCT OF MONTHU
Botanic Garden of Thutmose III
Small Temple of Thutmose III
East Gateway
Portico
Central Court
Pillars of Thutmose III
Top of Hatshepsut's Obelisk
Cachette Court
Sacred Lake
Seventh Pylon
Eighth Pylon
Festival Hall of Thutmose III
PRECINCT OF AMUN
Temple of Opet
Temple of Khonsu
Ninth Pylon
Temple of Amenophis II
Tenth Pylon
0 100 yards
0 100 meters
North-South Axis
Avenue of the Sphinxes

hall. Like others, the sanctuary is divided into three parts for the cult of the Theban Triad.

Resuming the progress of the compound's main axis, the **Second Pylon** was built during the reign of Horemheb (18th Dynasty). Most of the pylon was filled with blocks dismantled from buildings of the heretic pharaoh Akhenaten.

The second pylon opens onto the **Hypostyle Hall**. Note, before you plunge into this fantastical court, the statue of Amun-Re, in the company of a king, on the left. Then wander into what seems like a stone forest—with its breathtaking 134 columns. Not only are the dimensions gigantic, but the colors and hieroglyphs are remarkable. The 12 columns alongside the processional way have open-papyrus capitals, while the remaining 122 columns have papyrus-bud capitals and are smaller. New Kingdom pharaohs built the elaborate hall: Ramesses I began the decoration in the 19th Dynasty; Ramesses III completed it some 120 years later in the 20th Dynasty.

Amenhotep III (18th Dynasty) constructed the **Third Pylon,** which leads to the **Obelisk of Thutmose I** (18th Dynasty), inside the **Court of Amenhotep III**. The **Fourth Pylon,** erected by Thutmose I, gives access to the hypostyle court of Amenhotep III. In this court, one of two **Obelisks of Hatshepsut** (18th Dynasty) still stand. The lower part of the obelisk is well preserved, because Thutmose III, Hatshepsut's hostile successor, encased it with a brick wall—probably not to preserve it, because in other places he usurped her monuments and tried to erase her name from history. Perhaps the intention here was to mask its presence within the temple proper. *See* **Deir al-Bahri,** Hatshepsut's mortuary temple, *in* the Theban Necropolis section, *below,* for more of Hatshepsut's story.

Pass through the Fifth and Sixth pylons. In the vestibule that follows, look for the two **Pillars of Thutmose III**, before the sanctuary, representing the union of Egypt. The papyrus (left) signifies Lower Egypt, and the lotus (right) Upper Egypt. There is also an elegant statue of the gods Amun-Re and Amunet, carved during the reign of Tutankhamun. The red granite **Sanctuary of the Sacred Barques,** behind the vestibule, was built by Philip III Arrhidaeus, brother and successor of Alexander the Great. The sanctuary is made of red granite.

At the end of the main axis rises, transversely, the **Festival Hall of Thutmose III**, also called the Akhmenu. This unusual building was erected to commemorate the king's military campaigns in Asia. The columns are exceptional—massive representations of tent poles used during those campaigns. On the left side of the hall is the famous **Botanic Garden of Thutmose III**. The reliefs on the walls show exotic plants and animals that the pharaoh brought back from his expeditions. The hall was later reused as a Christian church. At the end of the west–east axis is one of the eight monumental gates that gave access to the complex of the Temple of Karnak. This one was erected by Nectanebo.

Southeast of the temple lies the **Sacred Lake,** which is fed by the Nile. The morning rituals of the priests included purifying themselves in this lake. At the northeast side of the lake, a large scarab dates from the reign of Amenhotep III and symbolizes the newborn sun. Legend has it that a woman who runs around it three times, clockwise, will get pregnant in the near future. Farther on the left lie the remains of the other obelisk of Hatshepsut (its partner is back between the Fourth and Fifth pylons).

The **north–south axis** begins from an entrance between the Third and Fourth pylons and continues outside of the Precinct of Amun with a southbound avenue of sphynxes. The **Cachette Court,** at the top of the axis, was so named because thousands of statues were found in it in 1903. South lie pylons seven to 10, each pair separated by a court. All elements of this axis date from the 18th Dynasty and are not accessible at present.

Besides fragments of temples and statues recovered from the Temple of Karnak itself, the **Open-air Museum** contains the small, white, well-preserved **Chapel of Senwosret I**, dating from the Middle Kingdom 12th Dynasty (1938–1759 BC). It was used during Senwosret I's reign to receive the sacred barques. Its new location and reconstructed state is due to the fact that Amenhotep III (18th Dynasty) dismantled the chapel and used it to fill his Third Pylon. Two other small chapels lie beside it, also found inside the pylon. One of these is the Red Chapel of Hatshepsut (18th Dynasty), currently undergoing restoration. The museum is rather small, and its chapels and fragments are totally swallowed up in the gigantic complex of Karnak, which by its size detracts from the beauty of the museum's elements.

Karnak's **Sound-and-Light Show** is the best in Egypt. The first part includes a walk through the temple, with several monuments illuminated successively, and ends at the Sacred Lake, where the second part begins. From a tribune, the entire complex can be seen, with, once again, different temples lighted, music, and a narrated history of the site. On a rotating schedule throughout the week, shows are conducted in Arabic, English, French, German, Italian, Japanese, and Spanish. English shows run each night, the other languages less frequently.

It is best to visit the Temple of Karnak early in the morning: massive groups of people begin arriving around 9 AM, the slanting light calls relief carvings into better focus, and later the heat can be overwhelming. ⊠ *From the Temple of Luxor, follow the Corniche north 2 km (1.25 mi), then turn right; the temple lies 100 yards ahead;* ☎ *no phone.* ▦ *Temple £e20; Open-air Museum £e10; Sound-and-Light Show £e33.* ☉ *Temple: Oct.–May, daily 9–5:30; June–Sept., daily 6 AM–6:30 PM. Sound-and-Light Show (in English): Mon. and Thurs. 8 PM; Tues., Wed., and Fri.–Sun. 9:15 PM.*

Dining

EAST BANK RESTAURANTS

$$$$ ✕ **The 1886.** Play lord or lady of the manor beneath the Venetian crystal chandeliers of this fin de siècle dining room. Candlelight plays on the heavy silver plate and thick linens. Twenty-three-foot-high windows open to a garden. In massive gilt mirrors observe yourself or the other diners struggling with a gigantic menu bearing complicated French names that sound terribly pedestrian in their English translations. White-gloved waiters are a bit disconcerting, but the food is fine, if overpriced. Dress and go for the ambience. ⊠ *Sofitel Old Winter Palace, Corniche al-Nil,* ☎ *095/380–422. AE, MC, V. No lunch.*

$$$–$$$$ ✕ **Miyako.** Luxor is getting more and more cosmopolitan, and Miyako's elaborate and leisurely meals with their element of spectacle offer proof. The room is sedately but luxuriously decorated in teal, gold, and deep green marble. There is a formal tea area and a sequestered alcove for romance or business. A variety of Asian specialties are available, but *teppan-yaki* (Japanese grill), prepared by a Japanese-trained Egyptian chef in flamboyant, percussive style, is a signature. It begins with salads, a choice of soup (pumpkin with a hint of coconut milk and vinegar is quite good), a terrifically complicated fried rice, and fresh shrimp, fish, or beef fillet quickly grilled and served on elegant Japanese pottery. ⊠ *Sonesta St. George, Corniche al-Nil,* ☎ *095/382–575. AE, MC, V. No lunch, closed Mon., Thurs.*

$$$ ✕ **La Mamma.** With its casual, garden-patio ambience, La Mamma is
★ extremely popular, and for good reason—ingredients are fresh and authentic, and service is swift. Antipasti include prosciutto (the genuine article) served with melon, and *insalata del mare* (fresh shrimp and calamari in a sauce of parsley, lemon, and olive oil). The pizzas are a tad thick if you're a fan of the Neapolitan style, but they're baked in pizza ovens. The pastas are all fresh, and the *gnocchi* (potato-based pasta) baked with butter and Parmesan is tasty. ⊠ *Sheraton Hotel, Corniche al-Nil South,* ☎ *095/374-544. AE, DC, MC, V.*

$$$ ✕ **The Flamboyant.** This modern hotel hosts a constant stream of group travelers, but the Flamboyant, with its large bay window overlooking the Corniche, is an intimate place for dining by candlelight. A Continental menu includes the tasty *soupe des pecheurs,* a creamy fish and shrimp bisque accompanied by croutons, grated cheese, and *aioli* (a garlic mayonnaise); ravioli stuffed with Red Sea lobster, served in a peppery sauce; a thick tender beef fillet flambéed tableside; and an excellent rack of roasted lamb. Main dishes are delivered in dome-covered silver salvers, but the atmosphere is casual. Several French wines are available. Service is friendly but rather slow. ⊠ *Hotel ETAP Mercure, Corniche al-Nil,* ☎ *095/380–944. Reservations essential. AE, DC, MC, V. No lunch.*

$$–$$$ ✕ **Bellavista.** If you like your pasta served in placid riverbank surroundings beneath the shade of thatched umbrellas, this beautifully sited Italian restaurant is for you. Bellavista's pastas, pizzas, and main dishes are all well prepared and generously portioned. Paper-thin *carpaccio* (raw beef) is a good starter, as is the tomato and mozzarella salad sprinkled with basil from the hotel's gardens. Roast chicken in olive sauce with garlic-sautéed spinach and fresh fettuccine is superb. A homemade Sicilian-style cassata ice cream with its bits of candied fruits is copiously served and delicious. ⊠ *Luxor Hilton, near the Temple of Karnak,* ☏ *095/374–933. AE, DC, MC, V, DC.*

$$–$$$ ✕ **À la Carte.** A buffet or an à la carte menu awaits in this indoor dining room decorated in cane and wood with a profusion of green outside its windows. The formal à la carte area is great for a pleasantly upscale lunch or a candlelight dinner, but the more casual breakfast and dinner buffets are better for their variety and skillful preparation. A complimentary shuttle will drive you to and from the island until sunset. ⊠ *Hotel Mövenpick Luxor, Crocodile Island,* ☏ *095/374–8555. AE, MC, V. No buffet at lunch.*

$$ ✕ **Sheherazad Terrace.** The Sheherazad has a 1,001 qualities, especially
★ if you count the multitude of sparrows that visit your table for bits of oven-baked bread. Sit on the riverbank terrace and watch the tall rushes wave in the breeze. The food is delicious, the vegetables are organically grown, and the ice cream is legendary. The local *shamsi* (bread) is thick and crusty and turned out by a gaily dressed crone. The pita-bread sandwiches stuffed with roast beef or grilled meats are a favorite. A complimentary shuttle will drive you to and from the island until sunset. ⊠ *Hotel Mövenpick Luxor, Crocodile Island,* ☏ *095/ 374–8555. AE, MC, V.*

$$ ✕ **The Classic.** A small dining room with windows overlooks a tree-lined street. The standard Upper Egyptian and Western fare comes at reasonable prices. Try the *kobbeba:* fried crushed-wheat balls stuffed with spiced minced meat. Ask for a lime to squeeze on top. The moussaka is a tasty and filling eggplant-and-minced-meat dish smothered in béchamel sauce. Eat five meals and get one free. ⊠ *Shar'a Khaled Ibn Walid, beside St. Joseph Hotel,* ☏ *095/381–707. AE, MC, V.*

$ ✕ **El Hussein.** One of the best values in Luxor serves both Egyptians and foreigners. This no-frills restaurant is clean, the service is friendly, and the location is ideal for a break from shopping or sightseeing. Choose from grilled meats, vegetarian and meat tagines, soups, salads, pizzas, sandwiches, and Western-style breakfasts, all competently prepared and served in large portions for remarkably low prices. There is an air-conditioned dining room and a shaded, streetside veranda from which you can observe Luxor city life. No alcohol is served. ⊠ *Luxor Temple St., near the New Tourist Market,* ☏ *095/376–166. No credit cards.*

$ ✕ **McDonald's Luxor.** The moon rises above the Temple of Luxor and from the distance you perceive a flash of yellow light between its monumental columns. Is this some strange visitation of the gods of old? Sorry, it's the golden arches heralding the long-awaited arrival of "civilization" in Upper Egypt. It's small, poorly ventilated, and you know the menu. ⊠ *Behind the Temple of Luxor,* ☏ *095/379670. No credit cards.* ☉ *Daily 10 AM–2 AM.*

WEST-BANK RESTAURANTS

$ ✕ **Mohammed Abdullah's Place.** Pass the ticket windows for the West Bank monuments and you'll find the colorful entry to the Antiquities Police Headquarters. Beside it is a pathway with a vine-covered arbor leading to a courtyard where baby ducks and chicks scuttle in front of the mud-brick home of Mohammed Abdullah. You'll be given a warm welcome and shown into a high-ceilinged room lined with tables. Mohammed's daughters prepare meals to satisfy the most voracious appetite. The menu depends on whose neck's been wrung that day, but call ahead if you really have a preference for fowl or grilled meat. Ask for beer if you desire. Fresh water-buffalo cheese (as much as you can eat), bread baked in the backyard, salads, and vegetable tagines—down-home cooking and shockingly modest prices make this a favorite with the archaeologists and ex-pats who live nearby. ⊠ *Beside the ticket office for West Bank monuments,* ☏ *095/311–014. No credit cards.*

$ ✕ **Tut Ankh Amon Restaurant.** This mud-brick shanty with its rag-carpet
★ interior and rooftop terrace is a West Bank institution. So is Mahmoud,
the owner, former chef at a variety of local hotels and archaeological
missions. His great meals are served up quickly and so bountifully that
two hungry people can share them. The standard menu consists of a
salad, followed by several savory vegetable tagines—okra, zucchini,
spinach, and eggplant, each in its own slightly spicy sauce. Dip in with
flat wheat bread. The main dish could be a charcoal-grilled chicken
cooked with fresh rosemary, a meat tagine, or Mahmoud's specialty:
an outstanding chicken curry made from his own blend of souk spices,
flavored with coconut, raisins, and bits of apple and banana. Finish
up with a slice of cool watermelon. Along with the bill, you'll probably be presented with a battered guest book full of enthusiastic scrib-
blings in seven languages. Three meals are served daily. ✉ *At the ferry
landing,* ☎ *095/310–918. No credit cards.*

Lodging

EAST-BANK HOTELS

$$$$ ⊞ **Sofitel Old Winter Palace.** This noble edifice, built in 1886, exudes
★ the heady scent of colonial luxury. Designed to accommodate the fes-
tive proclivities of the Egyptian monarchy, the Winter Palace, with its
pale-brick facade and wrought-iron balconies, gazes serenely out
toward the tombs of the kings and queens across the Nile. Many an
august personage has passed through these revolving doors, including
Russian tsars and tsarinas, Tito, the shah of Iran, and Jane Fonda. One
look at the vast lobby with its monumental staircase will tell you why:
the Winter Palace provides a backdrop grandiose beyond the dreams
of Hollywood. Each room is slightly different in decor and form, but
all are large and elegant and contain a scattering of antiques. The entire hotel and grounds seem suspended in time, a fugitive from some
more gracious era. The rooms of the charmless New Winter Palace are
modern, fairly small, and functional. The Pavilion annex accommodations are larger, more luxurious, and enjoy a garden view. The 1886
(☞ East Bank Dining, *above*) is one of the Winter Palace's restaurants.
✉ *Corniche al-Nil,* ☎ *095/380–422 or 095/380–425; 800/763–4835
in the U.S.;* 🖷 *095/374–087. 102 rooms. 5 restaurants, 5 bars, pool,
2 tennis courts, health club, squash. AE, MC, V.*

$$$$ ⊞ **Sonesta St. George.** Neopharaonic ostentation squeezed into a
small parcel of Nile real estate developed to within an inch of its life—
that's the St. George's modus vivendi. Exceedingly popular with Far
Eastern travelers because of the high standard of service and profu-
sion of colored marbles, the Sonesta is known throughout the region
for its excellent cuisine (☞ Miyako *in* East Bank Dining, *above*).
Rooms are well appointed but small, and those with Nile views have
balconies and graceful, lotus-motif wrought-iron railings. Elevators are
decorated to resemble the interiors of Egyptian tombs, and there is a
luxurious shopping arcade in the lobby. ✉ *Corniche al-Nil South,* ☎
095/382–575; 800/700–3782 in the U.S.; 🖷 *095/382–571. 224
rooms. 5 restaurants, 2 bars, pool, valet, beauty salon, health club, dance
club. AE, DC, MC, V.*

$$$ ⊞ **Luxor Hilton.** Unpretentious comfort and quality service character-
ize this peacefully located hotel. Set well back from the road directly
on the Nile, the low, rectilinear beige building is unobtrusive and im-
mersed in palms and gardens. Earth tones and shades of rose and
green are used for the standard-size rooms with small balconies. Club
Rooms, for about £e50 per night more, have considerably more bal-
cony space and direct access to the hotel's lovely Nile-view pool.
Bellavista (☞ East-Bank Dining, *above*) is one of the Hilton's restau-
rants. ✉ *Corniche al-Nil (north of the Temple of Karnak),* ☎ *095/374–*

933; 800/445–8667 in the U.S.; FAX *095/376–571. 261 rooms. 3 restaurants, 2 bars, pool, 2 tennis courts, beauty salon, shops. AE, DC, MC, V.*

$$$ ⚄ **Sheraton Luxor.** The lobby of this transplanted modern American institution is full of the hustle and bustle of group travelers. Rooms in the main building are small and functional; those in the white, semi-detached chalets have the advantage of a garden setting and escape the generic high-rise feel of the main building. A large circular pool is built onto a peninsular extension in the Nile. The lively bar, disco, and restaurants (☞ La Mamma *in* East Bank Dining, *above*) contribute to an overall atmosphere of conviviality. A playground is provided for children. The Sheraton also operates its own, medium-capacity cruise boats, which make regular journeys to Aswan, stopping at the monuments at Esna, Edfu, and Kom Ombo en route. ✉ *Corniche al-Nil South,* ☎ *095/374–544 or 095/374–463; 800/325–3535 in the U.S.;* FAX *095/374–941. 204 standard rooms, 92 chalets. 4 restaurants, bar, pool, beauty salon, shops, dance club. AE, DC, MC, V.*

$$–$$$ ⚄ **Luxor Mövenpick Jolie Ville.** Mother nature reigns supreme at this ★ garden-of-paradise resort, whose timeless, unsullied Nile vistas are a short distance from Luxor's bustling center. Occupying 60 acres of the pastoral Crocodile Island, the Mövenpick's exotic plants and flowering trees are filled with a multitude of migrating and local birds—if you're an environmentally sensitive traveler, you'll appreciate the admirable green-thinking practices of the hotel's efficient Swiss management. The resort's restaurants use organically grown vegetables cultivated on the property. The low, vine-covered clusters of bungalow-style rooms dispersed about the property are simply appointed and immaculate. There is a zoo, one of whose residents is a lonely female crocodile purported to have eaten her mate, and a full program of activities for children. Complimentary binoculars are provided for bird-watchers. À la Carte and Scheherazade Terrace (☞ East Bank Dining, *above*) are two of the Mövenpick's restaurants. ✉ *Crocodile Island,* ☎ *095/374–855 or 095/374–937; 800/344–6835 in the U.S.;* FAX *095/374–936. 332 bungalow-style rooms. 4 restaurants, 3 bars, pool, 4 tennis courts, jogging, billiards, travel services. AE, MC, V.*

$$ ⚄ **Luxor Club Med Villa.** The cool, dim lobby area with its lounges and bar sets the casual tone that prevails at all Club Med operations. Although the semidetached bungalows are very basic, this French-managed outfit has a five-star location directly on the Nile facing the mountains of the western bank. The pool is gorgeous, and while you swim in it the river is at eye-level. The buffet-style cuisine is attractive and appetizing. An extremely capable, multilingual staff caters to your needs and can arrange cruises to the wonderful Club Med in Aswan via Esna, Edfu, and Kom Ombo for prices comparable to the extraordinarily reasonable ones you pay at the Club Med itself. ✉ *Corniche al-Nil South,* ☎ *095/380–850 or 095/384–000; 212/977–2100 in the U.S.;* FAX *095/380–879. 138 rooms. Restaurant, bar, pool. AE, MC, V.*

$ ⚄ **Hotel St. Joseph.** This cozy hotel is one of the preferred stopovers ★ for demanding, budget-minded British travelers. Low-key decor, a high standard of cleanliness, very decent food, and a friendly staff are among the advantages. Add the small pool on the eight-story-high rooftop, one of the best views on this end of Luxor, fresh and welcoming rooms with spacious balconies and full baths, and you've got one of the best low-cost lodging options in Luxor. ✉ *Shar'a Khaled Ibn Walid,* ☎ *095/381–707,* FAX *095/381–727. 75 rooms. Restaurant, bar, pool. AE, MC, V.*

$ ⚄ **Philippe Hotel.** Leave the clamor of a shop-filled downtown street and enter what appears to be an outsized refrigerator: the Philippe succumbed to the local predilection for glaring white marble lobbies. Everything from the elevators on up adheres to the same liliputian, but pristine, standard. The Philippe's major asset besides value for money is a swimming pool on the remarkably spacious sixth floor roof. ✉ *Labib Habashi St. (just off the Corniche near the Hotel Etap),* ☎ *095/ 372–284,* 𝖥𝖠𝖷 *095/380–050. 55 rooms. Restaurant, bar, pool. V.*

WEST BANK HOTELS

$ 🏨 **El Gezira Hotel.** If you want to drink deeply of the remnants of an-
★ cient Thebes, stay at the El Gezira. It is a small, turquoise-colored pension on the bank of a canal. Rooms are spartan but comfortable, and
there is a delightful rooftop restaurant with a corn-husk awning and
a charming multilingual host, named Gamal, who can help arrange your
forays into the past. ✉ *From the West Bank ferry landing, take the
main road about 200 yards; a sign on the left points to the hotel, which
is down a small sand path,* ☎ *095/310–034,* 𝖥𝖠𝖷 *095/310–034. 11 rooms.
Restaurant, bar. No credit cards.*

$ 🏨 **Habu Hotel.** Reach out from the second-story arcade of this thick-
walled mud-brick structure and touch the Temple of Ramesses II. It is
an absolutely minimalist lodging, low on comfort, but the ambience
is nonpareil. The tiny domed rooms are like monk's cells with their
metal beds and darting lizards. The only touch of modernity is electricity, which seems to work most of the time. Visit the terrace for a
cool drink or a beer after you see the temples. ✉ *Medinet Habu,* ☎
095/372–477. 23 rooms with shared baths. No credit cards.

Shopping

The New Tourist Souk. This shopping area runs parallel to the Old Souk
but lacks it's charm. You'll find the full gamut of souvenirs and spices
minus the fruit, vegetables, and animal and car traffic of the Old
Souk—which makes for more contemplative bargaining. ✉ *Shar'a al-
Karnak.* ⊘ *Daily 8 AM–midnight.*

The Old Souk. Early morning is the best time to hit this fairly calm provincial *souk* (bazaar) and mingle with the locals doing their grocery shopping. It's a long narrow street running between concrete dwellings and
lined with shops, carts, and turbaned men and black-robed women sitting on the street hawking their wares. You'll find brass trays, alabaster vases and bowls, leather poufs, jewelry shops, and racks of
brightly colored cotton scarves (around £e7) and *galabeyya*s (cotton
shifts, around £e17)—mixed with hardware stores, displays of cow heads,
and great piles of fruits and vegetables in hemp baskets. Donkeys bray,
chickens cackle (sold live or with their necks wrung for a small additional charge), and people shuffle along calling greetings. All is redo-
lent of pungent spices, incense, tangy mint, and the occasional whiff
of offal and freshly butchered meat. Bargaining rules: (1) never make
the first offer; (2) start negotiating from about half of what is asked if
the price sounds unreasonable; (3) try to look disinterested; (4) even
if the price sounds appropriate, bargaining is still customary. ✉ *Shar'a
al-Souk, from Abu Haggar Sq.* ⊘ *Daily 7 AM–midnight.*

The Queen Nefertari Museum (✉ Corniche al-Nil, corner just north
of Hotel Etap, ☎ 095/374–702) has a collection of fabulous fake antiquities, courtesy of Mr. Fuad Allam. Small- and medium-size statuary crafted in the last century that looks so real you must take a
certificate to the airport so you won't be accused of smuggling artifacts. The shop's hours are erratic.

Nightlife

King's Head Pub (✉ Corniche al-Nil, above Naf Naf Shop, ☎ 095/
371–249), like its logo—a portrait of British king Henry VIII with the
face of the pharaoh Akhenaten—is an anomaly, with an eclectic pub

atmosphere and a mixed crowd. The bar is hung with coasters from around the world, pewter mugs, mosque lamps, and an Australian flag, and Bob Marley posters abound. A small blackboard announces the cocktail of the week. Besides several kinds of beer and good liquor, you can order from a substantial menu or sample the Indian buffet.

The Royal Bar (✉ Sofitel Old Winter Palace, Corniche al-Nil, ☎ 095/ 380–422) is hardly a jumpin' joint, but it's worth a visit for its colonial panache—burgundy walls; mahogany woodwork; high, beamed ceilings; lavish drapery; and bookshelves stocked with such oddities as *Who's Who of 1938* and a hard bound Tom Clancy. Enjoy good mixed drinks in the lounge or at the semicircular brass-and-black-granite bar. Complimentary canapés and nuts are available.

Sabil Disco (✉ Hotel ETAP Mercure, Corniche al-Nil, ☎ 095/380– 944) is catacomb-dark and nondescript, except for the illuminated tiled arch that encloses the dance floor and looks like something out of a very old "Star Trek" episode. It's frequented by a volatile mixture of bleach-blond Brits, hopeful Egyptians, and a smattering of insomniacs. Sometimes there is a barefoot belly dancer: Oriental posturing accompanied by a shiver of beads. The music is loud, but not painfully so.

The Theban Necropolis

4 km (2.6 mi) west of Luxor.

At the edge of cultivated land across the Nile from what the ancients called Thebes—the City of 100 Gates—lies their City of the Dead, arguably the most extensive cemetery ever conceived. New Kingdom pharaohs built their tombs here in the secrecy of the desert hills, trying to counter the easy accessibility of the Old Kingdom and Middle Kingdom royal tombs, which had been robbed even by the time of the New Kingdom. The pharaohs had their sepulchres hollowed out underground, and workers isolated from the East Bank decorated them. These artisans had their own village, temples, and cemetery at Deir al-Medina.

To celebrate their own greatness, as well as the magnificence of the god Amun-Re, most New Kingdom rulers constructed huge mortuary temples surrounded by palace granaries. These monuments spread across the edge of the fields, as if to buffer the fertile land from the desert. The choice of the West Bank was based on its rugged landscape, which should have kept robbers away. But the overall rationale came from ancient Egyptian religious beliefs. Every night, the old sun set in the west and was reborn the next morning as Khepry, the young sun. By the same principle, the dead were buried in the west to prepare for their rebirth.

The West Bank is not only a royal necropolis, reserved for the sovereign and his family. A considerable number of tombs belonged to Egyptian nobles and other preeminent courtiers. Their sepulchres were of smaller dimensions, but the quality of their decoration was comparable to that found in the tombs of the kings.

Because the tombs of the nobles were dug into the limestone hills at the edge of an open plain, numerous objects were robbed over the centuries. The same destiny was reserved for most of the graves of the Valley of the Kings and Valley of the Queens, despite the extreme measures that were taken to avoid it. The remarkable exception to this, of course, is the tomb of Tutankhamun, which archaeologist Howard Carter discovered with its treasures nearly intact in 1922.

Start making your way around the West Bank at the Valley of the Kings, then move on to the Temple of Hatshepsut at Deir al-Bahri, the Temple of Seti I, the Valleys of the Nobles, the Ramesseum, the Valley of the Queens, and Deir al-Medina, and end with the splendid mortuary temple of Ramesses III at Medinet Habu.

The best times of day to see the monuments, especially in summer, are in the early morning or in late afternoon—to avoid the high heat of midday and, likewise the waves of sightseers who begin to arrive between 8:30 and 9 AM. In winter, the weather is perfectly bearable, and the main obstacle to seeing the monuments is other tourists. Again, early morning and late afternoon forays are best for avoiding crowds. At sunset, the mortuary temple of Ramesses III at Medinet Habu is extremely pleasant—there is nothing better than relaxing on one of its terraces after a long day of monument hopping.

June through September are only for the brave—come then if you thrive on high heat and sweat. In these months, bringing a large bottle of water is even more essential than at other times. October, November, and May are the nicest months. From December to April, you might want to to carry a sweater with you.

Purchase tickets to enter the sites at one of two kiosks: at the ferry landing by the Old Winter Palace, or 3.5 km (2 mi) west of the West Bank landing (just off the main road after the second road to the left). Tickets for the sites are sold separately and are valid only on the day you purchase them (no refunds), so don't plan the day's sightseeing overzealously. All West Bank sights are open daily from 6 AM to 5 PM.

All tombs on the West Bank are numbered according to their positions in their respective valleys: the Valley of the Kings, the Valley of the Queens, and the Valleys of the Nobles.

Valley of the Kings

Encircled by majestic hills, the New Kingdom royal necropolis is slightly isolated from the other West Bank monuments. A mountain overlooks the valley. This was the domain of the goddess Meretseger: "She-who-loves-the-silence." Meretseger was honored mostly during the New Kingdom as one who punished criminals. Her cult began to decline after the Valley of the Kings fell out of use as a burial site.

The valley's 62 tombs can be dated between the reigns of Thutmose I (18th Dynasty) and Ramesses XI (20th Dynasty). For most of the royal tombs, the internal structure is the same: a long corridor sloping downward and leading to a burial chamber. There are exceptions, of course, such as the tomb of Tutankhamun, which is smaller because it was not designed to be a royal tomb.

The texts and decoration inside royal tombs are very different from those inside private tombs. The royal tombs contain illustrations of complex spiritual texts—the *Book of the Dead* among them—intended to accompany the deceased during his journey though the afterlife and to aid with the long-term expectation of rebirth. Private tombs, by contrast, were decorated with meaningful scenes from daily life.

The Valley of the Kings is 10.5 km (6.5 mi) from the ferry landing: take the main road 3.5 km (2 mi), then turn right. After 3 km (1.8 mi), turn left into the limestone hills. The valley is 4 km (2.5 mi) farther on.

Tickets cost £e20 and must be used on the day of purchase. One ticket admits you to three tombs, with the exception of Tutankhamun's tomb, which requires a separate ticket.

Tomb of Ramesses IV (Nr. 2). Son and successor of Ramesses III, Ramesses IV (20th Dynasty) is considered the first of a series of weak pharaohs whose declining power brought about the end of native kingship in Egypt. Ramesses IV's tomb was robbed in antiquity and must have been accessible during the Ptolemaic and Coptic periods, because graffiti from those times are found on the walls at the entrance of the tomb.

The tomb's first striking scene is the sun disc containing a scarab and Amun-Re represented with a ram's head. Both are adored by the divine sisters Isis and Nephthys. The first two corridors contain several parts of the *Litany of Re*—a celebration of the god Re identified as Osiris. The third corridor is dedicated to the *Book of Caverns,* which relates the journey of the sun god Re through the 12 hours of night, before he is reborn in the morning, and which was to instruct the deceased on his own passage to rebirth. The fourth corridor includes passages from the *Book of the Dead*—a better title for which would be "Spell for Coming Forth by Day"—and parts of the *Negative Confession,* the purpose of which was to prove to the gods that the deceased was pure of heart. The walls of the sarcophagus room are decorated with passages of the *Book of the Gates,* similar to the *Book of Caverns.* The goddess Nut is represented two times on the ceiling. On the left side, she is supported by Shu: this half relates parts of the *Book of Nut.* The other half is called the *Book of the Night.* Both narrate the nighttime journey of Re through the netherworld (again, like the *Book of Caverns*). Ramesses IV's sarcophagus is still inside the tomb. ⊠ *Main path, the second tomb on the right.* ▨ *£e20 (includes three tombs).*

Tomb of Ramesses IX (Nr. 6). Ramesses IX was the last great pharaoh of the 20th Dynasty and the New Kingdom. As with the tomb of Ramesses IV, the outer lintel (here badly preserved) is decorated with a sun disc, inside of which is a scarab, adored by the king and surrounded by the goddesses Isis and Nephthys. The first corridor has four undecorated side rooms, but on its left wall are scenes from the *Book of the Dead*—composed of a series of spells supposed to aid the deceased in getting into the next world —and parts of the *Book of Caverns* on the right side. The same divisions apply in the second corridor. Two niches border the corridor, and inside the niches are representations of different divinities. The third corridor, on the left, contains passages of the *Am-duat* ("The Book of What Is in the Duat," *duat* meaning netherworld) and images of rows of kneeling captives, some of whom are shown with their heads cut off. The third corridor is followed by three largely undecorated halls, the last of which is the burial chamber. Nut is represented on the ceiling as part of the *Book of the Night.* No sarcophagus remains. ⊠ *Main path, beginning of the court on the left side.*

Tomb of Merneptah (Nr. 8). Merneptah, successor of Ramesses II and fourth king (1213–1204 BC) of the 19th Dynasty, is called by some scholars the pharaoh of the Exodus. His tomb is composed of five corridors, three halls, and several side rooms. On the left wall, in the first corridor, are three scenes. The first shows the king before the god Re-Harakhte. It is followed by three columns of the *Litany of Re,* and it ends with a disk surrounded by a crocodile and a serpent, adjoining the rest of the *Litany.* The wall opposite is completely devoted to the *Litany.*

On both sides of the second corridor are figures of gods with texts from the *Book of the Gates* and the *Am-duat.* The jackal god Anubis is in the company of Isis on the left side, Nephthys on the right side. Most of the following chambers are decorated with passages from the *Am-duat.* The sarcophagus chamber has eight pillars. The inner lid of the sarcophagus, which is made of red granite and is decorated with scenes from the *Book of the Gates,* is still preserved. ⊠ *Main path, first small path on the right off the central court.*

Tomb of Thutmose III (Nr. 34). Thutmose III (18th Dynasty), successor of the pharoah queen Hatshepsut, was one of the great warrior kings of Egypt. During his reign, he reestablished Egypt's authority over Syria and Palestine. Before climbing the stairs leading to his tomb, ask one of the guards if it is open.

Several undecorated corridors lead to the pillared antechamber that has a sudden 90° change of axis to the left before you reach the burial chamber itself. On the walls is a list of divinities described in the *Am-duat*, scenes from which decorate the sarcophagus chamber. Note the curviness of the decorations—a remarkable feature of 18th-Dynasty royal burial chambers. The chamber is atypically shaped like a cartouche. The sarcophagus and lid, made of red sandstone, are still in the tomb. ⊠ *From the central court, go straight ahead; after 50 yards, turn left at the first fork; at the second fork, after another 100 yards, take the left path; the stairs are about 150 yards ahead.*

Tomb of Tutankhamun (Nr. 62). Why Tutankhamun's tomb went undiscovered and unraided for some 3,200 years might forever remain a mystery, but there's no doubt that the treasures that Howard Carter pulled out of it in 1922—after digging in vain for six seasons—have made it the most famous tomb of the valley in this century. The artifacts found inside, now housed in a discreet section of the Cairo Museum, are so astonishing that it is hard to imagine the luxury of the tombs of more important kings.

What is known about Tutankhamun's reign is so vague that it is almost impossible to retrace the life of this young king. He was enthroned at the age of eight, and died under suspicious circumstances around the age of 18. Tutankhamun was buried in a hurry, in a smaller-than-average sepulchre for a pharaoh, because his original tomb (Nr. 23) was not completed by the time of his death. Tomb 23 was usurped by his successor, Ay.

The tomb has four small rooms, and only the burial chamber is decorated. One of the scenes, from the *Am-duat*, represents the god Khepri in a sacred barque, followed by three registers with four baboons, which among other functions "scream" at the sunrise, each. Inside the burial chamber, in one of the gilded coffins, rests the mummy of Tutankhamun. Compared with other royal tombs, this one is somewhat disappointing, often crowded, and rather expensive. You can safely skip it if time is short or interest lacking. ⊠ *Main path, on the west side of the court.* ☞ *£e40.*

Valley of the Queens
The Valley of the Queens was also known as *Ta Set Neferu*, the "Place of the Beautiful Ones." Although some 17th- and 18th-Dynasty members of the royal family were buried here, the valley was more widely used for royal burials during the Ramesside period of the following two dynasties.

Seventy-five tombs were cut into the valley rock. A great number are anonymous and uninscribed; others have extremely delicate and well-preserved paintings. The tombs below are at various points on the path through the valley, starting on the right side of the first fork to the right (Nefertari). That fork continues around a loop to Amun-her-Khepshef, and then to Thyti's tombs. Another path leads right before the loop returns to the first fork; at the end of that path is Khaemwaset's tomb.

Admission to Nefertari's tomb is an expensive £e100. Admission to other tombs in the valley is by the same three-per-ticket system as that to tombs in the Valley of the Kings; here tickets cost £e12.

Tomb of Nefertari (Nr. 66). The famous tomb of Queen Nefertari, wife of Ramesses II, was restored over more than 20 years. The result is astonishing and well worth a visit. Unfortunately, to preserve the tomb, and to prevent more deterioration because of salt encrustation, the tomb is accessible to only 150 people per day. Arrive before 10 AM to be sure to get tickets.

Like most tombs in the Valley of the Queens, Nefertari's consists of an antechamber, a corridor, various side chambers, and a tomb chapel. The walls of the antechamber are decorated with scenes showing Nefertari adoring several deities. One remarkable scene shows the queen herself seated playing *senet,* a popular backgammon-like game. ⊠ *Main path (turn right at the fork) on the right.* ▨ *£e100.*

Tomb of Amun-her-Khepshef (Nr. 55). Prince Amun-her-Khepshef was a son of Ramesses III (20th Dynasty). His tomb's wall paintings have very bright and lively colors and show scenes of the young prince, in the company of his father or alone, with a variety of gods. The anthropomorphic, uninscribed sarcophagus remains in the undecorated burial chamber. The tomb contains an interesting and unusual artifact inside a glass case: the mummified remains of a fetus (not the prince himself). ⊠ *Last tomb on the main road.*

Tomb of Thyti (Nr. 52). Another well-preserved tomb is the cruciform tomb of Queen Thyti. Her sepulchre dates to the Ramesside period, but it is not known to whom she was married. The corridor is decorated on both sides with a kneeling, winged figure of the goddess Maat (who represented truth, justice, balance, and order) and the queen standing in front of different divinities. In the chamber on the right is a double representation of Hathor (goddess of love, music, beauty, and dancing), first depicted as a sacred cow coming out of the mountain to receive the queen, then as a woman, accepting offerings from Thyti. ⊠ *Main path, after the little resting place, second tomb on the left.*

Tomb of Khaemwaset (Nr. 44). The wall paintings in the tomb of the young Prince Khaemwaset, son of Ramesses III, are another example of the fine workmanship of the Valley of the Queens tombs. The scenes represent the prince, either with his father or alone, making offerings to the gods. Texts from the *Book of the Dead* accompany the paintings. ⊠ *From the main path, take the left fork and continue left to the path's end.*

Mortuary Temples

Each pharaoh worked to assure his eternal life in the netherworld, as well as in the world of the living. One way of achieving it was to introduce a royal cult among the living. Offerings and rituals guaranteed the survival of the royal *ka* (the individual life force). For this purpose, several kings, from the 18th Dynasty to the 20th Dynasty, had mortuary temples built on the West Bank at Thebes. In these temples, deceased kings, like Amun-Re, the principal god of Egypt, were adored as gods.

Most of the mortuary temples are seriously damaged or utterly lost. Those that still stand demonstrate once again the ancient Egyptian mastery of architecture.

Deir al-Bahri (1465–1458 BC). The Mortuary Temple of Hatshepsut, built by the architect Senenmut, is a sublime piece of architecture—some say the finest on the planet for its harmony with its surroundings. It consists of three double colonnades rising on terraces that melt into the foot of towering limestone cliffs.

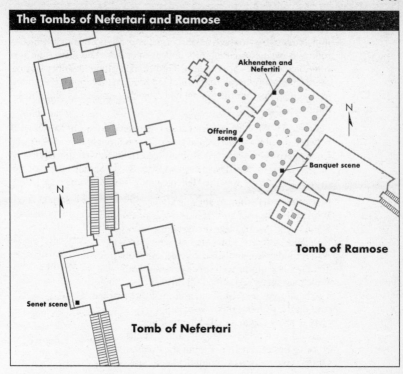

The Tombs of Nefertari and Ramose

Tomb of Ramose

- Akhenaten and Nefertiti
- Offering scene
- Banquet scene

Tomb of Nefertari

- Senet scene

Hatshepsut (18th Dynasty) was the most important woman ever to rule over Egypt as pharaoh. Instead of waging war to expand Egyptian territory like her predecessors, she chose to consolidate the country, build monuments, and organize expeditions to the land of Punt to bring myrrh, incense, and offerings for the gods. Prior to acting as pharaoh, she served as regent for her (then-young) successor, Thutmose III. As soon as Thutmose III came of age to rule over Egypt, he began a program of selectively eradicating her names and images from the monuments of Egypt. Curiously, he didn't erase all of her names, and in some cases the defaced and the intact cartouches are quite near each other.

The reliefs inside the first colonnade are damaged. They included a detailed scene of how the queen's granite obelisks were transported on boats from Aswan to Karnak. Take the large ramp that leads to the second court. The chapel on the left is dedicated to the goddess Hathor. The capitals of the columns are carved in the shape of the face of Hathor as a woman, with cow's ears surmounted by a sistrum. To the right of the chapel starts the second colonnade. Its first half is consecrated to the famous expeditions to Punt—modern scholars have yet to determine where Punt actually was—and shows scenes of the Egyptians traveling over the Red Sea to Punt. The colonnade on the right of the second ramp is devoted to the divine birth of Hatshepsut, with Hatshepsut's mother seated with the god Amun-Re, between the first and second columns. By showing that she was of divine origin, Hatshepsut proved she was able to rule over Egypt as pharaoh. The better preserved chapel to the right is dedicated to Anubis. The third terrace is closed for restoration and further excavations by the Polish Mission. ✉ *From the ferry landing, take the main road; after 3.5 km (2 mi), turn right; after 1.5 km (1 mi), turn left and the temple lies ahead.* 🎫 *£e12.*

The Ramesseum. The mortuary temple of Ramesses II (19th Dynasty) is one of the many monuments built by the king who so prolifically used architecture to show his greatness and to celebrate his divinity. The temple is a typical New Kingdom construction, which means that it includes two pylons, two courtyards, and a hypostyle hall, which is followed by the usual chapels and a sanctuary. The numerous surrounding granaries are made of mud brick. A huge quantity of potsherds, from amphorae that contained food and offerings, was found in situ. It shows that the temple had religious—as well as economic—importance.

Note the 55-½-ft-high (when it stood) broken **colossus of Ramesses II** between the first and the second courts. It was brought here in one piece from quarries in Aswan. A Roman historian's flawed description of the colossus is supposed have inspired Percy Bysshe Shelley's poem "Ozymandias"—its title was the Hellenic name for Ramesses:

I met a traveller from an antique land
Who said: Two vast and trunkless legs of stone
Stand in the desert. Near them, on the sand,
Half sunk, a shattered visage lies, whose frown,
And wrinkled lip, and sneer of cold command,
Tell that its sculptor well those passions read
Which yet survive, stamped on these lifeless things,
The hand that mocked them, and the heart that fed.
And on the pedestal these words appear:
"My name is Ozymandias, king of kings;
Look on my works, ye Mighty, and despair!"
Nothing beside remains. Round the decay
Of that colossal wreck, boundless and bare,
The lone and level sands stretch far away.

Shelley got the facial expressions (if not the sculptors' talents), the fictitious inscription, and the desert location all wrong, but the poetic evocations of ancient political might and its wreck do have their power. ✉ *From the ferry landing, take the main road; after 3.5 km (2 mi), turn right, then turn right again after 700 yards.* ▭ *£e12.*

Colossi of Memnon. Standing (sitting, actually) over 50 feet tall, these seated statues of the great Amenhotep III are the most significant vestiges of his mortuary temple. The missing pieces were taken away for use in other buildings as early as the end of the New Kingdom. Alongside the legs of the colossi are standing figures of the king's mother and his queen, Tiyi. Relief carvings on the bases of the colossi depict the uniting of Upper and Lower Egypt. Ancient grafitti also covers the ruined giants.

The poetry of these colossi is the sound that the northern statue emitted in earlier days. After an earthquake fractured the colossus in 27 BC, it was said to sing softly at dawn. That sound recalled for Greeks the time the myth of Memnon, who was meeting his mother Eos (Dawn) outside the walls of Troy when Achilles slayed him. In the 3rd century AD, Roman Emperor Septimus Severus had the statue mended. After this the colossus was silent. ✉ *From the ferry landing, the colossi are 1 km (.6 mi) west.*

Medinet Habu (1550–332 BC). The mortuary temple of Ramesses III is an impressive complex that was successively enlarged from the New Kingdom down to the Ptolemaic period. Hatshepsut built the oldest chapel. Ramesses III built the temple itself, which functioned as a temple to the deceased pharaoh.

Ramesses III, second king of the 20th Dynasty, had a certain admiration for his ancestor Ramesses II, so he copied the architectural style and decorative scheme of his predecessor. Following Ramesses II's example a century before him, Ramesses III consolidated the frontiers of Egypt. He also led successful campaigns against the Libyans and their allies, and against the Sea Peoples (the Phoenicians).

Enter the complex through the Migdol (Palestinian Gate). Two statues of Sekhmet (goddess of plagues, revenge, and restitution) flank the entrance. At the Window of Appearances, above the entrance, the living pharaoh received visitors or gave rewards to his subordinates. The path leads directly to the first pylon of the mortuary temple. The reliefs on this building, as well as in the first court, relate the king's military campaigns. On the back of the pylon, on the right side, a scene shows how the hands and tongues of the enemies were cut off and thrown in front of the king. The second court is dedicated to religious scenes, and the colors and reliefs in the court are well preserved. The remains of the hypostyle hall and the smaller chapels that surround the second court are less complete. On the left and right flanks of the temple, inside the enclosure, several mud-brick palaces are in need of immediate restoration. ✉ *From the ferry landing, take the main road; after 4 km (2.5 mi), turn left; the temple will be on the roadside 500 yards ahead.* 🎟 £e12.

Temple of Seti I. Seti I's 19th-Dynasty temple is the northernmost of the New Kingdom mortuary temples. Son of Ramesses I and father of Ramesses II, Seti I was one of the great kings who guaranteed safety inside the country and repelled the attempts of enemies to upset the balance of Egyptian supremacy.

The temple, which is extremely damaged, is dedicated to Amun-Re, Ramesses I, Seti I, and Ramesses II (who finished parts of it). Much restoration work has been accomplished, but the remains of the buildings are so poor that only lower parts of the walls were rebuilt. Nine impressive papyrus-bud columns of the peristyle hall, the hypostyle hall, and the sanctuary are the only massive parts of the temple still standing. ✉ *From the ferry landing, take the main road 3.5 km (2 mi), then turn right and follow that road for 3 km (1.8 mi); turn left and the temple is 400 yards ahead.* 🎟 £e12.

Deir al-Medina

Between the Valleys of the Nobles and the Valley of the Queens, in its own small valley, lies Deir al-Medina, the Village of the Workmen. Artians who inhabited the village were in charge of building and decorating the royal tombs of the Valley of the Kings between the 18th and 20th Dynasties. The site includes their houses, the tombs of many of the workmen, and a small temple dedicated to several gods. The temple was founded during the reign of Amenhotep III (18th Dynasty) and was rebuilt more than 1,100 years later during the reign of Ptolemy IV. Coptic Christians later turned the temple into a monastery.

The village is made up of houses of small dimensions, built against each other. They have similar plans, consisting of three or four rooms, some of which are decorated. Some have basements, and all, probably, had second floors, or used their roof space. Hygiene in the village is believed to have been good—there was a village doctor—and the villagers likely lived much as local people do today. Long lists of clothing items and the foods the residents ate have been found but have yet to be translated.

Although the tombs are small, they are jewel-like, with vibrant colors and beautifully detailed images—in other words, the workers applied the technical and artistic skill that they used on their employers' projects in their own as well. On the outside of many tombs stood small pyramids, where offerings were brought for the deceased. Since the artisans worked on the royal tombs, it is natural that there would be certain similarities between the decoration of the tombs of the Valley of the Kings and the decoration of their own sepulchres.

One of the most astonishing workers' tombs is that of **Senedjem** (Nr. 1), who was an artist during the reigns of Seti I and Ramesses II. The paintings on the walls of the burial chamber are extremely fresh looking. Notice on the opposite wall, left of the entrance, the god Anubis tending a mummy on a couch, surrounded with texts from the *Book of the Dead*. On the ceilings are several scenes showing the deceased kneeling in adoration before the gods. ⊠ *From the ferry landing, take the main road 4 km (2.5 mi); it leads directly to Deir al-Medina.* 🎟 *£e12.*

Tombs of the Nobles

The Valleys of the Nobles are divided into several necropolises distributed over the West Bank at Luxor. More than 1,000 private tombs have been found and numbered. Most of the them can be dated to the 18th through the 20th Dynasties, although some were reused during the 25th and 26th Dynasties (760–525 BC) and the Saite period (26th Dynasty, 664–525 BC).

As the name of the valley indicates, the necropolises were occupied mostly by nobles, but priests and officials were buried here as well. Funerary scenes appear in the tombs, but so do scenes of the daily life of the time. So it is not unusual in these tombs to admire the joy of a banquet, discover the leisure-time activities, and analyze the professional lives of the deceased.

Sheikh Abd al-Gurna is the most attractive and the largest necropolis. A present-day village was built on top of the cemetery. To protect the site, the government tried to relocate the local population to another village, made especially for them. In vain. The advantage of this is that you have the opportunity to get acquainted with the daily life of modern Egyptians even as you're looking back at how the ancients lived 3,500 to 2,500 years ago.

Local villagers will offer themselves as guides. They can be very useful, but of course you'll be expected to contribute a little baksheesh (a little pocket money, something like £e5–10) for their efforts. Tickets to the tombs cost £e12 and must be used on the day of purchase. One ticket admits you to three tombs.

Tomb of Nakht (Nr. 52). Nakht was a royal scribe and astronomer of Amun (high priest) during the reign of Thutmose IV (18th Dynasty). The tomb is somewhat small, and only the vestibule is decorated with bright, vivid colors. Before the vestibule is a small display of the finds inside the tomb.

Start with the first scene on the left of the entrance—which shows the deceased with his wife, who pours ointments on the offerings—and keep moving right scene by scene. Underneath the first is a butchery scene. Then three registers represent agricultural scenes in which Nakht himself supervises. The wall to the right of the agricultural scenes has a false door. The offering bearers are kneeling, two tree goddesses carry a bouquet, and other offering bearers stand before the gifts.

The wall opposite the harvest scenes presents a famous banquet scene with dancers and musicians—look for the blind harpist. The first scene on the right of the entrance represents, once again, the deceased and his wife pouring ointment on the offerings. To the right of the banquet scene, offering-bearers present gifts to Nakht and his wife. Farther right still, the wall shows hunting and fishing scenes in the Delta with the deceased and his family. ⊠ *Opposite the Ramesseum, second tomb on the left.*

Tomb of Ramose (Nr. 55). The tomb of Ramose is one of the finest tombs of Abd al-Gurna. Ramose was a vizier (high executive officer) during the reign of Amenhotep III and Akhenaten. His tomb is unusual for having both reliefs executed within the traditional norms of ancient Egyptian art, as well as reliefs done in the elongated Amarna style that the heretical pharaoh Akhenaten adopted.

The tomb was left unfinished. It has a court with a central doorway leading into a hypostyle hall with 32 papyrus-bud columns, most of which were destroyed, while others were reconstructed in modern times (full-height columns are all reconstructions). The inner hall that follows has eight columns and a shrine.

On the left side of the entrance to the hypostyle hall is a representation of the funerary banquet. The guests are seated in couples before the deceased. Their wigs are all different, and the eyes of the figures are accentuated with black contours. On the wall opposite, in an unfinished scene, Ramose presents the Theban Triad and Re-Harakhte to the king, Akhenaten, who is accompanied by Maat. To the right of this traditional scene, another bears the telltale Amarna influence: Ramose stands in front of Akhenaten and his wife, Nefertiti, adoring the sun disc Aten. ⊠ *From the parking area, the tomb is 100 yards ahead on the right side.*

Tomb of Rekhmire (Nr. 100). Another very important tomb is that of Rekhmire, governor of Thebes and vizier during the reigns of Thutmose III, Hatshepsut, and Amenhotep II (18th Dynasty). The tomb is well preserved, and the scenes are almost complete. The texts on the walls explain the installation, the duties, and the moral obligations of the vizier.

The right wall of the hall to the left of the entrance shows the deceased inspecting and recording foreign tributes. You will recognize people of Punt (☞ Hatshepsut's Deir al-Bahri, *above*) bringing animals and incense trees; the Kheftiu with vases and heads of animals; the Nubians with animals; and Syrians bringing vases, a chariot, horses, a bear, an elephant, and human captives. The second scene, on the left inside the chapel, represents several stages of various crafts. The making of jewelry and sculpture depicted here helped archaeologists understand the techniques used during the pharaonic period. The last group of scenes in the tomb tends to focus on funerary rituals, such as The Opening of the Mouth Ceremony. ⊠ *From the parking area, make your way to the top of the valley.*

Getting Around

There are several ways to cross the Nile. The cheapest is by local ferry (£e1; tickets are available from the kiosk in front of the East Bank launch), which leaves from in front of the Luxor Temple, near the Novotel. The ferry runs 24 hours a day. Smaller local boats docked around the ferry are also available; they also cost £e1. The problem with the ferry is that the boat leaves only when it is fully occupied. For a quicker crossing, special boats can take you across the Nile for £e5. Still another way to cross to the West Bank is by the new bridge, 12 km (7.5 mi) south of Luxor.

Once on the West Bank, there are a few ways to get around. The easiest, fastest, and most expensive is by private taxi, which will cost about £e40 per half day. Service taxis (group taxis) are a very cheap way (25 piasters) to get to the middle of the tourist area, but they only take main roads and skirt the monuments. To get a service taxi to stop and let you out, knock on the little window in the front.

Besides the motorized vehicles, cycling is always an option (rentals cost £e5); likewise donkeys. You can hire both at the West Bank docks. Cycling, or even walking, is definitely an option in winter, but either would be exhausting in summer. As for the donkeys, they will bring you through the local village to the sites, and they're an evocative form of transportation if time is not such a concern. Otherwise, taxis, cycling, and walking are more expedient.

Esna

54 km (34 mi) south of Luxor.

The town of Esna enjoyed some notoriety in the 19th century when quite a number of singers, dancers, prostitutes, and other similar folk were exiled from Cairo and resettled here. Flaubert visited Esna expressly to see and enjoy performances of the artists and professionals. He wound up becoming somewhat obsessed by a prostitute-dancer, and he spent a good deal of time describing her (and his opium-induced visions) in letters to his long-suffering wife.

Esna itself is an interesting town on the bank of the Nile and has some pleasant architecture. It is worth wandering about if you have time to spare. Esna is an easy day trip from both Luxor and Aswan, so there is little need to linger here. You'll find the usual food stands in the souk and the surrounding areas.

The Temple of Khnum (2nd century BC–1st century AD) is one of the most truncated and least attractively sited Egyptian temples that you are likely to see. It sits in a 30-ft-deep pit in the middle of town, and to get to it, you have to run the gauntlet down a short street from the river that's lined with souvenir sellers anxious to peddle their wares. Resist all temptation to go into a shop here, because salespeople are known to be unpleasantly aggressive. The reason that the temple is in a pit is because the level of the town has risen over time, sinking the excavated temple below the level of the modern houses. There is some fine stratigraphy, made visible from the excavations, in the soil behind the temple. The ticket booth is at the iron entrance gate that leads to a staircase descending into the pit.

Only the hypostyle hall of this Ptolemaic/Roman temple dedicated to Khnum (the god associated with creating people) is visible. There is a question as to what happened to the rest of it—was it never built, or was it robbed for its stone in antiquity? The portion of the temple that remains is completely decorated and has some very unusual cryptographic inscriptions that are hymns to Khnum. One is written almost entirely with hieroglyphs of crocodiles, another with rams. The columns are also inscribed with significant texts that provide an outline of different festivals held at the temple throughout the year. The ceiling is decorated with zodiacal motifs, and fragments of paint are still visible.

In the forecourt and around the temple lie picturesquely scattered fragments primarily of Roman and Coptic date, including a particularly charming lion-faced basin. ⊠ *Mabed Esna.* 🖼 *£e8, cameras free.* ☉ *Oct.–May, daily 7–5; June–Sept., daily 7–6.*

Getting Around

You can get to Esna from a cruise boat (☞ Chapter 5), or by taxi hired either in Luxor or Aswan for a set price (to be discussed at length and verified before you get into the car). If you come by taxi, you will also have time to stop farther south at the more rewarding temples in Edfu and Kom Ombo. You can also take a bus or a service taxi from either Luxor or Aswan; if so, be prepared to hire another taxi to get to the Temple of Khnum, which will involve crossing to the west bank. *See* Getting Around Luxor *and* Getting Around Aswan for costs.

al-Kab

32 km (20 mi) south of Esna.

Al-Kab, on the East Bank of the Nile, is the site of an impressive though imperfectly preserved town, temple area, and tombs. The site was first inhabited in around 6,000 BC and occupied thereafter. It was sacred to the vulture goddess of Upper Egypt, Nekhbet—the ancient name of al-Kab is Nekheb. Nekheb was allied to the town of Nekhen on the West Bank of the Nile (modern Kom al-Ahmar).

The only way to get to the ancient site is by private taxi. Service taxis go to the village, but not to the antiquities. You can include al-Kab in the general taxi fare on a trip from Luxor to Aswan (or vice versa), but a stop in al-Kab will raise the price of the trip.

The town of Nekheb is enclosed by a massive mud-brick wall and in-cludes houses, the principle **Temple of Nekhbet,** smaller temples, a **sacred lake,** and some early cemeteries, which are rather difficult to make out. About 400 yards north of the town are several **rock-cut tombs** that date primarily from the New Kingdom, although there are some earlier tombs as well. The most famous are those of **Ahmose Pennekhbet, Ahmose son of Abana,** and **Paheri.** The first two are noted for their historical texts, which discuss the capture of the Hyksos capital Avaris and various military campaigns of the pharaohs of the early New Kingdom. The tomb of **Paheri** is noted for its scenes, especially the small scene of a herd of pigs. Some distance into the wadis are the rock-cut **Sanctuary of Shesmetet,** a chapel, and a small **Temple of Hathor and Nekhbet** (these are not always open). ⊠ *Athar al-Kab,* ☎ *no phone.* 🎫 *£e8; still camera free in town, £e5 in tombs; video £e25.* ⊙ *Oct.– May, daily 6–5; June–Sept., daily 6–6.*

Edfu

115 km (72 mi) south of Luxor; 105 km (66 mi) north of Aswan.

Although the town itself is somewhat dull, Edfu's temple, dedicated to Horus, would make even Cecil B. De Mille gasp. It is the most in-tact of Egyptian temples you are likely to see, and it is a most unex-pected and breathtaking sight. Visiting Edfu's temple, set at the edge of the modern town of Edfu—portions of which peer over the temple enclosure wall—is the closest you can get to being an ancient Egyp-tian going on pilgrimage. To get the full effect of this marvel, buy your tickets and walk along the exterior of the temple, around the pylon, to the end of the courtyard toward the birth house, without turning around. At the end of the courtyard, turn suddenly to face the great Temple of Horus at Edfu.

Small restaurants and kiosks provide food in Edfu. There are also bak-eries and grocery stores if you want to make a picnic. The café at the temple gate provides light, inexpensive snacks and is relatively clean.

The **Temple of Horus** is mainly from the Ptolemaic period. The temple does, however, rest on earlier foundations, which might have dated from the Old Kingdom (2625–2130 BC). The exterior walls are covered with texts that give details of the temple's construction. It was started in 237 BC by Ptolemy III, and the entire building was completely finished and decorated in 57 BC. The temple is extremely unusual in being oriented to the south. Originally, access to the temple would have been from the south, but because of the growth of the town, it is now entered from the north.

The enormous **pylon,** fronted by a pair of statues of Horus as a falcon, leads into a columned courtyard at the end of which stands a single, better-preserved statue of Horus as a falcon. The doorway behind this leads to the **Hypostyle Hall.** The columns in this temple are typical of the Ptolemaic period, which means that they have varied capitals: palm-leaf capitals, lotus capitals, papyrus capitals, and a large variety of elaborate composite capitals. The bottoms of the column shafts, above the bases, are carved to show the leaves found at the bases of various plants.

Following the central axis, the Hypostyle Hall is succeeded by a series of rooms. The last in the series is the temple's sanctuary, which contains a finely polished monolithic syenite *naos* (shrine), which would have housed the statue of the god set in another smaller shrine made of gilded wood. An altar stands before the naos, and originally the naos would have been fronted by gilded wooden doors, the sockets for which are visible in the jamb area.

Rooms off of the central axis are thought to have been storerooms for various ceremonial items, such as perfume, vessels made of precious metals, wine, incense, and gold. A series of rooms in the rear of the sanctuary contain access, now blocked for the most part, to crypts made to store the most precious of the temple's possessions. The central room at the back contains a model barque (a modern reproduction) that is very probably identical to the one used in antiquity to transport the golden statue of the god in religious processions around town and on boats north to Dendera.

The inner rooms of the temple are dark, lit by shafts of light entering from narrow slits at ceiling level. Originally the temple would have been lit thus, with additional light coming from flickering torches. The richly colored walls would have shone and glimmered like jewels in the half-light; it is easy to imagine priestly processions passing through the temple on sandaled feet, chanting and praying amid clouds of incense.

The interior of the temple is decorated with scenes of divinities and pharaohs offering to one another, as well as some scenes of the founding of the temple. Elements of a celestial ceiling are visible in the hypostyle hall. A **side chapel** to the east with its own tiny courtyard contains a beautiful ceiling showing the course of the sun as it is swallowed by the sky goddess, Nut, and then born from her the following morning.

The inside of the temple's stone enclosure wall shows scenes of Horus fighting with and defeating his enemy, the god Seth. This is one of the few places where an illustrated version of the Horus and Seth myth is visible. There are several variations on the tale in which Seth killed his brother Osiris and set himself up as ruler in his stead. Isis, Osiris's wife, used her magic to bring Osiris back to life and to become pregnant. The result was Horus, who sought to avenge his father's murder and to rule, as was his right. He and Seth engaged in a series of battles using both strength and magic. Ultimately Horus was the victor, and he was rewarded by ruling over Egypt—hence the living pharaoh's identification with Horus—and Osiris ruled over the afterworld. Seth became god of deserts and distant lands.

The reliefs show Horus defeating Seth in his different guises (hippos, crocodiles, and so forth) and are quite entertaining. It is believed that a mystery play illustrating this struggle took place at a Horus/Seth festival at Edfu. Another amusing fact to note about this temple (and other Ptolemaic temples) is that many of the cartouches are left empty. This is because the Ptolemies overthrew one another so frequently and so speedily that the architects, contractors, and priests decided to leave blank cartouches that could be painted in with the ruling Ptolemy's name whenever the appropriate time arose.

On one side of the temple, between the outer and inner stone walls, is a Nilometer, a gauge used to measure the height of the Nile. Taxes were calculated accordingly. ⊠ *Mabed Edfu*, ☎ *no phone.* 🎫 *£e20, still camera free, video £e25.* ⊙ *Oct.–May, daily 6–5; June–Sept., daily 6–6.*

Getting Around
Visit Edfu either on a Nile cruise or by hiring a taxi in Luxor or Aswan for a set price. You will probably also want to stop at Esna and Kom Ombo. Buses and service taxis also run from Luxor and Aswan, but be prepared to hire another taxi to get to the temple. ☞ Getting Around Luxor *and* Getting Around Aswan for costs.

Kom Ombo

65 km (40 mi) south of Edfu; 40 km (25 mi) north of Aswan.

Kom Ombo is a fertile area, interesting because it supports not only its original Egyptian inhabitants, but also a large Nubian community that was resettled here after the construction of the Aswan High Dam and the flooding of Lower Nubia. As a result, the town has grown considerably in the past 20 years. Kom Ombo was an important town strategically, because it was one of the places where the trade routes to the Nile Valley, the Red Sea, and Nubia converged. Kom Ombo is the site of a very unusual double temple dedicated to the gods Sobek, depicted as a crocodile or a crocodile-headed man, and Haroeris, a manifestation of Horus represented as a falcon or a falcon-headed man.

The **Temple of Haroeris and Sobek** (2nd century BC–1st century AD) stands on a bend in the Nile. It is especially romantic to approach the temple in the moonlight, if you arrive on a cruise at the right time of the month. Virtually all the remains of the temple date to the Ptolemaic period and later, although evidence of earlier structures has been found, most notably an 18th-Dynasty gateway.

The temple is remarkable for its duality: it has two of almost everything, enabling its priests to conduct equal services for two deities simultaneously. The southern part of the temple, on the right when you face the entrance, is dedicated to Sobek, the northern part to Haroeris. The entrance and ticket booth are on the southeastern corner, at the Gate of Ptolemy XII, set into the mud-brick outer enclosure wall.

Immediately to the right of the entrance is a small shrine, dedicated to Hathor, which now houses some mummified crocodiles. Crocodiles, sacred to Sobek, were worshipped at Kom Ombo. The crocodiles were regarded as semidivine, and they were fed on the finest foods, provided with golden earrings, and given elaborate manicures, which involved gilding their nails. Areas in the northwestern parts of the enclosure are thought to have been the place where the sacred crocodiles were kept when alive.

The double entrance to the temple proper is from the southwest, leading into a large courtyard—the structure was oriented with its entrance to the river, rather than having a true east-west axis. This courtyard is the only shared space in the temple proper; from here, the building is divided in two. There are two doorways that lead to outer hypostyle halls, inner hypostyle halls, a series of offering halls, and twin sanc-

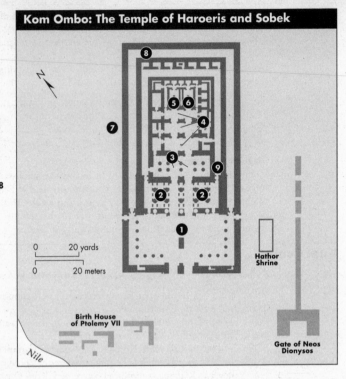

tuaries (the southern doorway's lintel was badly damaged in a 1992 earthquake but has since been restored). The sanctuaries contain a set of crypts from which priests provided oracular advice and the respective god "spoke" whenever necessary. Behind the sanctuaries are a series of storerooms now inhabited by bats.

The decoration of the walls is the usual type found in temples: pharaohs offering to divinities and divinities blessing pharaohs. The different gods being honored show to whom the temple is dedicated. Look for a calendar on the southwest wall of the offering hall, and a table laden with surgical implements on the back (northeast) wall of the outer stone enclosure wall. Surgical implements found at archaeological sites (and used worldwide until quite recently) can clearly be identified on the table. A rather charming relief of a pharaoh's pet lion nibbling on the unwillingly proffered hands of the king's enemies is carved on the exterior of the southeastern wall.

A large, deep well and a Nilometer are within the mud-brick enclosure west of the main building. This is also the area where the sacred crocodiles were supposed to have been kept. Fragmentary remains of a birth house stand at the temple's western corner (in front). Behind the temple is a yet-to-be-excavated area that was probably the site of priestly houses and a very modest town, built of mud brick. ⊠ *Kom Ombo,* ☎ *no phone.* ⌧ *£e12, still camera free, video £e25.* ☉ *Oct.– May, daily 6–5; June–Sept., daily 6–6 (if you arrive outside regular hours, it is sometimes possible to persuade the guard to open the temple for a small fee).*

Getting Around

You can visit Kom Ombo either on a Nile cruise or by taxi hired either in Luxor or Aswan for a set price, which can include stops in Edfu, al-Kab, and Esna. Buses, minibuses, and service taxis also run from

Luxor and Aswan. *See* Getting Around Luxor *and* Getting Around Aswan for costs.

Daraw Camel Market

5 km (3 mi) south of Kom Ombo; 35 km (22 mi) north of Aswan.

Known for its Tuesday camel market—the largest camel market in the Middle East—Daraw is otherwise a hot, dusty, and flyblown place. The camels come up from Sudan along the Forty Days Road. Traditionally, they made the trek on foot, but now more and more of them arrive in the backs of Toyota pickup trucks. Merchants from Cairo, mostly, make their way to Daraw to take the camels back to Cairo to sell, for about £e1,700 a head. The camels are sold to farmers or for slaughter, sadly not for the more romantic options of riding or racing.

The Daraw market sells not only camels, but also other livestock: sheep, goats, cows, bulls, and poultry. Full of dust, tumult, and herders with whips, market days are nothing if not colorful and crowded with people and animals. After you inspect the varieties of livestock and exchange views with Sudanese, Egyptians, and Beshari tribesmen about the animals, saunter over to the produce section for fresh fruit and vegetables before moving on to inspect the different sticks, staves, fly swatters, whips, and harness bits on sale here. Trading usually ends by noon. In summer, the market is very hot and very odorous.

Getting Around

The trip from Aswan by taxi will cost about £e50 per person, based on four passengers riding in a standard Peugeot taxi.

Aswan

880 km (550 mi) south of Cairo; 210 km (133 mi) south of Luxor.

It's worth going to Nubia to see the girls.
–Lucie Duff Gordon, 1865

For thousands of years Aswan was the "Southern Gate," the last outpost of an empire. Its name comes from the ancient Egyptian *swenet* ("making business"), and its reputation as a frontier emporium dates from the colonial era of the ivory trade and commerce in ebony, gold, slaves, spices, gum arabic, ostrich feathers, and, at least until 1929, panther skins. In today's souk, a variety of hoofed animals mingle freely with Sudanese in high white turbans, Bedouin camel traders, and black-clad women balancing impossible packages on their heads. The sound of singing and the beating of drums reminds you that this is a gateway to Africa, and that the Tropic of Cancer lies just a few miles to the south.

As seen in the climate-adapted architecture and gaily painted houses of the Nubian areas, Aswan town and its gracious inhabitants have an aesthetic sense rarely found in modern Egypt. This is a desert city, austerely clean, full of trees and gardens, the scents of baking sand and the Nile, oleander and frangipani.

It wasn't quite so shady when French troops arrived in 1799 on Napoléon's orders to capture or kill Mamluk leader Mourad Bey. By the time the exhausted regiment reached Aswan, the nimbler Mamluk cavalry had disappeared into the Nubian Desert. That gave the French time to take stock of the pharaonic and Greco-Roman monuments that even now seem strangely remote.

Although Aswan was a winter resort popular with Greeks, Romans, and Egyptians in antiquity, Europeans didn't come until Thomas Cook

Aswan

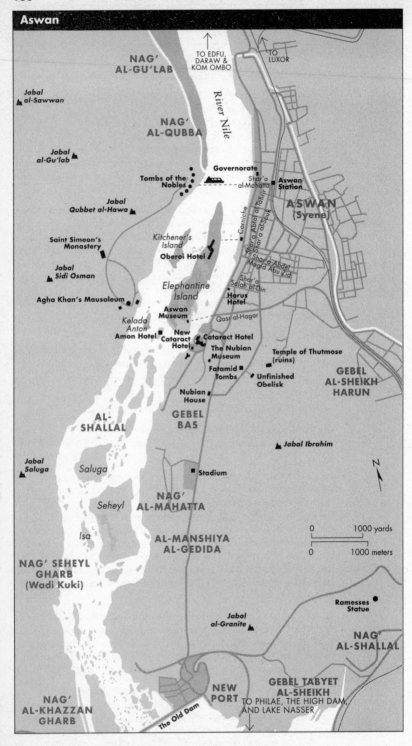

NAG' AL-GU'LAB

Jabal al-Sawwan

NAG' AL-QUBBA

River Nile

TO EDFU, DARAW & KOM OMBO

TO LUXOR

Jabal al-Gu'lab

Governorate

Tombs of the Nobles

Shar'a al-Mahatta

Aswan Station

Jabal Qubbet al-Hawa

ASWAN (Syene)

Coniche

Shar'a Abtal al-Tahrir

Shar'a al-Souk

Saint Simeon's Monastery

Kitchener's Island

Oberoi Hotel

Shar'a Abdel Magid Abu Zid

Jabal Sidi Osman

Elephantine Island

Shar'a Salah al-Din

Agha Khan's Mausoleum

Aswan Museum

Horus Hotel

Qasr al-Hagar

Kelada Anton Amon Hotel

New Cataract Hotel

Cataract Hotel

The Nubian Museum

Temple of Thutmose (ruins)

Fatamid Tombs

Unfinished Obelisk

GEBEL AL-SHEIKH HARUN

Nubian House

GEBEL BAS

AL-SHALLAL

Jabal Saluga

Jabal Ibrahim

Saluga

Stadium

Seheyl

NAG' AL-MAHATTA

Isa

N

AL-MANSHIYA AL-GEDIDA

NAG' SEHEYL GHARB (Wadi Kuki)

0   1000 yards
0   1000 meters

Ramesses Statue

Jabal al-Granite

NAG' AL-SHALLAL

NEW PORT

GEBEL TABYET AL-SHEIKH

NAG' AL-KHAZZAN GHARB

The Old Dam

TO PHILAE, THE HIGH DAM, AND LAKE NASSER

sent down his luxuriously outfitted and provisioned *dhabeyya*s (large feluccas) in 1869. Credited by some as having created the travel industry, Cook provided the means for wealthy Victorians to comfortably explore one of the outreaches of their realm while enjoying Aswan's excellent, dry climate.

Rich in granite, this area was quarried by Egyptians and Romans, the evidence of which stands in monuments up and down the Nile Valley. It continues to yield mineral wealth to this day—in addition to the distinctive pink-and-black-flecked Aswan granite there are iron foundries, aluminum mines, and important talc deposits that help fuel Egypt's development. The High Dam testifies to Egypt's modern determination and its unparalleled ability to renew itself, even to the extent that Egypt no longer ends at Aswan. The use of Lake Nasser for tourism and its open-air museum of salvaged monuments extends the grand tour well into what is appropriately, and poignantly, called the "New Nubia."

Aswan, like Luxor, is laid out along the Nile Corniche, but the West Bank here is undeveloped desert, accessible only by water. This means that you'll make short river crossings by felucca—which are wonderful preludes to visiting Elephantine Island and Kitchener's Island and the Tombs of the Nobles and St. Simeon's Monastery on the West Bank.

East Bank Sights

Nubia Museum. In 1954 the world learned that the High Dam was to be built, and that the resulting lake would submerge a large part of Egyptian and Sudanese Nubia. UNESCO responded to an appeal for assistance to salvage the many monuments by organizing 50 countries in "a work of peace founded on the intellectual and moral solidarity of all mankind."

The Nubia Museum, opened in November 1997, is the triumphant capstone of the effort to preserve Nubian culture and folk heritage, financed by the Egyptian government with technical assistance from UNESCO. Arranged chronologically, it takes you through Nubia's prehistory; the pharaonic dynasties, including the Kingdom of Kush, when Nubian kings ruled Egypt; and onward through its Christian and Islamic periods. The selection of statuary is extraordinary for its range and eclecticism. There is also a diorama with scenes of Nubian village life. There is lots to take in—allow about two hours for the well-curated displays.

The museum's harmonious architecture incorporates a Fatamid tomb. It comes from a group of poorly preserved monuments believed to date from the 8th to 12th centuries AD, located in the adjacent Fatamid Cemetery. ⊠ *Shar'a Abtal al-Tahrir (5-min walk south of the Old Cataract, Basma, and Kalabsha hotels),* ☎ *097/313–826 or 097/317–996.* ☒ *£e30, video cameras £e100.* ⊘ *Oct.–May, daily 9–1 and 5–9; June–Sept., daily 10–1 and 6–10.*

Aswan Souk. You won't find fresh elephant tusks here today, as in the past, but it's still a lively, colorful, Nubian music–filled marketplace. Juice shops churn out frothy *aa'saab* (yellow sugarcane juice)—highly recommended for a cool, sweet jolt of energy. Peaches, apples, melons, limes, and mint release their scents in the heat of the day. And huge baskets display local specialities: greenish henna powder, crimson hibiscus, small red-hot peppers, and sand-roasted peanuts.

Enter the souk beside the Benzion department store or start from the train station. You'll find better cotton fabrics here than in Cairo, either plain white or printed with African or pharaonic designs (about £e2.50 per meter). Ready-made buys include galabeyyas (£e15), tablecloths (£e30), and simple fine white cotton scarves that are so useful in the heat of the day (£e7–10). Stop in a café for tea and watch the traffic flow. ⊠ *Souk St. (parallel to the Corniche).* ⊙ *24 hrs.*

The Unfinished Obelisk. This site is an abandoned workshop, in which balls of greenish dolorite are still lying about. Dolorite is an extremely hard stone that was attached to rammers and used to pound and dress the surfaces of the quarried granite. Note the rows of slots where wooden wedges were driven in then soaked in water to expand and split the rock. The ancient techniques were so precise that once a stone was hewn it needed only finishing touches to ready it for its place in a temple wall.

In this case, a flaw was discovered in the massive obelisk-to-be, and it was left imprisoned in the bedrock. Had it been raised, it would have stood 137 feet tall—taller than any other obelisk—and weighed 1,162 tons. But the stone's supine potential makes it no less impressive and takes little away from the scale of the ambition of the builders of old. ⊠ *East of the Fatamid Cemetery (20-min walk from Nubia Museum).* ⊡ *£e10.* ⊙ *Oct.–May, daily 7–5; June–Sept., daily 7–6.*

NEED A BREAK? Famed in the previous century for its formal tea and dancing, **The Terrace** still continues the British afternoon tradition on its marvelous wood-pyloned terrace. These days a quartet of oriental musicians replaces the swing band, but the rarefied ambience of colonial leisure lingers. Birds roost in the wooden rafters, and the afternoon sun throws shadows and light though the balustrade. Lean back and watch the feluccas glide noiselessly by. Choose from a light menu of salads and sandwiches or sip a cardamom-scented Turkish coffee or a cool Stella beer as dusk settles on Elephantine Island's Temple of Khnum. Reservations are a good idea. ⊠ *Sofitel Old Cataract Hotel, Abtal al-Tahrir St.,* ☎ *097/316-000. AE, MC, V.*

Islands in the Nile

ELEPHANTINE ISLAND

Sources attribute the name Elephantine to three possibilities: the elephant cult symbol of a predynastic Egyptian tribe, the ancient Greek name *Abu* (Elephant Land), and more prosaically to the presence of gargantuan granite boulders that resemble the animals' rumps. The island was the site of a sanctuary to the gods of the flood and the home of noblemen whose tombs lie farther north on the West Bank. These days Elephantine is an open-air museum, brilliantly excavated and restored by the German and Swiss archaeological institutes.

Start with the **Aswan Museum,** built in 1912 to house the British engineer of the first dam. It is small and rather dingy, but you can pay your respects to the mummy of "the bearded man," whose horny toes peek out of the linen binding. The new **Museum Annex** (opened March 1998) is even smaller, but it is a revelation. Maps inside show the areas you'll visit as they appeared from 3000 BC to AD 300, along with some unsual finds, like a papyrus marriage contract, accompanied by its translation, and a hefty hoard of Ptolemaic coins.

The archaeological area is so jam-packed with debris of the old town that every time you move you crunch pottery shards beneath your feet. Highlights include the **Temple of Satis** (the goddess who "let fly the current with the force of an arrow"), a fine example of modern restoration techniques. The **Temple of Khnum** (ram-headed god of the flood and the whole locality) was the center of the ancient town and was recently cleared of rubble. On the southern tip of the island is a small Ptolemaic shrine dedicated to the Nubian god Mandolis. Beside it is a statue of an elephant. Back near the dock is the Nilometer, built by the Romans on the site of an older one and reused again in the 19th century to gauge the annual floods.

North of the archaeological area is a Nubian village, where you can go for a stroll to see how the local people live. You're likely to have kids approach you, and you might get invited for a cup of tea. ✉ *To get to the island, take a felucca from anywhere in Aswan (50p) or the public ferry from the south end of the Corniche.* 🎫 *£e10, £e15 for cameras, £e150 for video cameras.* ⏱ *Oct.–May, daily 8:30–6; June–Sept., daily 8–5.*

KITCHENER'S ISLAND

Also known as the Island of Plants, Kitchener's Island is named after Lord Horatio Kitchener, famed for his campaigns in the Sudan at the turn of the century, his role as Consul General in Egypt, and his love of exotic trees and plants. This enchanting **botanical garden,** which he endowed, is proof of the latter, and the birds just love it. ✉ *West of Elephantine Island, 15 min by felucca.* 🎫 *£e10.* ⏱ *Daily 8 AM–sunset.*

SEHEYL ISLAND

Seheyl Island is one of many islets (some of which are game preserves) in the cataract where the Nile narrows in the midst of dramatic outcroppings of pink and black granite—the felucca sail (£e40) through the cataract (rapids) is half the reason to come. Seheyl was sacred to the goddess Anukis, who wore a feather headdress and was entrusted with channeling the flood waters upriver. A mountain of crumbling rock on Seheyl's southeast corner is covered with 250 inscriptions, the graffiti of several thousand years of travelers. The **archaeological area** is gated, but the ticket kiosk is seldom manned. If the guardian isn't in, go to one of the nearby houses and someone will serve you tea (offer baksheesh in return for the courtesy) while you wait for him to return. ✉ *Seheyl Island is 40 min. south of Aswan by felucca; by taxi, 15 min to Gharb Seheyl, then a public rowboat-ferry to the island.* 🎫 *£e12.*

West Bank Sights

You can take in the West Bank sights in one half-day trip. Just sail to the West Bank dock for nearby Qubbet al-Hawa, and tell your felucca captain to pick you up at the Aga Khan Mausoleum (to the south) about four hours later. After visiting the Tombs of the Nobles, you can ride on a camel through the desert (£e30) to the Monastery of St. Simeon and onward, past the Aga Khan Mausoleum to the felucca landing at its feet. Bring a bottle of water with you (one per person) at all times of the year.

Mausoleum of the Aga Khan. The Fatimid-style tomb of Sultan Muhammed Aga Khan III (d. 1957), leader of the Shi'aa Isma'ili sect (Shi'ite), stands sentry over Aswan on a cliff of the West Bank. The tomb is closed to the public, but you can pass the outer walls on you way to or from St. Simeon's Monastery.

Tombs of the Nobles and Qubbet al-Hawa (Tomb of the Wind). The West Bank is the final resting place of the Keepers of the Southern Gate, the adventuresome ancient Egyptian noblemen of Elephantine who were entrusted with securing caravan routes, monitoring the granite quarries, and supervising trade shipments to the capital of Memphis. Take a camel or walk up the slope to the necropolis and enjoy a sense of discovery you rarely achieve when perusing Egyptian antiquities. Many tombs are closed or undergoing excavation but there's a great deal to see. The view as you make your way south along the cliff is stunning.

Start with the north-end **Tomb of Serenput I** (Nr. 36, 12th Dynasty, 1938–1759 BC), which is noted for its lovely forecourt, with six columns inscribed with male figures, and its 28-yard-long inner passageway, forged through bedrock (ask at the kiosk if this tomb is open; if not, they'll send with you someone who has a key). Move on to the **Tomb of Khounes** (Nr. 34h, 6th Dynasty, 2323–2150 BC), located beneath the ruins of a Roman wall. Traces remain of its conversion into a Coptic monastery. Look for the graffiti left by French soldiers in 1799. Continue south along the cliff to one of the best-preserved tombs of this era, that of **Serenput II** (Nr. 31, Middle Kingdom, 1980–1630 BC), grandson of Serenput I. Allow your eyes to adjust to the dim interior and watch the brilliantly colored reliefs (showing the deceased and his family) at the end of the 32-yard passage come to life. The last tombs are those of **Mekhu** and **Sabni** (Nr. 25 and Nr. 26, 6th Dynasty, 2350–2170 BC). These impressive rock-pillared chambers contain some frescoes and the occasional bat. Mekhu died in equatorial Africa on an expedition. His son Sabni went to punish the tribe who killed him and carry his father's body back home. Pharaoh Pepi II sent along mummification paraphernalia as a sign of appreciation for these exploits.

On your way back from the Tombs of the Nobles take a short hike up to the domed **Qubbet al-Hawa,** the tomb of a sheikh, for the best view in Aswan. ⊠ *West Bank access by felucca.* 🎟 *£e12 (for both tombs), cameras £e5, video cameras £e30.* ☽ *Oct.–May, daily 7–4; June–Sept., daily 7–5.*

St. Simeon's Monastery. This brooding mass dates from approximately the 7th century AD, and it is one of the largest and best-preserved Coptic monasteries in Egypt. Little is known of its origins, and although St. Simeon is said to have lived here in the 5th century, recent findings suggest that the monastery may have been originally dedicated to someone else. The place feels like an abandoned town, full of vaulted passages and crumbling arches. Some poorly preserved frescoes remain in the basilica on the lower level. A stroll through this austere and mysterious romantic ruin, with its awesome desert vistas, is memorable.

The monastery is 4 km (2.5 mi) through the desert from the Tombs of the Nobles; by camel the trip takes 40 minutes and costs £e30. From the Aga Khan Mausoleum, you can hike uphill to a footpath that leads from behind the mausoleum to the monastery, about a half-hour walk. 🎟 *£e12 (cameras free).* ☽ *Oct.–May, daily 7–4; June–Sept., daily 7–5.*

Philae Temple and the Aswan Dams

★ **Philae: The Temple of Isis** (4th century BC–1st century AD). The consequences of building the first dam on the Nile south of Aswan were alarming. In the case of Philae Island, water partially submerged the Temple of Isis when floods filled the dam as a result of seasonal rains upriver. Archaeologists feared that this periodic flooding would soften the monument's foundations, causing it to collapse. It was not until 1960, with the construction of the second dam, that UNESCO and the Egyptian Antiquities Service decided to preserve Philae and other important Upper Egyptian temples (☞ Lake Nasser Monuments, *below*). The dismantling of the Philae complex started in the early 1970s, when a huge coffer dam was erected around the island. Then nearby Agilqiyya Island was carved so the Temple of Isis would stand just as it had on Philae, and the whole complex was moved and meticulously re-installed on Agilqiyya. The process took until 1980, when authorities reopened the site to the public.

The oldest physical evidence, from blocks found on site, of the worship of Isis dates back to the reign of the 25th Dynasty Ethiopian pharaoh Taharqa (690–664 BC). During the 30th Dynasty, Nectanebo I built the temple's more imposing structures. The major part of the temple complex is the legacy of the pharaohs who ruled over Egypt between the reigns of Ptolemy II Philadelphos (285–246 BC) and the Roman emperor Diocletian (284–305 AD). The cult of Isis was upheld until the first half of the 6th century AD, when Justinian abolished the ancient Egyptian beliefs of the temple, by force.

Whereas most ancient temples are surrounded by modern habitations, the temple of Philae stands alone. The boat to the monument will take you past islands of rock, among which rises, as an image of order amid the natural randomness, the magnificent Temple of Isis.

The first sight that strikes you, once on the island, is the depth of the First Court, surrounded by a series of refined columns, all unique. The first building on the left is the **Kiosk of Nectanebo I**. The **West Colonnade,** built during the Roman period, leads up the west side of the island. In the **First Court,** turn east to admire, from right to left, the **Temple of Arensnuphis**, the **Chapel of Mandulis** (both are Nubian gods), the first **East Colonnade** (Roman period), and Ptolemy V Epiphanes's small **Temple of Imhotep.**

The First Court leads to the **First Pylon of Ptolemy XIII Neos Dionysos.** Both of the obelisks erected in front of the pylon are now at Kingston Lacy, in Dorset, England, taken there by Giovanni Battista Belzoni in 1819. Belzoni (1778–1823) was an Italian explorer, adventurer, and excavator. His unorthodox methods destroyed quite a lot of valuable material. Considering the techniques used in his day, he was no worse than other archaeologists.

The small *mammisi* (birth house) on the left side of the **Second Court** was erected in honor of the birth of Horus. Earlier New Kingdom (1539–1075 BC) counterparts of Greco-Roman mammisi are reliefs depicting the divine birth of the king, as in Hatshepsut's temple at Deir al-Bahri (Luxor West Bank) and Thutmose III's shrine in the Temple of Luxor (East Bank).

At the north end of the Second Court, through the **Second Pylon,** the **Hypostyle Hall** is the actual entrance to the temple of Isis. It consists of 10 columns and is mainly the work of Ptolemy VIII (Euergetes II). The majority of the reliefs on the walls are offering scenes. The king, by himself or accompanied by his wife, donates incense, vases, and wine to the gods to please them.

It is not uncommon to hear scholars call the art of the Greco-Roman period decadent and coarse. True, it is less classically *Egyptian* than the art of preceding periods. Nevertheless, it is an interesting mixture of Hellenistic and Egyptian traditions. At the same time, the religious beliefs—the most important part of the functioning of the temples— remained the same throughout the centuries, because the temples gained a degree of independence inside Egypt.

As with every temple, the **sanctuary** is the focal point in the complex. The **Pronaos,** behind the hypostyle hall, was a converted into a Coptic church, with an altar visible on the right—which also explains the crosses on the walls. To the east of the Temple of Isis, close to the river bank, the unfinished **Kiosk of Trajan** is a small open temple with supporting columns. Inside, once again, are offering scenes.

The **Sound-and-Light Show,** like the one at the Temple of Karnak, has two parts. The first is a walk through the partly illuminated temple, and the second delivers a brief history of the site combined with music and the light show. It is a pleasant spectacle, less showy than Karnak's.

Agilqiyya Island is in the basin between the Old Dam and the High Dam, 8 km (5 mi) south of Aswan town. Boats leave for Philae from

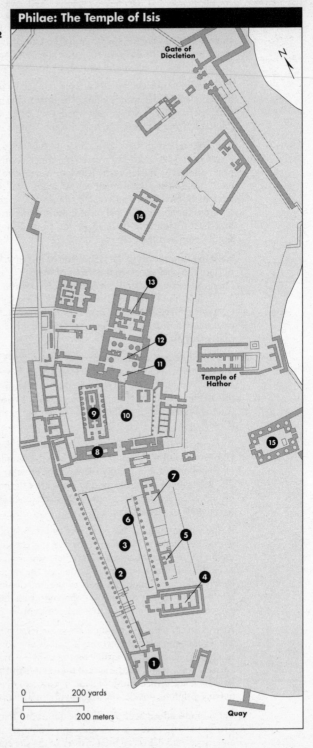

Philae: The Temple of Isis

the docks of Shellal, south of the Old Aswan Dam. The easiest, but also the most expensive way to get to the site is by taxi or with a group tour, which you can arrange at your hotel. Buy tickets for the temple before you board the boat at Shellal. ⊠ *Agilqiyya Island,* ☎ *no phone.* ▣ *Temple: £e20 (temple); boats (cost is divided among passengers): £e14 (daytime), £e16 (evening); sound-and-light show: £e33.* ⊙ *Temple: Oct.–May, daily 8–4; June–Sept., daily 7–5. Sound-and-light show: Oct.–May, daily 6, 7:30, and 9; June–Sept., daily 8, 9:30, and 11; 3rd show on Mon., 2nd show on Tues., and 1st shows on Wed., Fri., and Sat. nights are in English.*

The Old Dam. The British built the first Aswan Dam between 1898 and 1902 using blocks of local granite. The structure stands 130 feet high, 8,000 feet long, and has a capacity of 7 billion cubic yards of water. In its day it was one of the world's largest dams, and one of the sights to see in Aswan. These days the High Dam dwarfs it, and you can only drive over the Old Dam, because no stopping is allowed. The Old Dam is five minutes from town, on the way in from the airport.

Aswan High Dam. Jamal 'Abd al-Nasir's (Nasser's) vision of a modern Egypt rose and fell on the construction of the dam, which began in 1960. It took Soviet financing and engineering, plus the sweat of 30,000 Egyptians working around the clock, to complete the work by 1971. The volume of the dam itself is 17 times that of the Great Pyramid.

Lake Nasser is the world's largest man-made lake, 500 km long (310 mi), 150 km (94 mi) of which is in Sudan, and it has a storage capacity of 210,000 billion cubic yards of water. The dam doubled Egypt's power-generating capabilities, and it ensures a net surplus of 26 billion cubic yards as a reserve against low annual floods upriver.

The disadvantages of damming the Nile included the loss of fertile silt that the floods brought, which has made the use of chemical fertilizers a necessity. An incalculable loss is Nubia, which now lies beneath so many cubic yards of water, its 100,000 inhabitants relocated along the river valley. As one Nubian elder put it, "we cut off the arm to save the body."

Visit the stylized lotus monument commemorating the Russian-Egyptian collaboration, and try to convince the guard to take you up the tiny elevator for a view of surpassing splendor. The lake and Nubian desert stretch out to one side; on the other, the Nile, tamed.

The High Dam is 15 minutes from town by taxi. Allow 1 to 1½ hours to take in the spectacle. ▣ *£e5.* ⊙ *Oct.–May, daily 6–5; June–Sept., daily 6–6.*

The Fisherman's Port and Launches to Kalabsha. Just before you get to the High Dam, on the way out from Aswan, turn left down the road to the water to get to this ramshackle port, with its jumble of *African Queen*-style fishing boats and launches for the **Temple of Kalabsha** (☞ Lake Nasser Monuments, *below*). The launch to New Kalabsha Island costs £e25.

Dining

$$$$ ✕ **The 1902.** Inaugurated on December 10, 1902, on the occasion of
★ the completion of the first Aswan Dam, this palatial space, with its 75-foot central dome, is modeled after a 13th-century Mamluk mausoleum. Discreet service, candlelight, and pierced brass lamps suspended from the heights make this grand space more intimate. International menu items bearing the names of illustrious guests play up the restaurant's history. Start with a Princess Feryal (the daughter of King Faruq, who ruled the country from 1935 to 1952), a creamy pastel soup of

shrimp and saffron. For an appetizer, enjoy the famous Fayyum duck that garnishes the Lord Cromer salad (Lord Cromer was Egypt's sporting 19th-century British governor). Howard Carter, the man who rediscovered Tuntankhamun, lends his moniker to a Nile fish served in a pastry sarcophagus. King Faruq is piquantly commemorated with roasted pigeon stuffed with wheat. Reserve in advance, because priority is given to hotel guests. ⊠ *Sofitel Old Cataract Hotel, Shar'a Abtal al-Tahrir,* ☎ *097/316–000. Reservations essential. Jacket required. AE, MC, V. No lunch.*

$$$ ✕ **The Lotus.** Whether you choose the apricot-colored dining room, the outdoor terrace with its nighttime view of the lights of Aswan, or a table by the attractively lighted pool, the Lotus is nothing if not ambience. A Pan-European menu includes a creamy Veal Zurich, served with Swiss-style hash browns; an *escalope cordon bleu,* stuffed with cheese and beef-ham (the local alternative to taboo pork); and a Hungarian goulash full of fresh mushrooms, with homemade noodles on the side. Cheesecake for dessert is a better bet than the dense, buttery versions of French pastry popular in this part of the world. Breakfast, lunch, and dinner buffets are also served. ⊠ *Shar'a Abtal al-Tahrir,* ☎ *097/310–901. AE, MC, V.*

$$ ✕ **The Darna.** Decorated to resemble a Nubian dwelling, with Nubians strumming background music, Darna makes a good first foray into traditional Upper Egyptian food. A Discover Egypt menu covers the rather limited range of local dishes: mezzes (hot and cold appetizers), tagines, grilled meats, and pastries, each with a slightly haute touch. *Samboussek* (fried pastry triangles stuffed with cheese or spinach) are feather-light and flaky. Rice khalta, prepared with chicken livers and raisins, is flavored with a whiff of cinnamon. Cumin dominates the oniony sauce of *kebab hallah* (a beef tagine). *Om Ali* (a kind of bread pudding rich with coconut, raisins, and pistachios) is topped with a froth of oven-browned meringue. ⊠ *New Cataract Hotel, Shar'a Abtal al-Tahrir,* ☎ *097/316–000. AE, MC, V. No lunch.*

$$ ✕ **Club Med Buffet.** Hours are limited, but Club Med's food is prepared to please persnickety French palettes, and the dining area, with its intimate domed pavilion facing the West Bank, is charming. Come for the gorgeous swimming pool (which you can use for $6 a day, including a beverage), visit the island's gardens, and stay for lunch or dinner. Catch the Club Med launch from the south end of the Corniche near the Egypt Air office. ⊠ *Amun Island,* ☎ *097/313–800. Reservations essential. AE, MC, V.* ☉ *Daily 1–2 and 8–9* PM.

$$ ✕ **Al-Dokka.** There are several small islands around the cataract (rapids) of the Nile. One of them is occupied by this so-called Nubian restaurant, which is surrounded by the river, the gargantuan boulders of the adjacent Elephantine Island, and a view the desert beyond. The setting and the bright, airy dining room are hits, but the food itself is hit-or-miss. One sure thing is the tandoori chicken, which is tumeric yellow (a local adaptation?) but wonderfully spiced, marinated in yogurt, and baked to a crisp. A selection of Western and Middle Eastern items is also available. Call to have their boat pick you up. ⊠ *On a small island directly in front of Old Cataract Hotel,* ☎ *012/216–2379 (mobile). No credit cards.*

$$ ✕ **El Suono.** Opening onto the Old Cataract gardens, this brasserie serves a variety of Western dishes around the clock. Omelets, burgers, beef fillets, and fish, plus quick and friendly service and reliable cooking make the Suono a great solution to sightseeing-induced starvation. ⊠ *New Cataract Hotel, Corniche al-Nil,* ☎ *097/316–000. AE, MC, V.*

$$ ✕ **The Trattoria.** A basic Italian menu, and the pasta and main dishes make appetizing alternatives to Aswan's ubiquitous kebabs and tagines.

Tagliatelle served with a fresh tomato sauce and a remote relative of Parmesan cheese is fresh and surprisingly light. Although it's home-made, the lasagna is not always spinach-based, as advertised; this Upper Egyptian version is a hot, hearty tagine of spiced minced meat, pasta, and cheese topped with béchamel sauce. Breaded veal cutlets served in tomato sauce and still more cheese are tasty and substantial. ⊠ *The Isis Hotel, Corniche al-Nil, ☎ 097/315–100. AE, MC, V.*

$ ✕ **Al-Masri.** Frequented by Egyptians and foreigners, the well-known Masri is a cool refuge from the rigors of the souk. Charcoal-grilled meats are served preceded by a broth of lamb and beef, a plate of rice, a dish of veggies, and a basket of whole-wheat flatbread. Service is quick, and no alcohol is served. ⊠ *Just off Shar'a al-Souk, ☎ 097/302–576. No credit cards.*

$ ✕ **Panorama.** Sit outside or in at this sparkling-clean Nile-side restau-
★ rant, on a shady terrace or in a dining room full of plants and Nubian craft work: beaded amulets, brass fetishes, basketry, and camel sad-dlebags made from water-buffalo hides. The simple menu proposes Upper Egyptian tagines and charcoal-grilled *kofta* (ground beef), kebab, pi-geon, and chicken. There is no alcohol, so instead try one of the herbal teas; or fresh tangerine, mango, or guava juice; or one of Aswan's un-usual ice-cold libations: *karkadey* (hibiscus), tamarind, carob, or *dom* (a caramel-flavored affair made from the fruit of Sudanese palms). After the meal, don't miss the Bedouin coffee, a ritual drink associated with the Bishari tribe, and be sure to note the surprising way it's presented. ⊠ *Corniche al-Nil (just south of the Egypt Air office), ☎ 097/306–169. No credit cards.*

Lodging

$$$–$$$$ ⊞ **Sofitel Old Cataract.** The Old Cataract, which opened in 1900, is a living monument to the age of imperialism. Built on a granite bluff over-looking the temples of Elephantine Island and the stark mountains of the West Bank, it belongs to the Nile. The orderly sprawl of the brick-colored Victorian facade is dotted with wooden balconies painted a stately forest green. Birds flutter through the gardens, and the Orient of old reigns in the interior, with its keyhole arches, elaborate wood carvings, and the lofty spaces that characterize Islamic architecture. This was the preferred winter resort of the blue bloods of the early 20th century. Howard Carter stayed here after his discovery of Tutankhamun's tomb downriver. Later, Winston Churchill passed through, and the late French president Mitterand was a frequent guest. The hotel's fame was revived with the filming of Agatha Christie's *Death on the Nile,* and the current management has done much to restore the facility and its services to a high standard of elegance and efficiency. All rooms have character—the hotel's sumptuous suites most of all. A range of ac-commodations provides several price options, which might make a night at the Old Cataract a luxury that you can afford not to miss. Don't miss breakfast in the 1902 (☞ Dining, *above*), when sunlight filters though carved wooden screens. ⊠ *Shar'a Abtal al-Tahrir (south end of the Corniche), ☎ 097/316-000; 888/763–4835 in the U.S.; ℻ 097/316–011. 136 rooms. 2 restaurants, 2 bars, pool, tennis court. AE, MC, V.*

$$$ ⊞ **Isis Hotel.** This extremely well-located, riverside, bungalow-style hotel resembles a cruise ship with its terraced areas connected by staircases and the Nile-side rooms with water-level views. Rooms are small and the decor is dated, but the bathrooms are quite comfortable. The bun-galows are interspersed with gardens, and the large pool area is en-circled by multicolored flowering trees. ⊠ *Corniche al-Nil, ☎ 097/315-100 or 097/315–200, ℻ 097/315–500. 100 rooms. 2 restaurants, bar, pool. MC, V.*

\$\$ ☷ **Basma Hotel.** Occupying the highest point in Aswan, the Basma is an example of something seldom seen in Egypt: tasteful contemporary architecture. Several local artists helped decorate it, and throughout the grounds and the interior you'll come upon sculpture, murals, fountains, and mosaics. The large swimming pool is surrounded by gardens. Standard rooms are quiet, relatively spacious, and unpretentiously decorated. All have semi-enclosed, arched balconies, some of which overlook the pool and gardens and have a glimpse of the Nile. Others have a great view of the Nubia Museum, the Fatamid Cemetery, and the city. The staff is friendly and helpful. ☒ *Shar'a Abtal al-Tahrir,* ☎ *097/310–901,* ℻ *097/310–907. 179 rooms. Restaurant, minibars, pool, beauty salon, shops, travel services. AE, MC, V.*

\$\$ ☷ **New Cataract Hotel.** Off-putting utilitarian architecture here is redeemed by proximity to the Old Cataract, with which the newer sister shares management, a large pool, and gardens. The eight-story structure may be far from lovely, but the views from it are nothing short of sensational, and every comfortably spacious room has a large balcony from which to enjoy them. Request a room with a Nile view, because the others are a shade underwhelming. Service is well above average. ☒ *Shar'a Abtal al-Tahrir,* ☎ *097/316–000; 888/763–4835 in the U.S.;* ℻ *097/316–011. 144 rooms. 3 restaurants, pub, pool, tennis court, beauty salon, shops, dance club, travel services. AE, MC, V.*

\$\$ ☷ **Villa Amun.** This Club Med operation is on a tiny, idyllic island consecrated in antiquity to the Egyptian god Amun-Re. The present structure contains portions of its earlier mid-19th-century architecture. A salmon-pink villa houses 50 identical rooms (bathrooms with showers only) with balconies and splendid views of the West Bank, Elephantine Island, and Aswan. You arrive by motor launch from a small stone dock on the Corniche and pass through a corridor of imperial palms to the villa's veranda entry. The gardens are artfully landscaped, and the pool is a gigantic square of turquoise facing town. An energetic, multilingual staff makes you feel as if you're visiting your own vacation house. The food is good, if not superb, and the ambience in the dining and lounge areas is casual. Considering what else is available in town, it is an excellent value. ☒ *Amun Island (facing the Old Cataract hotel),* ☎ *097/313–800 or 097/313–850, 212/977–2100 in the U.S.,* ℻ *097/317–190. 50 rooms. Restaurant, bar, pool, steam room. AE, MC, V.*

\$ ☷ **Abu Simbel Hotel.** Another piece of boxy architecture from Egypt's socialist '60s, this hotel is central, right on the Corniche al-Nil, which makes it a low-cost favorite with no-frills travelers. A welcoming cane awning leads through the entry garden, where alcohol is served, to a tired lobby, where English is spoken. Rooms are unabashedly shabby though air-conditioned (if you prefer noise to heat), but the sheets on the twin beds are snowy white and views from the small balconies are great. The bathrooms are essentially closets with showers. Unlike other local hotels in the same category, the Abu Simbel does have personality. ☒ *Corniche al-Nil,* ☎ *097/302–327,* ℻ *097/315–931. 66 rooms. Laundry service. No credit cards.*

\$ ☷ **The Cleopatra Hotel.** A pleasant, modern, low-rise building with no Nile views, the Cleopatra allows you to experience the rhythms of Aswan. The lobby is decorated with low arches and small domes, and it houses a 24-hour restaurant. The rooms are disappointing, though clean, and they are undergoing refurbishment. Not all of the bathrooms have bathtubs: some are equipped with showers only. The Cleopatra's plus is its rooftop swimming pool—the only one in Aswan—with a panoramic, five-star view. Some rooms have small refrigerators. ☒ *Shar'a Sa'd Zaghlul (near train station and souk),* ☎ *097/314–001,* ℻ *097/314–002. 114 rooms. Restaurant, bar, refrigerators, pool. AE, V.*

$ 🏨 **Philae Hotel.** Once you get past the white marble lobby and its un-
savory furnishings, you'll be able to to better appreciate the budgetary
benefits of the Philae. The modern pink building (three floors, no elevator) is centrally located on the Corniche. Its shallow balconies have
Nile and Elephantine Island views. Despite dingy corridors and down-
at-the-heels furnishings, the rooms are of a decent size and standard
of cleanliness. Bathrooms have showers only. ⊠ *Corniche al-Nil,* ☎
097/312–090. 70 rooms. Refrigerators. No credit cards.

LAKE NASSER MONUMENTS

Until recently, Lower Nubia, the area south of Aswan below the First
Cataract, was much like to the Nile Valley north of Aswan—save for
the fact that the primary inhabitants were Nubian Egyptians, rather
than Egyptians of Arab, Turkish, or Bedouin descent. As in Upper Egypt,
Nubia's thin ribbon of green, fed by the Nile, was hemmed in by
desert. Nubians cultivated their fields, and massive pharaonic monuments line the riverbanks.

The Aswan High Dam and Lake Nasser put an end to that, of course,
forcing the Nubian population inhabiting the flooded areas to move
downriver to areas around Aswan and north of it. Many of the monuments from antediluvian Nubia were also relocated to higher ground,
or salvaged and removed to foreign countries like the United States (the
Temple of Dendur is in the Metropolitain Museum in New York), Spain,
Holland, and Germany. Unfortunately, others could not be saved, and
they were swallowed up by the waters of Lake Nasser—some were hastily
excavated first, while the rest were submerged without a trace.

The massive excavation, salvage, and relocation operation that took
place in Egypt in the 1960s is unique in archaeological history, and it
has been one of the most notable achievements of UNESCO. Until 1995
and the advent of Lake Nasser cruises, it was virtually impossible to
visit most of the rescued Nubian monuments, save for Abu Simbel (and
the relocated monuments accessible from Aswan: Philae, Kalabsha, and
Beit al-Wali). Now the superb lake cruises make all the sites equally
accessible.

For information on three- and four-day trips on Lake Nasser, *see*
Chapter 5.

New Kalabsha

30 minutes south of Aswan by taxi (or bus) and ferry.

The temples from the sites of **Kalabsha and Beit al-Wali** were moved
to the island of New Kalabsha near Aswan. This rocky island, redo-
lent of fish, is uninhabited save for a few dogs, foxes, and the Antiquities guards that care for the temple and monitor the ticket booth. The
view of the lake and the dam is very fine from the island, and especially charming from the landing dock.

The largest freestanding Egyptian temple in Nubia, **Kalabsha** was built
by Augustus Caesar (reigned 27 BC–AD 14) and dedicated to Osiris,
Isis, and Mandulis, a Nubian fertility god with a very elaborate headdress. Although the temple building was almost completed in antiquity, its decoration was never finished. Only three inner rooms, as well
as portions of the exterior, are completely decorated with reliefs. Kalabsha's half-finished column capitals and fragments of relief decoration do, however, provide a great deal of information about ancient
construction and carving techniques. And the view from the pylon and
the roof area is wonderful and well worth the climb.

The temple complex includes a birth house, in the southwest corner, and a small chapel in the northeast corner, dating to the Ptolemaic period. A large rock stela dating to the reign of Seti I has also been erected at this site. Its original location was Qasr Ibrim (☞ *below*).

Several large boulders covered with petroglyphs of uncertain date stand on the left side of the temple. The petroglyphs, which resemble those of the southern African San (Bushmen), include carvings of people and animals, including elephants and antelopes.

The small rock-cut temple of **Beit al-Wali** was removed from its cliffside home—the ancients had carved it out of the cliff, like Hatshepsut's temple on the West Bank at Luxor—and moved to New Kalabsha in the 1960s. A small path connects it to the Roman temple of Kalabsha. Ramesses II commissioned Beit al-Wali and dedicated it to Amun-Re and other deities. Originally the temple was fronted by a mud-brick pylon, which was not moved, and consisted of an entrance hall, a hypostyle hall, and a sanctuary. This small, jewel-like temple is a delight, because its painted decorations, its reds, blues, and greens—look almost as fresh as they did the day they were applied. The entrance hall contains scenes of Ramesses II quelling various enemies of Egypt, often accompanied by a pet lion. The columned hall shows the pharaoh interacting with different deities, chief among them being Amun-Re. The sanctuary contains carved seated statues of Ramesses II and deities, such as Horus, Isis, and Khnum.

The site is a stop on Lake Nasser cruises, and it is accessible from Aswan—by taxi to the fisherman's port east of the High Dam, then by boat (£e25) to the island. ☎ *No phone*. ✉ *£e12; cameras free*. ☉ *Oct.–May, daily 7–5; June–Sept., daily 7–6*.

Interior Lake Nasser Monuments

All Lake Nasser's interior monuments—those located apart from Aswan and Abu Simbal—can only be visited on a multiday lake cruise. They are set in rather bleak landscapes relieved only by the odd reed and bird. You don't need entry tickets, because they are included with the cruise.

The remains of the temple at **Gerf Hussein** are fragmentary. Built by Setau, a viceroy of Kush during the reign of Ramesses II, it was originally a combination rock-cut and freestanding temple, similar in plan to the temple of Abu Simbel (☞ *below*). It was dedicated to the deified Ramesses II, Ptah (a creator god), Hathor (goddess of love, beauty, and music), and Ptah-tanen (a Nubian-Egyptian creator god). Seated statues of the four were carved out of the rock in the sanctuary. Unfortunately, the portion of the temple that now remains is badly preserved, and it has little of the grandeur that it once did. For that you must travel to its counterpart at Abu Simbel.

Wadi al-Sebua is famous for being the site of two New Kingdom temples. The earlier temple, which had both freestanding and rock-cut elements, was constructed by Amenhotep III and added to by Ramesses II. It consists of a sanctuary, a court, a hall, and pylons. The temple was originally dedicated to a Nubian form of Horus, but was later rededicated to the god Amun-Re.

The more dramatic and larger site at al-Sebua is the temple of Ramesses II, Re-Harakhte (a sun god), and Amun-Re. It is yet another of Ramesses II's projects, and it once stood about 150 yards northeast of the Amenhotep III temple; it has been moved about 3 km (2 mi) to the west. This temple has both freestanding and rock-cut sections.

The Ptolemaic and Roman temple of **al-Dakka** has been moved from its original site to a new one not far from Wadi al-Sebua. Dakka was originally built by reusing fragments of an older temple dating from the 18th Dynasty.

The main part of the temple of **Amada,** dedicated to Amun-Re and Re-Harakhte, was constructed in the 18th Dynasty. Various 19th-Dynasty pharaohs repaired it and added to it. Between 1964 and 1975 it was moved here, about 2 km (1 mi) away from its original location.

Amada is noted for two important historical inscriptions. One dates to the reign of Amenhotep II; it appears on a round-topped stela on the eastern wall of the sanctuary. The inscription describes a definitive military victory over rebellious chiefs in Syria. The other is on a stela carved from the northern thickness of the entryway and dates to the reign of King Merneptah (1212–1202 BC). It describes how the king successfully repelled a Libyan invasion of Egypt in the early years of his reign.

The temple of **al-Derr** was moved in 1964 near the site of Amada. It is a rock-cut temple built by Ramesses II and dedicated to himself, Amun-Re, Re-Harakhte, and Ptah. The temple is well decorated, and its bright colors are still visible—particularly in the area before the sanctuary.

Qasr Ibrim is a large site on what is now an island. Not too many years ago the area was attached to the mainland by a spit of land. Because of the rise in the level of water in the lake, it is now impossible to land and walk around Qasr Ibrim, although archaeological work here continues (hastily). The site is interesting because it encompasses several periods of history: pharaonic, Roman, Christian, and Arab/Nubian, up to the mid-20th century.

The island houses the remains of temples from the 18th and 25th dynasties, as well as rock-cut shrines dedicated to different pharaohs and assorted gods dating to the 18th and 19th dynasties. Remains of a sizeable fortress of the Augustan period are also visible, as are portions of a large basilica. Foundations and standing portions of dwellings are also visible. Archaeologists working at the site have found much well-preserved evidence—leather, manuscripts, pottery, and animal and botanical remains—that sheds light on daily life during the various periods of occupation at Qasr Ibrim.

Abu Simbel: the Temples of Ramesses II and Nefertari

280 km (175 mi) south of Aswan.

★ Abu Simbel began as a small village of a few houses clustered at some distance from the temples of Abu Simbel. Now it is a lush oasis with hotels and a sizable settlement. Arriving by plane or bus steals some of the drama that is so much a part of Ramesses II's monument of monuments. The lake approach, on the other hand, fulfills every fantasy you might have about the grandeur of ancient Egypt.

Ramesses II's two enormous temples at Abu Simbel are among the most awe-inspiring monuments in Egypt. The pharaoh had his artisans carve the temples out of a rock cliff to display his might as the Egyptian god king and to strike dread into the Nubians—and the temples are most effective as such. They originally stood at the bottom of the cliff that they now crown (they're currently some 200 ft above the water level and ⅓ mi back from the lake shore). Their relocation required cutting the temples out of the cliffs in large sections, then fitting the pieces back together at the new sites—an amazing feat of modern engineering and international cooperation that took four years to complete.

The first of the two temples of Abu Simbel, the **Great Temple**, was dedicated to Ramesses II (as a god) and to Re-Harakhte, Amun-Re, and Ptah. The second was dedicated to the goddess Hathor and Nefertari, Ramesses II's wife and chief queen. The Great Temple is fronted by four seated colossi, about 65 ft tall, of Ramesses II wearing the double crown of Upper and Lower Egypt (one crown is broken). Around the legs of the statues stand smaller figures of Ramesses II's wives and offspring. The top of the temple facade is covered by a row of rampant baboons praising the sun as it rises. Between the two pairs of statues is a carved figure of Re-Harakhte that stands over the door to the temple.

The doorway between the colossi leads to the **first hall,** which contains columns decorated with figures of Ramesses II. The hall itself is carved on the right (north) with reliefs showing events from Ramesses II's reign, most notably his self-proclaimed victory at the Battle of Kadesh in Syria (his opponent might beg to differ). It shows the beseiged city, the attack, and the counting of body parts of the defeated enemies. The left (south) side shows Ramesses' battles with Syrians, Libyans, and Nubians, and it has some fine scenes showing Ramesses on a chariot. Vultures with outstretched wings decorate the ceiling. Several side chambers are accessible from this hall. These were probably used as storerooms for the temple furniture, vessels, linen, and priestly costumes.

The **second hall** contains four square columns and is decorated with scenes of Ramesses II and Queen Nefertari offering to various deities, including the deified Ramesses himself. This hall leads into a narrow room that was probably where the king made offerings to the gods of the temple.

Three chapels branch off the narrow offering room. The two side chapels are undecorated, but the central chapel, the **main sanctuary,** is decorated not only with scenes of the pharaoh making offerings and conducting temple rituals, but also with four rock-carved statues of the deities to whom the temple is dedicated. They are, from left to right, Ptah, Amun-Re, Ramesses II, and Re Horakhte. These were originally painted and gilded, but the paint and the gold has long since gone. The temple was originally constructed so that twice each year the first rays of the rising sun would pierce the dark interior of the temple and strike these four statues, bathing them in light. The temple was moved so that this still happens, albeit a day late, on February 21 and October 21.

The small temple at Abu Simbel is the **Temple of Queen Nefertari,** dedicated to Hathor. The temple is fronted by six colossal standing rock-cut statues of Queen Nefertari and Ramesses II. Each statue is flanked by some of their children. The temple doorway opens into a **pillared hall** that contains six Hathor-head columns much larger than those in Deir al-Bahri. The ceiling contains a dedicatory inscription from Ramesses II to Queen Nefertari. The hall itself is decorated with scenes of the royal couple, either together or singly, offering to or worshipping the gods. A narrow vestibule, decorated with scenes of offerings, follows the pillared hall, and the **main sanctuary** leads off of this vestibule. The sanctuary contains a niche with a statue of Hathor as a cow, protecting Ramesses. ⊠ *Mabed Abu Simbel,* ☎ *no phone.* ☎ *£e40, still camera free, video £e25.* ⊘ *Oct.–May, daily 6–5; June–Sept., daily 6–6.*

Getting Around

Egypt Air (☎ 095/380–580 in Luxor; 097/315–000 in Aswan) flies to Abu Simbel from Cairo (2½ hours), Luxor (1½ hours), and Aswan (½ hour). You can also hire a car or take a bus from Aswan (3½ hours each way). Lake Nasser cruises either begin or end here. As yet it is not possible to hire a private boat to get to Abu Simbel from Aswan.

NILE VALLEY AND LAKE NASSER A TO Z

Arriving and Departing

By Plane

Egypt Air is currently the only way to fly. Flight scheduling (usually at least two planes daily) can be unreliable and often late. Reconfirming tickets (in person or through your hotel) three days in advance is an absolute must. Domestic flights leave Cairo from the Old Airport, Terminals 2 or 3, which are adjacent to the new international terminal.

In **Cairo**, the best (meaning calmest) Egypt Air office is in the Nile Hilton on the Tahrir Square side of the building. ☎ 02/570–9703 or 02/579–3046. ⊙ Sat.–Thurs. 9–5.

In **Luxor**, the office is just beside the Winter Palace. ☎ 095/380–580. ⊙ Daily 8–8.

In **Aswan**, the Egypt Air building is a landmark on the south end of the Corniche. ☎ 097–315–000. ⊙ Daily 8–8.

Round-trip ticket costs and one-way flight times are **Cairo to Luxor** £e830, one hour; **Cairo to Aswan,** usually via Luxor, £e1,140, about 2 hours; **Luxor to Aswan,** £e190, 30 minutes; **Luxor to Abu Simbel** via Aswan, £e680, about 1½ hours; **Aswan to Abu Simbel,** £e300, 30 mintues.

Between the airports and downtown: Both the Luxor and Aswan airports are about 15 to 20 minutes from town, a taxi ride of about £e20.

By Train

Comfortable sleeper cars make the daily trip to Luxor and Aswan from the cavernous Ramses Station in central Cairo, departing at 7 PM and arriving the next morning first in Luxor at 8, then in Aswan at 11. Reserve tickets in advance, either at the station, if you feel adventurous, or at a travel agency such as **Hapi Tours** (✉ 17 Shar'a Qasr al-Nil, Downtown, ☎ 02/393—3562 or 02/393–3693). Return trains leave Aswan for Cairo at 4:45 PM, stopping in Luxor and departing at 9 PM, and arriving in Cairo at 6:30 AM the next day.

The cost of a single couchette with breakfast is £e490; a double with breakfast costs £e630.

By Bus

Government buses to Upper Egypt can be a pretty rough ride, because of the condition of the seats, the sporadic functioning of the air-conditioning, and the blaring of the on-board video machine. But buses are by far the cheapest way to go—about £e50 one way to either Luxor or Aswan. Purchase tickets in advance from the kiosk next to the Ramses Hilton, off Tahrir Square in central Cairo (☎ 02/574–6658).

Schedules are: **Cairo to Luxor** departs 8:30 PM and arrives around 6 AM the next day; **Cairo to Aswan** departs 5 PM and arrives 6 AM. Three daily buses make the 3½-hour run from **Luxor to Aswan** (£e15), departing Luxor from the station behind the Luxor Museum. Buses run from **Aswan to Luxor** every 40 minutes (£e10) from the station behind the Abu Simbel Hotel. Buses make the three-hour trip from **Aswan to Abu Simbel** twice daily (£e40 round-trip).

Getting Around Luxor

By Taxi

Luxor is rife with **taxis,** usually six-seater Peugeot station wagons. You can travel the length of the Corniche for about £e13, and shorter trips cost £e7. In practice, prices can fluctuate from driver to driver, but check with the tourist office or at your hotel to find out what the theoretically fixed rates are to all destinations. Everyone knows the rates, especially the taxi drivers, but it's a good idea to agree to a price before you set out. Tipping is customary.

The same Peugeot station wagons that work the town can be hired for longer trips to temples at Dendera, Abydos, Esna, Edfu, and Kom Ombo. The Tourist Information Office can advise on rates, as can Thomas Cook and the American Express offices, which can arrange cars for you. **Sinderella Cars** (☏ 095/381–068 or 095/379–700) advertises English-speaking drivers and air-conditioned vehicles at just slightly higher prices than the public Peugeots.

Approximate costs of private taxi service for a minimum of two people, and the time required for the trips, are as follows: **full day in Luxor,** £e136; **Luxor to Aswan,** full-day, 225-km (140-mi) trip with stops at temples at Edfu, Esna, and Kom Ombo, £e150 one way; **Luxor to Dendera,** 60-km (38-mi), half-day trip, £e70 round-trip; **Luxor to Edfu,** 230-km (144-mi) trip, with stop in Esna, £e100 round-trip.

In Luxor, support the local caleche drivers and take a Nile-side ramble in a **horse-drawn carriage.** As they will point out, unlike taxi drivers, they *have* to feed their horses. The entire 45-minute Corniche promenade will set you back around £e14.

Luxor's new **bridge,** 12 km (7.5 mi) south of town, opened in 1998, putting an end to the perilous car ferry that used to make regular crossings and now limps across occasionally. If you decide to take a taxi to the West Bank, the ride plus four hours time on the West Bank will cost about £e55.

By Boat

You can still take the **public pedestrian ferry** in front of the Luxor Temple for a few piasters. It plies back and forth every 15 minutes or so from early morning until about midnight. In Luxor, **powerboats** will also take you across the river a bit faster, for about £e17 per boat. You'll find them in front of the Winter Palace and at the car ferry landing near the Novotel.

Feluccas have fixed rates that tend to be highly negotiable and start at around £e24 per hour. You can find out these rates at the Tourist Information Office, hotels, Thomas Cook, and America Express offices.

Getting Around Aswan

By Taxi

You'll find plenty of **taxis** in Aswan, again the six-seater Peugeot station wagons as in Luxor. You can travel the length of the Corniche for about £e13, shorter trips will cost £e7.

In Aswan, prices quoted by the Tourist information Office for six-seater Peugeots cover up to four people in the same car: **Aswan to Kom Ombo,** a half-day, 90-km (56-mi) round-trip: £e50; **Aswan to Luxor,** a full-day, one-way (225-km, 140-mi) trip, including temples at Esna and Edfu, or Edfu and Kom Ombo: £e150; **Aswan to Abu Simbel,** a very full day (280 km, 175 mi): £e238; **Aswan to Philae,** including the driver's three-hour wait while you look around: £e70; **Aswan to the High Dam,** including a stop at the rest area: £e35.

Thrifty Limosine (☏ 097/316–000) has air-conditioned cars with drivers; a full day around town for costs £e300.

By Boat

Aswan has no West Bank roads, so you'll have to travel by felucca to visit the sights across the river. Powerboats also run between sights, but they are a less romantic, more expensive, and essentially unnecessarily expedient, coming at about twice the cost to cut travel time in half.

Public felucca ferries cross regularly to Elephantine Island for a couple of pounds from early morning to midnight. Catch them by the public park on the south end of the Corniche.

Feluccas have fixed rates that tend to be highly negotiable and start at around £e24 per hour. You can find out these rates at the Tourist Information Office, hotels, Thomas Cook, and America Express offices.

For longer felucca trips from Aswan, consult the Tourist Information Office for help in arrranging tours to Kom Ombo (a full day and night); to Edfu (two days and nights); and Esna (three days and nights). Prices for these trips are reasonable, from about £e35 to £e100 per person, depending on the length of the journey (note that captains can be reluctant to sail all the way to Luxor, because the return trip upriver takes longer; if you are going to end the trip south of Luxor, be sure to arrange to be picked up). You need a group of six people for one of these lovely, rustic, camp-out-style journeys. For information on arranging multi-day felucca trips, *see* Chapter 5.

In Aswan, **powerboats** leave for New Kalabsha Island (its temples are Kalabsha and Beit al-Wali) from beside the entry to the High Dam; the £e30 fare will allow about an hour's visit. Philae has its own dock about a 15-minute drive from town, on the east side of the basin between the Old Dam and the High Dam. Powerboats make the trip for about £e50, but they offer to wait for only two hours. It's advisable to allow three hours to see Philae's Temple of Isis, so mention this in advance.

Contacts and Resources

Currency Exchange

Most hotels have cashier desks to change money. Exchange offices tend to be open long hours and banks open shorter hours. American Express and Thomas Cook also change money. Rates are the same everywhere.

Luxor: Bank of Alexandria. ⊠ *Corniche al-Nil (near the Etap Hotel),* ☏ *095/380–282.* ☉ *Sun.–Thurs. 8:30–2.*

Aswan: Bank of Alexandria ⊠ *Corniche al-Nil (across from the Isis Hotel),* ☏ *097/302–765.* ☉ *June–Sept., daily 8–2 and 3–10; Oct.–May, daily 8 AM–9 PM.*

Emergencies

LUXOR

A new **hospital** is scheduled to open in Luxor in 1999, but it could be delayed. Meanwhile, rather than taking chances in the old hospital, contact a doctor directly: **Mazhar Wardi, MD** (⊠ Station St., ☏ 095/373–717), or **Maurice Suleiman, MD** (⊠ Station St., ☏ 095/372–036).

Police (☏ 095/372–066 or 095/373–845); **Ambulance** (☏ 095/372–474); **New Hospital** (⊠ Television St., ☏ 095/372–698).

ASWAN

The German Hospital in Aswan has a good reputation.

Police (☏ 097/303–163); **Ambulance** (☏ 097/302–176); **German Hospital** (⊠ Corniche al-Nil South, ☏ 097/302–176).

Guided Tours

If you haven't arranged an itinerary from Cairo, your best options for guided tours in Upper Egypt are Thomas Cook or American Express. Thomas Cook is particularly flexible in arranging tours to suit a variety of desires and budgets. Either office can arrange day trips, such as taxis taking you around town. The Tourist Information Office in Aswan is extremely helpful in this respect, whereas the office in Luxor only provides bus and train schedules. Travel office services are as follows (☞ Travel Agencies, *below*, for addresses and telephone numbers):

LUXOR

American Express's very helpful staff changes money, makes hotel and plane reservations, and arranges guided tours by car and boat. A full-day trip from Luxor to Dendera by powerboat, with lunch and guide, costs £e150 per person. An air-conditioned car from Luxor to Aswan via Esna, Edfu, and Kom Ombo, including a guide and temple tickets, costs £e350 per person.

Thomas Cook's courteous staff changes money and arranges guided tours and cruises. A trip from Luxor to Aswan and Abu Simbel by air—a super-full day that includes visits to the Aswan High Dam and the Unfinished Obelisk—costs £e1,120 per person. Thomas Cook can also arrange balloon trips over Luxor for approximately £e640 person.

Carlson WagonLit runs plenty of tours but has fewer price options and comprehensive services. One of its tours runs from Luxor to Dendera and Abydos, a full-day trip including a guide, temple tickets, and an air-conditioned car, for £e135 per person.

ASWAN

American Express changes money and arranges tours, hotels, and plane tickets. This office is not as helpful as the Luxor Amex office, but staff can arrange tours, such as a day at the Tombs of the Nobles, including felucca and camel rides, a guide, and admission tickets, for £e70 per person. Full-day excursions to Abu Simbel by air cost £e500 per person.

Thomas Cook can tell you most anything you need to know about Aswan and arrange tours for any budget. The office also changes money and provides other standard services, including Lake Nasser cruises, although it is advisable to book Nile and Lake Nasser cruises in advance from Cairo (☞ Chapter 5).

Pharmacies

Luxor Pharmacy. ⊠ *Behind Luxor Temple,* ☎ *095/372–051.* ☉ *Mon.– Sat. 8–3 and 5–11.*

Pharmacy al-Nil. ⊠ *Aswan, Corniche al-Nil (in front of the Isis Hotel),* ☎ *097/302–674.* ☉ *Daily 7 AM–1 AM.*

Travel Agencies

LUXOR

Agencies in Luxor are all alongside the Winter Palace Hotel on the Corniche. **American Express Travel** (☎ 095/378–333), ☉ open daily 9–5; **Thomas Cook** (☎ 095/372–402), ☉ open daily 8–8; **Carlson WagonLit** (☎ 095/372–317), ☉ open daily 9–5.

ASWAN

American Express Travel (⊠ New Cataract Hotel, Shar'a Abtal al-Tahrir, ☎ 097/316–000), ☉ open daily 9–5; **Thomas Cook** (⊠ Corniche al-Nil, ☎ 097/306–839 or 097/304–011), open Oct.–May, daily 8–8, and June–Sept., daily 8–2 and 5–8.

Visitor Information

Luxor Tourist Information Center (✉ Corniche al-Nil, between Luxor Temple and the Winter Palace, ☎ 095/372–215), ☉ open daily 9–2, though hours vary, has less than enlightening staff, but you'll find bus and train schedules posted and lists of fixed taxi rates, in Arabic. Staff should be able to help you figure them out.

Aswan Tourist Information Center (✉ Beside the train station, ☎ 097/312–811), ☉ open daily 9–2 and 6–9, has a very helpful, multilingual staff that can tell you about fixed taxi and felucca rates for short and long trips. The staff can also recommend guides and provide most any other infomation about Aswan.

5 Nile and Lake Nasser Cruises

Roman emperors and their ladies, medieval travelers and historians, 19th-century romantics and antiquarians—all have fallen for the legendary Nile, the majestic ghostly presence of its pharaohs, its healthy climate. Until the completion of the High Dam at Aswan in 1971, the land of Nubia was the age-old link between Egypt and the Sudan. Now it lies under Lake Nasser, on the shores of which stand fabled monuments like Ramesses II's great temple at Abu Simbel.

CRUISING ALONG THE NILE was once the only form of travel in Egypt, and there is still nothing like it. Rural areas succeed one another on the banks of the river in a pattern of life that has not changed for thousands of years. The Nile Valley farmer today, as in ancient times, tends his land with a wooden plough, transports produce from place to place on his faithful donkey, and draws water by such ancient devices as the hand-powered *shaduf* and the waterwheel, driven by patient buffaloes. His life is adjusted to the predictable rhythm of the seasons, and there is a timeless, almost biblical quality to the scene that unfolds as you follow the river. A Nile cruise affords the triple pleasure of comfortable relaxation on board, witnessing age-old ways of life on the riverbanks, and visiting some of the most famous and beautiful monuments in the world.

The Lake Nasser cruise is a different experience. "Lake" Nasser, of course, is a reservoir. Popularly known as the Nubian Sea, because of the land that surrounds it, the lake is 500 km (312 mi) long: 370 km (230 mi) in Egypt and the rest in the Republic of the Sudan. It takes its shape behind the Aswan High Dam from the spread of water around sun-baked hills and into dry riverbeds.

The cruel irony of the Nubran Sea is that today the neat, domed houses of the Nubian people, their villages, their places of worship, and their burial grounds along the banks of the Nile are under water—in the 1960s the entire population of nearly 100,000 people was relocated to Kom Ombo in Egypt and to Kashm al-Girba in the Sudan before the completion of the dam.

For millennia, the Nile was the trade route into the continent, and ancient Egyptians called Nubia the "corridor to Africa." It is a barren land, rich in minerals, especially copper and gold, and its richness in ancient monuments attests to cultural links to Egypt from the earliest times. Here the Nile carved its way through the native sandstone, creating cliffs over which the river never rose in flood season to deposit its rich, silt-laden soil along the banks, as it did in Egypt. Ramesses II's Abu Simbel temple was carved into those cliffs—until the rising waters of Lake Nasser forced the government to cut the temple from its former location and move it 200 feet higher up the banks.

The High Dam—a vast rock-filled structure 11,790 ft long, 375 ft high, and with a base thickness of 3,200 ft—separates the reservoir from the upper reaches of the Nile. Cruisers do not have access from one to the other.

Note: The ancient temples are all easily accessible; some you can actually see while cruising on the Nile or Lake Nasser. The monuments are covered at length in Chapter 4.

CHOOSING A CRUISE

The traditional Nile cruise is recommended if this is your first visit to Egypt, not only because of the greater diversity of monuments, but also because of the opportunity to see rural Egyptians, their villages, and, in places, local crafts. The Lake Nasser cruise is recommended if you have an archaeological bent, or if you simply want to get away from it all in the wide-open spaces of the lake.

On the Nile there are three-, four-, and seven-night cruises. The first two ply the river between Luxor and Aswan, taking in the towns and temples en route. The seven-night cruise extends north of Luxor to Dendera, the site of the Temple of Hathor, and goes from there on a day trip overland to that holiest of ancient cities, Abydos. An advantage of a seven-night cruise is that you will be sailing along parts of the Nile that are not so congested with cruise boats, past stretches of the valley that make for very impressive sightseeing.

Typically, Lake Nasser cruises start from Aswan on Mondays, in which case they last four nights, or from Abu Simbel on Fridays, in which case they last three. From north to south, sights viewed are the relocated temples of Kalabsha, Beit al-Wali, and Kertassi near the High Dam; the temples of Sebua, Dakka, and Meharakka reconstructed at Wadi al-Sebua; the temples of Amada, Derr, and the tomb of Penout reconstructed at Amada; Qasr Ibrim on its original site; and at Abu Simbel the famous temples of Ramesses II and his wife, Nefertari—hallmarks of the UNESCO-funded Nubian salvage operations.

Options

If you are taking a Nile cruise and don't want to miss Abu Simbel, a flight can take you there and return you to Aswan the same day. Likewise, if you are taking a lake cruise, you can fly to Luxor for a day to see its famous East and West Bank monuments. The Aswan–Luxor flight lasts 30 minutes. Aswan–Abu Simbel takes 30 minutes; Luxor–Abu Simbel takes 90 minutes. Cruise costs do not include these flights.

If a week or more on the water is your goal, some travel agencies are now offering combined river and lake cruises.

Types of Ships

Floating Hotels

The so-called "floating hotel" is the standard Nile and Lake Nasser cruiser. These tiered boats look like boxes with windows stacked on low-slung hulls—the waters are calm enough not to require seagoing vessels—and they are essentially the same, differing only in size and decor. The craft are air-conditioned and have pools, hot tubs, excercise rooms, saunas, Turkish baths, restaurants, and panoramic halls for viewing the passing scenery. The newer luxury boats are of a smaller class and are more intimate.

There are some 250 cruise vessels on the Nile. For reasons of safety and security, we recommend that you use only vessels with solid reputations, which are generally more expensive. These also most closely meet American standards for hygiene and sanitation. The government intends to restrict the number of cruisers on Lake Nasser to five to safeguard against pollution. All five vessels are of a high standard.

Feluccas

Felucca is the name given to those single-masted sailboats that are the romantic symbol of Nile travel. They have cushioned benches along the sides, sometimes a table at the center, and are a pleasant way to spend an hour or two sailing along the Nile, especially at sunset. They are decidedly *not* the standard vessels for taking multiday cruises.

For adventurers, nature lovers, and those who want to sample a simpler life, larger feluccas can be hired for a three-day cruise between Aswan and Esna only, when the locks at Esna are closed in the spring, or a longer cruise (between three and four days depending on your interests) between Aswan and Luxor at other times of the year. The vessels always sail from south to north, with the flow of the river, and on such trips you sleep in the open, on deck, wrapped in blankets. This trip is recommended only to the hardiest travelers, to whom a lack of privacy is of little concern. Also keep in mind that food is cooked by sailors and may not meet your normal standards of hygiene. Depending on the size and comfort of the felucca, the average cost is $25 per person per day, inclusive of food and sightseeing.

Two Egyptian companies can arrange such trips: **Apple Tours** (✉ 15 Abdel Aziz Gawish St., Abdeen, Cairo, ☏ 02/256–2517 or 02/594–0366, FAX 02/355–9814) make arrangements for groups of six to eight persons; and **Benu Travel** (☞ Booking a Cruise, *below*). You can also make arrangements directly with **Mohamed Awi** (☏ 097/306–6432) who owns a felucca fleet, has an expertise in making arrangements, and can get the necessary police clearance to take a group on the Nile.

The Cruise Experience

There is nothing more relaxing than spending an afternoon on a boat's partially shaded upper deck sipping a beverage. Lie back on a chaise longue and take in the wide valley of the Nile—its belts of palm groves and clusters of mud-brick houses passing in the foreground, its long ranges of limestone mountains stretching across the horizon. On a lake cruise, you'll look out on pristine deserts' tender, pale violet shadows patching ochre landscapes, the water turning to liquid gold from the reflection of the sunset.

Sailing on Nile or lake combines relaxation with sightseeing. Days are structured around the time of the year and the hours that your boat reaches towns and monuments. In summer, shore excursions start before breakfast to avoid the heat and resume in the late afternoon, when a fair breeze often picks up and cools the heat of the day. In cooler winter months, tours start after breakfast and continue after the midday meal.

Checking In

Check-in usually takes place before lunch, checkout after breakfast. Passports are registered at the reception area, then returned to you.

Entertainment

Entertainment is an important part of Nile cruises, and there is usually something different offered each evening: a cocktail party, a belly dancer, Nubian dancers (either a troupe from Aswan or the Nubian staff on board). One evening, guests arrange their own entertainment: a treasure hunt, a fancy dress party, a mime, a play, or a folkloric party in a tentlike setting where you sit on cushions and rugs, eat traditional food, smoke a *shisha* (water pipe) if you like, and men are encouraged to don *galabiyya*s, traditional male apparel that *fellahin* (rural people) still wear. Group photographs are taken as souvenirs. Candlelight dinner overlooking Abu Simbel temples is a Lake Nasser cruise highlight.

The lounge is the best place to read or to enjoy a drink. The larger vessels generally afford a panoramic view, the smaller provide a cozy, drawing room–like atmosphere. Most boats have small libraries with a selection of books about Egypt, largely in English, as well as novels, magazines, and newspapers.

Meals

Most meals are buffet style, with a wide variety of hot and cold food, as well as a selection of international, Egyptian, and vegetarian dishes. (There is plenty of choice if you follow a special diet.) Staff take professional pride in these buffets, and each is more like an excessive dinner celebration than an ordinary meal. Whether you will have buffet-style meals or set menus served by waiters depends on the boat's management. All three daily meals are served in a dining room unless a barbecue is set up on the sun deck, and afternoon tea or coffee is generally served in the open air.

Precautions

Water on board is safe for bathing, because boats have their own pu-
rification systems built with the latest technology. However, tap water
is not recommended for drinking, and bottled water is available.

The "gippy tummy" has its place in Nile cruise lore. Locals attribute
it to excessive consumption of iced drinks immediately after touring
in the hot sun, or sitting in direct sunlight for an extended time. The
syptoms are diarrhea, sometimes severe, combined with feeling slightly
queasy. It is almost certainly attributable to contaminated water, which
makes drinking bottled water and not taking ice in drinks strongly advisable. *See* the Health section of the Gold Guide for further food-re-
lated cautionary advice, as well as information on avoiding dehydration
and overexposure to the sun.

Security

Because of the troubled situation in Middle Egypt, where serious warnings against travel persist, cruises from Cairo to Aswan are generally
not running. Travel in Upper Egypt and Nubia is safe. At the end of
May 1998, the Egyptian Tourist Administration invited a large group
of foreign tour operators to come to Egypt on a fact-finding mission,
and they declared themselves satisfied with facilities and security arrangements in popular tourist areas. This security includes armed police strategically placed at popular tourist sites along the Nile, vessels
manned by Egyptian security forces accompanying tourist vessels between Assyut and Qena on a Cairo–Luxor cruise, and armed Bedouin
on the hills overlooking the monuments of Nubia. (Armed guards are
not an uncommon sight in Egypt and should not cause alarm. They
are also evident outside embassies, museums, and the residences of foreign diplomats.)

Tour Guides

Gone are the days when *dragomen* (a 19th-century term given to locally hired tour managers) conducted tourists to the monuments telling
them tall tales of ancient kings. Today's guides are bi- or trilingual professionals who are granted official licenses only after successfully passing an examination that covers pharaonic, Greco-Roman, Islamic, and
modern history. They are personable young men and women with a
sound knowledge of political and social events in Egypt, and they are
informed about environmental matters and the flora and fauna of
their country. Traveling with a cruise is a sought-after job, and cruise
operators choose only top performers, whose professionalism is eval-
uated by the travelers themselves.

Most boats have a resident guide for small groups and for individuals
who do not have their own accompanying guide. When there are different nationalities on board, more than one guide is provided. Guides
speak English, French, Italian, Spanish, and German to accommodate
travelers from around the world.

What to Pack

Be modest, travel light, and remember that Egypt is a conservative country. Egyptians dress modestly and respect those who observe their customs. When walking around Luxor and Aswan, it is wise to wear T-shirts
with short sleeves rather than sleeveless tops, and trousers or skirts that
come to the knee. (Sleeveless blouses for women are entirely acceptable on board.) A one-piece bathing suit is preferable to a bikini, and
topless sunbathing is forbidden. Although the weather is sunny in
winter, the evenings can be very cool, so bring clothing that you can
layer, with at least one medium-weight woolen sweater for the nighttime chill of the after-dark Sound and Light performance at Karnak.

You'll need a windbreaker in winter for the daytime. Proper walking shoes are a must—sandals are uncomfortable when walking in the sand—and take hats, sunglasses, sunblock, tissues, and a small bottle of water on shore excursions. It doesn't rain, so rain gear is unnecessary.

Although casual wear is acceptable at meals during the day, four- and five-star vessels have a casual-but-elegant standard at night. This does not necessarily mean jackets for men, merely long trousers and a collared shirt, rather than a T-shirt. Laundry service on boats is excellent. Laundry bags are picked up in the morning and returned by the evening of the same day.

There is a great deal to photograph, so be sure to bring enough film. Though available in Nile cities and towns, film is expensive.

Itineraries

Daily itineraries are geared around visiting monuments. Bear in mind that cruise organizers, in order to maximize profits by running back-to-back cruises, tend to rush visits around Luxor and Aswan, the two cities with the heaviest concentration of ancient sights.

On Nile cruises, for example, Luxor itineraries are necessarily rushed because there enough to occupy even casual sightseers for several days. The monuments lie on both sides of the Nile and spread over a vast area—the two major Luxor and Karnak temples are on the East Bank, and the Theban Necropolis on the West Bank includes the mortuary temples (such as Deir al-Bahri and Medinet Habu), the Valley of the Kings, the Valley of the Queens, and Tombs of the Nobles. Guides are obliged to keep to schedules and might not give you as much time at sights as you would like. Consider spending one or two nights at a hotel in Luxor at either the beginning or end of your cruise to give you time to see sights not included on the boat's itinerary, or revisit monuments that you want to see in greater depth.

On Lake Nasser cruises, although the boat docks at Kalabsha near Aswan, itineraries do not include most Aswan sights. You will see Nubian monuments reconstructed near the High Dam, but you should stay an additional night or two in Aswan to see the High Dam itself, the new Nubia Museum, the Temple of Isis at Philae, the famous granite quarries, the tombs of the nobles on Qubbbet el-Hawa, Elephantine Island, and the 5th-century St. Simeon's Monastery.

Cruise Costs

Each season, cruise companies determine their prices based on what they expect upcoming demand will be. Prices listed below are therefore guidelines. At press time, prices per person per night, double occupancy, ranged from $55 to $255, depending on the boat. Note that prices increase 25% to 40% during Christmas and Easter.

Transfers from airport to boat are not included; round-trip transfers cost $15 per person. On board, a special gratuity box might be displayed at the reception area for the boat crew; tour guides might take it upon themselves to pass a separate envelope among members of their party, with a suggestion that $3–$5 per passenger per day would be appropriate. This is what the guide hopes to receive; tip whatever you feel is appropriate based on the service provided. The same applies for gratuities to the boat crew.

Payment for beverages and other services such as laundry and outside phone calls are not included in cruise prices. The charge for drinks and laundry is reasonable, in line with any hotel, of any calibre, in Egypt.

You will sign bills when drinks are presented and services rendered, and you pay these at trip's end. Egyptian and some foreign currencies are accepted and most boats accept credit cards and traveler's checks. Banking facilities are not always available on board, but you will find them in Luxor and Aswan.

When to Go

The best time of year for a cruise is from the beginning of the winter season in October to the first half of April. In the second half of April, locks are closed because the river is at its lowest point; this happens just before the seasonal release of water for agricultural purposes. May is not recommended because of the likelihood of the *khamaseen*, sand-laden storms accompanied by scorching winds that make sightseeing all but impossible. Summer weather, especially in July and August, is dry. Temperatures in Upper Egypt and Nubia can soar to 108°F. Weather between November and February, when the mercury hovers between 75°F and 80°F, is ideal. Temperatures drop at night, both summer and winter.

BOOKING A CRUISE

Using a Travel Agent

If you intend to take a Nile cruise, make your bookings through a recognized international travel agency, preferably one that is a member of ASTA or SITE. With more than 200 vessels in operation, the majority owned by individual small businessmen, the choice of boats is vast, and standards among them vary considerably. The use of an established travel agent as a go-between is the best insurance that you will get what you think you are paying for.

Checklist: Get a printed itinerary with full details of communications, excursions, meals (whether included or not included), and availability of an English-speaking guide when you book your cruise.

Agencies to Contact

IN EGYPT

There are hundreds of travel agencies in Egypt that can book Nile cruises. The following are among the most reliable.

Abercrombie and Kent. Apart from having good connections with many cruise companies, Abercrombie and Kent has its own five-star vessel on the Nile. The company also can combine Nile cruises with other sights throughout Egypt and the Middle East and Africa. ⊠ *Cairo: 18 Shar'a Youssef El-Guindy, Boustan Centre,* ☎ *02/393–6255 or 393–6260,* ℻ *02/391–5179.*

American Express. ⊠ *Cairo: 15 Qasr al-Nil,* ☎ *02/574–7991;* ⊠ *21 Shar'a Giza, Nile Tower,* ☎ *02/739–673 or 02/735–856; or* ⊠ *72 Shar'a Omar Ibn el-Khattab, Heliopolis,* ☎ *02/418–114 to 46.* ⊠ *Luxor: Winter Palace Hotel,* ☎ *095/372–862 or 095/581–1301.* ⊠ *Aswan: Old Cataract Hotel,* ☎ *097/322–909.*

Benu Travel. This local representative of Imaginative Traveller, a British-run company based in London, specializes in tailor-made tours in Egypt that include regular cruises on the Nile and Lake Nasser, as well as felucca cruises in Upper Egypt. ⊠ *Cairo: Benu Travel, 6A Lebanon St., Hegaz Tower (Apt. 53), Mohandesin,* ☎ *02/344–0000 or 02/304–4802,* ℻ *02/304–4803.*

Egypt Panorama Tours (Ted Cookson). Panorama Tours has a good reputation among expatriates for efficiency and reliability. ⊠ *Cairo: 4 Road 79, Maadi, (mailing address:* ⊠ *11728 Box 222, Maadi),* ☎ *02/350–5880 and 02/351–0200,* ℻ *02/351–1199.*

Emeco Travel. Emeco is a well-established company that ranks with the best. ✉ *Cairo: 2 Shar'a Tala'at Harb,* ☎ *02/574–9360 or 02/574–4599,* ℻ *02/574–4212.*

Seti I Travel. This company has a fleet of Nile cruisers of excellent standard. ✉ *Cairo: 16 Shar'a Ismail Mohamed, Zamalek,* ☎ *02/341–9820,* ℻ *02/340–2419.*

South Sinai Travel. Many U.S. travel agencies work with South Sinai Travel because of their expertise, efficiency, and reliability. ✉ *Cairo: 79 Shar'a Marghany, Heliopolis,* ☎ *02/418–7310,* ℻ *02/290–9189 or 02/418–7396.*

Travcotels. Travcotels owns a fleet of 12 cruisers, 11 on the Nile, the other on Lake Nasser. ✉ *Cairo: 19 Shar'a Yehia Ibrahim, Zamalek,* ☎ *02/342–0488,* ℻ *02/340–4897.*

Thomas Cook. Thomas Cook was the first company to run Nile cruises, and it owns two vessels. One operates on the Nile and the other on Lake Nasser. Thomas Cook himself personally conducted his first Cook's tour up the Nile in 1869, the year the Suez Canal opened. His son John later built his own fleet of ships, finer, it was said, than anything that had floated on the Nile since Cleopatra's barge of burnished gold. ✉ *Cairo: 12 Maydan el-Sheikh Youssef, Garden City,* ☎ *02/356–4650,* ℻ *02/356–4654.*

IN THE UNITED STATES
A number of travel agents arrange special-interest and tailor-made cruises.

Abercrombie and Kent. ✉ *1520 Kensington Rd., Oak Brook, IL 60521-2141,* ☎ *630/954–2944 or 800/323–7308,* ℻ *630/954–3324.*

African Travel. ✉ *1100 E. Broadway, Glendale, CA 91205,* ☎ *818/507–7893,* ℻ *818/507–5802.*

American Express Travel Service. ✉ *: 420 Lexington Ave., New York, NY 10170,* ☎ *212/687–3700;* ✉ *2338 N. Clark St., Chicago, IL 60614,* ☎ *773/477–4000;* ✉ *Downtown Omni Hotel, 901 W. 7th St., Los Angeles, CA 90017,* ☎ *213/627–4800.*

Aslan Adventures. ✉ *25 North Wenatchee Ave., Wenatchee, WA 98801,* ☎ *509/665–2440,* ℻ *509/665–0664.*

Destinations & Adventures International (James Berkeley). ✉ *Box 46698, 8489 Crescent Dr., Los Angeles, CA 90046,* ☎ *213/650–7267,* ℻ *213/650–6902.*

Geographic Expeditions. ✉ *2627 Lombard St., San Francisco, CA 94123,* ☎ *415/922–0448,* ℻ *213/650–6902.*

Journeys of the Mind (Temma Ecker). Journeys sets the highest standard in educational adventures for discriminating travelers. The focus is on understanding another culture, not only on sightseeing. Apart from the cruise between Luxor and Aswan, with on-board lectures by a well-known Egyptologist, you will spend time in Cairo and learn about Coptic and Islamic periods on cultural tours. Journeys books a limited number of guests on 16-day excursions. ✉ *221 N. Kenilworth Ave. No. 413, Oak Park, IL 60302,* ☎ *708/383–9739,* ℻ *708/254–5154.*

IN THE UNITED KINGDOM
Abercrombie and Kent. ✉ *Sloane Square House, Holbein Pl., London, SW1W 8NS,* ☎ *0171/730–9600,* ℻ *0171/730–9376.*

Imaginative Traveller. This company arranges custom-designed trips throughout Egypt that include cruises on the Nile and Lake Nasser and felucca cruises in Upper Egypt. ⊠ *14 Barley Mow Passage, Chiswick, London, W4 4PH,* ☎ *0181/742–8612,* ℻ *0181/742–3045.*

Noble Caledonia Limited. An 11-day itinerary takes in Cairo, including the Egyptian Museum and the pyramids; a Nile cruise between Aswan and Abydos with an extension to Sohag to visit two Coptic monasteries; and a flight to Abu Simbel. The cruise is on one of the smaller Thomas Cook vessels, and a professional guest lecturer travels with the group. ⊠ *11 Charles St., Mayfair, London, W1X 8LE,* ☎ *0171/409–0376,* ℻ *0171/409–0834.*

Thomas Cook. ⊠ *Oxford St.,* ☎ *0171/493–4537;* ⊠ *4 Henrietta St., WC2,* ☎ *0171/379–0685.*

Voyages Jules Verne. This well-established company offers a unique Nile cruise on the intimate (17-cabin), restored steamer **SS *Karim,*** which Sultan (later King) Fu'ad commissioned in 1917. Voyages Jules Verne also has a comprehensive ancient Egypt itinerary that includes three nights at the Mena House Hotel overlooking the pyramids in Giza and two variations on the cruise itinerary: either four nights on the Nile followed by three on Lake Nasser, or four on the lake and three on the river. ⊠ *21 Dorset Sq., London NW1 6QG,* ☎ *0171/616–1000,* ℻ *0171/723–8629.*

Payment

You must pay the full cost of the cruise up front. On the whole, travelers are more than satisfied with their cruise experience, lauding it in glowing terms as a trip of a lifetime, an experience never to be forgotten. Of course, some customers go away more than dissatisfied. If that turns out to be you, and you feel that your experience was beyond atrocious, consider requesting a refund.

THE CRUISE FLEET

Nile Cruises

Floating Hotels

All Nile cruisers listed below were built after 1983 and those on Lake Nasser after 1992. (The older Hilton boats, the *Isis* and *Osiris,* and the Sheraton fleet have been fully upgraded but are not reviewed here.) Dates of construction and the size of the vessels are included wherever possible. Costs listed at the end of each review are per person, per night, based on double occupancy.

MS *Regency* and **MS *Royale.*** These two five-deck deluxe cruisers, which belong to the 12-ship fleet of Travcotels, are at the top of their range and are among the best that navigate the Nile. The vessels' neoclassical decor looks superb, and the large lounge, three bars, and panoramic windows add a spacious new dimension to relaxation on the Nile. Set meals are served twice a week. Mention the need for an English-speaking guide at time of booking. ⊠ *Cairo: Travcotels, 19 Yehia Ibrahim St., Zamalek,* ☎ *02/342–0488,* ℻ *02/340–4897. Built: early 1990s. Size: 235-ft length, 45-ft beam. 50 double cabins and 2 suites. Restaurant (capacity 110), 3 bars, luxurious lounge, 2 sundecks with large pool and whirlpool on upper deck, excercise room, gift shop, beauty salon, library. $55.*

MS *Nile Goddess* and **MS *Sun Goddess.*** One of the great advantages of these two five-deck boats (owned by Sonesta) is that they have private docking areas. This means that when other boats are moored five deep at Luxor and Aswan, and the outer boats' passengers have to pass through the reception areas of three or four boats to reach the shore, you'll be able to step right ashore. From practical and aesthetic points of view these two vessels rank with the best on the Nile. Sonesta caters to discerning leisure and business travelers. The vessels' junior suites are in fact the biggest cabins on the Nile. There is always an English-speaking guide on board, whether for a single person or for groups of up to 30 people. Rooms have private telephones, three-channel music systems, TV, and VCR. Bathrooms are equipped with tubs (shower also included); hair dryers and safe deposit boxes can be supplied on re-quest. ⊠ *Cairo: 4 El-Tayaran St., Nasr City,* ☎ *02/262–8111,* FAX *02/ 261–9980. Built: 1989 (Nile Goddess); 1993 (Sun Goddess). Size: 235-ft length, 44-ft beam (Nile Goddess); 252-ft length, 46-ft beam (Sun Goddess). 68 junior suites, 2 presidential suites with private lounges (Nile Goddess); 58 junior suites, 2 senator suites, 1 presiden-tial suite, 1 royal suite with private lounge (Sun Goddess). Nile and Sun Goddess: Room service, restaurant, barbecue, 2 interior bars, sundeck bar, piano bar, sundeck pool, discotheques, conference room. $100.*

MS Shehrazad and **MS Philae.** These three-deck Mena House Oberoi vessels have a reputation for comfort and service. They were built to the latest Germanischer Lloyd classification, which means that they meet the highest international standards for fire-safety and lifesaving equip-ment. Of the two ships, *Philae* is slightly more spacious. Single-room cabins are large enough to allow for roomy sitting areas and a pair of twin beds. Each cabin has a radio, TV, telephone, controllable air-conditioning, and attached bathroom with shower. The vessels' elegant restaurants serve Continental and Middle Eastern cuisines, and there are bars, lounges, and dance floors. ⊠ *Cairo: Hotel Mena House Oberoi, Pyramids Rd.,* ☎ *02/383–3222 or 02/383–3444,* FAX *02/ 383–7777. Sizes: 235-ft length, 38-ft beam (Shehrazad), 236-ft length, 43-ft beam (Philae). Built: 1987 (Shehrazad), 1996 (Philae). 59 twin cabins, 10 triples, and 2 slightly larger suites (Shehrazad); 54 doubles, 4 suites (Philae). Restaurant, bar (Shehrazad only), pool, beauty salon, shop, library. $156 (Sherhazad), $255 (Philae).*

MS Radamis Mövenpick Nile Boat. This vessel is operated by the Mövenpick Hotel group in Egypt, a Swiss company whose reputation for efficiency, warmth, and hospitality has become proverbial inter-nationally. The vessel combines luxury and high-quality service with a certain informality—the sort of atmosphere that encourages people to be friendly. The cruise is particularly popular among European travelers. Cabins have in-house music and closed-circuit video chan-nels, internal telephones, minibars, and bathrooms with tubs, hair dryers, and shaving sockets. Varied menus demonstrating typical Mövenpick excellence—buffet or à la carte—are presented in the gra-cious Orangerie, which seats 150 diners. A satellite telephone is avail-able on board. Children under age 5 sleep free in their parents' cabin. ⊠ *Luxor: Mövenpick Hotel Jolie Ville, Crocodile Island,* ☎ *095/374– 855 or 095/374–937,* FAX *095/374–936. Built: 1991. 70 deluxe and 4 suites. Restaurant, bar, barbecue, pool, exercise room, beauty salon, shop. (Price not available at press time).*

MS Alexander the Great. If you remember the TV series "Love Boat," *Alexander the Great* was the Love Boat in 1985. It is run by Jolley's Travel and Tours and has some of the highest standards for a luxury liner of its size. Add to this superb service, dining, and entertainment that includes dancing. The boat was designed and built to suit dis-criminating clients by Eimbcke Trading and Shipping of Hamburg, Ger-many, known for its technological standards and quality craftsmanship and materials. Cabins have twin beds and are equipped with TVs, video circuits, radios, telephones, and bathrooms with showers. The restaurant seats 133 passengers. ⊠ *Cairo: 8 Shar'a Tala'at Harb,* ☎ *02/579–4619 or 02/579–4620,* ℻ *02/771–670. Built: 1980. Size: 225-ft length, 38-ft beam. 62 cabins. Restaurant, bar, pool, beauty salon, shop.* $55.

MS *Nile Vittoria,* MS *Champollion,* and MS *Pyramiza 4.* These three vessels are operated by Egyptian-run Pyramiza Hotels, Resorts and Nile Cruises. The interior decor of each vessel is distinctive: if you want to travel in elegant Italian style, chose the *Vittoria;* for French classical, it's the *Champollion;* and the *Pyramiza 4* is furnished in traditionally English fashion. All suites have TVs with in-house movies and satellite channels, sound systems, safe boxes, and bathrooms with showers and hair dryers. The ships also have panoramic halls. ⊠ *60 Shar'a Giza, Dokki, Giza,* ☎ *02/336–0791 or 02/336–0792,* ℻ *02/336–0795. Built (all boats): 1995. Size (all boats): 239-ft length, 45-ft beam. 65 junior suites, 2 presidential suites (all boats). Facilities (all boats): Restaurant, pool, hot tub, excercise room, room service, shop.* $80.

MS *Liberty.* This is the kind of boat that turn-of-the-century travelers used, but it also incorporates the latest refinements—an evocative blend of 19th-century ambience and modern conveniences. All suites have private balconies, TVs, and international video systems, as well as minibars and individual safe-deposit boxes. All bathrooms have showers and hair dryers; presidential suites also have whirlpool baths. Telephone, fax, and telex services are available, and there is always an English-speaking guide on board. ⊠ *Cairo: 15 Shar'a Hassan Sabry, Zamalek,* ☎ *02/340–6820 or 02/340–6822,* ℻ *02/341–0432 or 02/341–5737. Built: 1995. 66 junior suites and 6 presidential suites. Restaurant, pool, hot tub, nightclub.* $145.

MS *Nile Romance* and MS *Nile Beauty.* Flotel, a privately run Egyptian firm with a sound reputation in the business, owns and manages these two lovely Nile cruisers. The vessels were granted licences to operate following inspection by American technicians who graded them "A1"—meeting the highest international standards in every respect. Both have five decks; the *Romance* is the larger of the two, and its cabins are slightly more spacious. Cabins on both vessels are configured as junior suites with sitting areas, minibars, TVs, music systems, telephones, and bathrooms with showers. The attentive staff meets your every need, and there are large common areas, discos, and unisex hairdressers. ⊠ *Cairo: Egypt Panorama Tours, 4 Road 79, Maadi, (mailing address:* ⊠ *11728 Box 222, Maadi),* ☎ *02/350–5880 or 02/351–0200,* ℻ *02/351–1199. Built: 1989 (Romance); 1983 (Nile Beauty). Size: 237-ft length, 39.3-ft beam (Romance); 201-ft length, 33-ft beam (Beauty). 75 junior suites (Romance); 52 junior suites (Beauty). Facilities (each vessel): Restaurant, pool, 2 bars, lounge, nightclub, beauty salon, shop; Romance only: whirlpool, excercise room.* $125.

MS *Sherry Boat.* This three-deck craft, built according to Germanischer Lloyd's specifications—which implies the highest international standards—is operated by the private Egyptian firm Sherry Nile Cruises. High standards are evident throughout this delightful vessel, including the quality and presentation of the meals, and the staff is friendly and efficient. Cabins are comfortable and are fitted with music systems, TVs with three video channels, telephones, and bathrooms with showers. The sundeck has ever-attentive waiters. ⊠ *Cairo: Egypt Panorama Tours, 4 Road 79, Maadi, (mailing address:* ⊠ *11728 Box 222, Maadi),* ☎ *02/350–5880 or 02/351–0200,* ℻ *02/351–1199. Built: 1989. Size: 198-ft length, 38-ft beam. 59 cabins, 4 junior suites. Restaurant,*

2 bars, lounge, pool, hot tub, nightclub, beauty salon, individual safes, and international telephone and fax service. $125.

Lake Nasser Cruises

MS *Eugenie*. This three-deck vessel was the first boat to be built above the High Dam and carry passengers on a lake cruise. The work of the al-Guidny brothers, the *Eugenie* is the last word in taste and refinement, with an attentive crew and decor reminiscent of turn-of-the-century warmth and elegance. ✉ *Cairo: Eugenie Investment Group, 17 Shar'a Tunis, New Maadi,* ☎ *02/516–9649 or 02/516–9653,* FAX *02/516–9646. Built: 1993. Size: 242-ft length, 44-ft beam. 50 standard and 2 suites, one with private whirlpool and terrace. Restaurant, 3 lounges, pool, hot tub, 2 sundecks, health club, sauna, Turkish bath, shop. $105.*

MS *Qasr Ibrim*. This four-deck vessel is larger than its sister, *Eugenie*, but it has the same sophistication and elegance—in this case Art Deco furnishings—high standards, and attentive staff. The boat's additional space is a plus, because it allows panoramic views of the desert from on deck, in the lounge, and in the cabins. All cabins have bathrooms with tubs. Executive, upper, and main deck cabins have their own private balconies. Junior suites can be used as triple cabins, and all suites have whirlpools and minifridges. *Qasr Ibrim*'s restaurant is also spacious, yet manages to remain intimate. ✉ *Cairo, Eugenie Investment Group, 17 Shar'a Tunis, New Maadi,* ☎ *02/516–9649 or 02/516–9653,* FAX *02/516–9646. Size: 258-ft length, 46-ft beam. 55 twin bed cabins, 7 junior suites, 2 royal suites, 1 imperial suite. Restaurant, lounge, bar, pool, hot tub, health club, sauna, Turkish bath, shop. $105.*

MS *Nubian Sea*. Cabins are equipped with telephones, radios, piped-in music, and bathrooms with showers. On the three decks of the *Nubian Sea*, you'll find spacious and elegant reception, lounge, and deck areas, and panoramic windows present splendid moving vistas of the lake. A canopied area is sometimes, depending on the weather, used for lavish buffet meals. Lounge chairs on deck provide plenty of comfort, and a refreshing drink is always at hand. ✉ *15 El-Shaheed Mahmud Tala'at, Doqqi, Giza,* ☎ *02/361–3680,* FAX *02/361–0023. Built: 1996. Size: 282-ft length, 46-ft beam. 66 standard cabins, 4 suites. Restaurant, 2 bars, pool, gift shop. $60.*

MS *Tania*. This luxury boat is the only member of the considerable Travcotels fleet on Lake Nasser. This boat was built according to the exacting Germanischer Lloyd's specifications; it has a complete water-purification station (you might want to drink only bottled water nonetheless), and all partitions and ceilings are soundproof and fire-resistant. The spacious lounge area has panoramic windows and comfortable sofas, chairs, and padded stools. Its elegant cabins have TVs, closed-circuit video, internal telephones, sound systems, minifridges, and adjustable air-conditioning. There are also large, luxurious lounges (with bar and restaurant) and a two-level sundeck. The pool, on the lower-deck, also has a bar. ✉ *Cairo: 19 Shar'a Yehia Ibrahim, Zamalek,* ☎ *02/342–0488,* FAX *02/340–4897. Built: 1995. Size: 195-ft length, 33-ft beam. 30 double cabins. Restaurant, 2 bars, lounge, pool. $55.*

6 The Sinai Peninsula, the Red Sea Coast, and the Suez Canal

Leaving Cairo, at first you see nothing but a flat sandy landscape that seems to extend beyond the horizon. A barren desert, seemingly lifeless—and the beauty is just beginning. Cross the Suez Canal and the Sinai Desert will take your breath away. As you snake through the rust-colored mountains toward the coast of the Gulf of Aqaba, the crystal sea peeks out through peaks that join it to the sky. Mysteries both on land and under the sea fairly beg to be explored.

FOR CENTURIES, European traders and Arab merchants had to sail around the Cape of Good Hope to travel east to Asia from Europe and the Mediterranean. Two thousand years earlier, ancient Egyptians had that problem licked. The records of the Greek historian Herodotus speak of a canal begun around 600 BC that connected the Nile to the Gulf of Suez. The canal was used during the time of Alexander the Great, left to ruin, then reopened during the Arab domination that began around AD 645. The canal was the primary route between the Nile Valley and the Arab world's trading center in Mecca, on the west coast of Saudi Arabia. Then the ancient canal was forgotten, and traders returned to the desert, risking their goods and camels. Aside from the accounts of historians, all traces of that canal have vanished. The Suez Canal—an effort of thousands of Egyptian men who with shovels manually removed tons of sand between 1859 and 1869 to create a 110-km (66-mi) trench through the desert—follows a different course.

By Magda Abdou and Nora El Samahy

Since the dawn of human culture in Africa and the Middle East, the Sinai and Red Sea region has been an important crossroads—then a land bridge, now a sea bridge—connecting East and West, North and South. Enormous container ships and fancy ocean liners now line up, waiting to pass through the Suez Canal. Canal towns like Ismailiya and Bur Sa'id (Port Said) make interesting day trips from Cairo, if you have the time. But the novelty of passing ships can wear off rather quickly, leaving little else to do.

Not so the Sinai Peninsula and the Red Sea coast, where relaxing on the beach, trekking through the desert, and diving amidst a wealth of marine life are the opposite of what you'd expect from a trip to Egypt. The desert itself, inland Sinai, has changed little since the times when Bedouins moved from one watering hole to the next. It remains awe-inspiring, especially if you get up for sunrise and catch the mountains changing from purple to red, then orange to yellow. The Red Sea continues to be an underwater haven, a living aquarium, in spite of the impact that a rush of divers has had on the reefs. If you want all the amenities of resorts and the option of escaping to virgin desert spotted with shady acacia trees and lazy camels, this is the spot to go. If you want to see ancient monasteries and biblical sites, or follow Moses' path from Egypt to Jordan, this is the place to go. Or if you just want to lie out and enjoy the sun, again this is the place to go.

Pleasures and Pastimes

Archaeology

The Christian monastic movement began in Egypt around the 4th century, which explains the number of beautiful monasteries buried deep in the mountains throughout the country. The most famous is St. Catherine's, at the foot of Jabal Moussa (Mount of Moses, or Mount Sinai) in the Sinai Desert. The summit of Jabal Moussa is reputedly where Moses received the Ten Commandments. The Greek Orthodox monastery—with its icons, ornate chandeliers, and unique mosaics—still functions, 12 monks living in its quarters.

There are two other monasteries in the ranges of South Qabala near the Red Sea coast. Both St. Anthony's and St. Paul's are Coptic monasteries dedicated to saints who spent most of their years as hermits living in caves and devoting their lives to God. These monasteries are open and have monks who provide tours of the grounds.

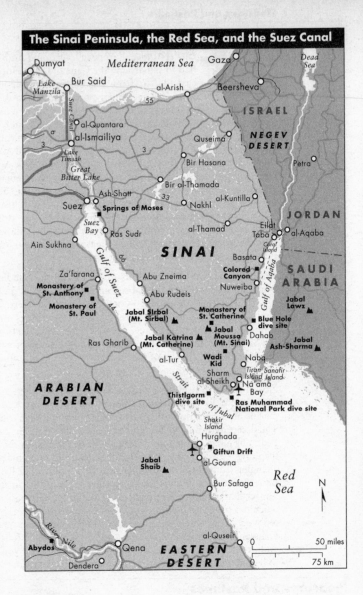

The Sinai Peninsula, the Red Sea, and the Suez Canal

Dumyat
Lake Manzila
Bur Said
Mediterranean Sea
Gaza
Dead Sea
al-Arish
Beersheva
55
al-Quantara
al-Ismailiya
Suez Canal
Quseima
ISRAEL
NEGEV DESERT
Petra
Lake Timsah
Bir Hasana
Great Bitter Lake
Bir al-Thamada
Ash-Shatt
33
Springs of Moses
Nakhl
al-Kuntilla
JORDAN
Suez
Eilat
al-Aqaba
Suez Bay
Ras Sudr
al-Thamad
Taba
Coral Island
Ain Sukhna
SINAI
Basata
SAUDI ARABIA
Za'farana
Abu Zneima
Colored Canyon
Nuweiba
Monastery of St. Anthony
Abu Rudeis
Jabal Lawz
Monastery of St. Paul
Jabal Sirbal (Mt. Sirbal)
Monastery of St. Catherine
Blue Hole dive site
Jabal Moussa (Mt. Sinai)
Dahab
Jabal Ash-Sharma
Ras Gharib
Jabal Katrina (Mt. Catherine)
Wadi Kid
al-Tur
Naba
Strait
Sharm al-Sheikh
Tiran Island
Sanafir Island
ARABIAN DESERT
Thistlgorm dive site
Na'ama Bay
of Jubal
Ras Muhammad National Park dive site
Shakir Island
Hurghada
Giftun Drift
Jabal Shaib
al-Gouna
Red Sea
N
Bur Safaga
River Nile
Abydos
Qena
al-Quseir
EASTERN DESERT
0 50 miles
0 75 km
Dendera

Dining

The Sinai and the Red Sea areas consist of a series of resort towns strung along the coast that cater primarily to European tastes. Culinary offerings include Continental fare, buffet breakfasts, Italian, Korean, and quick sandwiches. Typical Egyptian food is most readily available in the cities of Bur Sa'id and Ismailiya along the Suez Canal; harder to find in the resort areas. Local *koshary* is a quick solution to sudden pangs of hunger. It's a popular, inexpensive Egyptian meal of rice, lentils, and pasta sprinkled with grated browned onions and served with a fresh garlic tomato sauce. If you ask for extra-hot sauce, get a spare napkin to wipe away the sweat.

In Sharm al-Sheikh, the Na'ama Bay boardwalk is restaurant central. Grilled sea bass marinated in lemon juice, pepper, onions, and fresh garlic, served with french fries, is a local favorite. If you'd rather not bother with fish bones, look for flounder grilled or fried, served with lemon juice and a tasty garnish.

When out on a desert safari or Bedouin dinner, expect a hearty meal. Heaps of rice, grilled lamb, and chicken, tahina (a thick sesame-seed paste), freshly baked bread, salad, and plenty of Coca-Cola. Top this meal off with a Bedouin tea, brewed in front of you on an open flame with *habak,* desert-grown mint. Don't pass up the tea, but remember that it's likely to be shockingly sweet—try asking the tea-maker to go light on the sugar—and that "light" is a relative term.

A few words of caution: water is not always potable, so stick to bottled water to be safe. Likewise, vegetables are not always washed properly, so stay away from uncooked greens, especially lettuce and cucumbers. Oil, ghee, and butter, along with anything fatty, is very popular. A dish that you would expect to be light, like sautéed vegetables, may come dripping with oil.

CATEGORY	COST*
$$$$	over £e100
$$$–$$$$	£e50–£e100
$$–$$$	£e35–£e50
$	under £e35

per person, excluding drinks, service, and tax

Diving

The Red Sea's wealth of marine life brings divers here from around the world. Pegged as Jacques Cousteau's favorite body of water for recreational diving, it has withstood years of careless use and, at times, abuse. There are strong hopes that increasing education and increasingly fierce regulations will help preserve the 1,000 species of fish, 25% of which are exclusive to the region, and more than 137 species of coral.

The reef formation here changes as you travel south from the gulfs of Aqaba and Suez to Hurghada and beyond. Along the northern Sinai coast, the underwater environment is a series of coral patches that reach a maximum depth of 99 ft. Moving into the sea itself, around Sharm al-Sheikh and Ras Muhammad, flat reef tables are bounded by walls that drop down 330 ft and more. These underwater walls are often pitted with caves and large crevices that are home to such shy but menacing creatures as lionfish and large moray eels.

Spreading north from Hurghada, the underwater scene changes again. You will find large islets and small islands of corals whose reefs barely break the water's surface. This is the site where shipwrecks like the World War II SS *Thistlegorm* and the ancient spice ship *Dunraven* lie in thier watery graves. The marine life here flourishes in the strong currents that bring in plankton, a staple for a healthy, colorful underwater world. Horizontal visibility extends on average to a spectacular 83 ft.

Outdoor Activities

The abundance of outdoor adventure in the Sinai and the Red Sea makes them unique to Egypt. Fresh air and dramatic landscapes—everything from richly green desert oases to towering salmon-colored granite, limestone, and sandstone mountains—provide an ideal background. Sunset trips into the desert on horses, camels, or quad-runners (four-wheel dirt bikes) are unforgettable.

The southern Sinai Peninsula has the most diversity. You can climb Mount Sinai, arrange an intense trip into the Tih Desert, take an overnight jaunt by camel to Wadi Kid, or day-trip through the narrow paths of the opulent Colored Canyon. You can take on these areas yourself, or go on fully guided treks, even a Bedouin safari.

If resort life has more appeal, almost every hotel has a water-sports center that can set you up wave-running (jet-skiing), waterskiing, windsurfing (most popular in Dahab and Nuweiba), banana boating, parasailing, or, less actively, riding on a glass-bottom boat.

Lodging

Around the Sinai and the Red Sea you'll find everything from fancy, five-star resorts to motels and seedy areas for camping. Keep in mind that prices are considerably higher in season (September–November and April–June). In Suez, lodging options decrease greatly. The Helnan in Bur Sa'id and the Mercure Hotel in Ismailiya are the best hotels, and both are comfortable and have waterfront views. Bear in mind that, like elsewhere in Egypt, there is a precipitous drop in quality between high- and low-end hotels, with a conspicuous absence of midrange hotels that provide a comfortable standard.

CATEGORY	COST*
$$$$	$200 and over
$$$–$$$$	$150–$200
$$–$$$	$100–$150
$	under $50–$100

All prices are for a standard double room, excluding 17% tax.

Exploring the Sinai Peninsula, Red Sea Coast, and Suez Canal

Egypt is conservative when it comes to everyday attire. In the resort areas of the Sinai and the Red Sea, feel free to walk around in shorts and tank tops. Some people choose to dress up for dinner, although it is not mandatory. If you plan to visit any of the monasteries, wear modest attire. The Suez is not a resort area, so don't walk around in shorts, women especially; long, loose clothing is a better idea. If you are driving around the area, and definitely if you are taking buses, wear long pants and short sleeves.

Remember that you will be in a desert, and prices will necessarily be higher than elsewhere in the country because so many things have to be imported. If you plan to shop, plan to haggle. Always carry identification, and if you go out for a Bedouin dinner and camel ride, take along some candy to give to Bedouin children.

If you are a woman traveling alone or in a group of women, be alert and street smart. You are likely to be heckled—just ignore it.

Great Itineraries

Because the Sinai Peninsula and Red Sea coast both have seaside activities and ancient monasteries to see—the most impressive mountain scenery is in the Sinai—you don't need to go to both areas. It also happens that travel options between the two are limited, infrequent, and not entirely reliable. The Sinai has the greater variety of outdoor pursuits, but if diving is your sole aim, the Red Sea has the better sites.

Getting around the Sinai Peninsula and on the Red Sea coast requires bus, car, or jeep travel, which can take a fair amount of time. With three days or less, stick around one or two towns in either area. In the Sinai, you can visit the desert, swim in the Red Sea, and get plenty of sun all in a day, which makes it a great option if you have little time.

Take on the Suez Canal in a day trip from Cairo, or stay overnight in Ismailiya (which would give you a place to leave your bags while you explore) and continue the next day to Sharm al-Sheikh on the Sinai Peninsula.

If you are scuba diving, remember to give yourself 12 hours from the moment you finish your last dive before you board a plane or climb Mount Sinai, to allow all the nitrogen to clear your body.

IF YOU HAVE 3 DAYS

A three-day trip in the Sinai is enough time to see a few of the main sights in the desert and to dive or snorkel. If you plan to dive or snorkel from a boat, make arrangements from Cairo with a dive center, so you can be out at sea your first day. When you get to 🖼 **Sharm al-Sheikh,** check into your hotel if there's time, or go straight to the dive center (you can leave your things there while you dive). On the second day, find out which hotel or tour company will have a trip to **St. Catherine's Monastery** the next day, and sign up for it. If there are no trips scheduled, then you can arrange to rent a car and go on your own. Or if you'd rather go into the desert than visit St. Catherine's, go to the **Colored Canyon** and **Wadi Kid**—you will need a jeep and a guide. Make time on your second day to enjoy the beach. Windsurf or parasail. In the evening, head into the desert on horseback, camel or quad-runner to see the sun set.

If you want to do nothing but spend a few days lazing about in the sun, then go to the Red Sea towns of 🖼 **Hurghada,** 🖼 **al-Gouna,** or 🖼 **Quseir** on the Egyptian mainland.

IF YOU HAVE 5 DAYS

With five days to explore the region you need to prioritize. Do you want to relax, or do you want to see as much as possible? Again, choose between the Sinai or the Red Sea coast on the mainland.

If you're going to the Sinai, get to 🖼 **Sharm al-Sheikh** by plane, bus, or car in the morning. Check in and spend your day wandering around Na'ama Bay, swimming, and doing some easy snorkeling. On day two, plan to climb **Mount Sinai:** in winter, see **St. Catherine's Monastery** and climb Mount Sinai by daylight; in hotter months, leave your hotel at midnight and climb the mountain so you can see the sunrise from the summit. On the third day, dive or snorkel out of Sharm al-Sheikh. Then head north on the next day to 🖼 **Dahab** or 🖼 **Nuweiba** or 🖼 **Basata**—Dahab if a mellow, retro-hippie scene appeals; Nuweiba for a bit of luxury; Basata for a waterside, camp-like sojourn. All the resorts have access to great diving. On day five stay at the beach or trek into the desert to the **Colored Canyon** or **Wadi Kid.** Don't forget to take in the fresh air—you'll miss it when you get back to Cairo.

The second option will keep you on the Egyptian mainland. On the first day, go to Bur Sa'id and Ismailiya, wander around both towns for a couple of hours. Be adventurous and take the bus from Bur Sa'id to Ismailiya. Return to Cairo that night. Fly to 🖼 **Hurghada** the next morning. Hire a taxi to take you to 🖼 **al-Gouna,** and spend the day at the beach, then head back to Hurghada for dinner at Felfela's. On day three, hire a car and driver to take you to the monasteries of St. Anthony and St. Paul. On the next morning, make your way to 🖼 **Quseir,** the perfect place to end this part of your trip. Spend the day by the water, snorkeling or diving, and spend the night in one of the hotels. Start day five with a swim, then look around the town and **Quseir Fort.**

WHEN TO TOUR THE SINAI, RED SEA, AND SUEZ CANAL

April through October are the hot months, when temperatures get as high as 113°F. It's a great time to come for diving, because the visibility is at its best. November through March is cooler, with temperatures as low as 46°F. The desert gets very cold at night, and temperatures may even drop below freezing, so bring warm layers to put on in winter. The Sinai's high season is during the hotter months. The Red Sea, on the other hand, is great in winter, which is its most popular time.

Except in March, during the *khamaseen* (sandstorm) season, the sun shines here almost every day of the year, so don't forget a hat and sunscreen. Always carry a bottle of water with you (they're cheaper at supermarkets than from hotels). Because temperatures drop at night (not so drastically in summer), it's a good idea to bring a sweater.

THE SINAI PENINSULA

The Sinai Peninsula is a bridge between continents, and for ages travelers from Europe, Africa, and Asia have crossed and recrossed it. On its desert sands ancient Egyptian expeditions, more than 4,000 years ago, set out in search of copper and turquoise. Here Moses led the Israelites across the arid wastes before moving north to their promised land. Christian Europe's crusaders marched through the Sinai from the 11th through the 13th centuries, trying to take the Holy Land from the Muslims who ruled it. In this century, Egypt and Israel traded the land back and forth in war as they fought for it in 1967 and 1973, launching the desert once again onto the world's strategic stage. The Sinai is one of history's hotbeds of conflict, where time and the elements have weighed in on the harsh terrain, leaving behind majestic landscapes cradled by the crystal blue waters of the Red Sea and the gulfs of Aqaba to the east and Suez to the west.

There are two theories regarding the origin of the name Sinai. The ancient inhabitants of this desert worshipped *Sin,* a moon goddess, therefore naming the land in her honor—perhaps. Or it could be that the Semitic word *sin* (tooth) gets the credit; the peninsula indeed has the shape of a tooth.

Forty million years ago, the Sinai was part of the African-Asian landmass. Then seismic activity began a process that split the landmass into two separate plates—Saudi Arabia and Yemen on one side and Egypt and Sudan on the other—each plate pulling equally in opposite directions. Ongoing plate motion tore at and wrinkled the region, creating a protected underwater ecology, and leaving vast uninhabited areas of rugged mountain terrain and arid desert.

The Sinai is divided into three geological areas. The first lies to the north and consists mainly of pure, shifting, soft sand dunes. Herein lie ancient *wadi*s (dried up riverbeds), where you can find fossils from the Mediterranean. The second area is in the central part of the peninsula, a flat elevated plateau broken occasionally by limestone outcroppings and water sources. Toward the south of the central massif, the landscape begins to change to a granite and volcanic rocky region—the beginnings of the third area, which forms a natural barrier between desert and sea. If you are driving into southern Sinai through the mountains, look out for that breathtaking view of the blue sea when it peeks out from behind the mountains.

Sharm al-Sheikh

510 km (320 mi) southeast of Cairo.

Sharm al-Sheikh's old-timers remember when Na'ama Bay consisted of one hotel, two dive centers, and one snack bar—13 years ago. Now there are more than 40 hotels in the area, with attached dive centers, malls, and restaurants, and even more growth is expected. This exponential expansion marks the town as Egypt's key resort, what marketers like to think of as the Riviera Middle East. "Sharm," as it is fondly referred to, is known for having some of Egypt's most lavish hotels, world-renowned dive centers, as well as an active nightlife. If you have preconceived notions of visiting a barren wasteland rich in archaeological sites and a simple desert lifestyle, get rid of them. This town is chock-full of hotels, beaches, a brick boardwalk, and more Europeans than Egyptians. If your aim is to dive, snorkel, enjoy outdoor and water activity, or simply lounge, you're in the right place. Sharm also makes a solid base for nearby desert sites, which can be visited on day trips.

There are three main areas within the vicinity of Sharm al-Sheikh. The most popular is known as Na'ama Bay, the central hub with the majority of hotels (two- to five-star resorts), restaurants of various culinary merit, souvenir-filled shops, key nightspots, and excellent dive centers. South of Na'ama Bay is the expanding region of the Hadaba (the word means plateau), where the main highlight is the view of the surrounding area, and the number of hotels is increasing. South of Hadaba, Sharm al-Maya is often called downtown Sharm al-Sheikh. This is set on the more down-to-earth Sharm al-Sheikh harbor, where the dive boats dock at night and there are even more hotels, as well as typically Egyptian *kahwa*s (cafés) where men smoke *shisha* (water pipes) and play backgammon. The famous Sinai Star fish and chips place is here.

Sharm itself isn't a place to come for sightseeing: the resorts don't have any sights to see. As for shopping, prices for Egyptian goods to take home are likely to be double what they are in Cairo. It's the seaside activities—windsurfing, parasailing, waterskiing, and diving and snorkeling—and side trips to the desert that make boredom an unknown quantity here.

Dining and Lodging

NA'AMA BAY

$$$$ ✕ **Kokai.** The kitsch decor—fake plants, red lanterns, and Stella beer bottles plastered into the wall—is a bit much, but the food is very good, and entertaining in that (also kitsch) Polynesian-Japanese way. The menu includes everything from vegetable spring rolls with a tasty sweet-and-sour sauce to teppanyaki. In one corner, a Japanese chef smacks dough against a table to prepare noodles; in another, a deft Egyptian chef cooks omelets at supersonic speed. Adjacent to the boardwalk, Kokai has sea views as well as good people-watching. It's a five-minute walk from the shopping area, popular bars, and discos. Portions are huge, so come with an appetite. ⊠ *Ghazala Hotel, Na'ama Bay,* ☎ *062/600–150. AE, MC, V.*

$$$ ✕ **Liwa.** Make your way to the north end of the Na'ama Bay strip for a five-star dinner buffet with different themes each night. Seafood is the best of the menus, with grilled sea bass, crab, shrimp, fried sole, fish kebabs, sautéed vegetables, basmati rice, and the usual salad bar and scrumptious desert bar. If you aren't staying at the Sofitel, then it is three minutes from Na'ama Bay by cab or 15 on foot to walk off that second dessert you couldn't resist. ⊠ *Sofitel Sharm al-Sheikh Coralia, Na'ama Bay,* ☎ *062/600–080. AE, MC, V.*

$$$ ✕ **Rangoli.** If a couple of weeks travel have your stomach crying out
★   for vegetarian fare, of if you're just craving an Indian fix, make a beeline for Rangoli. Start with a glass of sweet lassi, the thick yogurt delight that comes sweet, plain, or flavored with mango; they're equally delicious. Move on to a pleasantly spicy *dal tarkiwali* stew; or to *biryani* for its promise of abundant peas, carrots, and long-grain rice; or to *aloo parantha*, a tasty flat bread stuffed with potatoes. Finish your meal with a soothing cup of *chai*, the tea infused with cardamom. Sit indoors or outside on the terrace. ⊠ *Sofitel Sharm al-Sheikh Coralia, Na'ama Bay,* ☎ *062/600–080. AE, MC, V.*

$$ ✕ **Da Franco.** As you're strolling on the boardwalk, an aroma of brick-oven-baked pizza wafting through the air is sure to turn your head. If you follow it here, you can get that dose of Italian cooking you've been craving, while watching passersby (the picture windows will make you wonder whether you're inside or outside a fishbowl). Da Franco is known

mainly for its pizza, and there are plenty of pizzas to choose from, the Da Franco being one local favorite. It's an ideal place for lunch and a popular evening hangout. ✉ *Ghazala Hotel, Na'ama Bay,* ☎ *062/600– 150. AE, MC, V.*

$ ✕ **Novotel Coffee Shop.** This is the only restaurant in Na'ama Bay that is open 24 hours—others will tell you they're open 24 hours, until they close their doors at 2 or 3 AM. So if you want to grab a bite after you've done the late-night circuit, come to this boardwalk café for light snacks, hamburgers, salads, and drinks. ✉ *Novotel Aquamarine, Na'ama Bay,* ☎ *062/600–173. AE, MC, V.*

$ ✕ **TamTam.** Finding authentic Egyptian food in a resort town is no mean
★   feat. At TamTam, fresh falafel is wrapped with locally made pita bread—be sure to ask for it without salad and with extra tahina sauce instead. Or try a ful sandwich, that classic Egyptian dish that's eaten for breakfast, lunch, or dinner. Its fava beans, flavored with olive oil, cumin, salt, pepper, and a dash of lemon, make for a protein-filled snack if you need a boost of energy. For a complete carbohydrate fix, order koshary, the local rice, macaroni, lentil, and tomato-sauce dish topped with a sprinkle of browned onions. TamTam is decidedly basic, its facade decorated with leftovers from building projects and wooden cafeteria-style tables with like chairs inside. The second-floor roof deck is perfect for watching people on Na'ama's boardwalk. ✉ *Ghazala Hotel, Na'ama Bay,* ☎ *062/600–050. AE, MC, V.*

$$$$ 🏨 **Conrad International.** Eighteen kilometers (11 mi) north of Na'ama Bay center, this resort stands on 37 landscaped acres fronting a 1,600-ft stretch of gorgeous beach. All but 30 of the oak-furnished and dark-tiled rooms have a beachfront view. Don't take cues from the brown buildings as you drive up; it's the lobby, with the relaxing sound of water from its fountain, that really sets the tone. And with everything you need on site, you won't need to go into town at all. Airport transfers are by shuttlebus or taxi, and a hotel bus makes scheduled trips into town, if you decide to go. ✉ *Ras Nasrani, Sharm al-Sheikh,* ☎ *062/601–585; 800/445–8667 in the U.S. and Canada,* 🄵🅇 *062/640– 465. 340 rooms, 11 suites. 7 restaurants, 4 bars, in-room safes, room service, pool, hot tub, massage, sauna, steam room, 2 tennis courts, excercise room, dive shop, snorkeling, waterskiing, shops, billiards, travel services. AE, DC, MC, V.*

$$$$ 🏨 **Hilton Fayrouz.** With the biggest stretch of sand of any hotel in the middle of Na'ama Bay, the Hilton and its Sun 'n' Fun Center provide a great beach and water sports for guests and nonguests. Privacy is key here, and each room, with its own patio, is fitted with pine furniture and faces either the pool or the boardwalk. Sign up for a Bedouin dinner trip, which is prepared once a week deep in the mountains behind Sharm. ✉ *Na'ama Bay, Sharm al-Sheikh,* ☎ *062/600–136,* 🄵🅇 *062/ 601–040. 150 rooms. 3 restaurants, 1 bar, 2 pools, hot tub, sauna, tennis court, horseback riding, squash, dive shop. AE, MC, V.*

$$$$ 🏨 **Sofitel Sharm al-Sheikh Coralia.** This fully equipped five-star is
★   perched on the northeasternmost tip of the Na'ama Bay cove. The Arabesque theme gives it the desired Mediterranean effect: a stark white exterior, Moorish architecture, Moroccan tiles, and brass chandeliers, none of which is done in excess. After checking in and being met with a complimentary glass of cold hibiscus tea, you'll find your room tastefully decorated with oak furniture, *mashribiya* (fretted handmade Egyptian woodwork) windows, and simple brass accessories. From your private balcony, take in views of the Red Sea and daily sunsets. Service is cordial, helpful, even generous—if you happen to be here on your birthday, you'll find a birthday cake, candles, a knife, and a couple of plates awaiting you in your room. The stables of the hotel have gorgeous, well-bred, carefully tended stallions and mares for desert rides.

✉ *Na'ama Bay, Sharm al-Sheikh,* ☎ *062/600–080,* 𝖥𝖠𝖷 *062/600–085. 340 rooms, 11 suites. 7 restaurants, 4 bars, in-room safes, pool, hot tub, massage, sauna, steam room, 2 tennis courts, dive shop, snorkeling, waterskiing, shops, billiards, travel services. AE, DC, MC, V.*

$$ 🏨 **Sanafir Hotel.** Over the years, Sanafir has served as the central hub and a meeting place for people staying in Na'ama Bay because of its prime location and relaxed atmosphere. An expansion of the hotel left it with an oddly shaped pool with boulders surrounding it, supposedly giving the place a desert-like feel. Rooms are basic, clean, and equipped with two narrow beds, a dome overhead, little in the way of accessories, and at best a pool view. But Sanafir is not about staying in your room, because it provides the nightlife and action of Sharm al-Sheikh from its pseudo-Bedouin tent, its bar, restaurants, and its very popular discotheque, Bus Stop. ✉ *Na'ama Bay, Sharm al-Sheikh,* ☎ *062/600–197,* 𝖥𝖠𝖷 *062/600–196. 47 rooms, 22 suites. 3 restaurants, bar, pool. DC, MC, V.*

$ 🏨 **Sunrise Hotel.** This budget property is quite out of the way—7 km (4½ mi) south of Sharm, about a £e10 taxi ride—but meal packages mean that you can get a lot for your money. Spartan rooms in the unassuming, three-story modern buildings have white-tile floors and two twin beds. The hotel is miles from the beach, but it does have a strip that a shuttle serves. ✉ *El-Haddaba, Sharm al-Sheikh,* ☎ *062/601–721,* 𝖥𝖠𝖷 *062/601–727. 102 rooms, 4 suites, all with shower. 2 restaurants, 2 bars, minibars, dive shop. AE, MC, V.*

Outdoor Activities and Sports

DIVING

Tiran, one of Sharm's favorite sites, is a one-hour drive east off the coast. It can be rough as you cross the Straits of Tiran, but it is well worth the trip. On a day of diving you will cover two of the four reefs in this area: north to south they are Jackson, Woodhouse, Thomas, and Gordon. It is popular for its strong fly currents—there are drift dives only—and rich coral walls, and you may spot some big fish.

Ras Muhammad National Park, the southernmost tip of the Sinai Peninsula, is considered one of the world's top three dive sites. With great beaches and more than 10 reefs to choose from, the park is a great place for shore and boat diving. The yellow starkness of the desert contrasts wonderfully with the explosion of life and color under the water. The most popular boat dive plan will include Shark's Reef and Jolanda Reef, where you will see hordes of great fish, beautiful coral, and some toilets and sinks deposited by the Cypriot freighter *Jolanda,* which dramatically sank here in 1980. Whether you drive the 30 km (15 mi) south of Sharm or opt for a boat dive, this is a must.

The *Thistlegorm* is a British World War II ship that the Germans sank in 1942 off the western shore of the Sinai. The ship was carrying, among other things, a train, cannons, jeeps, motorcycles, crates of guns, and boots. Now the ship lies 100 feet down in the Gulf of Suez. The wreck is a diving safari favorite, and some companies in Sharm will organize a day of diving that begins at 4 AM and returns you to Sharm, exhausted, at 5 PM. Strong currents and low visibility make this a hard dive, but it's a fantastic site.

Ras Nasrani is a favorite shore dive 18 km (11 mi) northeast of Na'ama Bay that is also often done by boat. From the shore you may get lucky and get a private tour of the reef with the resident napoleon fish. He will take you around and bring you right back to the entry point. Remember *not* to feed him, or any other fish.

Dive Centers. Almost every hotel rents space to independent dive shops, most of which provide the same services for the same prices: PADI, NAUI, and CMAS courses from beginner to instructor levels, three- to seven-day safaris, daily trips to Ras Muhammad, Tiran, and other local sites. What sets the dive centers apart is their degree of professionalism, quality of guides and boats, and levels of hospitality. Supervised introductory dives, local boat dives, and shore dives (in Dahab and Nuweiba) cost about £e170 for two dives, weights included; longer boat dives cost about £e230; daily equipment rental costs £e100; a five-day open-water certificate course costs about £e1,100.

If you want to be pampered, check in with the **Aquamarine Diving Center** (⊠ Aquamarine Novotel, Na'ama Bay, ☎ 062/600–276), run by Diver's International (which has other centers in Sharm and Dahab). Aquamarine, one of the oldest centers in the area, is managed by a team of professional divers who have been here for more than 10 years. It owns its own boats, which means that even if you are the only diver booked, your excursion will not be canceled. The skipper of the *Apuhara* has arguably the best reputation in the area. Aquamarine will pick you up from your hotel and drop you off there at the end of the day. Or you can return to their dive center for a comfortable chat and coffee with the dive guides and instructors.

The Swiss-run **SUBEX** (⊠ Mövenpick Jolie Ville Hotel, Na'ama Bay, ☎ 062/600–100) has an international reputation for being tightly run (if a bit military) and well-equipped with staff, facilities, and gear. Guided dives go out with a maximum of four people, you must take a guide with you if you have less than 30 dives, and all divers have to go on an orientation dive to determine experience levels.

SNORKELING

Snorkeling is quite popular on the Sinai coast. All dive centers rent snorkeling equipment, and in addition to snorkeling from shore, some centers run specific snorkeling trips. You can also join diving trips with snorkeling gear as a non-diver; the downside is that you will be left to your own devices, snorkeling by yourself as the guide takes the divers into deeper waters. This could be disconcerting at best, dangerous at worst, especially if you are unfamiliar with the sea's conditions.

Unlike scuba diving, you do not *need* a license to rent and use snorkeling equipment. Wherever you snorkel, wear a T-shirt or even a wet suit to protect your back from the sun. Sunscreen alone absolutely does not provide enough protection.

Aquamarine Diving Center (☞ Dive Centers, *above*) has a one-day snorkeling excursion aboard the sailboat *Henry de Monfried*. From 10 to 5 you visit some of the area's most pristine locations, have lunch, and bask in the sun. The price including lunch and equipment is $50–$60 per person.

GOLF

What do California fan palms, Jerusalem thorns, Hong Kong orchids, flames of the forest, and sand dunes have in common? The **Sharm al-Sheikh Golf Resort,** Egypt's number one golf course, which is the only course in the Sinai, for now. Set along the Red Sea in between Sharm al-Sheikh International Airport and the center of Na'ama Bay, this Sanford Associates–designed expanse of green is a well-watered haven in the desert. The 18-hole course has 17 lakes, and PGA-qualified professionals are on hand to give lessons. Call ahead for tee times and to schedule lessons. ⊠ *Airport Rd., Sharm al-Sheikh,* ☎ *062/600–635,* FAX *062/600–642. AE, MC, V.*

WATER SPORTS

There are so many water sports to choose from here—waterskiing (you can take lessons or barefoot ski), windsurfing, parasailing, and pedalboating. Another favorite, banana boating, is great fun, with a hint of danger: five or six people straddle a yellow, banana-shape boat and hold on for dear life as a speedboat pulls them around the bay. The driver will try to throw you off by taking sharp turns. Just hope you don't fall onto any fire coral.

Be prepared to pay for whatever you choose to do: £e 50 for a 10-minute round of waterskiing, £e40 for an hour of windsurfing, £e 150 for 10 minutes of parasailing for a single, £e200 for two. Ask your hotel what activities it offers. If it doesn't have what you're looking for, head over to **Sun 'n' Fun** (✉ Hilton Fayrouz, Na'ama Bay, ☎ 062/600–137).

Shopping

The **Sharm al-Sheikh Mall,** in Na'ama Bay center across from the Sanafir Hotel, has more than 20 stores that sell everything from carpets to expensive jewelry, water pipes to T-shirts. Most hotels have their own shopping arcades, but their prices will be at least double what you would pay in Cairo. The only thing you might have an easier time finding in Sharm would be Red Sea/Sinai T-shirts. So if you plan to spend any time in Cairo at all, save your shopping for there.

St. Catherine's Monastery

★ *240 km (150 mi) northwest of Sharm al-Sheikh.*

The very image of the walled monasteries pictured in luxurious medieval tapestries, St. Catherine's rests at the foot of Mount Sinai, nestled in a valley between jagged granite mountains. The monastery-cum-fortress was commissioned by the Byzantine emperor Justinian in AD 530 to protect those of Greek Orthodox faith. It also served as a strategic post on a bandit-ridden caravan route connecting Africa to Asia.

Buildings within the monastery have been erected and expanded upon throughout the centuries. The most important of these are the basilica, the Chapel of the Burning Bush, the monks' quarters, the Skull House, and the library, with its treasury of rare books that includes a 4th-century translation of the Hebrew Bible commissioned by Constantine the Great (the library is closed to the public). All buildings are enclosed by the fortress wall, which ranges in height and thickness as it adapts to the shape of the encompassing mountains.

Stepping through the modern-day north-side entrance, you see the fountain of Moses to your left. It serves as the main source of fresh water. To the right, a minaret of a mosque was built in the 10th century in order to protect the church from the Fatimid Caliph's order to destroy all churches and monasteries. After passing the fountain, step through to the **basilica,** also known as the Church of the Transfiguration, in which the apse is adorned with an ancient mosaic of the Transfiguration of Jesus. Chandeliers and decorated ostrich eggs hang from the ceiling, and gilded icons from Crete decorate the walls. Take your time in here—there are treasured works of art all around. The basilica doors date to the 6th century.

The **Chapel of the Burning Bush** remains the holiest of buildings in the monastery, but access to the inside is not always granted. The chapel, covered inside with icons, dates to the 4th century, which makes it the oldest part of the church. It is believed that God spoke to Moses by the bush outside this chapel, and many attempts to transplant branches of the bush have failed.

The **Skull House** contains the bones of deceased monks, which are kept here after their bodies deteriorate. The nature of the brittle earth, combined with limited burial space, means that monks' bones are transferred here from the cemetery after five years of interment. The skulls number around 1,500 and are arranged neatly in rows.

☉ The monastery is open daily from 9 AM until 11:45 PM. You cannot spend the night on site, but at the nearby **Wadi al-Raha Hotel** (✉ Village of St. Catherine, ☎ 065/470–325, FAX 065/470–323; no credit cards) a double room costs £e530, breakfast and dinner included. For reservations call the Cairo office (☎ 02/356–4565).

Jabal Moussa (Mount Sinai)

240 km (149 mi) northeast of Sharm al-Sheikh.

From the base of Mount Sinai, any fellow hikers who have preceded you look like dots 7,504 ft ahead of you, and the prospect of reaching the top begins to assume biblical proportions. As you step up to the mountain, the serenity of the surrounding hills is disturbed only by other passersby and the odd camel driver seeking your patronage. Stop every now and then to notice how the clean desert mountain air awakens your senses. The dusty rose tone of the granite mountains and the absolute peace makes it no surprise that this land has fostered so many religious expeditions and revelations.

Mount Sinai rises above St. Catherine's Monastery to the spot where Moses is supposed to have received the Ten Commandments. Scholars have debated the legitimacy of this claim for years and resolved nothing. Other locations have been suggested for the biblical Mount Sinai, but the mountain's position on the chief ancient trade route, and the accounts in the journals of pilgrims do seem to substantiate the claim for this mountain.

In 1934 a small chapel dedicated to the Trinity was built on the summit of Jabal Moussa, covering the ruins of a Justinian temple. Looking southeast from the peak, you'll have a crystal-clear view of the top of Mount Catherine, which is the highest point on the Sinai Peninsula at 8,652 ft. With granite mountains in all directions, it may feel like you're at the center of the Earth.

There are two routes up the mountain, and two essential times of day at which to start. The climb takes between 2½ and 3 hours. For a very steep climb, take the 3,750 steps that begin behind the monastery and lead directly to the summit. Please note that this is not exactly a proper staircase, and if you have knee problems, this will only increase them. There is another route that is also a camel track; its last 230 ft consists of 700 steps. If you take this route, you can bet that drivers will ask—repeatedly—if you want a ride. If you opt for the camel, ask around for the going rate, then haggle. Expect to pay £e30 tops.

The climb is strenuous, and you'll need to take water along and a snack to eat at the top (bring a backpack if you can). People often begin this climb around 2 AM to arrive at the summit at sunrise. If you are here during the months of January, February, or March, it won't be too hot for a midday trip; at other times, it will be. If you're going to do the night hike, take long pants, because it gets cold, and wear layers that you can take off and put back on as you warm up and cool down. A solid pair of shoes (preferably hiking boots) is also essential.

Dahab

100 km (55 mi) northeast of Na'ama Bay.

The drive from Sharm to Dahab snakes through the mountains of south Sinai. Look for Bedouin women, dressed in traditional colorful dresses and cloaked in black, herding goats and camels across the desert.

Dahab itself is another world, still half stuck in the 1960s, with roaming, long-haired hippies decked out in grungy tie-dyes. Compared with Sharm, the pace here almost runs backwards, with little more to do than hang out and snorkel and dive.

Dahab stretches along a small bay. Its three main areas include **Assla,** where you'll find camps and myriad stores all selling the same tie-dyed draw-string pants and cotton tank tops; **Masbat,** a stretch of Bedouin-style cafés that all look the same but blast different music, resulting in a strange cacophony; and **Mashrab,** a combination of both the Assalla and the Masbat.

If the promise of resort holidays brought you to the Sinai, then Dahab might not be for you. Stray cats and dogs might snuggle up to you as you eat dinner. In Assla at night, be careful not to step on people stretched out on the ground-level couches. Don't worry, these bodies are definitely alive, if of questionable consciousness. Some 5 km (3 mi) outside of town, big-name hotel chains have all the amenities you would find in Sharm.

Dahab is known for its windsurfing. Diving here is all done from the shore and is much more serious than in Sharm, with entries requiring balance and good footing. And Dahab has easy access to some superb inland sights, like the Colored Canyon. As with any off-the-beaten-path desert excursion, it is a good idea to go with a guide.

Getting around Dahab is an experience all on its own. Peugeot taxis are available at a premium (£e10). Instead, hop onto the bed of a pickup truck and pay only £e1 per person (if more than two are riding, or pay £e5 for two people).

Wadi Kid is approximately 20 km (12 mi) south of Dahab. The wadi itself is a gorgeous trek that leads to Ain Kid. Ain in Arabic means "spring." As is often the case in the Sinai, the wadis lead to springs, where the fresh water gives life to luscious green trees and grazing areas. On the way you'll drive through a Bedouin village. Stop off for a tea in the shade of an acacia tree. This is a great photo op. Your hotel can arrange a trip to the wadi.

Dining and Lodging

Don't come to Dahab looking for a gourmet meal. Restaurants and cafés in the Masbat all offer the same thing: pizza, pasta, fish, and chicken, all tasting the same and all served with a heavy cheese garnish. At the resorts you'll find a typical breakfast and dinner buffet as well as beach bars serving sandwiches and salads, perhaps even a theme lunch.

If you don't mind roughing it, you can find inexpensive rooms in the Assalla at any of the camps. Be prudent about what you pick because cheap doesn't imply clean and rarely will it include private bathrooms. If you must stay at any such establishments, wear flip-flops when you shower. At the hotels, although they are far from the mellow center of town, you can count on four-star quality, comfort, and services.

$$ ✕ **Pizza 'n' Pasta.** This quaint Italian restaurant, near the dive center on the beach, is a great place for a midday meal, which is about all you can get here, because it is open only from noon until 5 PM. ⊠ *Novotel Coralia Dahab,* ☎ *062/640–301. AE, MC, V.*

$ ✕ **Shark Club.** It might seem strange that this restaurant comes highly recommended. Its decor is—interesting, with small bonfires and floor seating. You might feel like going to one of the hotels instead, but don't. In spite of the grilled chicken drowned in cheese, fried chicken drowned in cheese, and wilted steamed veggies drowned in cheese, its oddities have great entertainment value. ⊠ *Masbat,* ☎ *no phone. No credit cards.*

$$ ⊞ **Novotel Coralia Dahab.** If you're coming straight from Cairo, it might take a few hours for you to acclimate to the tranquillity of the 1,600-foot beachfront of the resort's private lagoon. Mountain and sea views here are superb, and the layout of the rooms, which are admittedly on the tacky side, suits the environment. The buffet breakfasts and dinners are simple and tasty, although the overeagerness of the waiters can become trying. ⊠ *Box 23, Dahab,* ☎ *062/640–301,* 𝔽𝔸𝕏 *062/640–305. 141 rooms with shower. 3 restaurants, 3 bars, minibars, pool, dive shop, windsurfing. AE, MC, V.*

Diving

DIVE SITES

The three sites below are about 30 minutes north of Dahab, so you might want to dive with one of the hotel dive centers, which can arrange transportation. Bring water with you, and plan to pass some time relaxing under the awning of the Bedouin cafeteria that provides basic refreshments. No toilet facilities are available, so follow the cardinal rule of the desert: women to the left, men to the right.

A phenomenal dive plan begins at the **Bells** and ends in the **Blue Hole.** This is one of Egypt's most spectacular underwater havens. Although you are unlikely to see sharks or big fish, the plate-like coral formations, which run to nearly 1,000 ft below sea level, are gorgeous settings for other awesome marine life. The dive finishes at mouth of the remarkable Blue Hole, a cone-shaped coral enclave that seems to go on forever. Don't miss this dive.

The Canyon, right around the corner from the Blue Hole, is another great dive. You feel like you're sky diving as you descend through 100 feet of coral cliffs on either side of you.

DIVE CENTERS

Divers' International (⊠ Ganet Sinai Hotel, Dahab, ☎ 062/640–415) All trips are daily jeep or truck trips to local sites in the vicinity of Dahab. **Sinai Dive Club** also has a base in Sharm al-Sheikh (⊠ Novotel Coralia, Dahab, South Sinai, ☎ 062/640–301). All trips are daily jeep or truck trips to local sites in the vicinity of Dahab.

Water Sports

The bay at the **Novotel Coralia Dahab** (⊠ Dahab, South Sinai, ☎ 062/640–302) glistens with the colorful sails of Windsurfers, which rent for £e70 per hour.

Other **water sports** include jet-skiing, wave-running, pedalboating, and canoeing (a canoe here is a one-person, kayak-surfboard hybrid). Water-sports centers at any of the major hotels rent to guests and non-guests. An hour of canoeing will cost £e50.

Nuweiba

70 km (44 mi) north of Dahab.

The town of Nuweiba serves as both a crucial Gulf of Aqaba port and a resort with a couple of hotel areas and a quaint town center. Maagana Bay, the main port city, sees constant traffic from trucks full of goods and equipment, travelers making their way to Mecca, and tourists going to Jordan. This is where you'll find a post office, telephone central, bus station, and beckoning taxi drivers—exactly the picturesque part of town. The nearby Hilton resort, east along the bay, is something of a refuge by comparison, with all of the typical Sinai-coast amenities.

About 6 km (4 mi) north of the port lies the city center, commonly known as Tarabin by the Bedouin tribe that has settled here. The tightly packed center has simple stores filled with cheap local clothing, trinkets, souvenirs, and household goods. Cheap restaurants serve basic food, and supermarkets carry an adequate range of supplies.

You can hire a taxi in Maagana Bay (drivers understand "dolphin") to take you farther into the area settled by the Muzeinas. There you will find the much-loved and now-famous solitary dolphin, Holly. A few years back, Abdallah, a local fisherman, befriended her, and Holly stays in the bay of her own will. You might say that she even enjoys being a local entertainer, and she doesn't mind people swimming with her—she just makes her usual rounds, playing in circles. Her presence has been a boon for the local Bedouin, because people who come to see her spend money in cafés on the beach. For around £e10 you are invited to put on a mask and fins and plunge into the water and swim with her.

Because of its central position on the Sinai coast, Nuweiba makes a good base for trekking into the Sinai interior to the Colored Canyon, or going farther afield across the Gulf of Aqaba and into Jordan to see the ruins at Petra.

Getting a glimpse of the **Colored Canyon**'s red, yellow, rose, brown, and purple hues deep within the mountains northwest of Nuweiba is something that you can do only by camel or four-wheel-drive vehicle. The Abanoub Travel Agency (☞ *below*) or your hotel can arrange a trip here, or take one from Sharm al-Sheikh or Dahab.

Dining and Lodging

$$$ ⊡ **Hilton Coral Resort.** Being five minutes by taxi from Nuweiba Port makes the low-rise beachside Hilton an ideal place to station yourself in Nuweiba. Rooms are spartan, with white tiles, wooden furniture, and underwater photographs; all have large balconies. With an eye toward ecological friendliness, the hotel asks that you limit your use of water to what's necessary, and there are power cards to activate your room's electricity. The Hilton also arranges day trips to Jordan to see Petra. Its high-speed catamaran crosses the Gulf of Aqaba in 45 minutes (which shaves two hours off of the standard ferry crossing) and departs Friday mornings at 6 AM. ⊠ *Maagana Bay,* ☎ *062/520–320,* FAX *062/520–327. 100 rooms. 2 restaurants, 2 bars, minibars, 2 pools, spa, tennis court, horseback riding, squash. AE, DC, MC, V.*

Outdoor Activities

Abanoub Travel Agency (☎ 062/500–140, FAX 062/520–206), at the new commercial center in Nuweiba, runs camel, jeep, and trekking tours of varying durations to all parts of the Sinai.

Basata

20 km (12 mi) northeast of Nuweiba.

Remember *Gilligan's Island*? As the most serene spot in the Sinai, Basata feels very much like that—you hear only the crashing of surf and the chirping of birds; only the occasional distant rumbling of vehicles on the road breaks the spell. Sunrise is picture perfect; ditto the sunset.

Dining and Lodging

✕⊡ **Basata.** At this family-oriented, back-to-nature resort, seventeen bamboo huts span a 1,600-ft bay protected on three sides by red-rock hills and mountains. Across the Gulf of Aqaba you can see the mountains of Saudi Arabia. Basata is ruled by the honor code. The main hut, with its kitchen, covered dining area, and sun patio of sorts, is open 24 hours. Nightly communal house dinners alternate day to day between fish and vegetarian meals. Or prepare your own meals in the kitchen—just remember to sign for everything you consume and wash all dishes and utensils you use. Basata's specialties are its breads, baked fresh several times daily on the premises. Huts are decidedly simple, with beds (mattresses on the floor), a mirror, and a candle holder—in Arabic, *basata* means simplicity, and you should expect just that. In the shared bathrooms, taps and showers provide desalinated water—hot water is available when (after, that is) the sun shines—and toilets use salt water. Only the bathrooms and main tents have electricity. The flipside to Basata's cozy earthiness is that management does little to make you feel comfortable. Upon arrival you are questioned, then lectured on house rules and regulations, to which you are required to adhere. Then you are sent to your hut unaccompanied, and left to lug your bags through the sand. For the slightest infraction of the rules, expect a stern word and smug attitude. If you are really bad, you might be asked to pack up and leave. Remember to follow the rules and you will have a wonderful, relaxing stay. The resort arranges jeep and camel trips into the desert (for an additional fee), snorkeling gear is available to rent, but scuba diving is not permitted. Alcohol is also not allowed. ⊠ *Basata, South Sinai,* ☎ FAX *062/500–481; 02/350–1829 in Cairo. 17 bungalows with shared bath and beachside camping. Restaurant, snorkeling, beach. MC, V.*

Taba

43 km (26 mi) north of Basata.

Taba borders Israel, and is a sister city of the Israeli resort town of Eilat. It has been important since biblical times as a stopover for travelers entering or leaving Egypt. There is little to do here beyond poking around Pharaoh's Island—or, even better, snorkeling off it.

Pharaoh's Island, so-called because it was first used during the reign of Ramesses III (1194–1163 BC), is a long rocky island surrounded by reefs and the turquoise waters of the gulf. The best-known period of the islands occupation was during the Crusades, when it was an outpost for the warring Christians. For 55 years, from the safety of the island, the Crusaders controlled both the trade and pilgrimage routes that passed this way. Then, in AD 1170, soon after coming to power, Salah al-Din captured the island. Despite repeated attempts, Crusaders never again regained control of it.

The island is 250 yards offshore—a distance to travel if you're interested in diving or snorkeling around the excellent reefs off the north end of the island (where currents are strong). The fortress itself is perhaps best viewed from the mainland, in part because the view of the Salah al-Din motel back on land is unsightly. A boat runs from the resort every 15 minutes from 9 to 5 and costs £e14 round-trip. The island can get quite crowded with tourists from Eilat and Aqaba. ⊠ *5 km south of Taba.* 🎫 *£e10 (fortress).* ⊙ *Daily 10–4.*

The Sinai Peninsula A to Z

Arriving and Departing

BY BUS

Long-distance bus travel is recommended if you have time and a high annoyance threshold. Obnoxious dramatic movies play for the six-hour duration, and despite NO SMOKING signs everywhere, even the driver lights up.

Buses run daily from Cairo to Sharm al-Sheikh, Dahab, and Nuweiba. From Sinai Station in Abbasia, the **East Delta Bus Company** (☎ 02/482–4753 in Cairo) goes to Sharm; tickets cost from £e50 to £e65, depending on when you leave (morning buses are cheaper). Buses leave every 45 minutes between 7 AM and 6:30 PM. There are also daily buses to Taba and Nuweiba at 8 AM for £e50 one way.

Super Jet (☎ 02/772–663 in Cairo) buses run to Sharm al-Sheikh once a day at 11 AM from Cairo's Maydan Tahrir (Tahrir Square); return buses leave Sharm al-Sheikh for Cairo at 11 AM. A one way ticket costs £e50.

BY PLANE

Egypt Air (☎ 02/390–2444) has daily flights from Cairo to Sharm al-Sheikh. The 45-minute trip costs approximately £e1,000.

To get from the airport to Sharm al-Sheik, first look for your hotel's shuttle bus before approaching a cab, because the shuttle will save you the £e60 taxi fare.

Getting Around

If you plan to make your way up the coast, staying in a couple of towns on the way, it's best to have a car. There are plenty of rentals in Sharm al-Sheikh. Getting to the more remote sights in the desert requires four-wheel-drive vehicles and knowledge of how to drive them in the desert, which makes going with a guided group the best option.

BY BUS

The cheapest transportation within towns is local transportation. In Sharm al-Sheikh it's microbuses, in Dahab it's pickup trucks. In Sharm a one-way microbus from Sharm al-Maya to Na'ama Bay is 50p per person. Have change in hand and stand out on the street and flag down a bus or pickup. It's a slice of local life, and quite lot of fun.

BY CAR

Roads are mostly two lanes wide up and down the coast, and turnoffs are not always marked. Getting to remote sights requires some skill. Be careful when you negotiate winding turns through the mountains because local drivers tend not to stay in their own lanes. Renting a car is no different than it is in the United States, Canada, or Europe, and you will need to bring both your domestic license and an international driver's license.

BY TAXI

Taking taxis around the peninsula can get expensive. The seven-person Peugeot station wagons are ubiquitous, and drivers will practically harass you to hire them at the airport, at bus stations, ports, and outside hotels, bars, discos, and restaurants. There seems to be an understanding among them that foreigners will pay what often amounts to five times the regular fare. If you end up needing to take a taxi to St. Catherine's Monastery or any of the coastal towns, fill the cab to capacity with passengers to lower the per-person price.

Within Dahab, Nuweiba and Na'ama Bay, taxi rides cost £e10. There are no meters, so be sure to agree on a price with your driver before you get in the car. Estimated taxi fares are:

Sharm al-Sheikh–Dahab: £e120; **Sharm–St. Catherine's:** £e200; **Sharm–Nuweiba:** £e180; **Nuweiba–Taba:** £e90.

Contacts and Resources

CAR RENTAL

Max Europcar (✉ Ghazala Hotel, Na'ama Bay, ☎ 062/600-150, FAX 062/600–140). Daily rates start at £e170 for a compact car, excluding insurance and taxes, with an additional 58p per kilometer over the daily 100 km allowance.

EMERGENCIES

Police. ☎ *062/600–415.*

Ambulance. ☎ *062/600–554.*

Sharm al-Sheikh New Hospital. ☎ *062/660–425.*

Hyperbaric Medical Center treats diving conditions. ☎ *062/660–893.*

TRAVEL AGENCIES

Thomas Cook. ✉ *Gafy Mall, Gafy Land, Sharm al-Sheikh,* ☎ *062/601–808.*

THE RED SEA COAST

The Red Sea is one of the few seas on earth that is virtually closed, surrounded in this case by arid land: the Sinai to the north, the Eastern Sahara on the west, and the Arabian Peninsula to the east. The sea pours into the Gulfs of Aqaba and Suez to the north; to the south its mouth narrows into the strait of Bab al-Mandeb—The Gate of Tears. The Red Sea is 1,800 km (1,200 mi) long and 350 km (over 200 mi) wide. Along its central axis, depths reach 10,000 ft. The combination of minimal tidal changes, currents and wind, and almost year-round sunshine fosters the growth of a unique underwater ecology.

The Red Sea has been an important conduit for trade throughout human history. Along its coasts, new archaeological sites now being excavated date as far back as the earliest ancient Egyptian gold and turquoise expeditions, made more than 4,000 years ago. Ottoman outposts are being renovated and will reopen another chapter of life on the edge of the Eastern Sahara. Deeper in the mountains, Christian monastic life began at the Monastery of St. Paul, founded by the eastern church's first known hermit-priest.

Ain Sukhna

120 km (75 mi) southeast of Cairo; 45 km (29 mi) south of Suez.

The waters of Ain Sukhna ("hot spring") originate at Jabal Ataka, a mountain on the Red Sea coast. The turquoise water is clear and warm year-round. There is little to do here in the way of sightseeing, but it's a convenient day trip from Cairo or the Suez Canal zone if, like picnicking Cairenes, you're looking for a seaside day in the sun. Although public beaches are accessible the best option is to rent chairs and umbrellas for £e10 at either the Ain Sukhna Village Hotel or the Mean Oasis Hotel. The food here is dreadful, so be sure to bring some along with you.

The Monasteries of St. Anthony and St. Paul

Egypt's oldest monasteries stand at the forefront of Christian monastic history. Isolated in the mountains near the Red Sea, they have spectacular settings and views of the coast. Getting to the monasteries isn't exactly a picnic, but their remoteness was the reason the saints chose the caves at these sites for their hermitages. The saints' endurance in the desert, against Bedouin raids, changing religious tides, and physical privation, give them an allure that is augmented by paintings and icons that add color to their otherwise stark appeal.

The Monastery of St. Anthony
110 km (69 mi) southwest of Ain Sukhna.

St. Anthony is a prominent figure in Coptic Christianity because of his influence on the monastic movement. And even though his contemporary, Paul (☞ St. Paul's Monastery, *below*), was the first hermit, Anthony was the more popular. He was born in the middle of the 3rd century AD to wealthy parents who left him with a hefty inheritance upon their death, when he was 18. Instead of reveling in his riches, he sold all his possessions, distributed the proceeds to the poor, sent his sister to a convent, and fled to dedicate his life to God as a hermit in the mountains overlooking the Red Sea.

Disciples flocked to Anthony, hoping to hear his preaching and to be healed. But the monk sought absolute solitude and retreated to a cave in the mountain range of South Qabala. After his death in the 4th century—the hermit lived to age 104—admirers built a chapel and refectory in his memory. St. Anthony's grew. In the 7th, 8th, and 11th centuries, periodic Bedouin predations severely damaged the structure. It was restored in the 12th century.

St Anthony's stands deep back in the mountains. Its walls reach some 40 ft in height. Several watchtowers, as well as the bulky walls' catwalk provide for sentries. The **Church of St. Anthony** was built over his grave, and it is renowned for its exquisite 13th-century wall paintings of St. George on horseback and the three Desert Fathers, which have recently been restored.

Four other churches were built on the grounds of the monastery over the years. The most important of them is the 1766 **Church of St. Mark**, which is adorned with 12 domes and contains significant relics.

A 2-km (1¼-mi) trek will lead you to **St. Anthony's Cave**, 2,230 ft above sea level, where he spent his last days. Views of the Red Sea and the surrounding mountains are superb, and you're likely to encounter interesting local birdlife on the hike to the cave. Inside the cave, among the rocks, pilgrims have left pieces of paper asking the saint for intervention.

The Monastery of St. Paul
112 km (70 mi) south of Ain Sukhna.

St. Paul made his way into the desert to live as a hermit, having had a wealthy upbringing in Alexandria. It was his fellow penitent Anthony who reavealed his sainthood to him. The monastery was built in the 5th century, after the saint's death. A thousand years later St. Paul's was abandoned, after having been raided several times. Again Anthony came to Paul's aid: monks from the Monastery of St. Anthony eventually reopened St. Paul's.

A 7-km (4¼-mi) drive west from the Red Sea coast highway twists through the rugged mountains and deposits you near the entrance of St. Paul's Monastery. Thought to have been built sometime during the 6th century, the monastery was abandoned in the 15th century, then reinhabited 200 years later.

The high walls of the monastery are surrounded by a village, which has a bakery, mills, and a few surrounding fields. The buildings of the monastery are believed to encompass the cave in which St. Paul lived for nearly 80 years. In the **Church of St. Paul** paintings of the Holy Virgin cover the walls.

Arriving and Departing
To get to the monasteries you will need to rent a car or, preferably (because driving in Egypt is such a harrowing experience), hire a private

taxi from Cairo (£e300) or Hurghada (£e150). Note that Copts fast for 43 days in advance of Christmas, during which time most monasteries are closed to visitors. Call before you set out to confirm that the gates will be open.

Thomas Cook runs tours to the monasteries from Cairo and Hurghada. *Hurghada:* ✉ *8 Shar'a al-Sheraton,* ☎ *065/443–500 or 065/443–338. Cairo:* ✉ *12 Maydan al-Sheikh Youssef, Garden City, Cairo,* ☎ *02/ 356–4650 or 02/356–4652.*

Hurghada

410 km (255 mi) south of Ain Suhkna; 530 km (331 mi) south of Cairo.

Hurghada is an old fishing town that became a popular base for diving in the 1960s. As a result of the 1967 war between Egypt and Israel, Hurghada was closed to tourism and did not reopen until 1976. By this time, Sharm al-Sheikh, which was under Israeli occupation, was flourishing as a diving town. Hurghada had a lot of catching up to do.

Now, with a population lurching toward 50,000 and some 75 hotels in and around town, Hurghada is definitely the Red Sea's hot spot. Vacationers flock here in fall and winter specifically for its mild climate. But if it's sun, sand, and sea that you're after, the Sinai coast has more appealing beaches and desert diversions. Come to Hurghada for the diving.

Hurghada spreads over 15 km (9 mi) from north to south along the sea. The first string of hotels was built right along the coast, and subsequent stages of development have grown back from the front line, along the highway that leads north to Cairo and south to Quseir. The oldest hotel here is the Sheraton, and it is used as a landmark. The main boulevard, with its 15 car-splitting speed bumps, is called Shar'a Sheraton.

This town is known for its strong north-northwesterly winds, so if you plan to lounge about, find a spot with a protective windbreak. From April to October, the hotter months, be prepared to battle the bugs: mosquitoes, light brown desert flies, and other flying insects have nasty bites. Bring bug repellent and spend your time in the sea.

Beaches

Beaches around Hurghada haven't acquired the cachet of those on the Sinai coast. Because public beach access is virtually nonexistent—and public beaches are not worth going to—it's best to stick with your hotel's beachfront. For a change of scenery, Sharm al-Naga, 20 km (12 mi) south of Hurghada and another 7 km (4 mi) to the beach from the main road, is a simple campsite overlooking a bay area, ideal for diving, snorkeling, swimming, and tanning.

Dining and Lodging

Not unlike Sharm al-Sheikh, Hurghada caters primarily to a European package-tour clientele. This inherently implies an abundance of kitsch decor with purple, pink, and green paint jobs.

$$$$ ✕ **Al Dente.** Popular among local expatriates, this elegant restaurant is great for a romantic interlude. It is one of the few places in the country where you'll find pasta, as the name suggests, properly cooked. ✉ *Inter-Continental Hotel, Hurghada–Safaga Rd., Km 17,* ☎ *065/443– 911. Reservations essential. AE, DC, MC, V. No lunch.*

$$ ✕ **Felfela.** A sister of the Cairo-based Felfela, this is the best place in town for a traditional Egyptian meal. The restaurant's four levels all have great harbor views. Sit down to a fresh lemonade and start choosing appetizers from the menu—tasty *ful,* the classic fava-bean dish, koshary, or the spicy vegetarian casserole of zucchini, potato, eggplant, and onions in a tomato sauce. From the grill dig into kebabs or wheat-stuffed pigeon. The grilled catch of the day is another delicious choice. Specialties here are the salads: tahina, humus, *baba ghanouj* (eggplant dip), cumin-spiced tomatoes, *labne* (a yogurt and mint dip), and stuffed grape leaves. Bring an appetite and allow two hours for dinner. ⊠ *Shar'a Sheraton (2 km [1¼ mi] north of the Sheraton Hotel),* ☎ *065/442– 410. No credit cards.*

$$$$ ⬛ **Inter-Continental Resort and Casino.** In spite of its size and the
★ proximity of other resorts in the area, the five-story, crescent-shaped Inter-Continental manages to have a feeling of privacy, and its views of the sea are fantastic. Amid the expanse of the hotel's main building and villas, the principal restaurants and bars are grouped together around the casino, (housed in a separate building from the hotel). Rooms come with either a balcony or an enclosed patio, both being equally appealing, and marble floors have a welcome cooling effect. All levels of the hotel staff, from bell captains to deck hands are pleasant and attentive. With tennis, horseback riding, diving, and the largest pool in Hurghada (heated in winter), there is plenty to keep you stylishly occupied. ⊠ *Hurghada–Safaga Rd., Km 17 (Box 36),* ☎ *065/446– 911,* ℻ *065/446–910. 252 rooms, 4 VIP suites, 5 terrace suites, 8 villas with private pools. 3 restaurants, 2 bars, pool, 3 tennis courts, horseback riding, squash, beach, dive shop, billiards, marina, casino, nightclub. AE, DC, MC, V.*

$$$ ⬛ **Sofitel.** You're guaranteed a comfortable room with a view at this nouveau-Moorish hotel. Be sure to specify what view you want—mountain or sea, both with a veranda, both equally gorgeous. At this expansive waterside property, you will find your every need satisfied. Among the range of activities—a boon for families—tennis, squash (including rackets and balls), windsurfing, pedalboating, and sauna and excercise facilities are included in room rates (a unique arrangement on the Red Sea). Horseback riding, massages, lessons (for all sports), and water sports that require gasoline (like waterskiing) cost extra. The only drawback here is the 15-minute trip into town if you want to do something that the hotel doesn't have available. ⊠ *Hurghada–Safaga Rd., Km 12 (Box 166),* ☎ *065/442–266,* ℻ *065/442–270. 312 rooms. 2 restaurants, 5 bars, minibars, pool, sauna, Turkish bath, miniature golf, 5 tennis courts, archery, excercise room, horseback riding, squash, beach, dive shop, nightclub, baby-sitting, children's programs. MC, V.*

Diving

DIVE SITES

Shu'ab al-Erg looks like a big crescent with big ergs (shifting dunes) on the tips of the crescent. This site is two hours from Hurghada. You'll find a gorgeous coral garden, and look out for dolphins.

Giftun Drift, on Small Giftun Island, is a beautiful deep wall dive one hour off shore east of Hurghada. This is one of the deepest sites in the local area, and there is beautiful marine life. **Abu Ramada,** south of Small Giftun Island, has remarkable multi-colored corals.

DIVE CENTERS

SUBEX (Corniche, ☎ 065/547–593, ℻ 065/547–471) specializes in safaris south of Hurghada. Ever in search of virgin reefs unpopulated by divers and boats, the guides will take you on week-long trips to the kinds of sites that make a splash in *National Geographic.*

Pioneers of technical diving and the rebreather in the Red Sea, **Divers' Lodge** (⊠ Inter-Continental Resort and Casino, ☎ 065/446–911, ℻ 065/446–910) has its own jetty, fully equipped live-aboard boat, and several contracted daily boats. The company runs PADI courses from beginner to instructor levels, and has night diving, technical diving, and NITROX and rebreather courses. The staff is warm and professional and includes divers from around the world. Divers' Lodge also has a the only courses in Egypt in sign language for the hearing-impaired, conducted by a hearing-impaired instructor.

One-day dives cost £e170, including two tanks; full gear rental per day costs £e100. Ask for diving packages of up to 10 days, which include 20 dives. Two-day safaris to Abu Nahas, *Thistlegorm,* and distant sites cost £e350, including full accommodation. An open-water course costs £e2,000.

Fishing

Deep-sea fishing is the way to go on the Red Sea if you feel like dropping a line into the water. **Red Sea Fishing** (☎ 065/442–316) can hook you up with a charter captain.

Water Sports

Waterskiing, windsurfing, parasailing, kayaking, and pedal boating are among the aquatic possibilities in Hurghada. Wave-runners are banned from the area for now. Inquire at your hotel about what activities it offers; the staff can direct you in the right direction if they don't have what you're looking for. Prices will range from £e170 an hour to £e185 for 15 minutes, depending how much equipment, machinery, and staff-power is involved.

al-Gouna

20 km (12 mi) north of Hurghada; 510 km (319 mi) south of Cairo.

Al-Gouna is the dream of an Egyptian businessman who has utterly transformed a secluded bay and its surrounding resources. Equipped with its own wells in the mountains, a hospital with a hyperbaric chamber for dealing with divers' decompression problems, four power plants, and an impressive array of services, this environmentally friendly resort town is practically self-sustaining.

The village center itself, called Qafr al-Gouna, or just al-Qafr, was designed with cobblestone walkways and sand paths to look like a typical Egyptian peasant town. Gates manned by traditionally garbed guards usher you into this impressive space. Within you will find all the amenities you can think of—a museum, an aquarium, restaurants, bars, banks, plenty of shops, a nursery. Make sure you taste the Löwenbrau, a local beer brewed in the village, and Sabil, the locally bottled spring water. Bear in mind that al-Gouna isn't only a tourist village: Egyptians and foreign residents have bought villas here and come to unwind from the hustle and bustle of Cairo. If it all sounds contrived, it is. At the same time, it has been tastefully executed, the infrastructure works, and it is set in a beautiful spot.

Water sports, desert excursions, and golf are available in al-Gouna. If you can't arrange these at your hotel, stop by the **Club House** (☎ 065/549–701) in al-Qafr for information. Transportation within the resort is free, whether by microbus, tuff-tuff (topless bus), or boat.

If the **museum** ever opens its planned Bedouin exhibit, it will be worth visiting. Otherwise its replicas of Ancient Egypt artifacts, monuments, and art merit a pass. ⊠ *Qafr al-Gouna.*

Beaches

Zeytouna Beach is an island—it is the only public beach in al-Gouna—with a very popular beach bar. In high season there are enormous parties for everyone in al-Gouna, hotel guests as well as locals. To get to

Zeytouna, hop on one of the boat buses that moor along the canals of al-Gouna.

Hotel beaches are for the use of hotel guests only.

Dining and Lodging

$$ ✗ **Kiki's.** Not only is this a great Italian restaurant, serving arguably the best food in al-Gouna, it's also a hip hangout. Kiki's opens at 8 PM, but it really comes alive around 11—and keeps kickin' through the night until the last person leaves. ⊠ *Museum Square, Qafr al-Gouna,* ☎ *065/549–701, ext. 2407. Reservations essential in high season. No credit cards. No lunch.*

$ ✗ **La Grolla.** This open-air disco is a full-blown restaurant during the off-season, and it serves an early dinner in season before the action starts up. Adjacent to the Khayamia shopping arcade and right on the Lagoon Beach, it is an ideal setting if you just want to lounge around and enjoy the company of friends in the casual Red Sea style. ⊠ *Qafr al-Gouna,* ☎ *065/549–701. Reservations essential in high season. No credit cards. No lunch.*

$$$$ ⊡ **Sheraton Miramar.** Outside the Qafr near al-Gouna's second marina, this huge hotel is the design of architect Michael Graves. Its pink, yellow, and blue paint job might be on the shocking side, but in a town of great mountain and sea views, it has some of the best. No expense was spared to build this luxury hotel. Pamper yourself at the Palace, a separate enclave within the resort with 25 rooms usually occupied by VIPs and royalty. ⊠ *Sheraton Miramar al-Gouna,* ☎ *065/545–701 or 065/545–705,* ℻ *065/549–065. 282 rooms. 2 restaurants, 3 bars, room service, 5 pools, aquasport center, dive shop. AE, MC, V.*

$$ ⊡ **Dawar al-Omda.** The name of this hotel within the Qafr means "the mayor's house," and that is its theme. The small reception area is lighted by a massive old brass and copper lantern, and the tables in the dining room are made of heavy wood. The pool seems to spill over into the canal, and views are gorgeous. The rooms are cozy, a bit too cozy, perhaps, but each has a balcony overlooking the canal and pool. ⊠ *Qafr al-Gouna,* ☎ *065/545–060 or 065/545–062,* ℻ *065/545–061. 64 rooms, 3 junior suits, 4 honeymoon suites. Restaurant, 2 bars, pool. AE, MC, V.*

$$ ⊡ **Sultan Bay.** This relative newcomer in the Qafr (across from Dawar al-Omda, *above*) has a North African theme to it, with plenty of domes and Moorish archways. The buildings are painted a sand color and have an old, weathered look. Rooms are bright and sunny, with blue-and-white curtains and large French doors that open onto small balconies. ⊠ *Qafr al-Gouna,* ☎ *065/545–600 or 065/545–602,* ℻ *065/545–601. 115 rooms. 2 restaurants, 2 bars, minibars, pool, beach. AE, MC, V.*

Diving

DIVE CENTERS

Diver's Lodge is right on the beach at the Mövenpick Hotel. The staff's passion for diving is infectious, and with them you'll learn about the local marine environment and improve your diving. Everything from introductory dives to Trimix Instructor courses and week-long safaris are available. Diver's Lodge continues to be a local pioneer in technical diving, recreational diving, and free diving. Remember to bring your logbook and certification card, or, if you plan to take a course, records of a recent medical examination. Payment is accepted only in £e, US$, or U.S. travelers' checks. ⊠ *Mövenpick Hotel, al-Gouna,* ☎ *065/545–160.*

DIVE SIGHTS

Um Gamar means "mother of the moon." Roughly 90 minutes offshore by speedboat, this is truly an amazing dive, with great walls and caves. The current here is light, making this one of the easier dives of the area.

Abu Nahas is a wreck diver's haven, with four large freighters sunk at reachable depths. Twenty years ago a ship carrying copper (*nahas* in Arabic) hit the reef and sank, hence the name of the site. The Tile Wreck carried Spanish tiles and sank in the same vicinity. And the Lentil Wreck became a smorgasbord for fish. You will encounter huge napoleons, groupers, schools of snappers, and catfish. *Giannis D.* hit the reef in 1983 and is a favorite; at 82 feet underwater you will find a large air pocket where you can speak to your buddy. Remember not to breathe the air, though, because it is stale and probably poisonous.

Bur Safaga (Port Safaga)

40 km (25 mi) south of Hurghada.

This commercial town has little to recommend it. The diving in the area is great, but it's also reachable from Hurghada. Just pass on through on your way to Quseir.

al-Quseir

85 km (53 mi) south of Port Safaga.

Until the completion of the Suez Canal, Quseir was a crucial port, principally because of the *hajj* (pilgrimmage to Mecca) and Middle East trade. With the canal in place, the port of Quseir was no longer needed as a stop for ships, laden with goods, passing from the Nile Valley across the Red Sea and beyond, and so it fell into decline. The current development boom along the entire Red Sea coast is turning Quseir into a resort town. The most recent construction aims to be environmentally conscious, not only of marine life, but also of land that is thought to be rich in artifacts, from bits of Roman-era glass to Mamluk archways. This suits the people of Quseir, who are known for their gentle temperaments and welcoming personalities.

Quseir Fort was one of many strategically located military posts that the Ottoman Turks built along the Red Sea coast, and it was one of the chief posts that the Napoleonic Expedition in 1799 thoroughly bombed, then rebuilt. An international team of archaeologists is currently excavating the site of the old fort, hoping to regain the initial spirit of the place. It is estimated that the fort was commissioned in the early 16th century during Ottoman rule by the sharifs of Mecca and Medina. They wanted to protect the hajj route and maintain control of the passage of goods against the threat posed by the Portuguese fleet: the area around Quseir was a profitable granary for wheat, and coffee from Yemen and the most valuable spices of India and Persia were reloaded here. To get in, stop by between 9 AM and noon and try a little sweet talk.

Dining and Lodging

$$$ ☒ **Mövenpick al-Quseir, Sirena Beach.** This is one of the more tran-
★ quil settings on the Red Sea coast—even the buildings blend with the surrounding environment. One of Egypt's more prominent architects, Ramy Dahan, used the granite of the nearby mountains to give the buildings the same rose tint found in the surrounding area. No building is more than one story tall, and each is complemented with a large terrace facing either the sea or the garden. Rooms are fitted with terracotta tiles, a high dome over the desk and TV areas, and comfortable beds with shelves set into the wall. The Seagull Restaurant serves an excellent fish tagine, richly spiced with cumin and garnished with caramelized onions. The decor is tasteful and the service attentive. ☒ *Sirena Beach, al-Quadim Bay,* ☏ *065/432–100 or 065/432–120,* 🖷 *065/432–128. 175 rooms, 3 suites. 3 restaurants, 3 bars, minibars, pool,*

sauna, hot tub, 2 tennis courts, beach, dive shop, boating, children's programs, laundry service. AE, DC, MC, V.

DIVING

The tightly run Swiss **SUBEX** (☎ 065/432–100 ext. 8080, ℻ 065/432–124) is on the grounds of Mövenpick hotel, and it is well-equipped with staff, facilities, and gear. Guided dives go out with a maximum of four people, you must take a guide with you if you have less than 30 dives under your belt, and all divers must go on an orientation dive to determine experience levels.

Red Sea Coast A to Z

Arriving and Departing

BY CAR

The advantage of renting a car and driving to the Red Sea coast is flexibility, but that might not outweigh the dangers posed by other drivers, including many trucks, and the hairpin turns before Ain Sukhna. If you don't have nerves of steel, fly to Hurghada or hire a taxi to take you to the monasteries.

BY PLANE

Egypt Air (☎ 065/443–592) makes the 45-minute flight from Cairo twice daily for about £e1,000 round-trip. Flights from Sharm al-Sheikh run twice a week and cost about the same. There are also chartered flights from London and Rome that land in both Hurghada and al-Gouna.

Hurghada International Airport is in the desert, 4 km (2½ mi) west of the Sheraton at the southern end of town. Most hotels offer free airport transfers, so if you fly into the airport, look for your hotel's van before you give in to a taxi driver badgering you for a £e15 ride.

Getting Around

To travel between al-Gouna and Hurghada, hire a cab or rent a car (driving around the resorts is less perilous). Within al-Gouna there are microbuses and boats that stop at all hotels and key hotspots. These are all free of charge.

BY CAR

If you plan to stay in Hurghada or al-Gouna, you will not need a car. If you are going to to travel south as far as Quseir, having a car will be helpful. The road is well marked and easy to drive.

BY TAXI

Cabs are only available on the street (not by phoning a dispatcher). Taxis will cost at least £e10 for the shortest distance in Hurghada. A better, if more communal, option would be to flag down a microbus, which will cost only £e1 per person.

Contacts and Resources

CAR RENTAL

Europcar's rates start at £e170 per day for a compact car, excluding insurance and taxes, with an additional 58p per km over the allotted daily 100 km (62 mi). ⊠ *Sonesta Beach Resort, Hurghada,* ☎ 065/443–660 or 065/443–664.

EMERGENCIES

Police. ☎ 065/442–2359.

Ambulance. ☎ 065/546–490.

Hurghada General Hospital. ☎ 065/546–740.

TRAVEL AGENCIES

Thomas Cook. ⊠ *8 Shar'a Sheraton, Hurghada,* ☎ *065/443–500 or 065/443–338.*

VISITOR INFORMATION

Egyptian Tourist Authority. ⊠ *Shar'a Sheraton, Hurghada,* ☎ *065/444–421.* ⊙ *Daily 9–2.*

THE SUEZ CANAL

The construction of the Suez Canal changed the nature of European trade by connecting the Red Sea to the Mediterranean. Ismailiya and Bur Sa'id were homes to workers and leaders of the expedition. The colonial feel lingers in the old buildings that remain, raised on high wooden beams and decorated with French windows. National museums with small halls and a limited but interesting collection will suffice as sources of historical information.

The Suez Canal was by no means the first attempt to bridge between the Mediterranean and the Red Sea. It is, however, the only canal that has bypassed the Nile. In 1855, after years of lobbying with Sa'id, the Egyptian khedive (viceroy), French consul to Egypt Ferdinand de Lesseps received approval to incorporate the Suez Canal Company. After the sale of shares to raise the necessary cash, a contract was signed by the company and Sa'id, namesake of Bur Sa'id, which granted the French a 99-year concession to operate the canal. Construction began in 1859. And pressure was on, as the international demand for Egyptian cotton grew exponentially. The canal would facilitate the transfer of cotton to Europe and America.

Ten years later, on November 17, 1869, the world celebrated the inauguration of the Suez Canal. These weeks of lavish celebration nearly broke Khedive Isma'il, Sa'id's successor. No expense was spared to make this grand affair run as smoothly and elaborately as possible. To pay for his debts, Isma'il sold most of his shares in the Suez Canal Company to the British. From this point on, a French and British consortium managed the canal, ushering in the British influence that lasted until 1956, when President Jamal 'Abd al-Nasir (Nasser) expelled them from the country.

In principle, the British agreed to let any nation at war or during peacetime use the canal. But in practice, during the two World Wars, they strategically positioned soldiers along the canal and permitted only Allied nations to pass. In 1950, because of the Arab-Israeli war, Egypt banned all Israeli vessels from the canal. After the British were expelled from the canal zone, and later the entire nation, they joined the United States in refusing to lend Egypt the funds with which to build the Aswan High Dam. In response, Nasser nationalized the canal and combined the income from the canal with loans from the former Soviet Union to construct the dam.

On October 29, 1956, after several border clashes, Israel invaded Egypt. Great Britain and France then attacked Egypt a week later in an attempt to restore international control over the canal. After United Nations interventions, the canal was reopened in 1957 under Egyptian management and was policed by the U.N. It was closed again in 1967 during the Arab-Israeli war by sunken ships, and it didn't reopen again until 1975. Three years later Egypt lifted the ban on Israeli ships, and in 1980, a 10-mi-long tunnel was built under the canal to facilitate the passage of motor vehicles into and out of the Sinai.

Ismailiya

120 km (75 mi) east of Cairo; 87 km (54 mi) north of Suez.

Halfway between Bur Sa'id and Suez, this quaint city on Lake Timsah was founded by Khedive Isma'il for those working on the canal. The director of the Suez Canal Company, Ferdinand de Lesseps, resided here until the completion of the canal, and his home still stands, off-limits, alas, to the public. Ismailiya's population is close to 700,000, and the city is known for its wide streets, expansive public gardens, and cleanliness.

There is a distinct colonial feel in the area known as Hay al-Afrangi (the foreign district), because of the French colonial architecture of the remaining buildings. Here you will find the modest museum on Shar'a Muhammad 'Ali in front of the expansive Mallaha Gardens. A stroll down Shar'a Muhammad 'Ali will lead you along the Sweetwater Canal and eventually to the house of Ferdinand de Lesseps.

Perpendicular to Shar'a Muhammad 'Ali, running away from the Sweetwater Canal, Shar'a Sultan Hussayn has a number of restaurants, stores, banks, and a Thomas Cook office. From here, turn left (southwest) onto Shar'a Sa'd Zaghloul, and walk to Maydan al-Gummhurriya, not an important site but serene because of the wide streets and calm pace of the town.

The small **Ismailiya Regional Museum** has a modest collection of pharaonic and Greco-Roman artifacts. The majority of its collection consists of coins, pottery shards, and jewelry. The most impressive piece is a 4th-century Roman mosaic that has been cleverly laid in the floor of the hall. The picture shows Phaedra sending a love letter to her son Hippolyte. Other exhibits cover the ancient canals from the Nile to the Red Sea and contemporary canal history. The museum is across from the Mallaha Gardens at the north end of Shar'a Muhammad 'Ali. ⊠ *Shar'a Muhammad 'Ali,* ☎ *no phone.* ⊡ *£e3.* ☉ *Daily 9–4; 9–2 during Ramadan.*

Dining and Lodging

$$ ✕ **George's Restaurant.** This small, dark restaurant, with its English pub–like feel, seats no more than 30 people. Its full bar is decorated with old signs for beer and liquor. Menu items like baba ghanouj and lightly sautéed calamari are hardly extravagant, but they are tasty. Beer and wine are available—or toss back a glass of ouzo. ⊠ *Shar'a Sultan Hussayn,* ☎ *no phone. No credit cards.*

$$$ ▦ **Hotel Mercure.** On the shores of Lake Timsah, the Mercure has a peaceful setting and a good list of amenities. The lawns and beach add a leisured air. Lacquered wood furniture and floral-print bedding give the rooms a feeling of the 1980s. Most rooms face the lake and have private balconies. ⊠ *Forsan Island, Ismailiya,* ☎ *064/338–040,* ℻ *064/338–043. 152 rooms, 8 suites. 2 restaurants, bar, pool, 2 tennis courts, waterskiing, playground, laundry service. AE, DC, MC, V.*

Bur Sa'id (Port Said)

88 km (55 mi) north of Ismailiya.

Seaside Bur Sa'id is a commercial town where Egyptians come to buy duty-free goods. Much of the architecture is turn-of-the century French-colonial style, bearing a slight resemblance to New Orleans's French Quarter. It is a pleasant town to roam around in, but it isn't the kind of place that screams for a stop if you're in Egypt on vacation. Even among Egyptians it has begun to decline as a place to come in summer.

The city was founded in 1859 by Sa'id, in time for the start of excavation. Much of the area is built on sand fills from the digging of the canal. During the Arab-Israeili wars, most of the city was bombed, and parts of it have yet to be restored.

The main shopping strip is on Shar'a Gummhurriya, where you'll find big-city-style electronic stores, shoe stores, and the local favorites: shops selling Levis.

At the north end of town, Bur Sa'id's Mediterranean beach has limited appeal, in part because of its unswimmably polluted waters.

Port Fouad, Bur Sa'id's sister town across the canal, is a 25p ferry ride away. You'll see large vessels and pretty homes from the slightly malodorous and run-down ferry. Port Fouad itself is a residential town with early 20th-century villas, many of which were bombed during the wars and have been left to ruin.

The **Military Museum** is small building housing relics of the wars with Israel and the Anglo-French invasion. There are bombs, guns, cannon, American tanks painted with Stars of David, and oddly enough some ancient Egyptian weapons as well. ⊠ *23rd of July St., ☎ no phone.* ☞ *£e2.* ☉ *Oct.–Apr., Sat.–Thurs. 9–2 and 7:30–8:30, Fri. 10–1:30; May–Sept., Sat.–Thurs. 8–2 and 7:30–8:30, Fri. 10–1:30.*

Suez Canal A to Z

Arriving and Departing
The best way to get to the Canal Zone is by bus. Take one early in the morning from Cairo to Bur Sa'id, walk around for a couple of hours, then hop on another bus to Ismailiya. Have lunch there, explore a bit, then head back to Cairo in the evening. Travel time on the buses will total around five hours.

Trains also run to the zone, but they are slower than buses and poorly maintained.

BY BUS
Superjet (☎ 02/772–663 in Cairo) and **East Delta Company** (☎ 02/482–4753 in Cairo) buses run from the Almaza Station in Cairo to Bur Sa'id and Ismailiya. They leave almost every hour—punctuality is not always a priority. The fare is £e15 to Bur Sa'id, and the trip takes an hour and a half. Buses leave from Bur Sa'id to Ismailiya on the hour until 5 PM; the fare is £e7. The Ismailiya–Cairo fare is £e10. Buses vary in cleanliness. Be sure to book front seats, and get to the station ahead of time to book your ticket. And be aware that the ticket salespeople are not always helpful.

BY TAXI
Taxis from Cairo to Ismailiya or Bur Sa'id should cost around £e200 for two passengers.

Getting Around
BY CAR
Renting a car in the area is unnecessary because both towns are walkable. There are also plenty of taxis, and fares are reasonable.

BY TAXI
Taxis are everywhere. Just flag one down, and agree with the driver on a price before you get in. In Bur Sa'id, you should pay no more than £e2 for any local trip. In Ismailiya, you might pay up to £e5. The drivers are usually pleasant, and they will turn down the music if you ask them to. But brace yourself: they drive very fast.

Travel Agencies
Thomas Cook. ⊠ *43 Shar'a Gummhurriya, Bur Sa'id, ☎ 066/227–559.*

7 Western Desert Oases

Turn west from the Nile, and the desertscapes seem to echo with the haunting melodies of the Bedouin flute. Start the day with bread baked in the hot sand, and finish it with a plunge into a hot spring with the moon as your lantern, shining out from the stellar sea of the Milky Way. You'll sip strong, sweet oasis tea or thick Arabic coffee roasted over a desert fire. Embrace all of this and feel like you've crossed into another world.

A FEW HUNDRED YEARS AGO the only outsiders interested in the oases were occasional desert raiders bent on stealing the fruits from the orchards, destroying water supplies, and abducting women. Generation to generation, life followed the seasons with little change. The most exciting events of the year were the autumn date harvest and the subsequent caravans that would assemble and trek to the Nile Valley.

In the 1970s, the government built an asphalt ring road joining Bahariyya, Farafra, Dakhla, and Kharga—the four southern oases—to the Nile Valley, and the tranquillity of thousands of years of isolation met the hustle of 20th-century Egypt. Over the next years telephones, electricity, televisions, and elements of the world as we know it began to enter the traditional lives of the oases. Now the small trickle of backpackers—the first travelers over the new road—is giving way to a travel industry that will open up the desert and change the people of the oases for generations.

Egypt's Western Desert makes up the northeastern third of the Libyan Desert, a 1-million-square-mile waste, nearly half of which is sand. Edged by the fertile soil of the Nile Valley, this desert joins its sister, the Sahara, in central Libya to make North Africa a most inhospitable land. In places the desert has faulted and dropped lower, bringing subterranean water nearer the surface. This fossil water has slowly made its way north from central Africa, traveling downhill for centuries as it follows the African continental slope into the Mediterranean Sea. It bubbles to the surface in the depressions, creating the famed oases. Just as it sustains life today, it provided the necessary water for human beings at the dawn of history. For millennia the oases accommodated the permanent settlements of farmers and passing traders and nomads. The strict boundaries of today's nation states have all but ended nomadic desert life, and Bedouins and farmers mostly live together.

If ways of life in the oases may seem backward, and individually the people may appear extremely unsophisticated, bear in mind that oasis dwellers possess qualities that seem to have vanished from the societies of the modern world: honesty, integrity, respect for tradition and the law, and a high moral code. Most do not drink alcoholic beverages, smoke, or curse, and they are extremely polite and generous. There is rarely a murder and never a theft, no adultery, and no rape. Renegades are held in check by family honor, and misconduct brands descendants for centuries. All of this makes for a very high standard of living indeed.

If you have fears in the desert, they should not be of people. As for animals, snakes exist, but they hibernate in winter, and they'll slither away from you most of the time. Large animals are rarely seen, because they have been hunted to near extinction—even camels are strangers in oasis towns. Birds, happily, are highly visible and in abundant variety. Spring migrations move north across the desert to Europe, and birds return south in the fall.

The most fearsome creature you have to worry about in the desert is yourself: if you do not fear the desert, you are your own enemy. This is true wilderness. So while traveling mainly on asphalt roads is safe, it is the off-road tours that face certain dangers and require permits. If you want to take on the adventure on your own, hire a guide and go in at least two vehicles.

Pleasures and Pastimes

Archaeology

The desert is full of ruins—huge ruins, not mere tracings on the ground—Roman forts in Kharga, Islamic fortress towns in Dakhla and Siwa, ancient underground aqueducts, desert monasteries, and Roman watering stations. Most desert sites remain unexcavated by archaeologists and are too remote to police on a regular basis. You may well be the only people at the site for an entire weekend. This is not a license to vandalize. Take care of this desert. It is one of the last places on earth where human beings can still taste total freedom and have a sense of genuine adventure. Keep the ruins intact for the future and for the archaeologists, who are surely not far behind. Keep that artifact out of your pocket and on the desert floor where it belongs.

Camping

There are a number of camps in the oases, where you pay a small fee for a water hookup and use of facilities like electricity and kitchens. All have their charm and are usually run by interesting characters. In truth, you can camp anywhere: on top of a dune, at a hot spring, near a ruined antiquity, or at some other beautiful spot. There is no charge to camp here. There are only two rules: clean up after yourself—when you leave there should be no indication that you were there; and again, don't take anything away with you. Leave that shark's tooth, small Roman oil lamp, or dinosaur vertebra right where you found it.

Dining

Gourmet eateries don't exist in the oases—and hopefully never will. Instead, you'll dine on wholesome desert fare, mostly vegetable stews, grilled chicken, plenty of rice, and fresh fruits. On the whole you will also dine alfresco, because the few restaurants that do exist are streetside affairs.

Villagers enjoy inviting guests to dinner. If you are lucky enough to receive an invitation, be prepared to remove your shoes before entering the home, and bring a small gift: tea, sugar, or candy. You will sit on cushions on the floor and probably never see the women of the house who have prepared your food. You might be served by your host, who, because of tradition, will likely not eat with you. The food will be brought on a large tray where a number of porcelain bowls will contain stews. When meat is served, it is often boiled and tough, and thought to be a sign of wealth. Everyone digs into the same dishes. Usually the flat bread is broken into pieces and used as a spoon to scoop up the rice or stewed green beans, potatoes, or okra.

If you plan to eat around a campfire, buying fresh fruit and vegetables from the local stands is perfectly safe. You will find that they taste better than back home—terrific tomatoes are available year-round. Fresh whole wheat flatbread is available each morning from local bakeries.

Two musts: don't miss out on oasis dates; likewise Siwa's olive oil, which is rich and heady and extra extra virgin—gourmet without trying to be. Dates come in a number of varieties: sweet, firm, and yellow; sweet, mushy, and dark brown; or bitter, crunchy, and red. Try them all.

The oases are still cheap compared to the Nile Valley, which in turn is inexpensive compared to Europe. Breakfast is less than £e7, lunch (the main meal of the day) is less than £e20, and dinner (essentially a lighter version of lunch) less than £e15.

CATEGORY	COST*
$$$	over £e24
$$	£e14–£e24
$	under £e14

per person including the variable city tax and service charge.

Hot Springs

The hot springs are a gift of the desert. They are actually hot or cold springs, they can be used day or night, and in other parts of the world people pay fortunes for their medicinal effects. Here they are free. But don't expect a spa atmosphere. Things are more primitive: a pipe gushes water into a cement enclosure in the open air. In every oasis one or two springs have been set aside for travelers. Be modest, and don't swim naked. Desert people are very conservative.

Lodging

In the past few years desert hoteliers have come of age. Excellent new hotels have opened, and older ones have been revamped. All are still reasonably priced. If you come to the oases with a companion who's not so keen on overland four-wheel-drive adventures, staying at a new hotel will allow one of you to sit around the pool with a novel, a cold drink, and the desert sun, while the other takes in the desert landscape. New hotels usually offer half board and, for better or worse, are bringing European food to the desert.

CATEGORY	COST*
$$$$	over $50
$$$	$30–$50
$$	$15–$30
$	under $15

All prices are for a double room, tax and breakfast included.

Shopping

You won't make a dent in your credit card in the desert—you won't even be able to use it. The only things to buy are crafts, and they are in limited supply. Most oases sell camel-hair products, including woolen gloves, hats, scarves, and blankets, at very reasonable prices. Rugs made on desert looms follow the traditional designs and natural dye combinations of individual Bedouin tribes. Some motifs are amazingly similar to those of Native Americans. All oases have hand-woven baskets, each oasis having its own designs. The traditional jewelry, dresses, and headgear have been pretty much picked over, but the occasional find is still out there. Siwa has the best and most abundant crafts.

Touring

There is always something interesting happening the minute you step into the desert. The setting changes constantly as you move from place to place. A stop at a dune for lunch is worth a whole trip—you might sit down next to a broken ostrich egg hundreds if not thousands of years old, or discover you are in a field of nummalites (small, coinlike fossils of sea creatures) and desert diamonds (small pieces of quartz that look like diamonds when polished).

Exploring the Western Desert Oases

Whether you're bound for Siwa, Bahariyya, or Kharga, desert trips begin at the pyramids. Before you watch the pyramids fade into the distance, check that your car is up to the trip—that you have spare parts (especially a working jack), an extra gerrycan, water for you and for the car, maps, guidebooks, and a new toy to play with: a good Global Positioning System. GPS is fun—for plotting your exact latitude and longitude to the second and the navigational tricks that allows—and it could end up saving your life. Always top your tank at gas stations, because they are few and far between. For example, there is only one gas station between Cairo and Bahariyya, and it is often out of gas.

If you are on a tour, let the leaders worry about gas and spare parts. If you are camping, you will be expected to help set up camp.

For a map of the Western Desert, *see* the pages immediately preceding the Gold Guide.

Great Itineraries

The minute you leave the Nile Valley you're *in* the desert, and there are thousands of miles of empty space where you can enjoy a short walk, or a climb, or camping.

IF YOU HAVE 3 DAYS

Some 310 km (194 mi) southwest of the pyramids at Giza along a well paved road, ⛺ **Bahariyya** is doable in three days. It will take you at least an hour to reach the pyramids from Cairo, because traffic is an abomination along Pyramid Road. Another four or five hours puts you in Bahariyya. The rest stop halfway to Bahariyya is a bit dirty and usually out of gas. You'll pass a number of oil rigs before the biggest thrill of the ride out—dropping into the oasis's depression through a pass in the cliffs. Once there you have choices: **Bawiti, Qasr** (pronounced *kas*-sur), and **Bir Ghaba** are half-day excursions; allow a full day to see **Black Desert.** On your return, leave the oasis no later than noon to avoid the unnecessary risks of driving the desert roads at night.

IF YOU HAVE 6 DAYS

You could see all the oases in six days, but you would be in the car more than on the ground and wouldn't be able to absorb a crucial element of the oases' spirit—the elongation of time itself—that focusing on one oasis or two will give.

Bahariyya and Farafra. Six days for two oases broadens your program considerably. Head directly to ⛺ **Bahariyya** from Cairo and arrive late afternoon. Refresh yourself in a hot spring and make tour arrangements through a hotel. Day two head to the **Black Desert** in the morning and continue to ⛺ **Farafra** after noon. Camp overnight in the incomparable **White Desert.** Pass the next day touring the desert at the **Monoliths, Ain al-Wadi,** and/or the **Magic Springs.** Save time for **Qasr Farafra** toward sunset and swim in **Bir Setta,** Qasr's hot spring. Day four, slowly work your way back to Bahariyya via Ain Hadra, a small spring in the desert, likewise Naqb el Silim, which is the pass out of Farafra, and the several ruins of al-Hayz, including a Roman fort and Christian church. Overnight in the Black Desert. Take day five in Bahariyya to see its villages of **Bawiti and Qasr,** the gardens, the mountains, and the hot spring, **Bir Ghaba.** Stay in town that night, then make your final rounds in the oasis before you start back for Cairo by noon.

Kharga and Dakhla. It takes a full day to get from Cairo to ⛺ **Kharga** on the new desert road (flying saves time but means having three, four, or seven days in the area, because of Egypt Air's schedule). When you arrive in Kharga, start in on the traditional sites: **Hibis Temple, Bagawat Christian Cemetery,** and the fortress at **Nadura** in the morning, then **Ghueita** and **Zayyan** temples after noon. On the third day, move on to ⛺ **Dakhla.** En route visit the **Rock Inscriptions at Tineida,** the ruins around **Bashindi,** and the fortress village of **Balat.** Overnight in Dakhla's village of **Mut.** Start day four in its village of **Qasr,** the ancient temple of **Deir al-Haggar,** and the **Muzawaka** frescos in the morning, then head all the way back to Kharga in the afternoon (this is a big program, so keep an eye on the time). That leaves day five for a visit to **Dush**'s fortress and temple, or for taking at least one great off-road excursion. To visit any of these off-road sites you must have permission from the antiquities department in Kharga, which will provide a guide (be sure to give him a tip). Day six, return to Cairo, or move on to Luxor.

Siwa. The route to ⊞ **Siwa** from Cairo takes you along the northern coast of Egypt to Marsa Matruh—which almost always becomes an overnight stop—then south into the oasis. From Bahariyya, the track over the desert, the Darb al-Siwa, is equally long. The northern approach passes white-sand beaches and the azure Mediterranean, the latter a procession of sand dunes and four small but fascinating oases—Sitra, Nuwamisa, Bahrayn, and Areg—for overnight options (you need permission to travel the Darb al-Siwa). You arrive in Siwa in the afternoon of day two, a good time to walk around **Shali,** the main oasis village. Set aside day three for the famed, traditional loop through the oasis: to the site of Siwa's ancient **Oracle,** the **date and olive groves** of Siwa's gardens, to Jabal al-Dakrour known for its sand cures for rheumatism, then back to Shali after stopping at one of the **hot springs.** Watch the sun set from **Fatnas** (Fantasy Island) over a salty lake. On the fourth day, strike west via Gelel al-Matwa past Jabal Bayda to several **Bedouin villages** along the Smuggler's Road to Libya. On the morning of the fifth day, pick up whatever jewelry, dates, and olive oil you want to bring home, then hit the road by noon.

WHEN TO TOUR THE WESTERN DESERT

It is just too hot to travel in the desert in summer. If heat doesn't bother you, it will your vehicle. The desert's finest days fall between November and March. April and May are not only hot, but the *khamaseen* (desert storms) are blowing, and they are beyond unpleasant. Light in the desert is best in October and November.

BAHARIYYA OASIS

310 km (194 mi) southwest of Cairo.

Ancient travelers had to cross a dune belt several miles wide (and hundreds of miles long) to reach Bahariyya Oasis from the Nile Valley. Then it took them an entire day to descend the cliffs that hem the oasis on all sides. Today we simply glide along an asphalt road at high speed and need to make an intentional effort to slow down to enjoy the descent cut through the cliffs into the oasis. You must also slow yourself down, for you are stepping back into a gentler time.

In Bahariyya it is ever so easy to blend into the rural way of life, not least because the people are so friendly and helpful. It is the only one of the four southern oases that is not part of the New Valley governorate (the northern Matruh governorate administers the oasis), so it is the least modernized. As a result, you'll get a better idea of how the people have lived in the oases for the past 1,000 years.

Bawiti is the current capital of Bahariyya, having usurped the position of the older capital of **Qasr** a few generations ago. Today the two communities have blended into one. The older sections of the villages go back hundreds of years and are now being abandoned for newer homes. Do not miss the ancient **aqueduct** that cuts through the heart of Bawiti, or the **gardens** that cascade down the cliffside to the depression floor. You can walk or drive on this tour through the villages of Bawiti and Qasr, either on your own or with a guide.

Bir Ghaba is the hot spring traditionally reserved for tourists. It lies some distance from Bawiti in a small forest of eucalyptus trees, which makes getting there a desert adventure. The drive, or hike, first passes through traditional oasis gardens where farmers plant, grow, and harvest a variety of crops interspersed between fruit trees—orange, apricot, mango, guava, olives, tangerines, bananas, and of course date palms. Then the road meanders over a desert track between the many black-topped mountains of Bahariyya, including Maghrafa (the Pot), and al-Dist (the Ladle), two of the most famous. When you're ready for a pause, the cold-water spring of Bir Ghaba comes into view on the left just in time to jump in for a quick, cooling swim. After covering more desert, you enter a garden and, suddenly, there is Bir Ghaba, its heat creating a mist in the morning coolness. Camping is welcome here. The terrain is navigable by regular car, but there is a lot of sand near Bir Mattar.

Bahariyya is surrounded by golden sand topped by black rocks of various kinds. All the hills (called mountains here) wear black caps, and in one spot south of Bawiti the rocks line up in a row along the ancient fault that created them. This is the **Black Desert.** Off-road travel to the right or left of the road is possible for short distances in a regular car, but a four-wheel-drive vehicle is recommended to climb the sand dunes and explore at length. So is a guide who can take you to places you will never find yourself.

Dining and Lodging

$$ ✕ **Popular Restaurant.** People have enjoyed this street-side café's traditional food since its owner came here from the Nile Valley on the newly built asphalt road. The wooden tables and chairs and green latticed walls make for rather basic atmosphere, but most desert explorers, both foreigners and locals, can be found hanging around. One special is prepared each day. A typical meal includes one or two vegetable stews, boiled meat or grilled chicken, rice, potatoes, bread, and tea. It is all served in hodgepodge of dishes, some plastic, some aluminum, some dented, some cracked. ⊠ *In the center of Bawiti, near the police station on the Qasr road,* ☎ *no phone. No credit cards.*

$$ ✕ **Rashid Restaurant.** At the newest restaurant in town, the owner specializes in grilled chicken and an array of Egyptian desserts made especially with foreigners in mind—locals seldom eat out. Both indoor and outdoor dining is available in a clean, well-lighted, ceramic-tiled area. The owner also offers the *shisha* (water pipe), which is becoming very popular in the Nile Valley once again. ⊠ *Main St. (Cairo Rd.),* ☎ *no phone. No credit cards.*

$$$ ⌸ **Kamil Group.** If you are looking for a little comfort in the desert, this white-domed hotel is built around a hot spring. The roof allows sun worship during the day and stargazing at night. Rooms are small, but they include bathrooms with showers. In addition to a pleasing atmosphere, the hotel offers massage, sauna, and a well-equipped excercise room. The owners staff the place with local people, and they are a breath of fresh air. Even women work here, which is a major change in the desert. There is no air-conditioning, but there are heaters for winter nights. Rates include breakfast and dinner. ⊠ *Bawiti, at base of Black Mountain on a nameless dirt road.* ☎ *018/802–322. 29 rooms. Restaurant, exercise room. No credit cards.*

$ ⌸ **Hotel Alpenblick.** If you want to feel like a desert traveler, this is the original hotel in Bahariyya. Conceived by a Swiss expatriate who spent his later years in Bahariyya, it is a traditional, no-frills desert hotel built of mud brick and stucco. Now the windows are screened, but it is primarily the province of backpackers. The owners will take you to a hot spring free of charge. Meals are available on request. ⊠ *Bawiti, on a hillside overlooking the main street,* ☎ *018/802–184. 22 rooms, 6 with bath. Restaurant. No credit cards.*

$ ☑ **Ahmed Safari Camp.** Purple flowers bloom abundantly over the lattice of the grand veranda, which heralds the peaceful surroundings of this pleasant camp in a pretty rural area called Tibyeniah on the road to Darb Siwa. The camp is a million cuts below the standards of a U.S. campground, but the gardens are lush with fruit trees and the owner is amiable, so a stay here will add rich detail to your trip. The comfort of a hot spring is nearby, and nearby dunes are easy to reach and great for campfires. There are 21 plain, clean rooms; a few huts for backpackers; an area in which to pitch tents; and free use of the kitchen. ✉ *Siwa Rd., 4 km (2.5 mi) south of Bawiti,* ☎ *018/ 902–770 or 018/802–090. No credit cards.*

Desert Tours

Not all people like the challenge of being bounced around in an off-road vehicle for hours at a time. If you do, this is what the desert is all about. Bahariyya has a number of traditional tours that take in the Black Desert, Bir Ghaba, and the White Desert in Farafra. Prices vary from £e300 to £e400 per vehicle per day (three–five persons per vehicle). Trips farther afield to almost any oasis or dune in the desert by four-wheel-drive, camel, or on foot are easily arranged at Bahariyya hotels. Independent operators' names change frequently, and some are not licensed. They are the same faces and vehicles you will see if you book through the hotels, so you won't go wrong either way.

FARAFRA OASIS

100 km (62 mi) southwest of Bahariyya; 340 km (213 mi) northeast of Dakhla.

Farafra is what most people think of when they think of a desert oasis: a small patch of green, a desert spring, a few palm trees, and a vast desert all around. There are only a few ruins at Farafra, none of them interesting enough for the layperson to spend much time viewing, especially with the White Desert at hand. The White Desert, a dynamic natural wonder that you can explore in numerous ways, is the centerpiece of any trip to Farafra.

The small oasis village of **Qasr Farafra** once had the atmosphere of the frontier. No longer. The discovery of water is changing its demographics, as people from the Nile Valley homestead in new villages nearby. The increase in population is making the people more prosperous—enough to expand the village and build a new mosque to replace the 19th-century Sanusi mosque in the old main square. Being frugal and practical by tradition, the people tore the old mosque down, not seeing its aesthetic or historic value. Despite this loss, Qasr Farafra remains one of the most enchanting places in the desert. Just sitting in the village is an experience, because locals like to mingle with travelers, and there are seldom 20 travelers in Farafra at one time.

The best way to savor the village is by walking. You'll come across giggling children playing with push toys made of old tin cans and sticks and see old men in traditional clothing squatting on the ground chatting to each other while they make camel wool yarn with homemade spindles. With luck you might even spot an old woman, complete with black embroidered dress, tattoos, and small gold nose ring, hurrying through a passageway in the Roman fortress in the center of the village. Gardens, where the men cultivate their crops, cascade down the northwestern banks of the depression.

★ About 8 km (5 mi) outside town, the **White Desert** is legendary. Covering most of the northeastern portion of the Farafra depression, it is a white-chalk land of enchantment, where everything is white: the ground, the cliffs, the mountains, even the horizon. Erosion has left bizarre and comical outcroppings scattered about in twos and threes, tens and twenties. Some are a mere 2 ft high and look like crickets. Others are 14 to 20 ft high and look like elephants or whales or squirrels. Still others tower hundreds of feet into the air, true inselbergs (isolated mountains) housing seashells in their steep, straight sides. Two of the best have been named the Monoliths and are landmarks visible from a great distance. At the full moon, the entire desert shimmers in pale light. You can stay an hour, a day, a week, or a year. It is endlessly enlightening. You can explore the White Desert on foot or using a motorbike, a car, or a 4x4. Two small oases in the White Desert that offer shade and water are **Ain al-Wadi** and **Magic Springs.** They make good rest stops, just as they have for centuries, when the Bedouin rested their caravans on their way to the Nile Valley.

Dining and Lodging

Five years ago there were no restaurants in Farafra. There are three street-side restaurants in the main square of Farafra, just to the side of the main Cairo-Farafra loop road. The **Nicetime Coffee Shop** and **Ashraf's** both serve one traditional, inexpensive peasant dish that is delicious, energizing, and filling: *ful* and *tamayia*. Ful is the first national dish of Egypt: fava beans stewed, or with tomatoes, or with eggs, or even as a sandwich. Tamayia is falafel: fava beans ground with a variety of fresh herbs and spices then deep-fried. Both restaurants use rush mats for walls, have a few unorthodox tables and chairs, and present their food on plastic dishes. Meals will cost between £e2 and £e4. ⊠ *Main Square,* ☎ *no phone. No credit cards.*

$$ ✕ **White Desert Restaurant.** The White Desert serves the second national dish of Egypt: *koushari,* a mound of macaroni topped by a mound of rice, topped by a scoop of black lentils, all generously oozing with a rich, hot, tomato sauce and garnished with fried onions. This restaurant is, in fact, a kiosk with a few tables and chairs around it. The koushari is available whenever the owner feels like cooking. ⊠ *Main Square,* ☎ *no phone. No credit cards.*

$ 🏠 **Farafra Bedouin Village.** A Hassan Fathy delight hundreds of miles from the Nile (Hassan Fathy was Egypt's greatest 20th-century architect), this village is the only hotel in Farafra. Newly opened, its two-story, split-level, white-stucco bungalows sit under domed ceilings. Beds, covered with mosquito nets, are on the upper floors. The dining room is tucked into a series of open-air arches, which are covered with rugs whenever the weather turns cold or sandstormy. A typical Bedouin breakfast of tea, scrambled eggs, honey, jam, white cheese, and flat bread is included in the rates. Lunch and dinner can be arranged with advance notice. Occasional evening entertainment includes Bedouin flute-playing and desert dancing. ⊠ *Main Rd., at the entrance to Qasr Farafra, just before the main square,* ☎ *02/377–4600 or 02/377–4601 (Farafra); 02/345–8524 or 02/214–8343 (Cairo). 20 rooms, 12 with bath. No credit cards.*

$ ⛺ **White Desert Camping.** One major reason to come to Farafra is to camp in the White Desert, so leave your Walkman, checkers, and badminton at home, and let nature be your entertainment here. All tour groups include the desert in their itineraries. If you do it on your own, stick close to the road and be sure to bring your own food, fuel, sleeping bags, and water, then just pick a spot (there are no fees). Supplies, including warm camel blankets, are available in Farafra. A few rules:

keep tents and vehicles out of your site so others can enjoy the view—hide them behind a white monolith. Pick up all your debris before you leave. And don't take away any rocks or fossils.

Desert Tours

El Badawia Safaris. Co-owner of the Farafra Bedouin Village hotel and quite a character, Saad Ali is proud of his desert and its heritage. He and his brothers offer any type of desert tour you want, and very good service in the bargain. Specialties are camel tours to the White Desert, Ain Della (a famous remote waterhole), and the Great Sand Sea (hundreds of square miles of constantly shifting sands to the west), but he also has four-wheel-drive trips. Prices are roughly £e100 per person per day for a four-person trip. ☎ 02/377–4600 or 02/377–4601 (Farafra); 02/345–8524 or 02/214–8343 (Cairo).

DAKHLA OASIS

340 km (213 mi) southeast of Farafra; 150 km (94 mi) west of Kharga.

Dakhla remains a breadbasket, just as it was in Roman times. Its rich, red farmland is tucked under a pink-and-white desert cliff. Although it has a striking number of ancient ruins—like the restored Egyptian temple at Deir al-Haggar (☞ *below*), the ruins of an entire Roman community called Amheida, and a recently discovered Old Kingdom link to the Nile Valley near Bashindi—the Islamic fortress towns remain its crowning glory. The central village of Mut (pronounced moot) has five main streets and five *maydans* (squares). Some have names, but most do not. And even if you ask directions from locals, they're not likely to know the newly adopted street names anyway.

★   You approach **Qasr Dakhla** through a pine grove. Once you reach the old village you must walk. The striking medieval village streets are but paths that lead past still-occupied mud-brick and stucco houses to an Ayyubid mosque, its ancient minaret still intact, and a *madrasa* (medieval school) still used as a town meeting hall. The most important antiquities in Dakhla are carved, wooden Islamic beams erected in medieval times over entrances to the houses of prominent citizens. There are a number of them in Qasr Dakhla. One famous beam contains pharaonic and Islamic inscriptions, which means that Dakhla was known and occupied by the ancient Egyptians. Prudently, the people of the old village have ordered that no buildings are to be torn down and no new buildings built within the old town of Qasr Dakhla. Considering that this was done without government cooperation, it is a major step in desert preservation.

At the edge of the village is a **pottery factory** where potters have used their feet to turn ancient wheels to make unique pots for centuries. The pots are fired in hand-built kilns in the nearby potter's garden.

Deir el Haggar is a small desert temple west of Qasr Dakhla. One of its most interesting features is graffiti—19th-century explorers carved their names into its soft sandstone, including the entire Rohlfs Expedition of 1874. Rohlfs was the first major exploration in the Western Desert. Nearby Deir al-Haggar is **Muzawaka,** two colorful tombs dating to Roman times—the name *muzawaka* actually contains the word for color. Decorations here combine stylized ancient Egyptian art with more realistic Roman figures and motifs. ☒ £e20. ☉ *Dawn–dusk.*

Rock Inscriptions at Tineida. Dakhla Oasis is divided in two by a small stretch of desert. Eastern Dakhla contains a number of communities like **Balat,** similar to Qasr Dakhla; **Bashindi,** a small community with pharaonic-style houses; and **Tineida**, where the asphalt road from Kharga, the Darb al-Ghabari, enters Dakhla. There are also a number of ruins currently under excavation, like the Temple of Amun-Nakht at Ain Birbiyeh and the 6th-Dynasty (2323–2150 BC) mastabas at Qila al-Dabba. The latter are the first evidence that the ancient Egyptians knew of and inhabited Dakhla Oasis. They will soon be open to the public. For now the Rock Inscriptions at Tineida remain the most accessible and interesting site in this area.

Along the base of a number of rocks near the south side of the road east of Tineida are ancient rock inscriptions. Rock art exists throughout North Africa, but much of it is found in places so remote that most of us will never see it. Here, the ancient art is a few feet from the modern road. It is an amazing hodgepodge of Bedouin giraffes, tribal brand markings, Coptic inscriptions, Islamic writings, and even a drawing of a pregnant woman. To preserve the inscriptions, do not add to them or take rubbings.

Dining and Lodging

$$–$$$ ✕ **Anwar Restaurant.** In the center of Mut, about a block away from just about everything, this hearty, no-frills restaurant is open all day, every day. Grilling is the specialty, and it's done right on the maydan. The friendly owner also offers tours to nearby sites. ⊠ *Anwar is on a nameless maydan; natives can direct you to the restaurant,* ☎ *092/941–566. No credit cards.*

$$–$$$ ✕ **Hamdi Restaurant and Ahmed Hamdi Restaurant.** Two brothers run two clean and friendly restaurants practically side by side near the Mubarez Tourist Hotel. The food is good, the prices modest, the brothers friendly rivals. (A third brother runs tours that you can book at either restaurant.) You can dine inside or out, move your table to one side of the buildings to view the nearby fields, and eat from 6 AM to 11 PM. For breakfast try the tomato omelet along with your ful and tamayia. The locally famous, original Hamdi Restaurant stood in the main square of Mut and was run by the father. ⊠ *Third St. (the Farafra road),* ☎ *092/940–767 (Ahmed Hamdi). No credit cards.*

$$–$$$ ▦ **Mut Three Chalet.** The formerly government-owned Hot Springs Resthouses—the old chalets that line the perimeter of a very large hot spring—have been entirely renovated and are now equipped with air-conditioning and a bathroom. A pool-side restaurant is expected to serve such nontraditional fare as sandwiches and soups, which you might welcome after a diet of desert food. ⊠ *3 km (2 mi) north of Mut on the way to Qasr Dakhla. For reservations:* ☎ *092/907–982 or 092/907–983 (Kharga);* ⊠ *Rowad Oases Tourism Development Co., 12 Abdel Moneim Riyad St., Mohandeseen, Cairo,* ☎ FAX *02/349–6244 (Cairo). 6 chalets, 1 4-bedroom garden villa. No credit cards.*

$ ▦ **Mubarez Tourist Hotel.** This four-story hotel has a nondescript lobby and a nondescript dining room. What makes it noteworthy, and a possibly welcome site, is that it brings the standard of midrange interchangable international hotels to the desert, where a nondescript hotel is in fact unique. If you are weary of camping, you'll get a good night's sleep here. There are some air-conditioned rooms. ⊠ *Third St.,* ☎ *092/941–524. 40 rooms. No credit cards.*

$ ▦ **al-Dahouz Bedouin Camp.** On a small desert mound with a spectacular view of both the cultivated land and the desert, this small, and pleasant Bedouin camp is inexpensive and clean—and exactly what you came to the desert to find. The owners like to entertain around the campfire at night, singing Bedouin songs to the beat of the Bedouin drum. You may be awakened in the morning by the nearby farmer riding his donkey through his lush fields and thanking God for their bounty at the top of his voice. (This is a moving experience: look and listen and let your camera rest.) There are four thatched huts with twin beds and enough open space to accommodate 15 campers. Rates include breakfast; an alfresco, Bedouin-style dinner, served on the ground amid cushions and rugs, is available on request. ⊠ *The camp is along a desert track from the village of Dahouz, a few km west of Mut,* ☎ *092/941–151. 4 rooms. No credit cards.*

Desert Tours

Tours to the desert and around the oasis are not as plentiful as at Farafra and Bahariyya. They can be arranged through the restaurants in Dakhla (☞ Hamdi Restaurant, *above*) or through the Tourist Information Office. Most tours include the Islamic villages, but you can also go to the escarpment and various dune belts. **Al-Dahouz Bedouin Camp** (☞ *above*) runs camel tours (£e 100 per person per day, including meals), and everyone is friendly and very helpful. Your are their guest, and desert etiquette insists that you receive the best hospitality they can provide.

KHARGA OASIS

124 km (77 mi) southwest of Asyut.

As the capital of the New Valley governorate, Kharga has become very modernized, and its main village, Qasr Kharga, is now a city. If it's your first stop in the desert, you're likely to be disappointed because the the town is just an average town, and the antiquities (with paid admissions) pale in comparison to Nile Valley monuments. You have to move beyond the community to see that, in fact, Kharga possesses the best the desert has to offer. The capital's dominant features are its long lines of crescent dunes and mountains that rise up from the floor of the depression. Its major antiquities are not the ancient Egyptian ruins south of Kharga at Ghuieta or Zayyan—Luxor's are far better—but the Christian burial ground at Bagawat, a remarkable array of remote Roman forts that present more mysteries than answers, and a growing number of even more mysterious underground aqueducts that keep being discovered throughout North Africa. Combined, these are the most spectacular man-made ruins in the Western Desert.

The dozen or so **desert forts** of Kharga are also stupendous and should be on your must-see list. Three are outstanding: al-Deir, a 12-towered fortress with tons of graffiti from ancient times to World War I, is the easiest to access. Labeka, a site complete with fortress, two temples, rock-cut tombs, and aqueducts, is a little tougher to get to, but still easily done. The most difficult fort to access is, of course, the best—

★ **Ain Umm Dabadib** has a huge four-towered fortress, two villages, a temple, a Coptic church, and no less that four aqueducts, one more than 13 km (8 mi) long.

★ In **Bagawat,** hundreds of brown-domed Coptic tombs line the crest of a hill. They date from a time between the 4th and the 7th centuries AD when Nicaean and Arian Copts wrestled among themselves over the concept of God the Father, God the Son, and the Holy Spirit—was God one, or three in one? As each side rose to power it banished the other side to an oasis.

Bagawat is probably the oldest Christian cemetery of such magnitude in the world, and it is certainly the oldest in this desert. Two tombs' interior ceilings are painted with biblical themes. There is also a mudbrick church. Behind the cemetery are a number of ruins that have yet to be excavated. They dot the plain like lonely sentinels in a place that once bustled with caravans. Bagawat is on the northern outskirts of

Qasr Kharga, above the Temple of Hibis (☞ *below*), along the Kharga–Asyut highway. ◙ *£e20.* ☉ *Dawn–dusk.*

The Temples of Hibis and Nadura. Darius I dedicated the Persian temple Hibis to the god Amun-Re. Located in a palm grove, the temple is a miniature jewel. It has very good reliefs and plenty of graffiti, including edicts from the Roman governor to the people of Kharga. It is under restoration most of the time, and its hypostyle halls are often closed to visitors. East across the valley from Hibis, Nadura (the lookout) sits atop a hill and has a commanding view of the entire oasis. Its strategic importance in antiquity is obvious once you climb up to it. ◙ *Hibis: £e20. Nadura: free.* ☉ *Hibis: dawn–dusk; Nadura: 24 hrs.*

Getting to **Dush** is half the fun, because it lies along the famous **Darb al-Arbain,** the ancient slaver's trail out of sub-Saharan Africa. On the way you pass through a number of ancient towns and two major forts: **Ghueita** and **Zayyan,** which watch the road from their mountain perches. Hilltop Dush sits at the extreme southern end of the oasis, off of the Darb al-Arbain on another road, the Darb al-Dush, which in antiquity led to the Nile Valley. Dush is the modern name for ancient Kysis and its remains include a fortress, a sandstone temple, and an ancient cemetery. ◙ *£e20.* ☉ *Dawn–dusk.*

Dining and Lodging

Good restaurants are conspicuously lacking in Kharga. For fair attempts at Western cooking and basic meals of ful, falafel, and chicken, go to the restaurants at the Pioneer and Hamedalla hotels (☞ *below*).

$$$$ ✕🏨 **Pioneer Hotel.** The salmon-colored stucco Pioneer is the newest, biggest, and most impressive facility in the Western Desert. Standards of decor and service—from its dark marble floors, lush patio, and swimming pool to its outsourced staff—are imported from the Nile Valley, which for good or ill heralds a new era for the oases. Spacious rooms have sitting areas; some have balconies; all have large windows that give onto desertscapes. The hotel also offers desert tours of various durations that connect the oases to Luxor, Aswan, or Abu Simbel. ✉ *Shar'a Jamal 'Abd al-Nasir (north end of Qasr Kharga),* ☎ *092/927–982 or 092/927–983; in Cairo:* ✉ *Rowad Oases Tourism Co., 12 Shar'a Abdel Moniem Rayad, Mohandeseen, Cairo,* ☎ 𝖥𝖠𝖷 *02/349–6244. 102 rooms. Restaurant, coffee shop, bar, pool. AE, MC, V.*

$ ✕🏨 **Hamedalla Tourist Hotel.** Modest, clean, friendly, and on a par with a run-of-the-mill motor lodge, the Hamedalla, like the Mubarez Tourist Hotel in Dakhla, is another nondescript hotel that caters to tourists and businessmen. What it lacks in charm it (almost) makes up in personability. Some rooms are air-conditioned, and rates include breakfast. ✉ *Shar'a al-Nada,* ☎ *092/900–638,* 𝖥𝖠𝖷 *092/905–017. 30 rooms. Dining room. No credit cards.*

$ 🏨 **Nasser Resthouse.** South of Qasr Kharga along the Darb al-Arbain, the five refurbished bungalows here (each sleeps four) are pleasant havens nestled around a hot spring that's been converted into a bathing area. This cool, peaceful place has great views and friendly staff. There is also a caravan and tent area on site. ✉ *In Kharga:* ☎ *092/907–982 or 092/907–983; in Cairo:* ✉ *Rowad Oases Tourism Co., 12 Abdel Moniem Rayad St., Mohandeseen,* ☎ 𝖥𝖠𝖷 *02/349–6244. 5 bungalows. Pool. AE, MC, V.*

Desert Tours

No desert safari groups operate exclusively out of Kharga, but any of the Cairo-based organizations and most of the oases operators can take you to the off-road desert forts of Kharga (☞ Guided Tours *in* Western Desert Oases A to Z, *below*). Take the time to visit at least one of the local forts; al-Deir, Labeka, or Ain Umm Dabadib. You must have permission from the local **antiquities office** to visit any of these sites. They will provide a guide, who is an antiquities inspector. A £e50 tip is appropriate for a half day, small group tour.

SIWA OASIS

783 km (524 mi) northwest of Cairo.

★ **Siwa,** the northernmost oasis in the Western Desert, is leagues away from the loop road and near the Libyan border. Because of its location, Siwa's influences have come from North Africa, rather than central Africa or the Nile Valley. The people speak a Berber (an Afro-Asiatic language group) dialect, wear exotic clothing and adornment (the Traditional Siwan House in Shali is a good place to see them), and have aggressively fought for centuries to remain independent. The oasis was the home of the ancient Oracle that reportedly told Alexander the Great he was the offspring of the gods.

Shali is the main village of Siwa. Here you walk—first to its abandoned hilltop **fortress village.** The Siwans lived here for centuries, adding additional stories onto their mud-brick homes as the population increased. The fortress was occupied by two distinct groups—the westerners and the easterners—and they often broke into armed conflict over indiscretions. Today it is abandoned, and the people live in more modern and more convenient homes beneath its watchful eye. At night the fortress is illuminated. Take a guide to walk the village, because the ruins are dangerously close to collapsing. 🔲 *Free.*

Aghurmi, the original hilltop village of Siwa, is planted on a flat-topped rock. Most desert villages were built with defense in mind, which gave the high, flat rocks of the desert a haven-like quality. The **ancient Oracle**'s temple still stands at one of the corners. Below it, at the base of the rock, is the **Temple of Umm Ubayd.** Both sites figured prominently in the pageantry surrounding a visit to the Oracle. Leading lights from around the ancient world came to consult the Oracle at Siwa. Among them were Pindar (poet of Olympians), Lysander (Spartan general), Strabo (Greek geographer), and, of course, Alexander the Great. 🔲 *Small entrance fee.* ☉ *Daily dawn–dusk.*

Cleopatra's Bath. The Siwan springs are cooler than those at the southern oases. And where they are contained in rectangular enclosures, here the enclosures are circular; where the others emit fresh water, here the water is saline. But the Siwan springs are legendary. Ancient rumor had it that Cleopatra swam here. If she did, one would assume that either Julius Caesar or Mark Antony did, too. 🔲 *Free.* ☉ *24 hrs.*

Other oasis highlights are Jabal al-Mawta—the Mountain of the Dead, with its painted and inscribed 26th-Dynasty rock-cut tombs—and **Jabal al-Dakrour,** famous for easing rheumatism. **Fatnas** (Fantasy Island) is a must for watching the sun set over the salt lake. You can also make your way west past Bayda to several **Bedouin villages** along the Jabal Smuggler's Road to Libya and to visit the **rock-cut tombs** in the mountains and the **ruins of a small Doric temple,** which may have some connection to Alexander the Great.

Dining and Lodging

Private telephone lines are coming soon to Siwa. In the meantime, to reach any of the hotels, telephone the **central switchboard** (☎ 03/93–1026, 03/93–2026, or 03/93–3026) and give them the name of the hotel. The line may sound like it's dead—just hold on until someone picks up. Take into account that hotel rooms are scarce during Christmas, around the New Year, and at Ramadan. Reserve a room well in advance if you plan to come at these times.

$ ✕ **Abdou's and Kelani and Sons.** Restaurants come and go in Siwa. They are all in Shali below the ancient fortress. These two have remained for some time. Both are small affairs built of mud brick, with rush-mat verandas as seating areas. Both serve traditional desert fare with a larger menu than restaurants in the southern oases, but in the same plastic dishes that you find in all the desert's fledgling restaurants. Grills and stews are traditional; at Abdul's, try the banana crepes. ⊠ *Main Square. No credit cards.*

$$$ ⌂ **Arous al-Waha Locanda.** An old government hotel recently renovated, the Arous al-Waha (Bride of the Oasis) is a nondescript three-story building a cut below the motor-lodge variety in Dakhla. It does have a dining room and lobby, and rooms have private baths and hot and cold water—some even have air-conditioning. ⊠ *Main Rd., Shali. Dining room. No credit cards.*

$–$$$ ⌂ **Siwa Safari Paradise Hotel.** Everything is available at this newest facility in Siwa. And although there is good food in an interesting restaurant and the sparklingly clean, air-conditioned rooms have private baths, the most pleasing point about this hotel is that it is in one of Siwa's gardens. Palm trees dominate the scene, and you can witness an amazing year-round process: the tending and harvesting of the palm tree. In the spring the trees are pollinated by hand, in the fall they are harvested, and following the harvest the tree is trimmed and the wood and fibers are made into furniture and ropes. The owners can accommodate all price ranges and even have provided huts for campers. They also run safaris to all parts of the desert. ⊠ *Main Rd.,* ☎ *03/ 900–289 or 03/900–286; 018/490–006 or 018/490–027 in Giza,* FAX *018/491–394. No credit cards.*

Desert Tours

Desert tours are few in Siwa. The main off-road tour is to a spring set amid dunes on the outskirts of the Great Sand Sea, a wasteland of undulating dunes covering hundreds of miles in western Egypt and eastern Libya. Arrange tours at restaurants and hotels (☞ Siwa Safari Paradise Hotel, *above*).

WESTERN DESERT OASES A TO Z

Arriving and Departing

By Plane

Although there are dozens of World War II airstrips in the desert, there is only one operating airport, a few miles north of Qasr Kharga in Kharga Oasis. The 45-minute **Egypt Air** (⊠ 9 Shar'a Tala'at Harb, Cairo, ☎ 02/392–7444 or 02/392–7205) flight from Cairo arrives Sunday and Wednesday mornings and returns to Cairo almost immediately. Planes depart from the Egypt Air terminal (Terminal 1) at Cairo International Airport.

By Bus

The desert is backpacker heaven, and that means cheap transportation. Excellent bus transportation leaves various parts of Cairo to the different oases on a daily basis. Cairo travel agencies have schedules, although you probably will have to purchase the ticket yourself. You can buy reserved seats on air-conditioned buses one day in advance. The cost of bus transportation is minimal.

Distance is the major factor in touring the desert. It takes seven hours to reach Bahariyya, the closest oasis to Cairo; a full day to reach Kharga from Cairo or Luxor; and a day and a half to get to Siwa.

Upper Egyptian Bus Company runs to **Kharga** and **Dakhla** from Maydan al-Azhar in Cairo at 7 AM and 8 AM daily. The company's **Bahariyya** and **Farafra** bus leaves from Maydan al-Azhar daily at 7 AM, stopping at Maydan Giza at 8 AM.

West Delta Bus Company goes via Marsa Matruh to **Siwa** from Maydan Tahrir beside the Hilton Hotel in Cairo daily at 7:30 AM. It leaves Siwa at 4 PM for the return journey. From Alexandria, a daily bus departs for Marsa Matruh at 7 AM, then continues from Matruh to Siwa at 1 PM.

Microbuses also serve the oases. They, too, depart from different sections of the city—such as Baharia Café (✉ Shar'a Qasri, Maydan Sayida Zaynab), Maydan Tahrir, and Ramses Station—typically as soon as they fill up. There are seats for 12, but you can buy two or three seats to give yourself some extra room.

By Car

You can drive to the oases, and having a car affords the greatest freedom. A standard automobile will get you to any of the major oases and to most of the interesting sites. But you must rent a car that is in excellent condition, because the desert heat will wilt anything less than a sturdy and finely tuned vehicle, even in winter.

If you're fearless enough to take your life into your hands and can make it through the streets of Cairo to get to the desert, driving along the asphalt road in the desert is a relative breeze, and there is very little traffic. Off-road driving, however, requires skill and knowledge of local road conditions. We recommend that you use a guide for all off-road jaunts. Likewise, don't drive at night. Some drivers do not use their headlights, and those who do will blink them on and off at you as you approach, which is blinding. It's illogical and dangerous, but it is the local custom.

There are gas stations within the oases, but the rule is to top your tank whenever you see a gas station—absolutely, without fail.

By Four-Wheel-Drive Vehicle

If you want to do some off-road exploration, you can rent a four-wheel-drive vehicle to drive to the desert, or come by bus or car and book a four-wheel-drive tour through any of the oases hotels or restaurants. Every oases now has entrepreneurs and safaris to exotic and stupendous locations. If you do travel into the desert with your own four-wheel-drive vehicle, do not go off-road without a second vehicle and a guide. Between getting stuck and getting lost, the opportunities for fatal errors are abundant. If you're determined to sit behind the wheel yourself, any desert tour agency will be happy to put a guide in your vehicle or let your vehicle tag along on their tours.

Any desert trip off-road, outside the oases, especially to remote areas of the desert, requires permissions. These are available through travel agencies in Cairo (☞ Cairo A to Z *in* Chapter 2). Permits take two weeks to process, so plan ahead.

By Taxi

Service taxis used to travel to the oases on a regular basis, but microbuses have taken their place. There are no taxis in Bahariyya, Farafra, or Siwa. In Kharga Oasis, a few exist in the villages of Qasr Kharga and Mut, and Dakhla also has a few. Most are available for hire by the day.

Contacts and Resources

Car Rental

Good car-rental agencies in Cairo have a variety of vehicles. To rent a car, you must have an International Driver's License (☞ Driving *in* the Gold Guide for more information). The following rental agencies have outlets all over Cairo. Ask for the one nearest you when you call. **Avis** (⊠ 16A Mamal al Sukkar, Garden City, Cairo, ☎ 02/354–7400 or 02/354–7081); **Budget** (⊠ 5 al-Maqrizi, Zamalek, ☎ 02/340–0070 or 02/340–9474); **Hertz** (⊠ 195 26th July Street, Downtown, ☎ 02/303–4241 or 02/347–4172).

Emergencies

Police. Special tourist police patrol every oasis. They are so abundant, and the oases villages so small, that you will not have to search for one—in fact, if there is a problem, they will find you. Their English is not always good, so they may have to take you to someone who speaks English.

Ambulance and Hospital. New first-aid stations have been erected all along the loop road through the oases. Most are at or near communications towers, about 45 km (30 mi) apart. There are hospitals in every large village in the desert: Bawiti (in Bahariyya), Qasr Farafra, Mut (in Dakhla), Qasr Kharga, and Shali (in Siwa). There is no emergency system, but anyone can direct you to these facilities.

Guided Tours

Prices per person for Cairo-based tours range from $250 for three days to $450 for six. Oasis-based tours are much less—about $35 per person per day.

Cairo International (⊠ 21 Shar'a Mokhtar Said, Heliopolis, Cairo, ☎ 02/291–1491 or 02/291–1490, 𝔽𝔸𝕏 02/290–4534) has a number of itineraries to the oases, and you can design your own program.

Marzouk Desert Cruiser (⊠ 1 Maydan Abn Sandar, Hamamat al-Kuba, Cairo, ☎ 𝔽𝔸𝕏 02/258–8083) runs tours to all the oases. They specialize in Fayyum-to-Bahariyya off-road tours.

Zarzora Expeditions (⊠ 12B Mahmoud Azmi St., Zamalek, Cairo, ☎ 𝔽𝔸𝕏 02/341–0350) specializes in deep desert tours to Ain Della (the last waterhole before the Great Sand Sea). They run oases tours as well.

Visitor Information

Apart from tiny Farafra, all oases have tourist-information offices. All are (usually) open Saturday–Thursday from 8 to 2, again (often) in the evenings, and sometimes Fridays. They can help with hotels, tours, transportation, emergencies, and most anything else.

Kharga Tourist Information Office. ⊠ *Shar'a Gamal 'Abd al-Nasir, (near Mabrouk Fountain), Qasr Kharga,* ☎ *092/901–611.*

Dakhla Tourist Information Office. ⊠ *Third St., Mut,* ☎ *092/941–686.*

Bahariyya Tourist Information Office. ⊠ *Main St., Municipal Building garden,* ☎ *018/802–222.*

Siwa Tourist Information Office. ⊠ *Municipal Building, Shali,* ☎ *03/934–026.*

8 Portraits of Egypt

To Live and Die in Ancient Egypt

A Brief History of Egypt

Book and Videos

TO LIVE AND DIE IN ANCIENT EGYPT

Food, Drink, and Feasting

Ancient Egyptians were great lovers of plentiful food and drink. Tomb and temple reliefs show offering tables piled high with food, and tomb scenes depict stages of food preparation. Feasting and picnicking was an intrinsic part of ancient (and modern) Egyptian culture, and great varieties of foodstuffs were used as picnic fodder. Picnics were sometimes held on boats on the river, which you can do aboard a felucca.

Two ancient Egyptian staples were bread and beer, augmented by vegetables such as onions, squashes, cucumbers, and lettuce. Garlic and legumes, such as *mulukhaia* (lentils) and chickpeas, made up a large part of the diet of rich and poor alike. Cheese and yogurt were also eaten. Wealthier people, of course, were able to afford more varied diets.

The Egyptians ate domesticated animals, fished, and hunted animals and birds. The main domesticates were sheep, goats, cattle, and pigs. The hunted animals, which were often captured live and fattened up before slaughter, were antelopes, gazelles, and, particularly in the Old Kingdom, hyenas. Geese, ducks, pigeons, and other fowl were hunted or bred, and fish were caught from the Nile. Mullet roe was processed and eaten with pleasure; in fact, this roe, known as Egyptian caviar, has graced many gourmands' tables in the 20th century. Meats were generally grilled or stewed, or in some cases, salted and preserved for leaner times.

The Egyptians had more than 30 kinds of bread, including dessert breads. Fruit such as dates, dom nuts, grapes, pomegranates, cactus figs, and *nabk* berries were common. Fruit was fermented and used to make wine—date wine, pomegranate wine, grape wine, and palm wine (made from the sap of palm trees).

Tomb scenes often show Egyptians reveling at elaborate gatherings. Guests were greeted by their hosts, given scented flower garlands, and shown to a seat. They wore perfumed fat cones on their heads over their wigs, and servants brought them food and drink, all while they were entertained by conversation, music, singing, and dancing. Groups of musicians and scantily clad dancers performed for hours at these functions. Food and drink was placed on small tables to be shared between two or three people, and wine and beer constantly replenished whenever cups were empty. Some tombs show the unfortunate results of overindulgence: in one case a guest is being carried out of the party because he has passed out.

Religion

Egyptian religion is immensely complex, and it is not well understood by scholars. Beliefs and practices changed, sometimes radically, over 3,000 years of Egyptian history, and few easily understandable texts were left behind. On the surface the religion was polytheistic, with many gods derived from nature and natural elements that surrounded them, but the gods were all manifestations of aspects of one great divine force. During the course of Egyptian history several of the gods were syncretized.

The pharaoh was regarded as a living god closely identified with the falcon god, Horus. Apart from the pharaoh, there was generally one state (or major) god. People would also worship local city gods or patron deities relevant to their employment. This might be likened to the the Christian practice of having patron saints. The gods all had specific powers attributed to them, were associated with special animals, and had specific feast days. Gods were also often viewed in groups of trinities consisting of a father, a mother, and a child.

Ancient deities were worshipped in temples, in shrines in people's houses, and possibly on the wayside. Temples were of two types: cult and mortuary. **Cult temples** were located for the most part on the east bank of the Nile, and they were dedicated to the cult of a particular god. Their main focus was to house an image of the deity and to see to its comfort—temples were viewed quite literally as houses of the god. The temples were large, sprawling buildings to which successive pharaohs would add their own places of worship. In addition to the temple proper, there were libraries—buildings where doctors, astronomers, and botanists did their research—housing for priests, and storage areas for grain and other items. Temples owned land that they farmed or rented out, and they functioned as administrative and religious centers. A temple's high priest had many ranks of priests below him.

Mortuary temples were similar to cult temples, save for the fact that they were built on the west bank of the Nile and were primarily dedicated to the cult of the deceased pharaoh. Within their precincts there were also places of worship for various gods.

For most of Egyptian history the chief among the major gods was **Re,** or Amun-Re, a solar deity who saw to the balance and functioning of the world. Karnak at Thebes (now Luxor) was his primary temple. His wife was Mut, a goddess of queenship. Khonsu, his son, was the moon god.

From the Middle Kingdom (2040–1640 BC) onward, **Osiris** was one of the most important Egyptian gods. He is depicted as a mummiform figure and was the ruler of the afterworld. As such the dead pharaoh was associated with Osiris. His main sacred site is the fabulously elegant New Kingdom (1550–1070 BC) temple at Abydos, north of Luxor. His wife was **Isis,** goddess of magic and one of the most important figures in the Egyptian pantheon. Their child was **Horus,** often shown as a falcon, the symbol of kingship. Reigning pharaohs were always associated with Horus.

Seth was the brother of Osiris, and during the Late and Greco-Roman periods was regarded as Osiris's mortal enemy (☞ Abydos and Kom Ombo *in* Chapter 4 for the story of Seth's murder of Osiris). He was god of storms and deserts. His wife was **Nephthys,** a goddess associated with funerary rituals.

Jackal-headed **Anubis** was in charge of embalming and mummification and the actual trip to the afterworld. In the Hellenic and Christian eras he was associated with Hermes, then with the now-decanonized St. Christopher.

Maat was the goddess of truth, justice, balance, and order, all very important concepts in the Egyptian view of the world.

As well as being associated with kingship, **Hathor** was the goddess of love, music, beauty, and dancing. She was also goddess of remote places, such as turquoise mines. One of her sacred sites is Deir al-Bahri, Queen Hatshepsut's magnificent temple on Luxor's west bank.

Ptah was a creator god, associated with Memphis. **Sekhmet,** his wife, was goddess of plagues, revenge, and restitution. Their child was **Nefertum,** associated with rebirth in the afterworld.

Thoth was the ibis-headed god of writing and knowledge, and he was associated with the moon.

Ram-headed **Khnum** was associated with creation and fashioning people on a potter's wheel. His wife was **Anukis,** their daughter, **Satis.** They were all important in the region of the first cataract of the Nile, around Aswan, and therefore Khnum was associated with the river's annual inundation. It is interesting that there was no god identified specifically with the Nile, though the plump god depicted with pendulous breasts, **Hapi,** was the god of the inundation.

The Egyptian Way of Death

Most pharaonic monuments in Egypt are related to death. This was not because Egyptians had some morbid fascination with death, but rather because of their overwhelming love of life and a desire for its continuance. This is why the people took great care to prepare their tombs and their mummies in a manner that would ensure that they would be happy and well provided for in the afterlife. For poorer people, the preparations were limited to a simple tomb, a few grave goods, basic mummification, and some kind of grave marker or stela. For the wealthy, a more complicated, well-decorated tomb, abundant grave goods, and elaborate mummification were the standard.

TOMBS

The west bank of the Nile was the preferred location for tombs, and the east bank was for settlements—except when this was impractical because of the nature of local arable land. These preferences were based on the Egyptians' solar beliefs about death and rebirth. The sun rises—is born and reborn—in the east and sets—dies—in the west, and Egyptians organized their living and dying areas to coincide with the sun's path. Egyptian tombs tend to be in the desert, far from arable, and consequently usable, land. These desert locations also ensured that the bodies of the deceased would not be disturbed by the annual flood (which has stopped since the construction of the Aswan dams).

The earliest surviving graves are simple depressions scooped into the desert sand and gravel, dating to the period before 3000 BC. Bodies were placed in a fetal position and surrounded by grave goods such as pots, beads, knives, and so forth. As practices progressed, sand and stone was piled over the tombs in order to mark them. These tombs are known as **tumuli.** Throughout Egyptian history poor individuals were buried in such sandy graves, with a few grave goods to use in the afterlife as they had used them while alive.

The next step in tomb evolution is the **mastaba.** Mastabas—meaning bench in Arabic, so-called because of the similarity between the shape of the tombs and benches in village houses—were used as burial places for both royalty and nobles during the first two dynasties. Thereafter, with the advent of the pyramid, pharaohs were buried in pyramids, and others in mastabas. Mastaba burials consist of two parts, the substructure, the actual underground burial area, and the superstructure, the tomb building itself. The earliest mastabas were made of mud brick with solid superstructures and a small niche that contained a stela. In the 2nd Dynasty (2770–2649 BC) the superstructures were made to resemble houses, because the tomb was seen as the house for the soul. *Ka* (the individual essence) and *ba* (the active, immortal essence) were two of the aspects of an individual's soul.

In the 3rd Dynasty (2649–2575 BC), some mastabas were made of stone and others of mud brick, with niches set in the south and northeast faces. These niches contained stelae and offering tablets for the dead. The substructures, often reached from the roof of the superstructure, were simple rooms with space for a body and some grave goods. This form of substructure remains mostly the same throughout mastaba construction, with small changes made to the access routes to the building.

By the end of the 4th Dynasty (2575–2465 BC), many superstructures were accessible and decorated with scenes of daily life, such as hunting, fishing, feasting, manufacturing jewelry and pottery, making bread and beer, and butchering animals. The decorated portion of a tomb is generally called the chapel, the place where offerings were brought to the deceased by family members or friends. The actual burial place would remain sealed after the body had been interred.

Pyramids were the burial places of pharaohs. The ancient Egyptian word for pyramid is *mer,* derived from the verb *mr,* meaning to ascend. But the modern word *pyramid* is most likely derived from the Greek word *pyramis,* the name of a wheat cake that the pyramids were believed to have resembled. Pyramids are oriented to the cardinal points and generally entered from the north. Their shape was probably suggested by the sun cult: their triangular profile is reminiscent of the sun's rays seen through clouds. They might also have derived their shape from the ben-ben stone, a sacred stone, perhaps a meteorite, that served as the focus of the sun cult. The fact that pyramids were often topped by pyramidions (small pyramids) covered in gold further supports this idea.

Pyramid complexes consist of a central pyramid; satellite pyramids for female family members; subsidiary pyramids for cenotaphs for the pharaoh; boat pits; a mortuary temple to the east, facing the rising sun; a covered causeway leading to a valley temple, and a quay for boats to land. From the end of the 5th Dynasty, the burial chambers inside pyramids were decorated with pyramid texts, a series of spells that helped the pharaoh to achieve a successful afterlife. Pharaohs were buried in pyramids during the Old and Middle Kingdoms.

Rock-cut tombs were common from the Old Kingdom onward, and they were constructed all along the Nile Valley, especially in areas blessed with good stone cliffs. Rock-cut tombs consist of chambers cut into the rock, decorated with painted or carved scenes, and used as chapels. Burials took place inside the chambers, down a deep shaft, where the body and grave goods were placed. During the New Kingdom, pharaohs were buried in rock-cut tombs on the west bank of Thebes. These Valley of the Kings tombs were decorated primarily with religious scenes and instructions for the afterlife, while the tombs of nobles continued to be decorated with scenes of daily life. The pharaohs' mortuary temples were erected at the edge of the cultivated areas of the west bank, far from their tombs.

Shaft tombs were often used by poorer individuals or were constructed for security during the later periods of Egyptian history. These tombs consist of shafts cut into the bedrock that open into one or two (generally undecorated) chambers that contained the body and the grave goods. Often a stela placed at the mouth of the shaft marked it as a grave.

MUMMIFICATION

The earliest mummies were likely made by accident, when bodies were placed in the dry desert sand. These mummies were probably accidentally found by the ancient Egyptians (when disturbed by robbers or animals) and gave birth to the idea of mummification. The ancient Egyptian word for mummy was *saah*. The present-day word is derived from the Persian/Arabic word *mum,* which means pitch or bitumen, which was thought to have been used in making mummies. It was believed that the preserved body would provide a permanent house for the soul in the afterlife. The process of mummification changed throughout Egyptian history, reaching an acme in the 21st Dynasty.

The classic method of mummification was as follows: a slit was made in the left side of the body and the lungs, liver, stomach, and intestines were removed. The heart, believed to be necessary for rebirth, was left in place. The viscera were mummified separately, wrapped, and placed either in canopic jars, or back in the body cavity prior to burial, depending on the period. Then a chisel was inserted up the nose and through the ethmoid bone. A long, slim metal instrument was then used to poke, prod, and punch the brain before it was teased out of the nostril. The brain cavity was then filled with resin to purify it.

The body was first washed with palm wine, then packed with natron (a mixture of salt and carbonate found in the Wadi Natrun, northwest of Cairo), incense, and herbs. This process was repeated a few times over the course of 40 days. Then the body cavity was emptied, packed with resinous bandages and herbs, and sewn up.

After it was clean, the body was adorned with amulets and jewelry, wrapped elaborately in bandages while being prayed over by priests, annointed with oils, and enshrouded. The wrapping and annointing took another 30 days—a total of 70 days were required to make a good-quality mummy. During certain periods of Egyptian history a mask made of cartonnage (linen, papyrus, and plaster prepared like papier-maché) or gold (like that of Tutankhamun) was placed over the head and shoulders of the mummy.

The body package was then put into a wooden coffin, which, in turn, was placed in a sarcophagus (like a coffin, but larger and generally of stone), before being placed in the tomb. The canopic jars with the viscera were buried next to the body. Sometimes a funerary text containing spells to help the deceased in the afterlife was written on papyrus and placed within the coffin.

Writing

Egyptian writing, hieroglyphs, started in about 3000 BC; it consists of a series of signs derived from nature and common utensils. Hieroglyphics are read left to right, right to left, or top to bottom: You read into the beaks of the birds or into the faces of the animals.

There are two main types of signs: phonograms, which signify sounds, and determinatives, which signify what type of word it is. Phonograms have different sounds attached to them: single letter sounds, biliteral, and triliteral sounds. Thus, a hoe has the sound *mr,* and depending on its determinative can mean hoe, love, or be part of another word. Determinatives come at the end of words and help define what the word is or means. Thus, a pair of legs at the end of a word indicate that the word is a motion word meaning (depending on the spelling of the word itself) walk, move forward, or run.

Egyptian grammar and vocabulary changed throughout ancient history, with Middle Kingdom Egyptian being the most classic and widely used. Hieroglyphs (sacred images) were generally used only for important inscriptions on monuments or on papyri. Everyday accounts, letters, and even many religious texts were written in hieratic, a cursive form of hieroglyphs.

Jean-François Champollion deciphered ancient hierogylphics in 1822. Other scholars had come close to accomplishing this, but Champollion was the first one to publish his results. He managed to do this by using the Rosetta Stone, a large granite stone carved with hieroglyphs, demotic (everyday script of the Late and Greco-Roman periods), and Greek. The stone was discovered in the port city of Rosetta on Egypt's Mediterranean coast. The ancient Greek, still a known, if not spoken, language, provided Champollion with a clue as to how to break the code. When he broke it, Egyptology became a literate discipline.

—Salima Ikram

A BRIEF HISTORY OF EGYPT

Pharaonic Egypt

The recorded history of Nile Valley civilization begins more than 5,000 years ago, with the Palette of Narmer, a stone tablet that dates from 3100 BC. The tablet states that Narmer, also known as Menes, is the first pharaoh to unite the kingdoms of Upper (Southern) and Lower (Northern) Egypt. To commemorate the unification, he established his new capital at Memphis, just south of present-day Cairo, where the Nile meets its delta. In the centuries that followed, Narmer's successors developed hieroglyphics and experimented with burial mounds built from mud brick. As it happened, these mastabas proved to be the precedent for the pyramids.

For the next 3,000 years, 30 pharaonic dynasties would rule ancient Egypt, with a few intermediate periods of foreign rule. The dynastic era has been divided into three periods: the Old Kingdom (2575–2134 BC), the Middle Kingdom (2040–1640 BC), and the New Kingdom (1550–1070 BC).

The **Old Kingdom** generally had strong central governments and efficient bureaucracy, and technological innovations allowed Egypt to reach new political, economic, and artistic heights. First among these rulers was Djoser, who, in an effort to consolidate his authority, was the first pharaoh to proclaim himself the gods' representative on Earth. He and his advisor Imhotep (often regarded as history's first architect) designed and built the impressive stone funerary complex at Saqqara that includes the Step Pyramid, considered the oldest structure on Earth. Later dynasties constructed the Great Pyramids at Giza, which were the world's largest buildings until the 19th century. Although their successors continued to build pyramids, none rivaled those at the Giza plateau, and a slow decline to the chaos of the First Intermediate Period ensued.

A return to stability and prosperity began the **Middle Kingdom.** Records show that in this era Egypt established diplomatic and commercial relations with the people of Libya, Sinai, Nubia, and Punt (present-day Somalia). It was during this period that Thebes (now Luxor) was founded, and the great temples to Amun, Egypt's principle deity, began to rise at Karnak—it would become the largest temple in the world. A series of bad harvests caused the disunity that allowed the West Asian Hyksos tribes to sweep across the desert and occupy the Nile Valley.

Thutmose I (1504–1492 BC) successfully extricated the foreign presence from Egypt, expanded its borders, and initiated the **New Kingdom,** considered the high point of pharaonic history. He also began building the elaborate tombs in the Valley of the Kings, west of Thebes. His daughter, Hatshepsut (1473–1458 BC), developed the monumental west-bank temple at Deir al-Bahri, which was cut out of the face of the mountain. Her stepson, Thutmose III (1479–1425 BC)—she reigned as his regent—made Egypt the regional superpower and Thebes the world's richest city.

Eighty years later, a king named Akhenaten (1353–1335 BC) lost interest in all this conquered territory. Instead, he established a new city, Ahketaten (present-day Tell al-Amarna), where he and his wife, Nefertiti, could worship their one god, the Aten. Consequently he ignored the old temples, causing much antagonism among the powerful priesthoods. When he died, the country reverted to polytheism, his name was removed from official records, and his city was razed to the ground. He was succeeded by the child Tutankhaten (1333–1323 BC), who was quickly convinced to change his name to Tutankhamun. This young pharaoh became famous posthumously for being so insignificant a ruler that grave robbers forgot about his tomb. In 1922, Howard Carter's team discovered his burial site.

Pharaoh Seti I (1306–1290 BC) was able to reconquer the lands lost during the reign of Akhenaten. He also built many temples, including the colossal Hypostyle Hall at Karnak. His son Ramesses II (1290–1224 BC) reigned for 80 years, siring more than 170 children and building temples from Nubia all the way to the Delta. His successors eventually lost administrative control of the country—in part to the priesthood of Amun at Karnak—leaving Egypt weak and ripe for the picking.

After centuries of incursions, Libyans finally took the Delta in 945 BC. Nubians took Upper Egypt in 747 BC. In 667 BC, Assyrians conquered Memphis and sacked Thebes. And Persians defeated the last independent native dynasty in 525 BC, holding onto the Nile Valley until Alexander the Great chased them out in 332 BC.

The Greco-Roman Period

Alexander the Great established his capital, at Alexandria, and appointed Ptolemy Soter, one of his Macedonian generals, as governor. With the leader's death, the governor established the **Ptolemaic Dynasty** (332–30 BC). During this time Alexandria became the preeminent Hellenic city, the site of both the famous Pharos Lighthouse, one of the seven wonders of the ancient world, and the Great Library, where Euclid, father of geometry, came to study. This era saw Hellenic and pharaonic cultures syncretized and their religious practices intermixed. The infamous Cleopatra (51–30 BC) was from this period, but she proved no match for the aggressive Romans and was the last of the Ptolomies.

With the **Roman occupation** (30 BC–AD 337), Egypt was relegated to provincial status, useful to the empire only as a source for marble and grains. In AD 61, St. Mark arrived in Alexandria, and within 200 years Egypt had a significant Christian community, which was considered a threat to the divinity of the Roman emperor. This prompted a massive wave of persecution that began during the reign of Diocletian (284–304 AD). Responsibility for Egypt passed to the eastern Roman Empire in Constantinople in AD 337. Like their Byzantine rulers, Egyptians were by this time largely Christian. In fact, Egypt may have been the first country with a majority Christian population. Constantinople, however, was too preoccupied to concern itself with Egypt. Thus, being heavily taxed and under constant threat from marauding neighbors, Egyptians, quite naturally, welcomed the Arab conquest.

Islamic and Modern Egypt

In AD 642, **'Amr ibn al-Aas** removed the Byzantine presence in Egypt after a brief siege of the fortress of Babylon. Local Christians and Jews, considered "people of the Book" were tolerated and allowed to thrive, provided they paid tax to the Muslim army. Immediately to the northwest of Babylon, 'Amr built his town of al-Fustat ("the encampment"), which quickly grew to a city of more than 200,000. It remained the commercial capital of Egypt until it was destroyed in 1168.

Ahmad ibn Tulun arrived in Egypt in 868, appointed to be its governor by the Abbasid caliph in Iraq. But within months ibn Tulun shored up his position and declared Egypt independent from the Abbasids. He ordered the construction of al-Qata'i, a new city that was of legendary splendor. His successors were not as capable as he, however, and when the Abbasids reassumed control of Egypt in 905, they had the city razed, sparing only the magnificent Mosque of Ibn Tulun.

The Abbasids in turn quickly surrendered Egypt to the **Fatimids**, a group of Shiite tribes from North Africa who swept into Egypt in 969. They set up the royal city of al-Qahira, just northwest of al-Qata'i. Later the various towns merged, and the name al-Qahira (Arabic for Cairo) came to represent them all. The early Fatimid rulers al-Mu'iz (969–975) and al-'Aziz (975–996) were tolerant, quick to establish good relations with the local Jews, Christians, and Sunni Muslims—a necessary ingredient to economic stability. It was during this time that the famous religious university of al-Azhar was founded. Subsequent caliphs, however, were less accommodating, in particular the possibly deranged al-Hakim (996–1021), whose maltreatment of non-Shiites was extreme.

When the **Crusaders** attacked Egypt in 1168, the Fatimids requested assistance from an army of the Seljuk Turks, commanded by the Kurd Shirkhu and seconded by his nephew Salah al-Din al-Ayyubi (1137–1193), who took over administration of Egypt when his uncle died two years later. This ushered in the 80-year **Ayyubid** period. After repelling the Europeans from Egypt, Salah al-Din founded a citadel fortress above Cairo and built a series of walls that enclosed all the existing settlements. He also began the tradition of building *madrasas* (religious schools), to reorient the populace to Sunni Islam after 200 years of Shiite rule. His relatives were to continue ruling Egypt in his stead when he left to battle the Crusaders in Syria, but they didn't do such a good job. By AD 1250, their slaves had usurped power and ushered in an era of Mamluk rule.

There are two **Mamluk** periods: the Bahari (1250–1382) and the Burgi (1382–1517).

Both groups derive their names from the area in which they were garrisoned—the former at the Island of Roda in the Nile (bahr means water, sea, or river in Arabic), the latter camped in a burg (tower) at the Citadel. The term mamluk literally means "owned": The Bahari were Qipchak slaves imported from the Caspian Sea, and the Burgi were Circassian, from present-day Russia. Mamluks were bought, converted to Islam, and educated in the houses of the rich and powerful. They eventually acquired positions of considerable influence. This era was a mixed blessing for Egypt, for while there was considerable infighting and fratricide in the struggle for ultimate power, this was also a time of great economic prosperity, as Egypt was finding itself at the center of the trade routes between Asia and Europe. During this time art and architecture were very heavily funded.

The most significant Bahari Mamluks are Baybars al-Bunduqdari (1250–1277)—the founder of the era, who defeated the Mongols in Palestine, thereby saving Egypt and the rest of North Africa from the fate that befell all of Asia—and al-Nasir Muhammad (1294–1340), whose long reign saw the construction of numerous mosques and other public monuments as well as the redesign and expansion of the Citadel. Qayt Bay (1468–1496)—a great statesman, military commander, and the greatest Mamluk patron of the arts—was a Burgi Mamluk. Qayt Bay extended Mamluk control into the Near East and Arabia and built monuments in Cairo, Alexandria, Damascus, and Mecca. Tumanbay was the last Mamluk ruler, in power for a year before he was hanged above the gates of Cairo on the orders of the conquering Ottoman sultan, Selim the Grim.

The **Ottomans** ruled Egypt for 300 years through viceroys, who, as long as they provided Istanbul an adequate share of their booty, were given free reign. This Ottoman period in Egypt happened to correspond with the European age of discovery, when seafaring nations began to open shipping lanes that bypassed the Middle East completely. Thus, the province of Egypt came to resemble more and more a feudal backwater. Gone were the days of it being a grand seat of empire.

The **Napoleonic invasion** of 1798 shook things up considerably. Napoléon's troops did quick battle with the greatly under-equipped Ottomans and their Mamluk vassals, which made the Middle Eastern powers realize just how behind the times they were. And as it happened, the academics who accompanied Napoléon renewed European interest in ancient and medieval Egypt. When it came time to fight the British navy, the French were roundly defeated.

Muhammad 'Ali Pasha (1805–1849), the next Ottoman viceroy to Egypt, took the lessons learned from the Napoleonic invasion to heart. The first step in modernizing the country was to consolidate his power. This he did by inviting all the Mamluks to a ceremony at the Citadel. Then as they were departing, Muhammad 'Ali Pasha had them ambushed and assassinated, removing any remaining threat to his rule in one bold stroke. He then organized all agricultural land, deeding the plots to himself and his family and, with the help of several foreign (mainly French) consultants, began to grow several new crops, including the very lucrative cotton. Muhammad 'Ali Pasha developed the country's infrastructure and transportation systems. He also made conscription in the army mandatory and as a result built an army powerful enough to threaten Istanbul. Instead of challenging the Ottomans, he decided to accept Turkish sovereignty in return for recognition of his family as the hereditary rulers of Egypt.

The effectiveness of the **Dynasty of Muhammad 'Ali** was mixed at best. Most noteworthy of Muhammad 'Ali's heirs was his grandson Isma'il, who served as khedive from 1863 to 1879. Isma'il made the most serious attempt to continue his grandfather's modernization program by creating new neighborhoods in Cairo and Alexandria, beginning an extensive industrialization process, modernizing transportation, and opening the Suez Canal. In the process, he accumulated extensive debt to European banks, which required that he sell his shares of the Suez Canal to the British. It was at this time that the French and English became heavily involved in Egyptian financial affairs.

Ibrahim's son, Khedive Tawfiq (1879–1892), was a weak ruler unable to control the nationalist general Ahmad 'Urabi, who in 1882 lead an uprising in protest of Ottoman and European influence. In retaliation, the British bombed Alexandria flat and invaded, beginning the period known as the **British Protectorate** (1882–1922), during which Egypt was ruled by a British High Commissioner and the khedive was merely a figurehead.

Following World War I and Woodrow Wilson's famous self-determination speech, **Egyptian nationalists,** lead by Sa'd Zaghlul, presented a delegation at Versailles to petition the Great Powers for independence. The British arrested Sa'd Zaghlul and sent him into exile, a move that triggered demonstrations across the country and forced the British to return him to Egypt. As a result, independence was proclaimed in 1922, the khedive was appointed king, elections were announced, and Sa'd Zaghlul's Wafd (nationalist) party won in a landslide. The British still maintained control of defense, communication, and the Suez Canal Zone, and continued to exert great influence over Egyptian politics.

Dissatisfaction continued after World War II, during which the Wafd party had agreed to support the British in exchange for complete independence. This failed to materialize, however, and a spate of demonstrations and assassinations ensued, culminating on **July 26, 1952**—major streets are named for this date—in a bloodless coup by a group of midlevel military officers who called themselves the Free Officers. The officers forced the ineffective king, Faruq I, to abdicate and declared the nation a republic. Within a few months it became clear that the real leader of the group was **Jamal 'Abd al-Nasir** (Nasser) who was made president in 1956. Nasser was a charismatic and shrewd nationalist who advocated land reform, nonalignment with the United States and the Soviet Union, pan-Arabism, and as time passed, socialism. In July 1956, Nasser announced the nationalization of the Suez Canal Company, expelling British and French experts and causing the wrath of their home countries, who colluded with Israel to attack Egypt in an effort to regain the canal. The Americans and the Russians jointly forced the aggressors to withdraw, and Nasser became an Arab hero.

Nasser became increasingly autocratic. He disbanded all political parties and brooked no internal dissent. He relied increasingly on the Soviets for second-rate assistance and became a victim of his own pan-Arab rhetoric. In the Six Day War of June 1967, after months of Nasser's saber rattling against Israel, the Israelis finally attacked, destroying the entire Egyptian Air Force and capturing the Sinai. With tears in his eyes, Nasser accepted responsibility for the defeat and offered his resignation. In an emotional outpouring of support, Egyptians took to the streets and demanded that he return to office. He died three years later at he age of 52, never having fully recovered from the defeat.

Nasser was succeeded by **Anwar Sadat,** a man who had been considered a joke during the revolution. But he surprised everyone with a series of bold policy changes. In the October War of 1973, his army caught the Israelis off guard by crossing the Suez Canal and penetrating into the middle of the Sinai before the Israelis could retaliate. Although this wasn't a clear military victory, Sadat had restored Egyptian confidence and gotten the world's attention. He then announced that Egypt would have an open-door economic policy, and imported goods that had disappeared from Egyptian markets for more than a decade were once again available.

Sadat's most striking move, however, was his trip to Jerusalem and the talks that lead to the Camp David Peace Accords of 1978, which brought about a fragile peace with Israel, massive U.S. assistance, and excommunication from the Arab League. It also cost him his life. In October 1981, at parades commemorating the 1973 war, Sadat was shot to death by a low-ranking military officer, disgruntled by the new directions of state policy and by the death of his radical Islamist brother at the hands of Egyptian security forces.

For the past two decades, Egypt has been ruled by Sadat's vice-president, **Husni Mubarak.** A cautious man, Mubarak has slowly worked Egypt back into the Arab fold without alienating the West by positioning himself as an integral broker to a larger Middle East peace process. He has allowed economic reforms that have begun to seriously dismantle the socialism of earlier years. He has also accepted a larger degree of free speech, partly in the form of opposition parties, provided they are not religiously based or calling for the overthrow of the state.

—Rami el-Samahy

BOOKS AND VIDEOS

Books

Ancient History. Even the most general reading on ancient Egypt can help you get more out of visits to ancient temples— first to get a handle on what rulers are known for what accomplishments, then to be able to recognize the images of gods and pharaohs' cartouches on the walls of monuments so it isn't all a meaningless blur. For a broad overview of the culture and history of ancient Egypt, John Baines and Jaromír Málek's *Atlas of Ancient Egypt* is arguably the finest, with maps, plans, chronologies, and subject-by-subject treatments of everything from pharaohs' armies to women's lives. Dietrich Wildung's *Egypt from Pre-History to the Romans* is well-researched, and it is graced with Anne and Henri Stierlin's superb photographs. The handsomely designed *Ancient Egypt*, edited by James Silverman, also covers a variety of topics with reliable scholarship. *Egypt: The World of the Pharaohs*, edited by Regine Schultz and Matthias Seidel, the best-priced of all of the coffee-table books, is very informative. *Women in Ancient Egypt* is Gay Robins's engaging study of the lives of women in the time of the pharaohs.

Two very different books on *the* archaeological finds in 20th-century Egypt are Howard Carter and A.C. Mace's 1923 *The Discovery of the Tomb of Tutankhamun* and Kent R. Weeks's 1998 *The Lost Tomb.* Carter's Tutankhamun outshines Weeks's dig at the tomb of the sons of Ramesses II, but, read together, the two books are a short course on the evolution of archaeological technology.

The Dictionary of Ancient Egypt, by Ian Shaw and Paul Nicolson, is an illustrated A to Z on gods, monuments, invaders, and just about everything in between. Cyril Aldred's general *History of Ancient Egypt*, updated by Aidan Dodson, is a traditional, period-by-period overview.

Richard Wilkinson's *Reading Egyptian Art* makes sense of the motifs that you'll see on the walls of the Temple of Karnak, for example. Cyril Aldred's *The Art of Ancient Egypt* provides a solid background for temple viewing. W. Stevenson Smith's pocketable *Art and Architecture of Ancient Egypt* taught today's Egyptologists some of their tricks. Gay Robins's *The Art of Ancient Egypt,* in coffee-table format, is splendidly illustrated and informative.

The Complete Valley of the Kings, by Nicholas Reeves and Conrad Wilkinson, covers the tombs and treasures of the valley in Luxor where New Kingdom pharaohs were buried. Likewise, Mark Lehner's *The Complete Pyramids: Solving the Ancient Mysteries* is a reliable, well-illustrated volume on Egypt's earlier pharaonic burial sites. *The Complete Tutankhamun,* by C.N. Reeves and Nicholas Reeves, includes excerpts from archaeologist Howard Carter's notes and color photographs of all of that gold and turquoise. Salima Ikram and Aidan Dodson's *The Mummy in Ancient Egypt: Equipping the Dead for Eternity* is the definitive book on one of the most fascinating practices of pharaonic times.

Stephen Quirke's accessible *Ancient Egyptian Religion* discusses the role of religion in everyday ancient life. Geraldine Punch's *Magic in Ancient Egypt* introduces the techniques, practices, texts, objects, and medicines used. For cat lovers, by cat lover and scholar Jaromír Málek, *The Cat in Ancient Egypt* is an appealing side door into the lives of the ancients.

Arab History. The classic history of modern Egypt is P.J. Vatikiotis's aptly named *The History of Modern Egypt,* and there is no better single general source. Those who like their histories from the actors themselves might prefer the versions presented by Egypt's three presidents: Muhammad Naguib's *Egypt's Destiny,* Gamal Abdel Nasser's *The Philosophy of the Revolution,* and Anwar Sadat's *In Search of Identity: An Autobiography.* To understand Egypt's place in a broader Arab context, consult two books by Albert Hourani, *A History of the Arab Peoples* and *Arabic Thought in the Liberal Age: 1789–1939.*

Max Rodenbeck's *Cairo: The City Victorious* is an excellent new urban history of Cairo, although James Aldridge's equally wonderful *Cairo,* written in the late 1960s and now out of print, is well worth the effort it takes to find it.

For an introduction to Islam, A.J. Arberry has written an engaging book called *The Koran Interpreted.* If you are interested in Islamic mysticism, try Arberry's *Sufism: An Account of the Mystics of Islam.*

Fiction. Egypt's most famous author is Nobel Prize winner Naguib Mahfouz, although his work in translation is less nuanced than it is in Arabic. For a sense of the social and political changes in Egypt during this century read his Cairo Trilogy—*Palace Walk, Palace of Desire,* and *Sugar Street*—which traces the transformation of a family from Mahfouz's native district in Islamic Cairo. More interesting are the works of Yusuf Idris, playwright Tawfiq al-Hakim, legendary man of letters Taha Hussein, and feminist writer Nawal al-Saadawi. The first half of Adhaf Soueif's lengthy *In the Eye of the Sun* gives an excellent feel for Nasser's Cairo; once the narrator moves to England, the book loses some of its momentum. If you have a taste for mystery, look for Agatha Christie's *Death on the Nile,* best read on the terrace of the Old Cataract Hotel in Aswan. Perhaps best of all is Waguih Ghali's quirky, hard-to-find *Beer in the Snooker Club,* which subtly mocks all the sacred cows of the revolution.

For Alexandria, the standard reading is Lawrence Durrell's *Alexandria Quartet,* which defined the city for a generation of readers that came of age in the West in the late 1950s. Andre Aciman's story of his Alexandrian Jewish family, *Out of Egypt,* reveals little about the city but is exquisitely written. Much more relevant is the poetry of the melancholy Alexandrian Greek Constantine Cavafy. His most celebrated poems are "Ithaka," "The City," and "God Abandons Antony."

The Desert. *The* book to read on Egypt's Western Desert is Cassandra Vivian's *Islands of the Blest.* A trip to the oases wouldn't be complete without it.

Guidebooks of the Past. For a sense of what Egypt was early in the 20th century, novelist E.M. Forster wrote his *Alexandria: A History and a Guide* when stationed in the city during World War I. For a crazy-adventures-in-the-colonies slant, try Gustav Flaubert's romp, *Flaubert in Egypt.*

Videos

Egyptian cinema. Egypt has always been the center of the Arab film world, and some of the films made in the 1940s and '50s were equal to anything then coming out of Hollywood. Sadly, those days are long over. Since President Gamal Abdel Nasser nationalized the industry in the 1960s, there has been a seemingly irreversible deterioration in technical and artistic quality. In addition, the climate of intellectual and artistic freedom in the country was severely constrained under Nasser, then later under Sadat through censorship and political detention. As a result, much of the industry migrated to Beirut, then scattered once more when civil war broke out there in the mid-1970s.

The best Egyptian films are older, which means that they will unfortunately be less available in most video stores. If you live in a city with an Arab neighborhood, go to a video store in that area, because they will be packed with Egyptian films—just be sure that they have subtitles. You might have some luck tracking down the films of Egypt's best-known director, Youssef Chahine, who recently won a lifetime achievement award in Cannes. His latest film, *Massir* (*Destiny*), is an antifundamentalist song-and-dance historical drama, if you can imagine such a thing. Much more impressive is a film Chahine made in the 1950s called *Bab al-Hadid* (translated in English as *Cairo Station*), an affecting story about a community of people who sell drinks and newspapers on the platforms of the main train station. His *al-Arda* (*The Land*) expresses the intense attachment to the land of a society that is still largely agricultural.

There is no need to trek to an Arab neighborhood to find films starring Egypt's most internationally renowned actor, Omar Sharif, because his most famous works (including *Lawrence of Arabia* and *Doctor Zhivago*) were made in the West.

Western cinema. The greatest film ever made about the region is *The Battle of Algiers,* by Italian director Gillo Pontecorvo. Shot in a documentary style in the 1960s, it treats the Algerian struggle for independence against the French. Don't let the fact that it is about Algeria put you off: it so powerfully captures the feeling of the Arab streets that it reflects life in Cairo better than most films that are actually about Cairo.

The most famous recent film involving Egypt is *The English Patient,* based on Michael Ondaatje's novel of the same name. Most of the Egypt scenes were filmed in Tunisia. When it played in Cairo cinemas, audiences burst out laughing at the way Egyptians were stereotyped on screen.

INDEX

Fodor's Travel Publications

Available at bookstores everywhere. For descriptions of all our titles and a key to Fodor's guidebook series, visit http://www.fodors.com/books/

Gold Guides
U.S.

Alaska

Arizona

Boston

California

Cape Cod, Martha's
Vineyard, Nantucket

The Carolinas &
Georgia

Chicago

Colorado

Florida

Hawai'i

Las Vegas, Reno,
Tahoe

Los Angeles

Maine, Vermont,
New Hampshire

Maui & Lāna'i

Miami & the Keys

New England

New Orleans

New York City

Oregon

Pacific North Coast

Philadelphia & the
Pennsylvania Dutch
Country

The Rockies

San Diego

San Francisco

Santa Fe, Taos,
Albuquerque

Seattle & Vancouver

The South

U.S. & British Virgin
Islands

USA

Virginia & Maryland

Washington, D.C.

Foreign

Australia

Austria

The Bahamas

Belize & Guatemala

Bermuda

Canada

Cancún, Cozumel,
Yucatán Peninsula

Caribbean

China

Costa Rica

Cuba

The Czech Republic
& Slovakia

Denmark

Eastern &
Central Europe

Europe

Florence, Tuscany
& Umbria

France

Germany

Great Britain

Greece

Hong Kong

India

Ireland

Israel

Italy

Japan

London

Madrid & Barcelona

Mexico

Montréal &
Québec City

Moscow, St.
Petersburg, Kiev

The Netherlands,
Belgium &
Luxembourg

New Zealand

Norway

Nova Scotia, New
Brunswick, Prince
Edward Island

Paris

Portugal

Provence &
the Riviera

Scandinavia

Scotland

Singapore

South Africa

South America

Southeast Asia

Spain

Sweden

Switzerland

Thailand

Toronto

Turkey

Vienna & the Danube
Valley

Vietnam

Special-Interest Guides

Adventures to Imagine

Alaska Ports of Call

Ballpark Vacations

The Best Cruises

Caribbean Ports
of Call

The Complete Guide
to America's
National Parks

Europe Ports of Call

Family Adventures

Fodor's Gay Guide
to the USA

Fodor's How to Pack

Great American
Learning Vacations

Great American
Sports & Adventure
Vacations

Great American
Vacations

Great American
Vacations for
Travelers with
Disabilities

Halliday's New
Orleans Food
Explorer

Healthy Escapes

Kodak Guide to
Shooting Great
Travel Pictures

National Parks and
Seashores of the East

National Parks of
the West

Nights to Imagine

Orlando Like a Pro

Rock & Roll Traveler
Great Britain and
Ireland

Rock & Roll Traveler
USA

Sunday in
San Francisco

Walt Disney World
for Adults

Weekends in New
York

Wendy Perrin's
Secrets Every Smart
Traveler Should
Know

Worlds to Imagine

WHEREVER YOU TRAVEL, *H*ELP IS NEVER FAR AWAY.

From planning your trip to providing travel assistance along the way, American Express® Travel Service Offices are always there to help you do more.

Egypt

Aswan
American Express Travel Service
New Cataract Hotel Lobby
Abtal El Tahrir Street
(20)(97) 306983

Luxor
American Express Travel Service
Winter Palace Hotel
Corniche El Nil Street
(20)(95) 372862

Cairo
American Express Travel Service
Nile Hilton Hotel
Tahrir Square
(20)(2) 5785001/2

American Express Travel Service
15 Kasr El Nil Street
Down Town
(20)(2) 5747991/2/3

American Express Travel Service
Nile Tower Building
21 Giza Street
(20)(2) 5693301/2/4-9

do more AMERICAN EXPRESS

Travel

www.americanexpress.com/travel

Fodor's Special Series

Fodor's Best Bed & Breakfasts
America
California
The Mid-Atlantic
New England
The Pacific Northwest
The South
The Southwest
The Upper Great Lakes

Compass American Guides
Alaska
Arizona
Boston
Chicago
Coastal California
Colorado
Florida
Hawai'i
Hollywood
Idaho
Las Vegas
Maine
Manhattan
Minnesota
Montana
New Mexico
New Orleans
Oregon
Pacific Northwest
San Francisco
Santa Fe
South Carolina
South Dakota
Southwest
Texas
Underwater Wonders of the National Parks
Utah
Virginia
Washington
Wine Country
Wisconsin
Wyoming

Citypacks
Amsterdam
Atlanta
Berlin
Boston
Chicago
Florence
Hong Kong
London
Los Angeles
Miami
Montréal
New York City
Paris

Prague
Rome
San Francisco
Sydney
Tokyo
Toronto
Venice
Washington, D.C.

Exploring Guides
Australia
Boston & New England
Britain
California
Canada
Caribbean
China
Costa Rica
Cuba
Egypt
Florence & Tuscany
Florida
France
Germany
Greek Islands
Hawai'i
India
Ireland
Israel
Italy
Japan
London
Mexico
Moscow & St. Petersburg
New York City
Paris
Portugal
Prague
Provence
Rome
San Francisco
Scotland
Singapore & Malaysia
South Africa
Spain
Thailand
Turkey
Venice
Vietnam

Flashmaps
Boston
New York
San Francisco
Washington, D.C.

Fodor's Cityguides
Boston
New York
San Francisco

Fodor's Gay Guides
Amsterdam
Los Angeles & Southern California
New York City
Pacific Northwest
San Francisco and the Bay Area
South Florida
USA

Karen Brown Guides
Austria
California
England B&Bs
England, Wales & Scotland
France B&Bs
France Inns
Germany
Ireland
Italy B&Bs
Italy Inns
Portugal
Spain
Switzerland

Pocket Guides
Acapulco
Aruba
Atlanta
Barbados
Beijing
Berlin
Budapest
Dublin
Honolulu
Jamaica
London
Mexico City
New York City
Paris
Prague
Puerto Rico
Rome
San Francisco
Savannah & Charleston
Shanghai
Sydney
Washington, D.C.

Languages for Travelers (Cassette & Phrasebook)
French
German
Italian
Spanish

Mobil Travel Guides
America's Best Hotels & Restaurants
Arizona

California and the West
Florida
Great Lakes
Major Cities
Mid-Atlantic
Northeast
Northwest and Great Plains
Southeast
Southern California
Southwest and South Central

Rivages Guides
Bed and Breakfasts of Character and Charm in France
Hotels and Country Inns of Character and Charm in France
Hotels and Country Inns of Character and Charm in Italy
Hotels of Character and Charm in Paris
Hotels of Character and Charm in Portugal
Hotels of Character and Charm in Spain
Wines & Vineyards of Character and Charm in France

Short Escapes
Britain
France
Near New York City
New England

Fodor's Sports
Golf Digest's Places to Play (USA)
Golf Digest's Places to Play in the Southeast
Golf Digest's Places to Play in the Southwest
Skiing USA
USA Today The Complete Four Sport Stadium Guide

Fodor's upCLOSE Guides
California
Europe
France
Great Britain
Ireland
Italy
London
Los Angeles
Mexico
New York City
Paris
San Francisco